Sources in Modern History Series:

Levy, *Antisemitism in the Modern World: An Anthology of Texts*
Lunenfeld, *1492: Discovery, Invasion, Encounter*
Other titles forthcoming

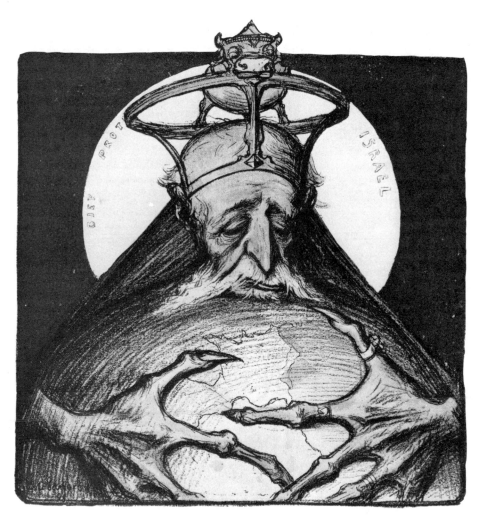

Baron Alphonse de Rothschild (1898) by Charles Léandre (1862–1930). Note the golden calf and halo, the claw-like hands clutching the globe with France at its center.

Antisemitism in the Modern World

An Anthology of Texts

Richard S. Levy
University of Illinois, Chicago

D.C. Heath and Company
Lexington, Massachusetts Toronto

Acquisitions Editor: James Miller
Production Editor: Bryan Woodhouse
Designer: Henry Rachlin
Production Coordinator: Mary Taylor
Photo Researcher: Billie Ingram
Text Permissions Editor: Margaret Roll

ILLUSTRATION CREDITS

Frontispiece Historical Pictures Service, Inc.
Page 137 (top) From Morton Seiden, *The Paradox of Hate: A Study in Ritual Murder* (New Brunswick, N.J.: T. Yoseloff, 1968)
Page 137 (bottom) University of Chicago Regenstein Special Collections
Page 138 From Eduard Fuchs, *Die Juden in der Karikatur* (Munich, 1921; reprinted Berlin: Guhl, 1985)
Page 139 From Morton Seiden, *The Paradox of Hate: A Study in Ritual Murder* (New Brunswick, N.J.: T. Yoseloff, 1968)
Page 140 Historical Pictures Service, Inc.
Page 141 Historical Pictures Service, Inc.
Page 142 Historical Pictures Service, Inc.
Page 143 From Morton Seiden, *The Paradox of Hate: A Study in Ritual Murder* (New Brunswick, N.J.: T. Yoseloff, 1968)
Page 144 Library of Congress

Published simultaneously in Canada.

Printed in the United States of America.

International Standard Book Number: 0-669-24340-X

Library of Congress Catalog Number: 90-81852

10 9 8 7 6 5 4 3 2 1

FOR MY MOTHER

Preface

Antisemitism appears, either withers or thrives, but seems never wholly to disappear from the modern world. The conditions of Jewish life that once called forth hostility may have altered dramatically. Yet antisemitism seems to have a life of its own, impervious to objective reality. Time and again, it has risen to the surface in particular societies, demonstrating its capacity to move sizable groups of people to action of an innately destructive nature. Knowledge of its history is the only weapon, fragile though it may be, against endless recurrence.

Given the political impact of antisemitism on modern history, it is rather surprising that until now there has been no collection of primary texts to use as a basis for discussion among serious students. Numerous anthologies exist for racism, slavery, the women's movement, nationalism, imperialism, and a great many other historical problems, bringing together the relevant documents and enabling the reader to reach an informed judgment on the nature of a specific problem. Unfortunately, the subject of antisemitism has not been so well served.

In my own teaching of German and European history over the past twenty years, I have been forced to lecture on, rather than discuss, the subject and have regretted the necessity of doing it this way. To me, decrying the evils of antisemitism smacks of sermonizing. I would much prefer to let the antisemites convict themselves out of their own mouths.

This anthology of antisemitic writings has been collected to fill the gap in the available literature. It rests, confidently, upon two assumptions: first, that antisemitism remains a continuing menace; second, that students, when given the facts and allowed full discussion of them, will arrive at the truth about antisemitism, and that that truth will have much more life to it than mere pious condemnations.

Along the way to its completion, the book has received the help of many individuals who deserve acknowledgment and thanks. To the best of friends and critics, Jonathan Marwil and David Jordan, I owe much. Our dialogues about style, content, and interpretation have enriched the book and my life. The thoughtful comments of Robert Melson helped refine the introductory argument and changed my mind about several key issues. My thanks also to John Kulczycki for making me think long and hard about the nature of Polish-Jewish relations, and for his excellent translation. Richard and Gerda Geehr helped unravel the mysteries of the Austrian-German idiom; Richard's biography of Karl Lueger was also a big help. Linnea Randolph Levy asked the right questions and relieved the prose of some of its heaviness and opacity. Robert Phillips enlightened me with his views on ethnicity. Hannah Decker, Rice University, and Bernard Wasserstein, Brandeis University, reviewed the final manuscript. And Susan Brown, Billie Ingram, James Miller, Henry Rachlin, and Bryan Woodhouse, all of D. C. Heath, helped see the book through the press. All these I thank sincerely for having given freely of their time and intelligence. Of course, the shortcomings that remain are entirely my own.

It is appropriate here also to thank two other groups of people. During discussions of several of the texts, my students taught me to see them in new ways and to present them in clearer fashion. For this instruction I am grateful. My own understanding of antisemitism has been formed by the seminal works of Hannah Arendt, Raul Hilberg, Jacob Katz, Paul Massing, George Mosse, and Peter Pulzer. Their influence upon me has been such that I now find it difficult to disentangle my own thinking from theirs. Cumulatively, their thought has worked toward a common aim—the understanding and overcoming of antisemitism. I will be happy indeed if the present work contributes in some way to this continuing process.

R.S.L.

Contents

Chronology

1710	J. A. Eisenmenger's *Judaism Exposed* is published.
1764	Voltaire's *Philosophical Dictionary* gives a secular basis to anti-Jewish thought.
1782	The Austrian Emperor, Joseph II, issues an Edict of Toleration, acknowledging Jews as permanent residents.
1807	Napoleon revises French provisions for Jewish equality enacted in 1790–91.
1845	Alphonse Toussenel, a socialist, condemns "Jewish money power" in his *The Jews, Kings of the Epoch*.
1850	Richard Wagner publishes *Jewry in Music* under a pseudonym.
1855	Count Gobineau provides a theoretical basis for racial antisemitism in *Essay on the Inequality of the Human Races*.
1867–1871	Germany, Austria, and Hungary institute legal equality for Jews.
1873	Financial crash causes a major depression in Central Europe.
1879	Wilhelm Marr introduces the term *antisemite* into politics while founding the first antisemitic party.
	Court Chaplain Stoecker and his Christian Social Party turn to antisemitism.
	The historian Heinrich von Treitschke publishes "A Word About Our Jews."
1881	Wide-scale anti-Jewish riots (pogroms) in Russia initiate a massive westward Jewish emigration.
1886	Edouard Drumont publishes *La France Juive*.
1889	Austrian university fraternities adopt the "Aryan paragraph," prohibiting Jewish membership.
1895	Captain Alfred Dreyfus, a Jewish officer on the French General Staff, is convicted of treason and sentenced to life imprisonment on Devil's Island (pardoned in 1906).
1897	Karl Lueger is elected Mayor of Vienna.
c. 1898	*Protocols of the Elders of Zion* is fabricated in Paris from old and new materials, probably by agents of the Okhrana (tsarist secret police).
1899–1900	Ritual-murder accusations lead to sensational trials in Austria-Hungary and Prussia.
1912	Roman Dmowski organizes the boycott of Jewish businesses in Poland.
1917	Balfour Declaration promises British support for a Jewish national home in Palestine.
1919	Minorities' Treaty, safeguarding Jewish equality, is signed by Poland and Romania.

Pogroms occur in Hungary, following the overthrow of the communist regime of Bela Kun, and throughout the rest of eastern Europe.

1920 A quota (*numerus clausus*) limiting Jewish attendance is established at Hungarian universities.

1921 Henry Ford reissues articles from his newspaper in a four-volume pamphlet, *The International Jew.*

1922 Radical rightists assassinate Walther Rathenau in Germany.

1933 January 30. Adolf Hitler becomes Chancellor of Germany.

April. Hitler's government institutes an official boycott of Jewish businesses in Germany, purges the civil service, and restricts admission to public schools and universities.

1935 Nuremberg Laws, defining German citizenship in racial terms, abolish Jewish emancipation in Germany.

1936 Cardinal Hlond's pastoral letter on the Jewish question in Poland condemns Jews as atheists and revolutionaries and lends church support for economic antisemitism.

1938 May. "First Jewish Law" in Hungary limits participation in economic and professional life.

November 9–10. During the *Kristallnacht* (Night of Broken Glass), stormtroopers burn 300 synagogues, loot and vandalize hundreds of Jewish shops, kill 91 Jews, and send 25,000 to concentration camps.

1939 Beginning in September, the Nazi policy of forced emigration of Jews is phased out in favor of deporting them to the East, where they are concentrated in ghettoes.

1941 January. The fascist Iron Guard instigates a wave of pogroms in Romania.

March. Commissariat-General for Jewish Affairs, created by the Vichy regime, directs anti-Jewish policies in France.

September 29–30. 33,771 Jews are massacred at Babi Yar, outside of Kiev.

1942 January 20. The Wannsee Conference systematizes the Final Solution of the Jewish question.

By April, *Einsatzgruppen* (mobile death squads) operating behind the advancing German armies have murdered 461,500 Soviet Jews.

July–September. First phase of mass deportations of western-European Jews to Auschwitz.

1943 January–April. Jews inside the Warsaw ghetto resist deportation.

October. Operation "Reinhard" ends; 1.5 million Jews have been exterminated in the death camps at Belzec, Sobibor, and Treblinka.

1944 By July 7, over 437,000 Hungarian Jews have been deported to Auschwitz.

October 7. Jewish prisoners revolt in Auschwitz.

1945 April–May. With the collapse of Nazi Germany, the Holocaust ends.

1948 Founding of the State of Israel.

1953 The manufactured "Jewish Doctors' Plot" against high-ranking officials exploits latent antisemitism in the Soviet Union.

1962 Antisemitic outrages occur in Argentina.

1967 The Six-Day War in the Middle East launches a sustained anti-Zionist campaign in the Eastern Bloc.

1979 *The Call*, Cairo newspaper of the fundamentalist Muslim Brotherhood, condemns a monolithic Jewish conspiracy against Islam.

1987 Several antisemitic works, including the *Protocols*, become bestsellers in Japan.

Antisemitism
in the
Modern World

Introduction
Antisemitism in the Modern World

In May 1988, Steven Cokely, an adviser to the mayor of Chicago and his link to the black-nationalist movement of Louis Farrakhan, accused unnamed Jewish doctors of purposely infecting blacks with the AIDS virus in order to further a plan for world domination. Nurtured by first the local, and then the national, media, the resulting furor escalated into successive charges and countercharges. As Cokely defended himself against Jewish critics, it became clear that (1) antisemitism had lost none of its emotional power and (2) neither the actors nor their audiences had any inkling of the long history that had set the stage for their ritual performances.

The accusation that Jewish doctors conspire to poison their trusting patients is nearly a thousand years old. Its most recent incarnation, the "Jewish doctors' plot" against powerful leaders of the Soviet Union in 1953, had lethal consequences for Jews. But it is not only the repetition of this and other ancient anti-Jewish charges that makes the "Cokely affair" relevant to this collection of antisemitic writings. The incident also reveals some of the mechanisms by which a specific, historically conditioned anti-Jewish prejudice can lead to much larger disturbances of political life.

Black and white leaders with no sympathy for antisemitism remained silent, and the controversy soon grew into more than a debate on the merits of Cokely's charges. His defenders urged blacks not to stand by while the white power structure condemned another of their courageous leaders to impotence. Showing solidarity with one of their own became far more important than the offending of Jews, who, if not engaged in medical experiments on blacks, "certainly dominated black economic existence." The mayor's reluctant dismissal of Cokely only added to anti-Jewish feeling. The ouster was seen—and not by blacks alone—as evidence of the control that Jews had over the media, and further proof of their power to exert political pressure. What had begun with the repetition of old accusations about Jews developed into a much broader conflict about justice, oppression, and the force of evil.

Doubtless the "Cokely affair" will soon disappear from memory, recalled, if at all, as no more than an inconsequential flurry on the political scene. Few people of goodwill would wish it otherwise. Yet the troubling issues the episode raised, and particularly the pivotal role of antisemitism in it, are worth considering carefully. Few would deny that blacks suffer from real problems or that these problems have real causes and, possibly, real solutions. But why clothe protest in this particular mode? Cokely, whether he intended to or not, succeeded in mobilizing a section of the black community—though a comparatively small one, it is true—to express its anger at victimization by Jews and whites in general. Antisemitism was central to this success. It gave Cokely instant access to people's emotions and riveted the attention of a larger, more passionately involved audience than less-inflammatory methods were likely to give him. The enduring power of antisemitism, at least in part, lies in its capacity to do exactly this.

For nearly a century, thinkers from many disciplines have struggled to understand antisemitism. The psychology of its individual practitioners and the dynamics of group action, the sociological basis of antisemitic movements and their economic underpinnings, the history of antisemitic organizations and the careers of notable antisemites, and the anti-Jewish stereotyping indulged in by religious and cultural institutions have been studied and elucidated. These investigations have sometimes yielded valuable, enlightening results. Too often, however, they have neglected what ought to have been the starting point for any serious understanding of antisemitism. Without knowledge of the literary tradition of antisemitism—what the antisemites said, did, and wanted to do—a sufficient explanation of the phenomenon will continue to elude us.

The aim of this anthology is to present antisemitism in its historical context. Antisemites may honestly think that they have discovered something entirely new to tell the world, but whether they realize it or not, they operate within a deeply rooted historical tradition. They avail themselves of a body of culturally transmitted literature comprising ideas about Jews and ever-changing suggestions about what ought to be done with them. These historical patterns of thought and action govern the form and content of individual antisemitic outbreaks. Antisemites may actually profit from a lack of historical perspective, but those who want to understand antisemitism cannot afford to do without it.

This collection of documents exemplifies the literary tradition of antisemitism. Section introductions present the social setting and the political, psychological, and socioeconomic motives of the producers and consumers of antisemitism. The ideas and policies of antisemites—the literature of antisemitism—and the great variety of social milieux into which they have been injected are the subjects of this book.

Antisemitism: A Definition

The documents in this book are not old; the first dates from the early eighteenth century, and most of the others were written in the last hundred years. Yet anti-Jewish sentiments, which range from raging hatred to mild disdain, have been voiced in a variety of forms for close to two millennia. I have emphasized the last century for one simple reason: anti-Jewish feeling, of whatever degree, and antisemitism differ from one another in significant ways.

Antisemitism is a modern phenomenon, the origins of which can be dated precisely. The word *antisemite,* and the abstraction "antisemitism" first appeared in Germany in 1879. Initially, the new terms coexisted comfortably with older expressions such as "Jew hatred," "Jew baiting," and "Judaeophobia." But soon anti-Jewish activists, their opponents, and neutral commentators began making frequent use of *antisemitism,* thereby gaining acceptance for the new word in most modern languages. Its extremely rapid adoption after 1879 reflected a wide recognition that traditional patterns and motives of persecution had so changed that a new word was needed to describe the new sort of activity.

This is not to suggest that there was a clean break with the past in 1879, or that the changes were precisely understood. The relationship between traditional Jew hatred and antisemitism was sensed at the time, and it still has relevance for the present: antisemitism proceeds from preexisting anti-Jewish feeling and indeed would not exist without this motive force of antagonism.

The authors represented here testify to this relationship. If not already conscious of the long history of anti-Jewishness, they were soon informed of it by their opponents, who ridiculed them mercilessly for their lack of originality. Unperturbed, most went on repeating charges against Jews and Judaism that were centuries old. Some openly drew inspiration from past Jew baiting and made it serve as an argument for the legitimacy of what they were now doing; others responded defensively, embarrassed about what their readers might regard as out-of-fashion religious bigotry.

Tone and style aside, however, all antisemites resorted to traditional sources of "knowledge" about Jews. Pre- and early Christian writings, medieval iconographic and modern literary expressions, pithy folk sayings, cartoons, and doggerel songs had created a reservoir of anti-Jewish thinking. The anti-Jewish stereotype that resulted was part of every European's cultural heritage. And yet many who were raised in that heritage and were clearly suspicious or contemptuous of Jews never became antisemites. To be anti-Jewish was not necessarily to be antisemitic.

The difference between Jew hatred and antisemitism, then and now, is not one of degree. Anti-Jewish feeling was too ubiquitous before and after 1879, too much a part of the common outlook of Westerners (including a good many Jews), to be considered the acid test for antisemitism. Although it might be tempting to conceive of someone's becoming an antisemite after a certain "critical mass" of hatred has been reached, the antisemites betray no consistency in this matter. Some were rabid and obsessional, others appeared to be no more than ordinarily prejudiced, and a few maintained cordial relationships with Jews while exploiting the anti-Jewish feelings of others.

Judged by prejudicial feelings alone, nearly everyone would have to be labeled an antisemite. Such a collective judgment makes little sense, however, because some people focused much more intensely on the Jewish problem than did others, and in qualitatively distinct ways. On one side stand the writers of tracts, like those represented in this collection, that prod the state, the political parties, or the public to intervene against Jewish power. In many instances, the lives of such people take on new meaning with the discovery of a Jewish conspiracy. On the other side stands the far larger group, composed of those who tell anti-Jewish jokes, blackball Jews from their social clubs, or shun them socially. For the latter it is casual prejudice, a peripheral concern, while for the former it is a central and life-shaping force, the means by which they have come to understand the world. These two have too little in common to live easily under the same classification.

Antisemitism is something other than inherited contempt, suspicion, or snobbery concerning Jews. Some of the most revered men of letters, champions of humanity like Voltaire, Diderot, Herder, Kant, Goethe, Hegel, Marx, Proudhon, and Nietzsche, made extremely hateful statements about Jews and Judaism. Paradoxically, most of them also advocated full and equal citizenship for Jews. This was not so much ambivalence as a compartmentalization of feelings about Jews. One and the same person might view Jews as a group as despicable (or meritorious) while considering an individual Jew a trusted friend (or sinister figure). Such mixed opinions were not the sole property of great thinkers, however; many ordinary Europeans of the middle and upper classes harbored all sorts of negative attitudes about Jewry in general without this mind-set seriously affecting their personal relations with individual Jews, even up to and including marriage.

In contrast to Jew hate, antisemitism implies more than a distaste for Jews, more even than bristling hatred. Antisemitism is not merely emotional; it is activist. Antisemites advocate long-term activity against Jews, the enemy. Irrational hatred may lead to such action, possibly to violence and murder; or it may not. To equate traditional antagonisms, however intense, with continuing goal-directed action by calling them both antisemitism is thus not only illogical but self-defeating. This was the error made by the early Jewish and non-Jewish opponents of antisemitism. Many saw it as an inexplicable but temporary throwback to medieval Jew baiting. Although they dimly sensed that this was not the whole truth, they failed to confront what was new and menacingly different about antisemitism: its politicization and embodiment in permanent political parties, voluntary associations, and publishing ventures—in short, its institutionalization.

Antisemitism entered the political culture of several European nations in the last quarter of the nineteenth century, because perceptions of the Jewish danger had changed. These new perceptions, along with the traditional ones, were often couched in racial terms. But to define antisemitism exclusively as racially motivated Jew hatred is also a mistake. Race, not just in cultural but in implicitly biological terms, appeared in anti-Jewish writings several centuries before the birth of antisemitism. Martin Luther's ruminations about Jewish perfidy centered on their irredeemable, uncanny otherness. More strikingly, the Spanish "pure-blood" laws of the sixteenth century located the source of Jewish evil in the blood. On the other hand, Court Chaplain Adolf Stoecker, "the second Luther" to his followers in Germany's first successful antisemitic political party, alienated racists when he suggested that conversion and assimilation could solve "the Jewish problem." He was an antisemite because he urged legislative restrictions on Jews and took action to that end. But he denied the central tenet of the racists by allowing the theoretical possibility that Jews could overcome biological and cultural traits to become "truly German."

Racism, although crucially important, does not serve as the distinguishing difference between antisemitism and Jew hatred, let alone as an all-embracing definition of the term. Racism existed before 1879 and is not universally a part of the new outlook after 1879. It rarely attained much influence in eastern Europe, and many antisemites slipped in and out of racial terminology without giving it special importance. Arguably the most influential twentieth-century antisemitic book, *The Protocols of the Elders of Zion,* owed little to racial conceptions of the Jewish question.

Although difficult, as the above discussion has indicated, it is important to arrive at a definition of antisemitism. The formulation I offer may perhaps best be thought of as a provisional one, a working hypothesis for readers to test as they study the documents that follow.

Contemplating the lives and writings of the authors collected in this anthology and trying to distinguish them from a great many others who shared their negative opinions about Jews, I suggest the following definition: *antisemitism is a willingness and a commitment to act against Jews over long duration for either of two aims:*

1. *to render Jews harmless by some means or other, thus negating the enormous power they had illegitimately gained* or
2. *to accomplish other political goals not directly bearing on the well-being of Jews*

An example of the latter was the frequent attempts of conservative parties to blackmail governments into changing their policies by claiming that they were under the thumb of Jews. Such pressure tactics did not necessarily call for curtailing Jewish rights but nevertheless drew strength from and nurtured anti-Jewish feeling.

This is a pragmatic rather than a precise definition. Antisemitism appealed to such a wide variety of people with such differing motivations—dabblers, cynics, and zealots alike—that no single formulation can embrace them all. But my definition has at least two virtues. First, by demarcating sentiment from the will to act, it places antisemitism and anti-Jewish feeling in their proper relationship without denying the formative influence of past anti-Jewish thought, discrimination, or violence. It also denies the notion of an "eternal antisemitism" by treating it in its proper late-nineteenth-century historical context as a response to Jewish emancipation.

Jewish emancipation, entailing the formal abolition of discriminatory laws and practices, was achieved in central Europe during the late 1860s and in eastern Europe during the first quarter of the twentieth century. It provided the catalyst for the development of antisemitism because, universally for the antisemites, emancipation signaled a critical reversal in the relations between Jews and non-Jews. It signified not mere *equality* but rather the definitive *empowerment* of Jews. Their enemies saw it as an invalidly bestowed legal right to belong to the nation—and then to dominate it. Their hostile response to this new situation included a body of traditional ideas about Jews that, although constantly and superficially updated, in fact changed remarkably little over the years. A less-studied feature of the response was the advocacy of practical solutions to the Jewish problem, and these do develop significantly over time, as the documents in this anthology will show.

The second strength of this definition is that it emphasizes the political character of antisemitic action. In the last analysis, the reason that we study antisemitism at all is because of its ability to activate people politically. Historically, it has operated in political life as both a "leavening agent," readily combinable with other issues, and as a conscious instrument of power, usable for all sorts of individuals who often care little about the Jewish question but nonetheless appreciate antisemitism's capacity to inflame the passions.

My definition stresses the *willingness*, rather than the *ability*, to act, because the power to effect one's beliefs through politics is not equally distributed in any society. Antisemitism clearly appealed to people no matter where they stood on the social scale. The powerful used it to defend or increase their power while contributing little or nothing to antisemitic ideology. On the other hand, the creators of the ideology were, for the most part, powerless "little people," who thought, mistakenly in most cases, that antisemitism offered them a means of obtaining power. With the passage of time, antisemitic political movements broadened the options for individuals between these two extremes to act upon their feelings about Jews, from participating in pogroms to signing petitions, from boycotting Jewish shops to voting for antisemitic parties. By the twentieth century, those willing to act found ample opportunity to do so.

The people who fit my definition of an antisemite, always relatively few in number, shared several common traits, no matter what their national origin or personal idiosyncrasies. Jean-Paul Sartre described their movement as "an attempt to give value to mediocrity for its own sake, to create an elite of the mediocre." It is true that many of the antisemites represented in this collection were thwarted intellectuals, career failures, or frustrated social dropouts. Yet it is equally true that several (for example, Richard Wagner, Court Chaplain Stoecker, and Henry Ford) had achieved worldly success and wielded considerable economic, political, or cultural influence before turning to antisemitism. In Austria, Hungary, Germany, Poland, and Rumania, university student elites became early converts to antisemitism and helped carry it to the broad public. Although it is consoling to think of such a mean-spirited phenomenon as the product of ignorant failures, such an approach is misleading.

Yet Sartre was correct in one respect: the ideology of antisemitism, which has so dramatically altered the world, has remained a barren field. Although antisemitism has again and again proved its power to excite and channel people's rage, its theory has confined itself to a few highly specious propositions about human nature and history. Endlessly repeated, these axioms have rarely been objectively examined by believers. Antisemitism makes few intellectual demands of its adherents; they need not master complex theories or engage in careful study of classic texts. Unlike the adherents of other ideologies, the antisemites have neither expanded our mental universe nor enriched our fund of truth.

Those who created antisemitic ideology were not, as a rule, stupid or uneducated—nor were they, for the most part, demonically evil. Although far from admirable as human beings, neither their intellectual nor their ethical shortcomings should disqualify them from careful study. Despite the poverty of their ideas, they have much to tell us about the thoughts, opinions, and worldviews of their contemporaries. Their powerfully articulated myths moved men at least as effectively as did the "great ideas." Because the antisemites knew how to reach broad audiences, at least temporarily, and exercised great immediate influence on the public, it is a mistake to trivialize them.

Although many antisemitic ideologues had originally been active on the Left, antisemitism as a movement found its home on the right side of the political spectrum, among Christian conservatives, extreme nationalists, and violence-prone reactionaries. Radical democrats and socialists might harbor and give voice to many anti-Jewish prejudices, but rarely did they become antisemites. They did not urge action against Jews or, with occasional exceptions, attempt to exploit generalized anti-Jewish feelings for political ends. The reason for this difference, however, is not to be found in any greater appreciation of Jews among leftists than among rightists. Both were schooled in the traditional anti-Jewish stereotype, and only a few overcame it. The difference has to do, not with Jews, but with contrasting views of the masses of humanity and their potential for democratic emancipation. Antisemites, no matter their other differences, were united in their rejection of democracy.

The antidemocratic thought and action that typified the antisemitic movement issued from many sources. A major constituent element came from the Protestant and Catholic churches. By the time antisemitism emerged in the last quarter of the nineteenth century, embattled Christian activists had come to identify democracy as one of the modern evils undermining religion. They put no faith in the autonomous decision-making capacity of the masses, and they believed that the common people, whether they knew it or not, required hierarchy and authority to be truly happy.

A large number of antisemitic intellectuals, however, came to antisemitism from an established left-wing worldview and experienced a prior loss of faith in the masses and the possibility of democracy. One of their constantly reiterated grievances was the inability of ordinary people to see the dimensions and dangers of the Jewish conspiracy. The thriving of newly emancipated Jews, often coupled with the personal setbacks of these men, could have no explanation other than the gullibility, bad taste, or apathy of the herd. That Jewish composers, writers, businessmen, or politicians should occasionally enjoy high popularity simply proved the lack of intelligence among the masses. This weak-mindedness, as much as Jewish evil, was responsible for the Jewish problem.

At times, antisemites appeared in the guise of populists or as protectors of the "little man" or as critics of the established authorities. Nevertheless, their programs were, in fact, uniformly antidemocratic. Their solutions to the Jewish question promised prosperity, national power, or moral regeneration but did not envision democracy as desirable or possible. The masses were too unreliable, too likely to fall victim to Jewish cunning, to be trusted with governing themselves. That they had been invested with voting rights in the first place—by Jewish radicals and revolutionaries— was one reason that the battle against Jewry had such poor prospects of victory. With such attitudes, antisemites could find little to attract them to democratic political philosophies.

As with their progressive posturing, the erstwhile liberals and democrats frequently denied any betrayal of formerly held principles or fundamental outlooks when discussing how and why they became antisemites. It was important for them to think of themselves as men of consistent principle. They had not simply dumped one inconvenient set of beliefs for a more promising one; rather, they had grown wiser. They had gradually become aware of destructive Jewish interference in world affairs and, only later, they claimed, detected this meddling in their own lives as well. Previous experiences, only dimly understood or written off as inconsequential at the time, assumed sinister new meaning as the ancient pattern of Jewish conspiracy became ever clearer. Acting on their new knowledge and speaking out against awesome Jewish power became their destiny.

A third group of antisemites, composed mostly of men who came of age after 1900, did not attempt to graft antisemitism onto older worldviews but rather made it central to their political outlook from the beginning. They also spurned democracy in all its forms. But they conceived of their coming to antisemitism differently, less as the organic process favored by the others and more as a quasi-religious experience. Because they had no need to explain a defection from former political beliefs, they acknowledged and relished an abrupt break with the past.

The formula was almost always the same: a dramatic conversion occasioned by an intense, usually providential, confrontation with Jews suddenly tore the veil from their eyes. Even after divine revelation, however, they had to struggle against their cosmopolitan or liberal upbringing. They had been taught (falsely) that Jews were unjustly persecuted in the past and that they were now simply fellow citizens of a different religious denomination. Such liberalism, they had come to understand, was no more than a Jewish plot under cover of which the aliens carried on their conspiracy of world domination.

Although freed of their fathers' liberal prejudices, the struggle was far from over. They had still to fight the complacent anti-Jewish prejudice of the common herd. Given the enormous growth of Jewish power since emancipation, this casual prejudice of the mob was altogether inadequate, even counterproductive. Historically, it had resulted in occasional pogroms and intermittent discrimination, but these outbursts of "healthy instinct" always yielded to "reactionary" periods of toleration, affording Jews time to recoup and strengthen their positions. Clearly, periodic persecutions, largely defensive actions, had not prevented Jews from achieving near-total victory. What was needed now, at the last hour, was not mindless mob violence but scientific rigor, careful study, and, most of all, lifelong commitment to overcoming the Jewish peril. The fecklessness of their countrymen, too, filled these antisemites with gloom. Eternal scolds, given to both self-pity and self-glorification, they thought of themselves, in a favorite metaphor of the times, as lonely prophets, "going against the current."

Common to all types of antisemites, as well as to the adherents of many other political movements, was unbending adherence to their beliefs. Occasionally, an individual might recant those beliefs, declaring that antisemitism had been "a childhood disease." But the normal case was beyond such redemption, beyond learning or changing. Having unearthed the Rosetta stone of universal understanding, he could not give up the ideas that infallibly deciphered the past, the present (which so bewildered the unenlightened), and the apocalyptic future. Antisemitism gave meaning to his life and provided him with a mission. He was to give unsparingly of himself to the desperately difficult task of enlightening his fellow citizens about the Jews. He sought nothing less than to make true antisemites out of the merely prejudiced.

How successful were these antisemites? This question is not open to a simple answer; however, it is certainly *not* true that popular antisemitism spread ever more strongly and deeply in society from the late 1870s until it resulted finally in the Holocaust. Evidence for such a linear development is lacking. Judging from election statistics, the size of avowedly antisemitic organizations, the readership of antisemitic periodicals, and the incidence of anti-Jewish violence, the popularity of antisemitism fluctuated dramatically. Periods of intense activity—1873–81, 1890–1905, 1918–23, 1930–45—alternated with years of popular disinterest and unresponsiveness. Levels of intensity also varied considerably from one country to another during these periods. As pogroms raged in Russia in the early 1880s and after the revolution of 1905, most of the rest of Europe was quiescent. Generally speaking, the times of wide-scale antisemitic action corresponded to general economic calamities—the crash and depression of the 1870s, the aftermath of World War I, and the Great Depression of the 1930s. But with the ebbing of these crises, the willingness to act against Jews, and even the public's *interest* in antisemitism, also waned.

As a group, the antisemites were a pessimistic lot, convinced that, in terms of achieving mass support, their movement was a failure. In Germany, pessimism did not wholly disappear even with the rise to power of Adolf Hitler and his Nazi party. There were substantial grounds for the gloom. Historians have begun to question whether antisemitism was the keystone to Hitler's movement. It was undoubtedly essential to Hitler's view of the world and to that of many of his followers, but it is arguable that rank-and-file Nazis were more powerfully drawn by the party's nationalism, economic promises, anticommunism, and anticapitalism than by its antisemitism. Although all of these components of Nazi ideology received an antisemitic emphasis, it is not certain that they were "properly" interpreted. Much evidence suggests that "the Jewish question" exerted only moderate influence on party members. Among ordinary Germans, antisemitic propaganda seems to have exercised even less attraction. Their lukewarm response to the regime's measures against Jews in the 1930s quickly persuaded the leadership to dispense with mass participation in the realization of its anti-Jewish objectives.

Hitler complained of his people's superficiality regarding the Jewish question right up to the end. He skillfully exploited the anti-Jewish feelings of the populace but never seriously envisioned a "democratic" solution to the Jewish question, one based on "enlightened" mass action. And when Hitler and his accomplices decided upon the Holocaust, they also decided to keep it as secret as possible. Its major implementors were convinced that neither Germans nor the rest of the world were ready for such drastic measures.

The antisemites may have failed in their goal of converting the prejudiced into antisemitic activists, but they nonetheless succeeded in an area vitally important to their aims. Although antisemitic political activity fluctuated in the period 1879–1945, antisemitic propaganda continued unabated. The volume and ready availability of printed matter produced by antisemites kept the anti-Jewish stereotype alive and disseminated it all over the world. Millions of copies of antisemitic works circulated throughout the period. The audience for libelous newspapers, political broadsides, and inflammatory speeches probably did not believe all they heard or read. It is unlikely that many placed Jews at the center of universal evil or believed that a solution to the Jewish question would automatically cure all ills. But the unremitting vilification had pernicious effects, and the anti-Jewish feelings they popularized had destructive consequences.

One effect of the barrage of propaganda was to obscure the line between anti-Jewish feeling and antisemitism. More people may have become willing to act against Jews during the interwar era, or at least to allow others to act in their name. With more certainty it can be said that the willingness to defend Jewish rights diminished, and in some countries, it disappeared altogether. Passive acceptance of political antisemitism became pronounced in Germany, where, if what Hitler said against Jews did not necessarily induce Germans to vote for him or join his party, neither was it sufficiently offensive for millions to withhold support from him or reject his leadership after 1933.

Passivity in the face of antisemitism was not unique to Germany. It became the norm in Europe and the world at large. Following World War I, antisemites everywhere depended upon popular hostility or indifference toward Jews to push forward their objectives. Genocide could not have succeeded otherwise. In addition to sadists and psychopaths, ordinary people of many nationalities, with no special indoctrination in antisemitic ideology, were prepared to staff extermination camps and assist the mobile death squads that followed the German army into eastern Europe. The Holocaust required the services of thousands of others who must have been well aware of the harsh treatment that awaited Jews. They ranged from statesmen with no prior public record of antisemitism and civil servants who accepted no moral responsibility for their collaboration to friends and neighbors who raised no protest at the brutalization of their Jewish countrymen. Under the right circumstances, toleration of antisemitism proved as devastating as active fanaticism.

Dissatisfied though they were, the antisemites could congratulate themselves on having contributed mightily to the wide tolerance for anti-Jewish activity. During the Holocaust, the risks attached to the rescue of Jews were enormous. The few who dared to help were authentic heroes. But well before the Holocaust unfolded, when it was far less risky to do so, too few people were willing to speak out against antisemitism. Antisemites had sown enough doubt about Jewish political reliability, unwarranted power, ethical inferiority, and conspiratorial ambitions to convince the great majority of people to do nothing to avert murder. For many, Jews stood outside the human community. It was this fact that made them eligible for catastrophe.

Jews and Non-Jews: A Sketch

Remarkably, Europeans' knowledge of Jews and Judaism remained generally scanty, despite an on-going fascination with them. Antisemites often boasted of their expertise but were actually the most ignorant of all. Interpretations of Jewish history formed one of the major ingredients of their ideology, a standing rationale for taking action against the enemy. Their versions of the Jewish past, however, were twisted to serve polemical purposes and typically dealt with Jews as symbols of exaggerated power and deviousness rather than as beings endowed with normal human qualities. The fabrications of the antisemites usually reveal more about individual and group pathologies than they do about Jews. The texts collected here are representative and virtually useless as sources of accurate information about their subjects. The grosser distortions can be addressed in notes and introductions, but a fuller perspective on Jewish history is necessary for a critical reading of antisemitic literature.

Jewish history is studded with tragic occurrences, yet collective tragedy is not uniquely Jewish. Throughout history many ethnic and religious groups have been subject to ruthless extermination. In modern times, the Armenians of the Ottoman Empire, the Ibo of Nigeria, and the Bengalis of Bangladesh have been victims of attempted genocide. Common to all these groups was their objective powerlessness. In the practice of genocide, however, objectivity exercises little force. The larger societies in which the victims lived converted their impotence into its opposite, investing them with an imaginary power so enormous and threatening that the most bloody "self-defense" appeared justifiable and, indeed, utterly necessary to their oppressors.

The case of the Jews fits this pattern but also diverges from it. Because they settled over a large part of the world, the effort to exterminate them assumed necessarily greater scope, extending over most of Europe, with plans eventually to include all the nations they inhabited. Unlike the Third World genocides, which assumed the character of tribal massacres and pitted a dominant ethnic group against a weaker one, the Holocaust required the cooperation of several such groups, each with ancient hatreds for one another to overcome before they could act against the common enemy.

Another difference is that, although it is historically rooted, the systematic murder of the Jews was a distinctly modern undertaking. It took "highly civilized" Europeans, employing every sophisticated technological means at their disposal, to attempt—and nearly accomplish—the annihilation of the Jews. The systematic registration, roundup, transport, and killing of such a widely dispersed people was not feasible before the twentieth century.

Yet the most distinctive element in the case of the Jews, and that which forms the subject matter of this book, is the long history of the ideas that prepared their destruction. The "problem" of the Jews has bedeviled Europeans, and the inhabitants of the colonies they founded, for nearly two thousand years. No other people has had such a continuous history of revilement or occupied such a prominent place in the consciousness of others. In contrast to the genocides of Third World peoples, which were carried out with a minimum of ideological justification, ideology was central to the Holocaust. A set of ideas upon which value judgments could be made and actions taken was in place long before the machinery of death began to operate.

Anxious to legitimize their own hate-filled actions, antisemites were fond of proclaiming that hatred of Jews was universal, rising to the surface of normally placid societies whenever Jews appeared in history and wherever they settled. Like so many of the other assertions by antisemites, this one does not survive analysis of the facts. The Jewish communities of India and China merged effortlessly with other population groups and left little record of their existence, precisely because of the absence of conflict. The lack of ideological Jew hatred in the Islamic world, at least until its recent transference from the West, is also striking. Historically the Jewish communities in Muslim lands, like other minority groups, have suffered inferior political status, humiliating legal discrimination, and occasional violence. But until the founding of the state of Israel, Jews had always played a wholly peripheral role in Islamic civilization. They were of minor importance to its theologians, philosophers, and politicians. The endless theorizing about them, the conscious dissemination of a negative stereotype, and their placement at the very center of world evil are foreign to Islam.

Thus the global claims of the antisemites were fallacious. In truth, the obsessional concern with real and imaginary Jews that culminated in murderous antisemitism is very much a creation of the Christian West. From its /inning, the existence of the Jews has been of pivotal importance to

Christianity. Judaism's genesis and subsequent rejection of the new religion, the role of Jews in the Crucifixion of Christ, and the competition for souls between church and synagogue imbued the relationship with an intensity of emotion rarely found among other rival groups. This was not merely an argument between religions but a contest between those who claimed exclusive rights to the same God.

Judaism clearly lost the contest. Christianity permeated the structure of the Roman Empire and then spread far beyond it, becoming a dominant religion, while Judaism remained a sect whose members were widely but sparsely distributed in the Islamic and Christian worlds. Where Christianity triumphed, the status of Jewry declined. By choice and necessity, Jews withdrew from the struggle with Christendom, adhering to their stigmatized religion and retaining their alien forms of language and dress.

Whether from the beginning hatred ruled the relationship between these two communities or whether it was confined to the religious leaders of both groups is not clear. Sociable contact, integrated living conditions, and even intermarriage were apparently still possible for Christians and Jews in the early Middle Ages, but they did not endure. To the Christian majority, the stiff-necked Jews were presented as a people guilty of deicide, a sinister and dangerous element within its midst. Demonized in the popular art of the Middle Ages, ridiculed and condemned by theologians, and sealed off from social intercourse with Christians by canon law, the Jews became social pariahs.

Jewish withdrawal did not end the conflict, however. Although left to themselves for long periods of time, Jews periodically withstood intense waves of violence, the first dating from the eleventh century. Accused of murdering Christians for ritual purposes, defiling the sacred host, and poisoning wells, they always lived in the shadow of sudden death. In close conjunction with the cyclical renewal of Christian enthusiasm represented by the Crusades, the rooting out of heresies, the Reformation, and Counterreformation, active persecution of the Jewish minority reappeared. Christian revival rekindled memories of ancient theological conflicts, especially "the original sin of the Jews," the Crucifixion. Centuries later, antisemites, even those disaffected from Christianity, could not refrain from drawing upon religiously inspired animosities of an earlier era to give their polemics special force. Faithlessness, perfidy, and unforgiving hatred of Gentiles remained basic attributes of the anti-Jewish stereotype.

Although in constant danger, Jews and Judaism were tolerated in the Christian world because they performed a necessary theological function. Jewish suffering bore witness to the superior truth of the Christian faith. Jews presented a living reminder to backsliders of the price of heterodoxy. Accordingly, their prosperity was an affront to God, but their misery was not. And while the church customarily condemned their murder, it taught the flock to loathe them as "the very tool of Satan." "Tolerance" on this basis brought with it no great security.

Other sources of dubious security in the Middle Ages were the economic functions allotted to Jewry. Although the way they made their living varied according to time and place, a fairly common pattern can be discerned in Western Europe. In an era of subsistence farming and restricted commerce, Jews were able to take advantage of religious contacts with farflung communities to engage in long-distance trade, and they mediated profitably between European and Islamic markets. Societies divided into landholding nobles and dependent peasants left room for Jews to act as middlemen, collecting rents, minting coinage, and trading in local markets. But as trade revived and towns began to prosper, a Christian middle class, usually supported by spiritual and sometimes by temporal powers, ousted Jews from the more lucrative endeavors, forced them out of the craft guilds, and excluded them from landholding.

From a central position in economic life, Jews as a group fell into marginal, "obnoxious" occupations, such as pawnbroking, peddling, or second-hand dealing. The process of pauperization could be gradual or sudden, aided by wholesale expulsions such as occurred in England (1290) and France (1392). The typical response of Jews was to move on, thus giving rise to the often-repeated charge that they were rootless nomads, wanderers without true attachment to the land in which they dwelt for the moment. In their search for more favorable situations, they carried this pattern of economic devolution with them into central and then eastern Europe, where medieval conditions prevailed into the twentieth century.

Because the church, at least theoretically, forbade the loaning of money at interest, Jews found profitable occupations at all levels of money handling, acting as particularly useful screens between territorial princes, local noblemen, and their subjects. Allowed to extract profit from resentful peasants and town dwellers as tax farmers, moneylenders, or holders of state monopolies, Jews were periodically relieved of their wealth, individually and collectively, by those who had the power to protect them. Diverse mechanisms accomplished this goal. Fines levied on the entire Jewish community, special head taxes, huge payments for the renewal of religious and economic privileges, and outright extortion under threat of expulsion recurred with regularity into the early modern era.

Although the privileges of the Jews occasionally produced legendary fortunes and influence for individual financiers, they also exposed the community at large to outbursts of popular fury. The mass of Europeans could scarcely be expected to appreciate that Jews were simply functioning as a convenient tax-collection system for their rulers, especially when princes took care to justify their own spoliation of Jewry as retribution for some religious or economic misdeed. Already exposed to contempt and suspicion because of their foreign religious practices, Jews repeatedly found themselves at the flash points of economic life, in positions at once precarious and provocative. By the dawn of the modern era, they had developed a cultural and economic identity that rendered them visibly separate from the majority.

Even after religion lost its primary influence on people's lives, the emotional antagonism of the early struggle between the faiths continued to poi- the relationship. Naturally, the weaker element in the hostile equation suffered the consequences. The mix of religious and economic grievances had embedded itself so firmly in the minds of Europeans that negative feelings about Jews easily survived the transition to a more secular age. When Jews and Gentiles encountered each other in subsequent centuries, their mutual preconceptions made it impossible for them to experience each other objectively.

For most Jews, the modern era began considerably later than for non-Jews. Not until the mid-eighteenth century did they begin the hundred-year quest for entry into the European mainstream. Why Jews should have wanted to do this always remained a mystery to antisemites. They speculated on the motivations and came up with sinister theories. But the emotional and material advantages of such a goal are not difficult to fathom. Individual motives, of course, varied greatly, but escape from economic and spiritual poverty, from narrowly constricted lives and primitive living conditions, appealed strongly to those willing to undertake the long journey.

The process of emancipation usually began and continued most smoothly with the mastery of their neighbors' languages. Yiddish-speaking Jews learned English, French, German, and Hungarian, unsettling non-Jews by the speed with which they began contributing to national cultures. Getting out from under the complex of medieval legal restrictions proved a much thornier problem, however. Freedom of movement, right of habitation, entrance into the crafts and professions, employment by the state, public office-holding or voting, matriculation in secondary schools and universities, and even the right to marry were in many places severely limited, or denied entirely, to Jews.

By the end of the eighteenth century, many of these barriers were falling of their own weight. Religious hostility remained strong, but the secular state began formulating its policies on a different basis. The Christian churches, though still a force, lost some of their unquestioned right to direct public life, and this trend improved the status of Jews. But new problems began to bear on the relations between Jews and non-Jews. Throughout the nineteenth century, Jews experienced a population explosion in Europe. In 1825 they numbered approximately 2.75 million, by 1900 nearly 8.5 million. The small towns and villages could not support such growth, and Jews began moving to large cities, where their presence exerted an unwelcome pressure.

Meanwhile, the rise of capitalism in western and central Europe acted as a powerful solvent on the economic restrictions that directly affected Jews and indirectly those who did business with them. Jews were particularly well placed to take advantage of this new economic development. Increasingly urbanized, literate, experienced in commerce and finance, and accustomed to keeping their assets liquid, they found their way onto stock exchanges and into banking, overseas trade, and merchandising.

Jews began living more modern lives, even though many obstacles to their equality stubbornly remained. Without the physical means to wage open warfare against discrimination, they were reduced to petitioning the authorities for relief, a hallowed, although rarely successful, strategy approved by the timid older generation of community leaders. The younger generation, yearning for the full rights of citizenship, grew impatient with this minimalist approach and sought to win over public opinion by tying Jewish emancipation to larger causes. They recognized the need for allies and sought them among the educated elite of Europe.

From the late eighteenth through the nineteenth century, the most likely advocates of Jewish equality were found among those with progressive political views. The cause enlisted support from enlightened bureaucrats, sympathetic clergymen, men of letters, liberals, democrats, and socialists. Almost imperceptibly, Jewish emancipation merged with the more general trend toward bourgeois emancipation from aristocratic and monarchical domination. The French Revolution and the European revolutions of 1848 hastened Jewish liberation and actually achieved it in a few places; but the movement was fitful, with temporary victories followed by periods of reaction and the loss of many of the gains.

When Jews began participating in politics, they naturally gravitated to the Left, where the forces of progress were fighting for the rights of all to live with dignity. Still, the alliance between Jews and the apostles of liberation was problematic. After all, the liberators had also been "educated" to look down upon "the common Jew." Although many of them championed Jewish equality for its own sake, as a right of human beings, others did so because they thought it was the best way to "improve" the Jews and to make them into useful citizens. For them, emancipation was not a right but rather an implicit contract arrangement. Jews had to demonstrate continued willingness to acculturate and to adopt the ways of the Christian majority. Baptism, a proof of compliance with these expectations, could ease the way to assimilation and lead to advancement for individuals, and there were some notable converts (Disraeli, Heine, Mahler). But the great majority of Jews maintained allegiance to their religion in its traditional form or in a modernized version. Many others, with no particular attachment to the faith of their ancestors, bridled at the implicit demand that they become Christians and chose instead to ignore all religion.

Continued adherence to Judaism, religious indifference, engagement in capitalist enterprise, and involvement in progressive politics awakened opposition to the granting of emancipation along a broad front. Churchmen, who took the inferiority of Judaism as an article of faith, argued that granting Jews political rights would weaken "the Christian state." Artisans, opposed to Jewish entrance into the already overcrowded crafts, rioted and petitioned, charging "unfair competition" and "dishonest business practices." Conservatives, frightened by the dismantling of traditional values and hierarchies, pictured Jews as inherently destructive agents of social turmoil. Even in the camps of sympathetic allies, individuals occasionally questioned whether Jews were deserving of equal rights. Socialists railed against "parasitical" Jewish bankers as the epitome of bourgeois society's shortcomings. Liberals doubted their national loyalties. Democrats decried Orthodox Judaism's clinging to superstition and empty ritual.

Opponents of emancipation usually spoke in the name of high-minded principle, reluctant to admit that they were also defending special interests against the threat posed by unfettered Jewish competition. Consciously or not, all of them appealed to inherited prejudice in order to strengthen their own positions against what they perceived as the "Jewish danger." In virtually a reflex reaction, they stigmatized new cultural trends, objectionable political movements, threatening economic developments, or rival interests as "Jewish." The presence of a few Jews in any of these phenomena constituted an argument against them. The argument was persuasive because society at large was still riddled with anti-Jewish feeling.

By the mid-nineteenth century, literature for and against emancipation created the contours of what came to be called the "Jewish question." There was a Jewish problem because Jews still appeared foreign to most Europeans. Some complained that Jews had not assimilated enough; others worried that they had adapted too readily to the ways of host peoples. Particularly for those whose national consciousness was of recent vintage, the exclusion of Jews from the nation became a means of defining nationality. In the language of integral nationalism, "Jewish traits" came to signify the very opposite of what it meant to be a Pole, Rumanian, or Ukrainian.

Most Jews living in central and western Europe refused to see a Jewish question; they had come to think of themselves as simply Germans, Frenchmen, or Englishmen of another religious denomination. They stood fully prepared to share in and contribute honorably to the national destiny. But their neighbors by and large did not share this conviction and resented the dogged demand for equality.

Had Jews truly been regarded as, for example, merely "German citizens of the Jewish faith," as their major organization proclaimed, there would have been little to object to in the great number of Jewish lawyers, physicians, and writers or in the few political personages who rose to prominence during the second half of the nineteenth century. Similarly, the absence of Jewish peasants and proletarians would have offered less of an opening for hostile speculation about alleged racial traits. But for a people so recently emerged from an inferior legal and social status, the Jews' progress and prosperity struck many of their countrymen as provocative and unjustifiable.

The strength of negative feelings about Jews became startlingly clear soon after emancipation was realized in central Europe during the second half of the nineteenth century and in anticipation of its accomplishment in eastern Europe. Emancipation was normally carried out by liberal parliaments or by administrative fiat, not by mass acclamation. At the time, the act of emancipation itself awakened only minimal public opposition, but the economic crisis that swept over Europe in the early 1870s revitalized and heightened anti-Jewish feeling. The politically motivated antisemitism that arose out of this crisis inherited rather than created an audience already inclined to believe the worst about Jews. In the Jew, antisemites found a figure groomed by history to occupy the role of villain.

Economic dislocation highlighted a number of deeply disruptive trends. The corrosive effects of urbanization on traditional values, disturbing examples of upward and downward social mobility, and the unsettling effects of the business cycle provided the basis for several kinds of political protest. The antisemitic movement distinguished itself from the rest by pouncing on a wide variety of grievances attendant upon modern development and in each case associating them with Jews.

Social observers might advance reasons for these disorienting features of modernity, such as the structural shift from an agrarian to an industrial market economy. But for the peasant and lower-middle-class casualties of the process, such objective explanations were too sophisticated. More important, they failed to answer psychological needs. The loss of certainty about their place in the world and the dawning recognition of their permanent insecurity opened masses of people to the politics of hysteria. Their decline in status coincided with the dramatic rise of Jewry. In their personal calamities, they were easily persuaded to see the workings of a sinister conspiracy directed by a historically despised group out for revenge. Such beliefs proved wholly invulnerable to rational argument. They had passion and the strength of "history" for support.

Jews were more urban, middle class, and commercial or professional than the peoples among whom they lived. These realities of Jewish existence fed suspicions and convinced some of the need to take political action against Jews. Prejudice made it certain that the economic abuses of Jews would come in for more attention than those of others, and wild claims of their sole responsibility for economic disaster accompanied every dislocation. To the gullible, they appeared to be the only ones prospering in evil times. Few asked if this were truly the case. Yet fewer were capable of sifting through the exposés of the antisemites for false or exaggerated claims. Jews participated in modern economic life, already bearing the reputation for sneakiness and excessive cleverness, especially in money matters. Many individuals overwhelmed or threatened by economic catastrophes were primed to see Jewish economic behavior as evidence of a carefully hatched plan of conquest.

In this context, the liberal political loyalties of Jews proved most inopportune. Liberals had engineered Jewish emancipation while the masses of Europeans remained largely apathetic or hostile to it. Liberals also stood in the forefront of laissez-faire economics and were held responsible by its victims, those who could not adapt to the new needs of industrial capitalism. Theories of conspiracy flourished in this atmosphere. Jews, with the help of non-Jewish liberals, so the argument went, had insinuated themselves into power positions with terrifying speed. Honest Gentiles had been thrown into confusion by the march of events, but the Jews, as a united people, always knew what they wanted and stood on the verge of achieving their goals. As a result of the lack of vigilance on the part of non-Jews, the enemy had already won emancipation and was using it to gain well-nigh unassailable positions of strength from which to carry out its designs.

One such advantage that appeared especially ominous to the antisemites was the extraordinary number of Jews active in journalism. Even before emancipation, this new field had offered attractive possibilities of advancement for Jews who were still excluded from many traditional occupations. From the 1870s on, they were instrumental in developing the mass-circulation daily newspapers of central Europe, profitable enterprises that relied on advertising revenues rather than subscriptions or sales. Antisemites, many of them newspapermen of the old school, found it difficult to adapt to the new style of journalism and condemned it as a falling away from the traditional high standards of the trade. Jews, they declared, were the sole perpetrators of this cultural degeneracy.

This "stranglehold on the press" was particularly vexing to antisemites in that it allowed Jews to dictate public opinion. The dim-witted masses could now be fed Jewish propaganda, weaned away from their healthy instincts, and softened up for Jewish conquest. Antisemites referred to the "Jewish press" as though it were a potent weapon in the hands of a conspiratorial band, following a premeditated, uniform policy. In fact, the many Jewish publishers, editors, and reporters, though generally liberal in their politics, were competitive rivals. They did not follow the same line and ignored or dealt gingerly with "Jewish interests." Nonetheless, in the recurrent crises of modern times, their inordinate role in the media rendered Jews suspect to their neighbors.

Antisemitic politics, which displayed many of the symptoms of paranoia, did not confine itself to misinterpreting the realities of Jewish existence, however. Jews were a tiny fraction of the national populations of western and central Europe, usually 1 percent or less; in eastern Europe they constituted a larger proportion of the population, approaching a majority in some urban areas. But antisemites insisted that their influence went beyond mere numbers. The presence of Jews near the seats of power, as the personal advisers or friends of highly placed personages, aroused profound fears. Antisemites, usually men with active resentments that went beyond Jews, were ever ready to accuse their own national leaders of being corrupted by or ensnared to do the will of the aliens. The international ties of Jewry, another factor that supposedly compensated for their small numbers, also provoked antisemitic attacks. Innocent philanthropic organizations were elevated into "secret governments." Behind-the-scenes "Jewish syndicates" were said to be calling the shots during the Dreyfus Affair (see Document 8), at the Paris Peace Conference ending World War I (see Document 17), and in the diplomatic crises of the interwar era (see Documents 18, 20–21).

Large Jewish settlements in capital cities like Budapest, Vienna, and Berlin contributed to antisemitic anxieties, but small Jewish populations could also be menacing to antisemites. In the kingdom of Saxony, for example, the antisemitic parties campaigned vigorously and successfully, even though Jews made up only 0.2 percent of the population. Small numbers were actually an advantage because they facilitated an allegedly absolute, iron-willed solidarity. The antisemites' faith in Jewish unity could not be shaken by the facts. For them, public disputes among Jewish spokesmen were nothing more than a smokescreen to confuse gullible Gentiles, to make them think that Jews were every bit as factionalized as their intended victims. At least one of the reasons for this skewed perception is obvious. The making of fine distinctions between individual Jews and the larger group, or seeing the group as anything but monolithic, would have robbed antisemitic polemics of their point and antisemitism of its rationale.

Yet the Jewish community had fallen into great disarray. As a consequence of emancipation and assimilation, Jews had lost any semblance of a unified outlook. Just as political antisemitism was gaining strength, the Jewish community was in the process of dissolution. Stark differences of custom, language, and religious orientation separated eastern- and western-European Jews. Apostates, Reformed, and Orthodox Jews warred openly with one another. Class conflict raged within the eastern European Jewish communities. Conversion and mixed marriage were on the rise, and birthrates began declining. Never were Jews less prepared to defend themselves against the onslaught of their enemies.

Jewish disunity was in large measure the natural result of assimilation and acculturation. However, antisemitism contributed to, and then exploited, two aspects in the breakdown of the Jewish community. The variable pace of assimilation—rapid in the West, slow or virtually nonexistent in the East—produced dramatic contrasts among Jews. From the 1880s on, a constant, sometimes hectic, flow of Jewish emigration from east to west brought *Ostjuden,* eastern European Jews, into contact with people who knew little or nothing about them. Coming from underdeveloped areas and bearing the marks of centuries of isolation and poverty, speaking Yiddish or heavily accented versions of modern European languages, they struck the native population as uncivilized. Their strange manners and elaborate religious customs reawakened fears as old as the Middle Ages. Antisemites pictured them as a dirty, dangerous threat, the scouting party for hordes of their fellows who stood poised to inundate Europe. They also insisted that the differences between *Ostjuden* and assimilated Jews were only superficial; to the practiced eye, they were simply different faces of the same Jewish conspiracy. The assimilated rejected this charge, and some even welcomed the revitalizing energy of the newcomers; but the more usual response was embarrassment or hostility toward the wretched newcomers.

Eastern-European immigration and the antisemitism it helped foster added a new dimension to the full-blown identity crisis among assimilated Jews. The great majority of them in western and central Europe wished for nothing more than equal participation in the life of their fatherlands. They responded to the antisemitic movement with disbelief or disappointment, denial or despair. They organized their legal and literary self-defense. As a group they refused to be deterred from their belief that dignified assimilation was both possible and desirable. A vocal minority, however, responded differently.

The Zionist movement, under the leadership of Theodor Herzl, a thoroughly acculturated Viennese, interpreted the emergence of political antisemitism as proof of the impossibility of assimilation. Rejecting the notion that Jews were evil incarnate, Zionism made a virtue out of the antisemites' insistence that Jews were different. Jews *were* a separate nation, a people with a proud history and culture. During their centuries of exile, they had become alienated from the soil and manual labor. They had developed a set of values and a social structure that was bound to irritate non-Jews. Until they possessed a state of their own, they would remain a thorn in the flesh of Europe, and antisemitism would not only continue but grow stronger, placing Jews in growing jeopardy. The assimilators cravenly denied their roots and the positive values of Jewish nationhood. Moreover, they deluded themselves in the belief that their neighbors would ever see them as Frenchmen, Germans, or anything other than Jews.

As in the case of the *Ostjuden,* the assimilationist majority again reacted with annoyance to these troublesome militants. They were playing right into the hands of the antisemites. They seemed to accept large parts of the antisemitic indictment of Jewry as being true, which undermined the very basis of assimilationism. Zionism drew its mass support from the oppressed Jews of the East and found sources of virtue in them that further alienated westernized Jews. The Zionists' illiberal nationalism was not the right way to fight antisemitism, and, in fact, their definition of Jewry smacked of racism, strengthening the hand of the enemy.

Antisemites certainly found Zionism useful. They readily accepted the contention that all Jews, even the highly assimilated who denied it, were part of the same people. Thus, "antisemitic Zionists" were justified in demanding the expulsion of all Jews from the places they had lived for centuries. The coerced return to Zion as an instantaneous solution to the Jewish question continued to appeal to some antisemites, but to others it was also cause for dread. Why drive the Jews from Europe, only to have them conduct their conquest from the safety of Jerusalem? In general, the antisemites used Zionism as corroboration for their claims about the "Jewish race" or identified the Zionist organizations as the engine of Jewish world conspiracy. The Nazis toyed with the Zionist solution to the Jewish question as long as they sought the massive emigration of Jews from Europe—that is, until they embarked upon the Holocaust in 1942.

Into the twentieth century, most Jews continued to hope that antisemitism was a temporary aberration that would inevitably yield to progress and enlightenment. Although political manifestations of the movement came and went without ever accomplishing anti-Jewish goals, antisemitism did not disappear. In stable times it slumbered on the fringes of political life, kept alive by crackpots, cultists, and splinter parties. But when tensions rose, antisemitism moved back toward the center of public discourse. Then true believers were joined and sometimes financed by governments seeking to deflect attention from social ills, by powerful groups gathering support from desperate people, or by ambitious politicians exploiting fear and hatred for personal aggrandizement. On the eve of World War I, it had become entrenched in the political culture of many countries—a familiar, if slightly disreputable, element of modern life.

The Great War replaced intermittent with near-permanent crises. Economic disruption, conflicts between nationalities, border disputes, and class war intensified, and then radicalized, antisemitism. Individual Jews in Germany, Austria, Great Britain, and America rose to powerful positions in the conduct of the war. In several of the new and reorganized states that came into being after 1918, Jews helped write democratic constitutions and held high public office. The massive resentment produced by the war and its aftermath fastened onto those "who had obviously profited from the conflagration." Only Jews, who bore a reputation for vengeful scheming, could rise to power by having non-Jews slaughter one another. Only Jews, logical thinkers declared, were to blame for the catastrophic war.

The war also put whole population groups to flight. Jewish civilian casualties in the eastern theater of operations were especially heavy, a fact never admitted by their enemies. Along with other refugees, they flooded into the West. This time they arrived in countries where economic distress was the rule. Willing to work for lower wages or longer hours, they competed with native labor forces and awakened much hostility. Most congregated in the miserable slums of the large cities, never becoming citizens or rising above a marginal existence. But a very few made it from rags to riches, and these, to the homeless and unemployed non-Jews, seemed outrageously typical, a swarm of predators descending upon the carcass of Europe.

Responding to popular fears, governments harassed the immigrants, occasionally expelling them or pressuring them to move on. They were now feared not only as creatures of inferior worth but as carriers of a new contagion, bolshevism. The Russian Revolution of 1917 and the attempted spread of communism following it were widely attributed to a Jewish conspiracy. Henry Ford and Adolf Hitler, Woodrow Wilson and J. Edgar Hoover, the *Chicago Tribune* and the *Times* of London were just a few of those who identified bolshevism with Jewry. Antisemites saw communism as final and absolute proof of the Jewish plan of world conquest.

The evidence for the connection between world communism and the Jews should not have been persuasive. It was at best a case built on circumstantial evidence. Many Jews were active in the leadership and rank and file of the Bolshevik party (although the key leaders, Lenin and Stalin, were not Jewish). But was their participation really cause for surprise? The tsarist regime had engaged in blatant persecution of Jews, used them as scapegoats for its own corrupt incompetence, and fomented bloody pogroms. In disproportionately large numbers, Jews responded by joining *all* the parties—not just the Bolsheviks—that were dedicated to fighting tsarism.

The attempt to overthrow tsarist oppression was not illegitimate. But despite the claims of many responsible people that "the Jews are in charge," their maltreatment continued after the revolution. Wherever communists exercised power in the interwar era, they acted harshly against Jews, expropriating or deporting them as the "bourgeois class enemy." Within Russia, Lenin pursued a policy designed to weaken both Judaism and antisemitism, succeeding only with the former goal. As a group, Russian Jews were particularly unresponsive to bolshevism before or after its victory. Orthodox Jews rejected the regime's atheism; Zionists and Jewish socialists rejected its denial of Jewish nationality.

Jews also figured prominently in the short-lived revolutionary governments of several other European states or in their communist parties. Even though most of these individuals had severed all connection to Judaism and were quite capable of dealing ruthlessly with other Jews and although the mass of Jews remained committed to middle-class liberal or democratic socialist parties, the stigma of revolutionary nihilism attached itself firmly to the whole group. Antisemitism had acquired a resonant new argument to use against Jews.

In the years between the two world wars, it was often difficult for Jews to assess their situation. The outward signs were mixed, with some seeming to promise continued progress toward integration. Immediately after the war, authoritarian regimes gave way to democracies with constitutions that afforded Jews access to higher education, public office, and the free marketplace. In the Soviet Union, Jews as individuals advanced upward into the middle class. Elsewhere, unhampered participation in the social, cultural, and economic life of several nations had been virtually realized for the first time. Jews won the Nobel Prize, fame in the arts, university chairs, and popularity in some political movements. But less-favorable trends were also visible.

Antisemitic fantasies notwithstanding, Jews remained essentially powerless, deeply divided and without the political, military, or territorial base to defend themselves. Their physical safety still depended on the goodwill of those among whom they lived, or, in the absence of this, the readiness of governmental authorities to protect them; both proved unreliable. The "red scare" that erupted in the United States and several European nations following the Russian Revolution revealed the limits of popular toleration that Jews could expect in times of stress. The myth of a Jewish world conspiracy had now achieved global currency. And the very familiarity of the many charges raised against Jews served to win broad public acceptance for them. They had become axiomatic, truisms that needed no proof beyond their utterance.

Economic stagnation in eastern Europe, the hyperinflation in Germany and Austria in the early 1920s, and influence-peddling scandals in France produced abundant evidence of popular anti-Jewish feeling. The democratic constitutions that protected the rights of Jews came under attack from many directions. Violence against them, which had been more typical of eastern Europe, made its way west. Ideologically motivated zealots practiced political assassination, physical intimidation, and vandalism with increasing impunity. Political parties of the radical and conservative Right had frequent recourse to antisemitic campaigning, and the political utility of antisemitism was demonstrated as never before.

The Great Depression helped remove the last defense on which Jews had come to rely. In eastern Europe, several of the insecure democracies gave way to authoritarian, military regimes that showed a special willingness to accommodate popular anti-Jewish feeling, exacerbated by the depression. The economic freedom of Jews fell victim to popular pressure or to compromises between radical and moderate rightist parties that came to power. Quotas in the professions or in admissions to universities, restrictions in awarding public contracts, and other sorts of discrimination further undermined their economic viability. In many places, the government not only no longer protected Jewish equality but proceeded to undo emancipation itself.

The rise to power of the Nazi party in Germany and its immediate legal persecution of Jews prompted radical rightists elsewhere into imitative actions. German expansion into Austria and Czechoslovakia produced a new wave of unwanted immigrants. Central-European Jews, vying for jobs in the depressed economies of France, Belgium, and the Netherlands, awakened predictable hostility. Few governments felt strong enough during the depression to welcome Jewish refugees, and the possible sanctuaries for them dwindled at exactly the time they were most needed. Wherever they did gain entry, it was usually as stateless aliens, and eventually these *Ostjuden* became the first victims of the Holocaust in Western Europe.

The Nazis' determination to exterminate the Jews of Europe met with individual and collective acts of resistance. Many people hid or helped spirit Jews to safety. Many governments protected native-born Jews, although usually at the expense of immigrants. But active collaboration and passive indifference were far more widespread. The deeply ingrained suspicion of Jews, perpetuated and disseminated over the globe by antisemites, contributed substantially to their murder. To millions of bystanders it must have appeared that, even if Jews were guilty of only a fraction of the crimes they had been continuously accused of, they were simply not worth the risk of saving.

Selection of the Texts

The documents collected here have been chosen to reflect the wide geographic scope of the antisemitic movement. Some of them, such as the *Protocols of the Elders of Zion,* were truly universal documents, translated into every major language. Selections from Russia, France, Hungary, Austria, Romania, Poland, and the United States could have, had space permitted, been supplemented by British, Italian, Lithuanian, Spanish, or Latin American literature. German-language documents predominate, both because of the vital part Germans played in the genesis of antisemitism and because of their extensive influence upon others. The political potential of antisemitism was also first demonstrated in Germany, and its development there served as a model in many other locales.

Antisemitic and anti-Jewish documents take many forms, from crude cartoons to abstruse philosophizing. Aside from the introductory section, which seeks to summarize the varieties of anti-Jewish thought that fed into the antisemitic movement, selections for this book came from the political or potentially political sphere. They were intended for a wide public audience. Parliamentary speeches, essays, journalistic pieces, party harangues and programs, protocols, and popular art indicate the many types of antisemitic theory and practice.

The documents included represent ideas or methods that were significant in the development of antisemitism, were recognized as important at the time they were produced, or gained importance later. They have been reproduced in their entirety or in large extracts, where completeness has been judged impractical or unrewarding. As a consequence, modern readers will confront numerous allusions to no-longer-familiar historical persons or events. I have dealt with this problem in explanatory footnotes in order to retain the original flavor of the sources and to do justice to the historical context which produced them. The translations, except where otherwise indicated, are my own. Parenthetical comments that appear within the texts are part of the original. My editorial comments appear in square brackets.

The texts I have chosen are certainly not the only ones that could have been included. The sheer volume of antisemitic literature, one of the movement's chief characteristics, made for some hard choices; space limitations have also forced some regrettable omissions. Examples from drama, fiction, and film scripts have been excluded. Shakespeare's Shylock, Dickens's Fagin, or Hemingway's Cohen may well have contributed to the general pool of anti-Jewish feeling and the perpetuation of stereotypical thinking about Jews, but their political intentions, if they existed at all, seem relatively innocuous when compared to the overtly action-oriented texts contained here. They have little to tell us about the practical or theoretical bases for action adopted by the antisemites. These forms of anti-Jewish literature are clearly significant in revealing the underlying emotions of the antisemitic movement, but the subject of this book is antisemitism as a conscious political activity.

Wherever possible, I have adhered to a chronological ordering of the documents. In the case of political-party antisemitism in pre–World War I Germany and Adolf Hitler on the Jewish question, however, more is to be gained by ignoring strict chronology in order to emphasize a relatively self-contained development of antisemitic thought.

Beyond chronology, the texts display a logical, historical progression. The content of antisemitism altered little from 1879 to 1945. With only slight variations, Jews are charged with nearly the same crimes at the end of the epoch as the beginning. And most of the accusations are a good deal older than antisemitism itself. In contrast, the practical solutions to the Jewish question hinted at or developed fully in the documents moved in ever-more-radical directions.

Radicalization of the vocabulary of antisemitism is also apparent. Coarseness of tone, the snide or threatening remark, runs through the documents from beginning to end. But Heinrich Class (see Document 14) introduces "the language of hardness," the demand that no exceptions be made to the implementation of anti-Jewish laws. The innocent must suffer along with the guilty, no matter the violence done to basic feelings of humanity. The language of hardness recurs with greater frequency in the later sections of this anthology, culminating in the grotesque statement of Heinrich Himmler, overseer of the Final Solution. The true measure of a man, he said, was his being able to look upon thousands of corpses "without losing his basic decency"—an attitude requisite for genocide.

It is impossible to measure accurately the influence of any one of these antisemitic writings. Some achieved massive national and international circulation; others spoke exclusively to the initiated elite. Edouard Drumont numbered his readers in the hundreds of thousands; Heinrich Class's book, by contrast, had a readership of approximately twenty-five thousand. In neither of these extremes nor in the many intermediate cases is it clear how seriously they were taken or what effect they had on anti-Jewish policies. But a careful reading will show that, at the very least, antisemites took other antisemites seriously. They were mindful of precedents. Despite their often-demonstrated vanities, they studied the documents collected here, as well as many others, and attempted to learn from past errors and successes. To Hitler, the most important antisemite, the central lesson of past antisemitism was that the Jewish question could not be solved "democratically" through the action of the masses. Political antisemitism, as developed by his predecessors, had all kinds of utility for him (see Documents 19–21), but it could not settle the Jewish question in a final way.

Aside from instructing Hitler, the antisemites represented here prepared for the Holocaust in concrete ways. All of the measures actually taken against Jews in the decade before their destruction had been suggested earlier. The Nuremberg Laws of the Nazis, which withdrew citizenship from Jews, realized goals first formulated by the German antisemitic parties in the 1880s (see Documents 10–12). Registration of Jewish property with an eye to future confiscation, a measure carried out by the Vichy regime, was advocated by Edouard Drumont fifty years before (see Documents 8 and 22). Measures taken against Jews on the eve of the Holocaust—economic quarantine, forced emigration, alien status, sexual and social isolation from non-Jews—all had their precedents in previous antisemitic literature.

Antisemitism appeared to many contemporaries as nothing more than an ignorant reaction to socioeconomic disturbances, a problem that would solve itself as people moved toward harmony and enlightenment. But the twentieth century disappointed these naive hopes. Old prejudices did not die; rather, they flourished in the era of permanent crisis. Fantasies and fears, cultivated over centuries and embodied in a many-faced political movement, led some to commit murder and millions of others to stand by as passive spectators. From deceptively modest beginnings in the late 1870s, antisemitism first served as an outlet for aggrieved individuals. It went on to demonstrate its utility to a broad range of political forces, and eventually its programmatic demands were realized through the authority and power of several governments. Nazi genocide, the most horrific evidence of antisemitism's potential to unleash murder, has not eliminated the willingness of some to use and others to respond to its lies.

A word here about fairness is in order. It is not my intention to exculpate Jews as individuals or as a group. Doubtless, individual Jews did many bad things, including some of the things antisemites accused them of doing. Even if Jews never constituted the monolith antisemites insisted upon seeing, it seems reasonable also to concede that they differed from those among whom they lived, or at least that they were perceived as different. Some of their alleged character traits, conditioned by their history, undoubtedly grated upon Gentile sensibilities. But this does not validate antisemitism, a movement that customarily dealt in blanket indictments, unqualified generalizations, and group punishments. Antisemites peopled their universe with all-powerful demons uniformly committed to a conspiracy of destruction.

For these reasons, antisemitism is not presented here as one ideology among many, with good points and bad. From its inception, it relied on false perceptions of reality, leading to faulty hypotheses, buttressed by erroneous data, and arriving at unwarranted conclusions. Once it resulted in mass murder, and it still has extraordinary power to harm the human community.

1 The Anti-Jewish Tradition

Medieval Jew Hatred

The following excerpt from Johann Andreas Eisenmenger's *Judaism Exposed* (1710) stands at the end of a long tradition of theologically based anti-Jewish writings and serves here to sum up its characteristic methods and points of view.

Eisenmenger (1654–1704) was a competent scholar, a professor of Oriental languages at the University of Heidelberg. His diligent reading of the Talmud and other rabbinic writings, and his by-and-large accurate quotations, are no longer seriously disputed. This expertise set him apart from most of the succeeding "unmaskers" of Judaism.

But Eisenmenger studied in order to confirm beliefs about Jews already deeply rooted in the Christian West. Writing to prove the superiority of Christianity, he failed to grasp the organic nature of rabbinic literature. The Talmud, for example, came into existence over a thousand-year period, from the fifth century B.C. to the fifth century A.D. No doubt it contained many sentiments that contemporary Europeans would have found barbarous (and some it would have found admirable). Commentary on its practical, ethical, and legal subject matter continued uninterruptedly, reflecting the differing opinions of Jewish scholars and answering the need to adapt from a life amid pagan peoples to life in Christian Europe and the Islamic Middle East. By Eisenmenger's time, Talmudic writings had become an object of study rather than a practical guide for Jewish behavior. Many parts of the tradition lost validity as the ethical sensibilities of Jews developed in ways similar to those among whom they lived as insecure minorities. Eisenmenger's reliance on the sources and his literal interpretation presented a distorted picture of contemporary Jewish life, suggesting that the religious and ethical values of the ancient Middle East still held full force among Jews. This false premise was to remain a permanent feature of anti-Jewish polemics.

Judaism Exposed appeared in 1710, six years after its author's death, and only when Jews in Frankfurt failed in their legal attempts to prevent its publication. Implicit in the two-volume work is the vindication of Christianity against the Satanic doctrines of Judaism and the desire to turn the Jews away from their absurd and destructive beliefs. Eisenmenger himself explained the writing of the book as the result of the disturbing impression made upon him by the conversion of three Christians to Judaism.

An equally strong motive for writing, he said, was the negative criticism of Christianity on the part of his Jewish teachers (of Hebrew). The subtitle of the book conveys this aspect of his intentions unmistakably: "thorough and truthful report concerning the manner in which the stiff-necked Jews blaspheme against and abominably dishonor the Holy Trinity, the Father, Son, and Holy Ghost, shame the Holy Mother of Christ, ridicule the New Testament, the Gospels, and Apostles and curse and scorn all of Christianity in the extreme." Individual chapters treated "ridicule of the sacraments and Christian clergy," "how they render the food of Christians loathsome and unclean," "their doctrine that all Christians be damned," "schemes and plots to deceive the authorities," "what to believe concerning the oath of a Jew," and so on. The purported hatred of Jews for Christians and, later, for non-Jews in general served as a frequent justification for many sorts of discrimination. Eisenmenger's call to retaliate against "Jewish misanthropy" recurs frequently in the readings that follow.

Among the calumnies of Jews repeated and "corroborated" by Eisenmenger, the one that probably did more than any other to render them sinister and positively dangerous in the eyes of the Christian majority, was the charge of ritual murder. The "blood accusation" emerged in the middle of the twelfth century and asserted that Jews required the blood of Christians, usually children, for ritual or bizarre magical purposes. Eisenmenger's variant of this fable contains most of the classic elements of the charge: sadistic cruelty practiced on a helpless child, "factual" details to enhance credibility, placement of the deed at Easter and Passover, and reference to the killing of Christ, which this murder was intended to celebrate anew. In other depictions, evidence is usually provided by a recently baptized Jew, and the blood is used to bake unleavened bread.

The ritual-murder allegation often led to serious violence against Jews and mass executions, with or without trials. Occasionally it provoked more widespread disorders. In the thirteenth century, when the charge was particularly rife, Frederick II, Holy Roman Emperor, instructed a commission of high churchmen to settle the question as to whether the Jews required Christian blood. He eventually summoned a number of converted Jews to bear testimony as well. His Golden Bull of 1236 declared the charges groundless. A decade later, Pope Innocent IV issued an official pronouncement acquitting the Jews of "blood guilt" and condemning the motives of those who raised the charge.

But the myth had taken hold of popular imagination and has never wholly disappeared. At the end of the nineteenth century, several ritual-murder trials, invested now with overtones of sexual depravity, seized public attention. From 1891 to 1900, no fewer than 120 stories of ritual murder received extensive coverage in antisemitic newspapers. The charge surfaced in upstate New York in the 1920s and in Argentina as recently as the early 1960s. Discussion of the issue in scholarly books by reputable theologians, while rejecting the charges, probably helped leave a residue of suspicion about the "otherness" of the Jews, even among the educated. If so many "honorable" people gave credence to the idea, Eisenmenger asks, could the accusation be wholly without foundation?

Eisenmenger's exposé became the chief source for all future attempts to ground theories of Jewish evil in the sacred writings of the Jews. In 1870, August Rohling, a Catholic priest with no serious knowledge of rabbinic literature, produced a blatant plagiarism of Eisenmenger and one of the most widely distributed antisemitic pamphlets of all time, *The Talmud-Jew*. The Nazis made frequent use of this work as well as the original.

For Further Reading

On Eisenmenger, Jacob Katz, *From Prejudice to Destruction: Anti-Semitism, 1700–1933* (Cambridge, Mass., 1980). On the charge of ritual murder and medieval conceptions of Jewry, see Jacob R. Marcus, *The Jew in the Medieval World* (New York, 1960). A fictional account of the Beilis ritual murder case in tsarist Russia is Bernard Malamud, *The Fixer* (New York, 1966).

1. Johann Andreas Eisenmenger
Judaism Exposed (1710)

[Chapter 9 begins by questioning whether it is permitted to Jews to rescue a Christian whose life is in danger: "... it is not only disallowed, but on the contrary, sharply forbidden." Eisenmenger goes on to give ten reasons that this is so, citing a wide range of Talmudic writings as proof.]

In addition to these [ten reasons], experience also shows that Jews do not scruple to kill a Christian. As history shows, this pertains not only to mature adults but also to young, innocent children. I shall communicate only a few such cases.

In his church history, Socrates[1] relates that in the year 418 A.D. the Jews of Alexandria conspired together in the night. As a distinguishing sign, they wove rings of palm bark and thereupon raised a cry that the Christian church, which was named the Alexandria Church, was on fire. When the Christians rushed there to put out the alleged fire, the Jews waylaid them and murdered all that they could catch. For this reason and on the next day, Bishop Cyrill expelled all Jews from Alexandria.

In the year 1321 A.D. the Jews of France caused lepers to poison the wells so that many men died therefrom. And all who were guilty of it were burned by command of King Philipp. Thus reported Heinrich Anselm von Ziegler in his [book] published in folio here in Frankfurt and Sebastian Münster in his *Cosmographia*, Book II, page 192, published in Basel in the year 1550. The Jews acted thusly also in Switzerland and Alsace. According to Ziegler, this crime has been confessed by the Jews. Concluding that the dissension between the pope and the emperor would lead to the destruction of Christianity, [the Jews] wanted to advance this eventuality through poison. But they received their well-deserved reward when many of them were burned at Basel, Strasbourg, and Mainz. In other places Jews

---

Source: From Johann Andreas Eisenmenger, *Entdecktes Judentum*, edited and reworked for the present day by Dr. Franz Xaver Schieferl (Dresden, 1893), pp. 367–71, 374–78.

[1]This was not the ancient Greek philosopher but Socrates Scholasticus, a Byzantine of the fifth century who wrote a seven-volume ecclesiastical history.

were put in these same poison sacks, which they had placed in the wells, and thrown into the water, whereupon they drowned. Others were stabbed or thrown from houses and otherwise executed by various lethal means, without regard to age or sex.

In the year 1349 the Jews of Meiningen wanted to fall upon the Christians and kill them as they prayed in their churches. A maid overheard the plot and exposed it. Thereupon the Christians left their churches, seized their weapons, and slew all the Jews.

In the year 1571 Joachim II, Elector of Brandenburg, was poisoned by a Jew with whom he was very intimate, as Schleidanus reports in the tenth book of his histories, page 60. In the same year M. A. Bragadinus was flayed alive and murdered in the cruelest fashion by the Jews. Beyond this Cluverius reports that, when the Persian King Croesus captured Jerusalem in the year 611 . . . and killed many Christians there, the Jews purchased 90,000 captive Christians for a little money and killed them all in piteous ways.

In the year 1665 on May 11 in the Jewish quarter at Vienna, a woman was cruelly murdered by the Jews. She was found in the watering trough used by horses in a sack weighted down by a fifty-pound stone. The corpse had many stab wounds. The head and shoulders and the thighs up to the knees had been slit open. Because the said murder had been accompanied by numerous robberies and other ruthless depravities, his imperial majesty, moved by praiseworthy Christian zeal, decreed the expulsion of the evil-doing Jews. In the year 1670 he had proclaimed with trumpet blasts in the public squares of Vienna that all Jews be eternally banned and that none be any more seen, upon pain of life and limb. Thereafter over 1400 Jewish persons withdrew, part going to Turkey, part to Venice.

Concerning the horrifying murders of tender, innocent little children by Jews there is much to write. . . .

In the year 1250 the Jews of Aragon also stole a child of seven years, crucified him on their Easter [Passover], stabbed him in the chest with a lance, and thus killed him. Cluverius also writes that in London in the year 1257, a Christian child was killed in their annual sacrifice.

In the year 1282 it transpired in Munich that an accused witch sold a little boy to the Jews, who punctured the body and murdered him cruelly. And when the suspected witch again stole a child and wanted to bring him to the Jews, she was this time caught by the father and accused. Thereupon, and after suffering torture, she made known the deed and the place where the murdered child had been buried. She was then judged. When now the people of Munich had seen the punctured and killed child, they were so embittered against the Jews that they killed all of them in the area.

In the year 1475 on Maundy Thursday, a Jew named Tobias brought the Jews of Trent, assembled in the house where they had their synagogue, a Christian child named Simon, not yet three years old. Thereupon an old Jew named Moses took the child on his lap, undressed him, and stuffed a cloth in his mouth so that he could not cry out. The others held his hands and feet. The said Moses made a wound with a knife in the right cheek and cut out a small piece of flesh. Those standing around caught up the blood, and each cut out a small piece of flesh until the wound had become the size of an egg. This they also did on other parts of the body. Then they stretched out the hands and arms like a crucifix and stuck needles into the half-dead body, while speaking a few words of this nature: "Let us kill him, just as we did the God of the Christians, Jesus, who is nothing. Thus must all our enemies perish." Finally, the child, having endured this martyrdom, which lasted a full hour, gave up the ghost. [The Jews] hid the body under some wine barrels and then, fearing a search of the house, threw it into the water flowing by the synagogue. This murderous deed, to the greatest derision of the Jews, is depicted under the bridge tower here in Frankfurt with the inscription: "Anno 1475. On Maundy Thursday the child Simon, two and one-half years old, was murdered by the Jews."[2]

... In the present day we no longer hear of such cruel deeds in Germany, aside from what, if I remember correctly, I read in a newspaper a few years ago, concerning a murdered child found in Franconia; the Jews fell under suspicion in the case. Because in former days Jews were dealt with very sharply when such crimes were committed, it is not to be doubted that they now refrain from shedding blood solely because of the fear of punishment. Certainly, their hatred of Christians remains as great as it ever was. It is clear from what has been said above, however, that the Jews do not scruple to kill a Christian and that it must be permitted to them, if only it can be done conveniently, secretly, and without danger.

As to the use of Christian blood in this context ... Pregnant Jewish women cannot give birth without it. The converted Jew Friedrich Samuel Brentz writes about this in his book: "If there is a Jewess present who cannot free herself of her womanly burden and who stands in great need, the rabbi or the eldest Jew takes a pure deerskin parchment and writes three (easily) discernible notes. The first he lays on her head, the next he puts into her mouth, and the third in her right hand. Then she gives birth. What kind of ink must be used for these notes is a complete secret. However, I have heard truthful and believable stories that the Jews sometimes buy or steal Christian children and then torture them. With their blood such notes are perhaps written; I know for a fact that they do not regard anything done against Gentiles, that is, against Christians, as a sin. They say also that it is better to deprive a Christian of life, for then a whole generation of Satan shall be prevented." These are the words of Brentz. However, that [blood] is used, and that it actually is effective in promoting birth, I cannot believe.

It is also mentioned that in former times during their Easter feast, Jews made use of [Christian blood] in their sweet cakes, which they call matzos, and mixed in their wine. We read that King Alphonso of Spain conversed

---

[2]Although skeptical of Jewish guilt in this, the most famous medieval allegation of ritual murder, the church lent credibility to the charges when the victim was beatified as the Blessed Simon of Trent in 1582. The scene of the murder became a site of pilgrimage and a commemorative chapel.

with the scholar, Thomas, undoubtedly a Jewish convert, about this. He said to him that a bishop had come to Madrid who preached publicly that the Jews could not hold their Easter feast without Christian blood. He asked whether it were true that such things happened. Thomas answered the king: "Lo, we have seen that a Jew may eat no blood of any living thing. Indeed, they are also forbidden to drink the blood of fish, even though the Talmudists say that it is not called blood. It is scorned and loathsome to them because a Jew is unaccustomed to it, even though he sees that other peoples eat blood. How much more so will he abhor the blood of men, since he has seen no other men who eat it. . . ." From this we can see that Thomas, who was probably a convert, declared the Jews innocent in this matter. [Eisenmenger presents a number of denials by Jewish writers concerning the use of Christian blood. He then delivers his last word on the subject.]

Because, however, many sound writers have written that the Jews do use Christian blood, and demonstrate this with examples, and because most of the children are murdered around Easter, we can suppose that not everything is untrue. I leave it at this as to whether or not the matter is true. Undoubtedly, the Jews murder Christian children mostly at Easter because our Savior Jesus Christ was crucified then. They do it as a mockery of Him. Let that be enough on this matter.

As to the question, whether a Christian, when he is ill, should entrust himself to a Jewish physician and use the remedies prescribed by him, I answer the following. No one should act thus. I shall prove this.

First, because Jews are the condign and bitter enemies of the Christian, as has been adequately shown in the seventh chapter of this book and in other passages, one can expect no good from an enemy. Second, I assert this because, as confirmed previously, it is allowed them to deprive a Christian of his life. Who would want to trust such men to care for them when, instead of restoring him to health with suitable remedies, he is concerned with killing him with unsuitable ones? The rabbis forbid that a Jew make use of a Christian physician. . . . If Jews will not trust Christians because they think that they possess souls as murderous as their own, why should we then entrust our lives to them, especially when we know how inimical they are toward us?

The Secularization of Jew Hatred

The preceding selection, written at the end of an era, expressed medieval superstitions regarding Jews and Judaism that struck many educated Europeans of the author's time as hopelessly benighted and anachronistic. The following excerpt, from the writings of Voltaire, nonetheless reveals the survival of many such attitudes in a more secular age and among those educated men who thought they had freed themselves from Eisenmenger's theological preconceptions.

François-Marie de Arouet, known as Voltaire (1694–1778), waged a long battle against injustice, superstition, and persecution. Jailed in the Bastille and exiled from France as a young man, he wrote dramas, philosophical tracts, romances, and histories in a rationalist and skeptical vein. His deft style, satirical and devastatingly ironic, made many enemies in high places. But he was also the confidant of kings, and by the end of his life, and certainly in succeeding generations, his courage in the cause of tolerance and freedom had won him undying fame. In 1791 his remains were enshrined in the Pantheon of Paris.

The Age of Enlightenment, linked inextricably with Voltaire's name, fostered significant improvements in the lot of European Jews and inaugurated their struggle for full and equal participation in European life. It was among the enlightened that Jews first emerged from the status of sinister aliens. For those of philosophical bent, a man or woman of talent, including individual Jews, could overcome the disadvantages of lowly birth and gain entry to the circles of the cultured all over western and central Europe. The plays of Richard Cumberland and Gotthold Ephraim Lessing, contemporaries of Voltaire, portrayed Jews as sympathetic human beings, possessed of normal, even noble, feelings, and as the victims of irrational religious persecution. But even among the educated elite, this was not a universally held view. Several prominent figures in the Enlightenment evinced a far from enlightened attitude toward Jews and Judaism. Of these, Voltaire was the most important. His writings on the subject, tinged as they are with the residue of medieval Jew hatred, seem strangely out of harmony with the general tenor of his thought and the causes that he championed.

The *Dictionnaire philosophique* is a wide-ranging compendium of Voltaire's thought on many subjects. Jews and Judaism do not play an inordinately large role in it, yet the general picture he presents in this and other writings is of "an ignorant and barbarous people," inferior in every category he deemed important. Judging from their own sacred writings and the accounts of ancient historians, he views the Jews as ethically, socially, politically, culturally, and militarily worthless. Fatally formed by their earliest experiences and the geographical factors of the ancient Near East, they had not developed in any significant way over the centuries. Although admitting that they were the victims of religiously inspired oppression, Voltaire assured his readers that the Jews had committed many atrocious acts and were therefore not entitled to sympathy.

Whereas Eisenmenger wrote to defend the superiority of Christian revelation, Voltaire was motivated primarily by hatred of Christianity and the
biblical Judaism that had spawned it. Pretending to reverence Scripture, he
judges and condemns it by eighteenth-century ethical standards. A great
part of the loathing he felt for Jews stemmed from his rejection of Christianity and its role in human subjection. Some commentators have even suggested that Voltaire's attack on Judaism was little more than a safe way to
attack his real enemy, the Christian Church.

Voltaire's emotional language and the sincere contempt he evidences
indicate something more than a mere stratagem to avoid the charge of
heresy or escape the censors. Perhaps his personal experiences with Jews
had something to do with his enmity. Voltaire was a sharp businessman—
he died a millionaire—and had had questionable business dealings with
two Jewish bankers, one of whom entangled him in a long lawsuit. This
experience, however, is too simplistic an explanation of hatred in a man
who could be notably fair-minded and tolerant. Moreover, Voltaire's first
anti-Jewish utterance predates by four years his conflict with the banker,
Medina, mentioned in the following excerpt.

Whatever the explanation of Voltaire's hostility, it is clear that he uncritically accepted a good deal of the medieval stereotype concerning
Jews. That he, the leading philosopher of the Enlightenment, could not free
himself from these prejudices shows how deeply they were entrenched in
the European experience. This cultural inheritance of Europeans proved
inescapable for many, and its consequences reappear often in the texts that
follow.

According to the definition I advanced in the Introduction, Voltaire
ought not to be considered an antisemite. He never urged action against
Jews or singled them out for special treatment, and he even, disingenuously
perhaps, called for harmonious coexistence with them. He differs from the
antisemitic zealot as well. Jews did not preoccupy him, and solving the
problem of the Jews did not provide his career with its substance or direction. He wrote little about them and, even in the document reprinted here,
he occasionally contrasts them favorably to the people among whom they
live.

But Voltaire's equivocation does not rob his negative views of their
force and effect. He is nonetheless a key figure in the survival and reorientation of Jew hatred in the modern era. He rejected the Christian conception of Jewish history that portrayed Judaism as the harbinger of
Christianity and the suffering of the Jews as divine retribution for their denial of the New Covenant. Despised though they were, the Jews functioned
usefully in the Christian world as living testimony to the costs of heresy.
Voltaire saw no truth in this conception and therefore preserved no function
for the Jews, no rationale for their continued existence.

Voltaire's influence helped undermine what was a promising new departure in the relations between Jews and non-Jews. Contemporaries cited
his arguments and employed his rhetoric in working against Jewish emancipation. For succeeding generations of antisemites, his enormous prestige

and talent legitimized a potent, secularized antisemitism. Particularly for antisemites with left-wing sympathies, he demonstrated that it was possible to hold progressive and antisemitic views simultaneously.

For Further Reading

On Voltaire's role, Jacob Katz, *From Prejudice to Destruction: Anti-Semitism, 1700–1933* (Cambridge, Mass., 1980). For a defense of Voltaire against the charge of antisemitism, Peter Gay, *Voltaire's Politics* (Princeton, 1959).

2. Voltaire
Philosophical Dictionary (1764)

Section I. Jews

It is certain that the Jewish nation is the most singular that the world has ever seen; and although in a political view, the most contemptible of all, yet in the eyes of a philosopher, it is, on various accounts, worth consideration.

The Guebers, the Banians, and the Jews, are the only nations which exist dispersed, having no alliance with any people, are perpetuated among foreign nations, and continue apart from the rest of the world. . . . but the Jews are dispersed over the whole face of the earth, and if they were assembled, would compose a nation much more numerous than it ever was in the short time that they were masters of Palestine. . . .

The learned have agitated the question whether the Jews, like so many other nations, really sacrificed men to the Divinity. This is a dispute on words; those whom the people consecrated to the anathema were not put to death on an altar, with religious rites; but they were not the less immolated, without its being permitted to pardon any one of them. Leviticus (27:29) expressly forbids the redeeming of those who shall have been devoted. Its words are, "They shall surely be put to death." By virtue of this law it was that Jephthah devoted and killed his daughter, that Saul would have killed his son, and that the prophet Samuel cut in pieces King Agag, Saul's prisoner. It is quite certain that God is the master of the lives of men, and that it is not for us to examine His laws. We ought to limit ourselves to believing these things, and reverencing in silence the designs of God, who permitted them.

. . . [The war against the Romans] was the last struggle of this nation, which has never lifted its head again. Its constant opinion, that barrenness

Source: From Voltaire, *Philosophical Dictionary.* Trans. William F. Fleming (New York, 1901), 6:266–67, 269–70, 278–81, 283–94, 301–6, 313.

is a reproach, has preserved it; the Jews have ever considered as their two first duties, to get money and children.

From this short summary it results that the Hebrews have ever been vagrants, or robbers, or slaves, or seditious. They are still vagabonds upon the earth, and abhorred by men, yet affirming that heaven and earth and all mankind were created for them alone. It is evident, from the situation of Judaea, and the genius of this people, that they could not but be continually subjugated. It was surrounded by powerful and warlike nations, for which it had an aversion; so that it could neither be in alliance with them, nor protected by them. It was impossible for it to maintain itself by its marine; for it soon lost the port which in Solomon's time it had on the Red Sea; and Solomon himself always employed Tyrians to build and to steer his vessels, as well as to erect his palace and his temple. It is then manifest that the Hebrews had neither trade nor manufactures, and that they could not compose a flourishing people. They never had an army always ready for the field, like the Assyrians, the Medes, the Persians, the Syrians, and the Romans. The laborers and artisans took up arms only as occasion required, and consequently could not form well-disciplined troops. Their mountains, or rather their rocks, are neither high enough, nor sufficiently contiguous, to have afforded an effectual barrier against invasion. The most numerous part of the nation, transported to Babylon, Persia, and to India, or settled in Alexandria, were too much occupied with their traffic and their brokerage to think of war. Their civil government, sometimes republican, sometimes pontifical, sometimes monarchical, and very often reduced to anarchy, seems to have been no better than their military discipline.

You ask, what was the philosophy of the Hebrews? The answer will be a very short one—they had none. Their legislator himself does not anywhere speak expressly of the immortality of the soul, nor of the rewards of another life. Josephus and Philo[1] believe the soul to be material; their doctors admitted corporeal angels. . . . The Jews, in the latter times of their sojourn at Jerusalem, were scrupulously attached to nothing but the ceremonials of their law. The man who had eaten pudding or rabbit would have been stoned; while he who denied the immortality of the soul might be high-priest.

It is commonly said that the abhorrence in which the Jews held other nations proceeded from their horror of idolatry; but it is much more likely that the manner in which they at the first exterminated some of the tribes of Canaan, and the hatred which the neighboring nations conceived for

---

[1]Flavius Josephus (b. 37 A.D.), a Jewish historian who wrote in Greek, lived in Rome after the destruction of Jerusalem in 70 A.D. His *The Jewish Wars* and other writings are an important source of knowledge concerning the ancient Near East. He was also critical of "Jewish fanatics" in the struggle against Rome. Philo of Alexandria (c. 20 B.C.–c. 50 A.D.) acted as mediator between Hellenistic philosophy and the Judeo-Christian religious outlook. His numerous works exerted influence upon both Jewish and early Christian writings.

them, were the cause of this invincible aversion. As they knew no nations but their neighbors, they thought that in abhorring them they detested the whole earth, and thus accustomed themselves to be the enemies of all men.

One proof that this hatred was not caused by the idolatry of the nations is that we find in the history of the Jews that they were very often idolaters. Solomon himself sacrificed to strange gods. After him, we find scarcely any king in the little province of Judah that does not permit the worship of these gods and offer them incense. The province of Israel kept its two calves and its sacred groves, or adored other divinities. . . .

You then ask whether the ancient philosophers and law-givers borrowed from the Jews, or the Jews from them? We must refer the question to Philo: he owns that before the translation of the Septuagint[2] the books of his nation were unknown to strangers. A great people cannot have received their laws and their knowledge from a little people, obscure and enslaved. . . . This people, after their captivity at Babylon, had no other alphabet than the Chaldean; they were not famed for any art, any manufacture whatsoever; and even in the time of Solomon they were obliged to pay dear for foreign artisans. To say that the Egyptians, the Persians, the Greeks, were instructed by the Jews, were to say that the Romans learned the arts from the people of Brittany. The Jews never were natural philosophers, nor geometricians, nor astronomers. So far were they from having public schools for the instruction of youth, that they had not even a term in their language to express such an institution. The people of Peru and Mexico measured their year much better than the Jews. Their stay in Babylon and in Alexandria, during which individuals might instruct themselves, formed the people to no art save that of usury. They never knew how to stamp money. . . . In short, we find in them only an ignorant and barbarous people, who have long united the most sordid avarice with the most detestable superstition and the most invincible hatred for every people by whom they are tolerated and enriched. Still, we ought not to burn them.

Section II. The Jewish Law

Their law must appear, to every polished people, as singular as their conduct; if it were not divine, it would seem to be the law of savages beginning to assemble themselves into a nation; and being divine, one cannot understand how it is that it has not existed from all ages, for them, and for all men. . . .

In this law it is forbidden to eat eels, because they have no scales; and hares, because they chew the cud, and have cloven feet. Apparently, the Jews had hares different from ours. The griffin is unclean, and four-footed

---

[2]The Septuagint was the translation of the Old Testament into Greek by Hellenistic Jews in Alexandria between 250 B.C. and 100 A.D. Greek-speaking Christians, including St. Paul, employed this version, as does the present-day Greek Orthodox Church.

birds are unclean, which animals are somewhat rare. Whoever touches a mouse or a mole is unclean. The women are forbidden to lie with horses or asses. The Jewish women must have been subject to this sort of gallantry. The men are forbidden to offer up their seed to Moloch; and here the term seed is not metaphorical. It seems that it was customary, in the deserts of Arabia, to offer up this singular present to the gods; as it is said to be usual in Cochin and some other countries of India, for the girls to yield their virginity to an iron Priapus in a temple. These two ceremonies prove that mankind is capable of everything. The Kaffirs, who deprive themselves of one testicle, are a still more ridiculous example of the extravagance of superstition.

Another law of the Jews, equally strange, is their proof of adultery. A woman accused by her husband must be presented to the priests, and she is made to drink of the waters of jealousy, mixed with wormwood and dust. If she is innocent, the water makes her more beautiful; if she is guilty, her eyes start from her head, her belly swells, and she bursts before the Lord. . . .

Section III. The Dispersion of the Jews

It has been pretended that the dispersion of this people had been foretold, as a punishment for their refusing to acknowledge Jesus Christ as the Messiah; the asserters affecting to forget that they had been dispersed throughout the known world long before Jesus Christ. The books that are left us of this singular nation make no mention of a return of the twelve tribes transported beyond the Euphrates by Tiglath-Pileser and his successor Shalmaneser; and it was six hundred years after, that Cyrus sent back to Jerusalem the tribes of Judah and Benjamin, which Nebuchadnezar had brought away into the provinces of his empire. The Acts of the Apostles certify that fifty-three days after the death of Jesus Christ, there were Jews from every nation under heaven assembled for the feast of Pentecost. St. James writes to the twelve dispersed tribes; and Josephus and Philo speak of the Jews as very numerous throughout the East.

It is true that, considering the carnage that was made of them under some of the Roman emperors, and the slaughter of them so often repeated in every Christian state, one is astonished that this people not only still exists, but is at this day no less numerous than it was formerly. Their numbers must be attributed to their exemption from bearing arms, their ardor for marriage, their custom of contracting it in their families early, their law of divorce, their sober and regular way of life, their abstinence, their toil, and their exercise.

Their firm attachment to the Mosaic law is no less remarkable, especially when we consider their frequent apostasies when they lived under the government of their kings and their judges; and Judaism is now, of all the religions in the world, the one most rarely abjured—which is partly the fruit of the persecutions it has suffered. Its followers, perpetual martyrs to their creed, have regarded themselves with progressively increasing confidence, as the fountain of all sanctity; looking upon us as no other than rebellious Jews, who have abjured the law of God, and put to death or torture those who received it from His hand. . . .

It is singular that the Christians pretend to have accomplished the prophecies by tyrannizing over the Jews, by whom they were transmitted. We have already seen how the Inquisition banished the Jews from Spain. Obliged to wander from land to land, from sea to sea, to gain a livelihood; everywhere declared incapable of possessing any landed property, or holding any office, they have been obliged to disperse, and roam from place to place, unable to establish themselves permanently in any country, for want of support, of power to maintain their ground, and of knowledge in the art of war. Trade, a profession long despised by most of the nations of Europe, was, in those barbarous ages, their only resource; and as they necessarily grew rich by it, they were treated as infamous usurers. Kings who could not ransack the purses of their subjects put the Jews, whom they regarded not as citizens, to torture.

What was done to them in England may give some idea of what they experienced in other countries. King John, being in want of money, had the rich Jews in his kingdom imprisoned. One of them, having had seven of his teeth drawn one after another, to obtain his property, gave, on losing the eighth, a thousand marks of silver. Henry III extorted from Aaron, a Jew of York, fourteen thousand marks of silver, and ten thousand for his queen. He sold the rest of the Jews of his country to his brother Richard, for the term of one year, in order, says Matthew Paris, that this count might disembowel those whom his brother had flayed.

In France they were put in prison, plundered, sold, accused of magic, of sacrificing children, of poisoning the wells. They were driven out of the kingdom; they were suffered to return for money; and even while they were tolerated, they were distinguished from the rest of the inhabitants by marks of infamy. And, by an inconceivable whimsicality, while in other countries the Jews were burned to make them embrace Christianity, in France the property of such as became Christians was confiscated. Charles IV, by an edict given at Basville, April 4, 1392, abrogated this tyrannical custom, which, according to the Benedictine Mabillon, had been introduced for two reasons:

First, to try the faith of these new converts, as it was but too common for those of this nation to feign submission to the gospel for some personal interest, without internally changing their belief.

Secondly, because as they had derived their wealth chiefly from usury, the purity of Christian morals appeared to require them to make a general restitution, which was effected by confiscation.

But the true reason of this custom, which [Montesquieu] the author of the *Spirit of the Laws* has so well developed, was a sort of . . . redemption for the sovereign, or the seigneurs, of the taxes which they levied on the

Jews, as mortmainable serfs, whom they succeeded; for they were deprived of this benefit when the latter were converted to the Christian faith.

At length, being incessantly proscribed in every country, they ingeniously found the means of saving their fortunes and making their retreats forever secure. Being driven from France under Philip the Long, in 1318, they took refuge in Lombardy; there they gave to the merchants bills of exchange on those to whom they had entrusted their effects at their departure, and these were discharged.

The admirable invention of bills of exchange sprang from the extremity of despair; and then, and not until then, commerce was enabled to elude the efforts of violence, and to maintain itself throughout the world.

Section IV. Letters in Answer to Some Objections

Gentlemen: When, forty-four years ago, your countryman Medina[3] became a bankrupt in London, being twenty thousand francs in my debt, he told me that "it was not his fault; that he was unfortunate"; that "he had never been one of the children of Belial"; that "he had always endeavored to live as a son of God"—that is, as an honest man, a good Israelite. I was affected; I embraced him; we joined in the praise of God; and I lost eighty percent.

You ought to know that I never hated your nation; I hate no one. . . .

Far from hating, I have always pitied you. If . . . I have sometimes bantered a little, I am not therefore the less sensitive. I wept, at the age of sixteen, when I was told that a [Jewish] mother and her daughter had been burned at Lisbon for having eaten, standing, a little lamb, cooked with lettuce, on the fourteenth day of the red moon; and I can assure you that the extreme beauty that this girl was reported to have possessed, had no share in calling forth my tears, although it must have increased the spectators' horror for the assassins, and their pity for the victim. . . .

You clearly see, then, that even so long ago I was your servant, your friend, your brother; although my father and mother had preserved to me my foreskin.

I am aware that virility, whether circumcised or uncircumcised, has caused very fatal quarrels. . . . I have read enough of your books to know that Hamor's son Sichem ravished Leah's daughter Dinah, who at most was not more than five years old, but was very forward for her age. He wanted to make her his wife; and Jacob's sons, brothers of the violated damsel, gave her to him in marriage on condition that he and all his people should be circumcised. When the operation was performed, and all the

---

[3]Medina, or Anthony Mendez daCosta, was a Jewish banker in London who went broke in the aftermath of the frenzied speculation associated with the name John Law and the bursting of the South Sea Bubble (1720). Voltaire arrived in London in 1726 with a letter of credit for 20,000 francs, on which Medina failed to make good. Voltaire's second unfortunate experience, for which there is any record, was with the Court Jew, Abraham Hirschel, in Berlin (1750–51). This time, it revolved around a shady speculation by Voltaire and issued in a lawsuit, which in turn led to his break with Frederick the Great of Prussia.

Sichemites, or Sechemites, were lying-in of the pains consequent there-upon, the holy patriarchs Simeon and Levi cut all their throats one after another. But, after all, I do not believe that uncircumcision ought now to produce such abominable horrors; and especially I do not think that men should hate, detest, anathematize, and damn one another every Saturday or Sunday, on account of a morsel more or less of flesh.

If I have said that some of the circumcised have clipped money at Metz, at Frankfurt on the Oder, and at Warsaw (which I do not remember) I ask their pardon; for, being almost at the end of my pilgrimage, I have no wish to embroil myself with Israel.

I have the honor to be (as they say),

Yours, etc.

Fifth Letter

> Jewish Assassinations. Were the Jews Cannibals? Had their
> Mothers Commerce with Goats? Did their Fathers and Mothers
> Immolate their Children? With a Few Other Fine Actions of God's
> People. . . .

JEWISH CALAMITIES AND GREAT ASSASSINATIONS Permit me, in the first place, to lament over all your calamities; for, besides the two hundred and thirty-nine thousand and twenty Israelites killed by order of the Lord, I find that Jephthah's daughter was immolated by her father. Turn which way you please—twixt the text as you will—dispute as you like against the fathers of the Church; still he did to her as he had vowed; and he had vowed to cut his daughter's throat in thanksgiving to God. An excellent thanksgiving!

Yes, you have immolated human victims to the Lord; but be consoled; I have often told you that our Celts and all nations have done so for-merly. . . .

I find that seventy brothers of Abimelech were put to death on the same stone by this Abimelech, the son of Gideon and a prostitute. This son of Gideon was a bad kinsman, and this Gideon, the friend of God, was very debauched.

Your Levite going on his ass to Gibeah—the Gibeonites wanting to violate him—his poor wife violated in his stead, and dying in conse-quence—the civil war that ensued—all your tribe of Benjamin extermi-nated, saving only six hundred men—give me inexpressible pain.

You lost, all at once, five fine towns which the Lord destined for you, at the end of the lake of Sodom; and that for an inconceivable attempt upon the modesty of two angels. Really, this is much worse than what your mothers are accused of with the goats. How should I have other than the greatest pity for you, when I find murder and bestiality established against your ancestors, who are our first spiritual fathers, and our near kinsmen according to the flesh? For after all, if you are descended from Shem, we are descended from Japhet. We are therefore evidently cousins. . . .

DID THE JEWS EAT HUMAN FLESH? Among your calamities, which have so often made me shudder, I have always reckoned your misfortune in having eaten human flesh. You say that this happened only on great occasions; that it was not you whom the Lord invited to His table to eat the horse and the horseman, and that only the birds were guests. I am willing to believe it.

WERE THE JEWISH LADIES INTIMATE WITH GOATS? You assert that your mothers had no commerce with he-goats, nor your fathers with she-goats. But pray, gentlemen, why are you the only people upon earth whose laws have forbidden such commerce? Would any legislator ever have thought of promulgating this extraordinary law if the offense had not been common?

DID THE JEWS IMMOLATE HUMAN VICTIMS? You venture to affirm that you have never immolated human victims to the Lord. What, then, was the murder of Jephthah's daughter, who was really immolated, as we have already shown from your own books?

How will you explain the anathema of the thirty-two virgins, that were the tribute of the Lord, when you took thirty-two thousand Midianitish virgins and sixty-one thousand asses? I will not here tell you, that according to this account there were not two asses for each virgin; but I will ask you, what was this tribute for the Lord? According to your Book of Numbers, there were sixteen thousand for your priests, and on the soldiers' share there was levied a tribute of thirty-two virgins for the Lord. What became of them? You had no nuns. What was the Lord's share in all your wars, if it was not blood? Did not the priest Samuel hack in pieces King Agag, whose life King Saul had saved? Did he not sacrifice him as the Lord's share?

Either renounce your sacred books, in which, according to the decision of the church, I firmly believe, or acknowledge that your forefathers offered up to God rivers of human blood, unparalleled by any people on earth.

Seventh Letter

> Charity which God's People and the Christians
> Should Entertain for Each Other

My tenderness for you has only a few words more to say. We have been accustomed for ages to hang you up between two dogs; we have repeatedly driven you away through avarice; we have recalled you through avarice and stupidity; we still, in more towns than one, make you pay for liberty to breathe the air; we have, in more kingdoms than one, sacrificed you to God; we have burned you as holocausts—for I will not follow your example, and dissemble that we have offered up sacrifices of human blood; all the difference is, that our priests, content with applying your money to their own use, have had you burned by laymen; while your priests always immolated the human victims with their own sacred hands. You were monsters of cruelty and fanaticism in Palestine; we have been so in Europe: my friends, let all this be forgotten.

2 From Jew Hatred to Antisemitism

A Cultural Danger

At the time he wrote the following essay in 1878, Richard Wagner (1813–83) was a world-famous composer whose musical genius was widely, if not universally, recognized. This had not been the case when he first attacked Jews in *Jewry in Music,* which he published under a pseudonym in 1850. At that time, struggling for recognition of his music, he was living as an exile because of his participation in the Revolution of 1848. During the revolution he had espoused democratic views and at least passively favored the progressive position on Jewish emancipation.

Yet he must have been harboring doubts even then, for in *Jewry in Music* Wagner condemns the idea of Jewish emancipation as an abstraction, not the product of real sympathy between Jews and non-Jews. Such sympathy was impossible, he maintained, because of the repellent character traits of the Jews as a whole; these could not fail to awaken an instinctive antipathy. Because all art, for Wagner, emerged from the artist's rootedness in the *Volk,* Jews, eternal strangers among the peoples of Europe, could not be artistically creative. This was especially true of Jews who dressed and spoke like Europeans. They were totally rootless, not even at home in their own tribe, able only to ape their hosts but never to assimilate their language and culture.

The reader might expect pity for the purported creative sterility of Jews; instead, Wagner's tone in *Jewry in Music* is angry and sardonic. He uses Jews as his foil and a means of self-advertisement. It is characteristic of this nation, he charges, that it cannot create an original culture yet knows how to exploit the art of others for profit; its "artists" are satisfied if they achieve popularity through cheap effects. Wagner's is the antithesis of "Jewish music," that is, rooted in the *Volk,* original rather than derivative, scornful of easy popularity. Personal animus toward his immensely popular competitors Meyerbeer, Mendelssohn, and Offenbach (all of Jewish origin) is easy to find in *Jewry in Music.* But as with most of the following documents, the argument goes beyond professional jealousy or personal grudges.

To account for the popularity of "Jewish art," Wagner coined the term *Verjudung,* meaning the Jewification or Judaization of culture. That such trivial and debased art could find a large audience in Europe, and particularly in Germany, was the best evidence of the degeneration of artistic taste. Jews knowingly fostered such decadence in all cultural forms and did so from positions of economic power within the cultural establishment. Yet they could not have succeeded so well, were it not for the apathy, ignorance, and philistinism of European peoples.

The concept of *Verjudung* gained wide currency in Germany because it expressed the fears of many intellectuals regarding Jewish emancipation and the breakdown of legal safeguards that had kept Jews and non-Jews living separate lives. The swiftness of Jewish acculturation appeared to be confirmation of sinister intentions. Mongrelization or, worse, the inevitable absorption of Germandom into Jewry, was the predicted outcome of this cultural conquest. Wagner's malicious attack fed these fears, denying the validity of Jewish participation in German cultural life, the single area in which Jews seemed to have gained acceptance during the nineteenth century.

In the following essay, Wagner cannot disguise his impatience with Germans who tolerated things Jewish, thus inviting the appearance of ruthless parasites. Christian conservatives in Germany had been complaining about the inroads made by the Jews since the 1850s. Yet, writing before Jewish emancipation, they were confident that the basically sound German body politic would reverse this worrisome development in time. Wagner, writing in 1878, is by no means so certain. Given legal equality, their "unquestionable" control of the mass media, the determined way in which they had "taken over" German cultural concerns, and the degeneration of public taste at all levels of society, he worries that Jews may succeed in their attempts to alienate Germans from their culture. He sees hope only in the fatal lack of originality among Jews and therefore the possibility that a German genius might bring about a cultural regeneration of the *Volk*. This, of course, was the special destiny Wagner assigned himself.

Wagner's antisemitism had no clearly political motives and little to do with Judaism as a religion. He framed his argument on racial grounds, condemning converts as well as practicing Jews and attributing ineradicable, uniformly negative tribal characteristics to them. Personal antagonism and career failure may account for his publishing *Jewry in Music* in 1850. But they cannot explain why he republished the booklet in 1869, this time under his own name, or why he wrote the following essay in 1878. By this time, he could no longer be considered a struggling artist, yet he did not abandon antisemitism.

Whatever its origins, Wagner's antisemitism remained constant. His diary and that of his wife, Cosima, reveal an unflagging concern with the Jewish question through the 1860s and 1870s. As a matter of course, several antisemites sent their writings to the "Master of Bayreuth," sure of a sympathetic reception. He was an inspiration for antisemites in Germany and abroad during his life and remained so in death.

The intensity of his antisemitism notwithstanding, Wagner was extremely cautious in his public behavior. He refused to sign the Antisemites' Petition in 1881 (see Document 10) and condemned the rowdiness of the antisemitic political parties that took shape in the early 1880s. He never publicly suggested that any sort of action be taken against Jews. This diffidence, however, was the result of what one historian has labeled, "honest paranoia." Wagner felt that after publication of *Jewry in Music*, he was the object of a Jewish vendetta. He did not dare to alienate the powerful Jews further. They formed too great a part of the audience for his musical creations, and their money dictated the reviews of critics and musicologists. It is true that Jews were among his severest critics, but generally they were also his sincere admirers and closest collaborators. That they continued to flock to performances of his works apparently fed, rather than softened, his hostility and fear.

For Further Reading

Jacob Katz, *The Darker Side of Genius: Richard Wagner's Anti-Semitism* (Hanover and London, 1986). Also George Mosse, "The Image of the Jew in German Popular Culture," in *Germans and Jews* (New York, 1970).

3. Richard Wagner
Modern (1878)

In a pamphlet sent in a short time ago, a "significant Jewish voice" is quoted as expressing the following opinion:

> The modern world must triumph because it is incomparably better armed than the old, orthodox world. The power of the pen has become a world power without which there is no survival in any area. And this power has almost completely passed you orthodox by. To be sure, your scholars write beautifully, intelligently, but only for their peers. Yet Popularity is the shibboleth of our times. The free-thinking Jewish and Christian world has completely conquered modern journalism and romanticism. I say the free-thinking Jewish world, advisedly, for, in fact, German Jewry works so energetically, so colossally, so untiringly within modern culture and science, that the greatest part of Christendom is being led, consciously or unconsciously, by modern Jewry. With few exceptions, there is no newspaper or piece of literature which is not directly or indirectly presided over by Jews.

How true! I have never read about this before and rather thought that our Jewish fellow-citizens would have preferred not to hear such things. Now, however, since we have been met with such open language, we may also perhaps be permitted to speak openly as well. And this without having to fear being made ridiculous, injured in various ways, or occasionally even tumultuously hissed off the stage, all because we are hateful oppressors of Jews. Perhaps, we will even succeed, with our "culture-guardians," the world power of which we do not deny, in reaching an agreement about basic principles which they may not use in quite the correct sense. For, then, if [the Jews] are being honest with us, their "colossal efforts" may have a good result for all involved.

Source: From Richard Wagner, "Modern," in *Bayreuther Blätter* (March 1878): 59–63.

All of a sudden, there is "the modern world." This does not apparently refer to the world of today, the time in which we live, or—as modern German puts it so beautifully—"nowadays." No, in the heads of our latest culture bearers, it signifies a world that has never yet existed, namely a "modern" world such as the world has never known at any time. Thus, a new world that previous worlds do not even approach and that therefore must be measured completely and arbitrarily according to its own standards. To the Jews, who, as a national entity, until half a century ago stood completely outside our cultural strivings, this present-day world, which they have entered so suddenly and which they appropriate to themselves with increasing force, this world must in fact seem a wholly new and hitherto nonexistent one.

To be sure, they should conceive of themselves as the only novelty in this old world. They seem, however, to want to fend off consciousness of this and prefer, on the other hand, to believe that this old world became brand new the moment they entered it. This strikes us as erroneous, and they ought diligently to enlighten themselves on this matter. This presupposes that they are being honest with us and that they want really to help us out of our degeneracy (which up until now they have only exploited and exacerbated). Let's give them the benefit of the doubt.

Scrutinized carefully, our world was a new one for the Jews. All they required to find their way in it was contained in the attempt to appropriate our hard-earned heritage. First and foremost this concerned our language—it would be gauche here to talk of our money. I have never met Jews who make use of their own original mother tongue [Hebrew] among themselves. On the other hand, I have noted again and again that in all the lands of Europe Jews understand German; unfortunately most of them speak it only in their own peculiar jargon [Yiddish]. When legally allowed entrance to the German world, I believe that this immature and incompetent knowledge of the German language, which an inscrutable world destiny bestowed upon them, may have made it particularly difficult for Jews to understand or really assimilate. The descendants of the French Protestants, who were cast out of their homeland, have become completely German. Chamisso,[1] who as a boy spoke only French when he came to Germany, grew up to be a master of German language and thought.

It is extraordinary how difficult this seems to be for Jews. We may suppose that they went too hastily to work in appropriating what was too alien to them and that their unripe knowledge of our language, that is, their jargon, may have led them astray. It belongs to another discussion to illuminate the character of language falsification and what we owe to Jewish journalism for the intrusion of "the modern" into our cultural development. To elaborate further on the present theme, however, we must point out the weighty destiny under which our language had to labor for

---

[1]Adelbert von Chamisso (1781–1838), a botanist, world traveler, and German writer, is most famous for his tale of the man who sold his shadow, *Peter Schlemihl* (1814).

so long and how it took the most ingenious instincts of our greatest poets and sages to restore it to its productive character. And how this remarkable, linguistic-literary process of development was encountered by decadents who frivolously abandon the deadly seriousness of their predecessors and proclaim themselves "Moderns."

We cannot, however, while awaiting their original creations, attribute the invention of the "modern" to our Jewish fellow citizens. This they found as a weed in the field of German literature. I witnessed the youthful first bloom of this plant. It was called, at the time, "Young Germany."[2] Its cultivators began with a war waged against literary "orthodoxy," by which was meant the faith in our great poets and sages of the previous century. They attacked the succeeding, so-called "romantics" (not to be confused with the above-mentioned "significant Jewish voice's" reference to journalism *and* romanticism!), went to Paris, studied Scribe and E. Sue,[3] translated them into a flashy, sloppy German, and ended in part as theater directors and in part as journalists for the philistines.

This was good preparation, and on its foundation, without further invention but well supported with the power of money, the "Modern" could easily be outfitted to become "the modern world," which could then stand victorious over "the orthodox old world."

For the Moderns to explain what we ought to think about this term "modern" is not so easy, especially if they concede that it is something quite lamentable and even dangerous, particularly to us Germans. We will not suppose this because we are assuming that our Jewish fellow citizens mean well by us. Shall we, on this assumption, believe that they don't know what they are saying and only talk twaddle? It is useless here to trace the historical paths of the concept "modern," a term originally coined for the plastic arts of Italy to differentiate them from those of the classical age. It suffices that we have come to know the significance of "modishness" for the French national character. With an idiosyncratic pride, the Frenchman can call himself "modern," for he creates fashion and thereby dominates the external appearance of the entire world.

---

[2]"Young Germany" was an amorphous collection of mostly Christian writers in the 1830s with whom Wagner had had close connections. What bound together people like Karl Gutzkow (1811–78), Heinrich Laube (1806–84), Heinrich Heine (1797–1856), and Ludwig Börne (1786–1837) was not any sort of formal organization but rather a generally critical attitude toward established religion and philistine morality. The first two were prosecuted for "immoral" writings and were hostile toward Jews; Börne and Heine, Jewish converts, lived as exiles in France to escape the censors and were ambivalent about their Jewishness. Young Germany's enemies in the 1830s tried to discredit the whole enterprise as "Jewish," suggesting that it was a French invention and ought to be called "Young Palestine." Wagner here suggests that, if not "Jewish," Young Germany was not properly German either.

[3]Augustin Eugène Scribe (1791–1861), the French dramatist and librettist, was exactly the kind of popular and "lightweight" luminary of French grand opera that Wagner despised. Scribe collaborated in the operas of Auber, Halèvy, and Meyerbeer. Eugène Sue (1804–57) was a popular French novelist, remembered in Wagner's time and today for his *The Wandering Jew* (1845). None were Jews.

If, presently, the Jews, by dint of their "colossal efforts, in common with liberal Christians," are making us into articles of fashion, then let the God of their fathers reward them for "doing so well by us" poor German slaves of French fashion! For the time being, it still appears otherwise, however. For, in spite of all their power, they have no remedy for their lack of originality. And this applies particularly to the employment of that power that they insist none can deny them: "the power of the quill." They can deck themselves out with foreign feathers [quills], just as they can with the delicious names under which our new Jewish fellow citizens come to us—as surprising as they are enrapturing—and this while we poor old peasants and burghers have to satisfy ourselves forever with quite wretched names like "Schmidt," "Müller," "Weber," "Wagner," etc.

Foreign names don't have all that much to do with the matter. But feathers must grow out of our own hides, especially if we do not merely want to decorate ourselves with them, but to write from within ourselves. This is especially true if we hope to conquer the entire old world, something that did not even occur to a Papageno.[4] This old world—or should we say—this German world still has its originals, whose feathers grow without benefit of second blooms. Our "significant [Jewish] voice" does concede that our scholars write "beautifully" and "intelligently." But, alas, we have reason to fear that the constantly obtruding influence of Jewish journalism will eventually undermine this beautiful/intelligent writing, too. It already speaks or remains silent, just as the modern pens would self-evidently have it. Yet "liberal Jewry" still has "colossal" efforts to make in this direction before all the original talents of their German fellow citizens have been completely ruined. They have a long way to go before the feathers grown out of our own hides can only play word games with incomprehensible slogans, badly translated and absurd pet phrases, etc., or before all our musicians have assimilated the remarkable art of composing without imagination.

Possibly, Jewish originality will reveal itself fully in the field of German intellectual life only when no one can any longer understand his own words. Among the lower classes, for example, among our peasants, thanks to the intercession of our colossally striving liberal Jewry, it has almost come to this pass. Even the most sensible [peasant] can no longer get out a reasonable word and thinks he understands the purest nonsense.

Honestly, it's difficult for us to expect much in the way of salvation from the victory of the modern Jewish world. I have got to know serious, gifted individuals of Jewish descent who have made real and strenuous efforts to support the striving of their German fellow citizens and to understand the German language and German history. They have so far turned away from the world-conquering struggles of their former coreligionists that they have even befriended me. These few abandon the "moderns," while the journalist and essayist have succeeded in gaining their full acclamation.

---

[4]Papageno is the comic bird catcher, decked out in feathers, from Mozart's opera, *The Magic Flute* (1791). Although timorous at heart, he is full of bluff and talks too much.

Unclear and difficult to discover is the meaning of that "orthodoxy" that "the significant voice" expects to conquer with his retinue of "Moderns." I fear that this word, like so many others in our current intellectual world, has been rather confusedly understood and vaguely employed. If it is supposed to refer to Jewish orthodoxy, we might then think it relates to the teachings of the Talmud. But our Jewish fellow citizens appear to have turned away [from the Talmud], and advisedly so, for what we know of it suggests that following its doctrines would make any well-meaning cooperation with us uncommonly difficult. [Such behavior] would antagonize the German nation, which, as we know, liberal Jewry only wants to help out. . . .

Certainly, it is not Christian orthodoxy that the liberal Jews are going after again. That would be like them undergoing baptism out of pure liberalism and in a weak moment. Therefore, it is probably the orthodoxy of the German spirit in general that they mean—orthodoxy with regard to the prevailing faith in German science, art, and philosophy. This faith, too, is difficult to understand and surely difficult to define. Many believe, many doubt. Even without the Jews, it has been much debated and much criticized, without resulting in much that is positive. The German, too, has his loves and joys. He enjoys the pain of others, and he "loves to blacken the radiant ones." We are not perfect. This is a fatal theme, better left untouched today. So, too, is the "Popularity" that the "significant voice" has elevated to the shibboleth of our times. I skip over this passage all the more gladly because this word *shibboleth* fills me with horror. On closer inquiry into the meaning of this word, I discovered that it was used by the ancient Jews to earmark the members of a tribe whom they intended to exterminate. Whoever could not pronounce the sound, "sh," was struck down.[5] This is a fittingly fatal word in the battle for popularity. If liberal/modern Jewry should ever wage all-out war for popularity, there could be no more fittingly fatal password, especially destructive for us Germans if we leave off the Semitic "sh" sound.

This ever-so-brief discussion must suffice for now as a closer illumination of "the modern."

---

[5]Judges 12:4–6 relates the story of Jephthah who used the Hebrew word *shibboleth* to distinguish the fleeing Ephramites, who could not pronounce the soft "sh," from his own men. The word has come to signify the pet phrase of a party or sect.

Destroyers of Traditional Values

From his days as a Lutheran theology student at Halle University, where he earned money on the side as a tutor to aristocratic families, Adolf Stoecker's path in life became fixed. Born in 1835 in humble circumstances, he rose to fame and wealth by first deferring to the Prussian noble class he revered and then defending its interests in the arena of German politics. On the strength of his stirring battlefield sermons during the Franco-Prussian War, he earned the favor of King Wilhelm I of Prussia, soon to be the German kaiser. Shortly after the war ended, the kaiser summoned him to become one of the chaplains of the Berlin Cathedral. Patriotism, conservative values, and spellbinding oratory were the elements of Stoecker's budding career, but it was his open espousal of antisemitism in 1879 that made him a prominent figure in national politics until his death in 1909.

In 1877 he took over leadership of the Berlin City Mission, a Protestant charitable institution that worked among the suffering masses. Rapid industrialization and the crash of 1873, followed by a long depression, created chaotic conditions in the capital of the new German Empire. Peasants, who became proletarians overnight, flocked to Berlin in search of work and a better life. Unprepared to deal with the influx, the municipal sanitation and housing systems broke down, forcing many worker families to find shelter in tents in the city's parks. Stoecker confronted working-class alienation in a period of economic turmoil by attributing it to a decadent, materialistic spirit, a falling away from traditional Christian values.

To win workers back to the fatherland and to snatch them away from the growing influence of the Socialist Workers' party, he established the Christian Social Workers' party early in 1878. The Christian Socials appropriated several of the socioeconomic demands of labor and contested three election districts in the capital. However, the left-liberals who commanded all of the seats for Berlin had no difficulty in beating back the threat. Nor did Stoecker's party, bound too closely to throne and altar, manage to lure workers away from the socialists.

By this time, however, Stoecker was no longer speaking to workers. When they attended his meetings, it was usually with the purpose of heckling the demagogue. Instead, his audience was now comprised largely of lower-middle-class elements. These "little people" had also suffered in the economic turbulence of the mid-1870s. Under the pressures of structural economic changes they did not comprehend, shopkeepers, artisans, low-level professionals, and minor bureaucrats had invested their small savings in the boom preceding the bust of 1873. Hoping to get rich quick or at least keep their heads above water, they were ruined.

These were the people who enthusiastically applauded the court chaplain's denunciations and the growing tendency to identify German woes with the rise of the Jews. Not only could the crash of 1873 and the corruption uncovered in its wake be conveniently and almost completely blamed on Jews, but declines in personal fortunes begged to be compared to their success. Their visible prospering since emancipation, stemming from their participation in the business, cultural, and educational life of the capital, appeared to be insupportable arrogance on the part of a people traditionally thought inferior and despicable. For Stoecker, especially, Jews came to epitomize the dangerous modern forces he had long feared.

Even before his electoral defeat, Stoecker had begun identifying liberal "Manchesterite Jews" as the chief opponents of his economic reforms. In 1879, as Wilhelm Marr's book (see Document 6) was creating a stir, several liberal newspapers—it is not clear that they were uniformly "Jewish"—subjected the court chaplain to scathing criticism. The speech reproduced here was his response, his first overtly antisemitic effort. It singled out assimilated ("modern") Jews for major attention, presenting them as agents of social discord, alienated from their own people and committed to destruction for its own sake.

The positive reception of the speech, combined with his party's failure to penetrate the ranks of socialist labor, persuaded him to set a new course. The Christian Socials dropped "Workers'" from their name and concentrated on organizing the disaffected lower middle class in town and countryside. Always closely allied to the German Conservative party, the Christian Socials never won many mandates. Stoecker, however, representing a rural west German district in the German Reichstag or Prussian parliament, played a significant role in right-wing politics for nearly thirty years.

Seen in the context of the wild street agitation that led to random acts of violence against Jews and Jewish property in Berlin and Dresden, Stoecker's speech strikes a moderate tone, but this moderation is misleading. His defense of the claims of Christianity against the pretensions of Judaism, his stressing of old-fashioned values, and his condemnation of Jewish arrogance, as much as they harked back to traditional forms of Jew baiting, nonetheless sought to utilize anti-Jewish sentiments for wholly modern political purposes.

As a minister of the Christian religion, Stoecker was bound to accept conversion as a solution to the Jewish problem, a position that separated him from his racist competitors. But he frequently fell into racial terminology ("Semitism" and the "Semitic spirit") and the consequences that flowed from this mode of thinking. For example, his talk of social reconciliation is offset by references to Jews as carriers of disease ("the cancer that is eating away at us" and "the social maladies which Jewry brought with it"). And it is difficult to be sure that his pious warnings about impending violence are not, in fact, a suggestion that violence might be warranted or at least understandable, given the seriousness of his charges against Jews as a group.

Stoecker's audience was at the point of believing that the whole German Empire was nothing more than a front for Jewish swindlers. Although the staunchly conservative court chaplain would never have stooped to spreading such revolutionary ideas, others in the antisemitic movement were ready to do just that. The court chaplain took care to except some

Jews from his blanket indictment and cautioned against extremism, but his revilement of Jews, and particularly Judaism, was an invitation to his followers to share his views and act accordingly.

In exploiting the existing hatred of Jews to shore up the authority of the state, Stoecker helped legitimize antisemitism as a political force. Although he qualified his rhetoric, he was no more fair-minded in his discussion of the Jewish problem or scrupulous in his handling of the facts than the other antisemites. Furthermore, in measuring his impact, it is important to bear in mind that it was not so much what he said as who he was. This was no failed journalist or social casualty but a man of the cloth, a chaplain to the imperial court with the highest social credentials. He put his enormous prestige at the disposal of the antisemitic movement and did more than any other individual to render that movement respectable in German society.

For Further Reading

Paul W. Massing, *Rehearsal for Destruction: A Study of Political Anti-Semitism in Imperial Germany* (New York, 1949). On Christian Socialism in general, William Shanahan, *German Protestants Face the Social Question* (Notre Dame, 1954). On Bismarck's equivocal relationship to the antisemitic movement, Fritz Stern, *Gold and Iron* (New York, 1977).

4. Adolf Stoecker
Our Demands on Modern Jewry (1879)

The Jewish question has long been a burning question. Amongst us it has flamed brightly for several months. It feeds on neither religious fanaticism nor political passion. The orthodox and the freethinker, the conservative and the liberal, write and speak about it with equal violence. None of them treats Jewry as the apple of discord because of religious intolerance but because of social concern. "The social question is the Jewish question," writes [Otto] Glagau.[1] "Elect no Jews!" cries W. Marr in his third pamphlet;

Source: Adolf Stoecker, "Unsre Forderungen an das moderne Judentum," in *Christlich-Sozial: Reden und Aufsätze* (Bielefeld and Leipzig, 1885), pp. 143–54. Speech given before the Christian Social Workers' party on September 19, 1879.

[1]Otto Glagau (1834–92) studied philosophy at the University of Königsberg and was a private tutor for ten years before he moved to Berlin in the 1860s. There he became a journalist for newspapers of varying political complexion. In 1875 he published a series of articles in a popular magazine, exposing what he claimed was the largely Jewish corruption behind the financial crash of 1873. Spurred on by popular acclamation, he published several books and a play that highlighted the economic power of the Jews as a

in the first he reported on the "Victory of Jewry over Germandom" and from the "Jewish Theater of War" in the second. His highly agitated appeal to the nation ended with Finis Germaniae—"the end of Germany is at hand" [see Document 6]. Well, now, we don't believe the death of the German spirit to be so near. Nations, like individuals, can be reborn. Germany, and even Berlin, will recover and free itself from alien spirits.

Yet symptoms of illness are present. Social evils are visible in all the limbs of the body politic, and social enmity is never without a cause. Christians and Jews must be seriously concerned that conflict does not grow into hatred. Here and there the summer lightning already flashes, heralding a distant storm.

It is quite remarkable that the Jewish-liberal press does not have the courage to answer the complaints and accusations of its attackers. It is usually all too ready to uncover scandals where there are none. They sharpen their poisoned quills on the sermons delivered in our churches and on the debates of our church assemblies. But they condemn the Jewish question to silence, and they avoid having their readers hear anything of those hostile voices. They adopt the air of scorning their opponents, pretending that they are unworthy of an answer. It would be better for them to learn from their enemies, to acknowledge their faults, and to work in common for the social reconciliation we so need.

It is with this intention that I would like to deal with the Jewish question in full Christian love but also in full social truthfulness.

Occasional utterances of mine on this theme in Christian Social gatherings have been conveyed to the public out of context, exaggerated, and always distorted—for partisan political reasons. Reporters from certain newspapers, a disgrace to the city of intelligence, have been equally ignorant and untruthful. Many of them falsify out of incomprehension but most out of malice. An occurrence that took place in the last year is both characteristic and instructive. In my absence, the Jews were discussed more than was necessary in our gatherings. The Jewish press wrote that the Christian Socials were animated by Jew hatred and that they were pushing for the persecution of Jews. I returned and seized the opportunity publicly and solemnly to declare: We hate no one, not even the Jews. We respect them as our fellow citizens and love them as the people of the prophets and apostles, out of which our Savior came forth. But this ought not stop us from identifying the danger when the Jewish papers assault our faith or when the Jewish spirit of Mammon ruins our people. This declaration was then distorted into the accusation that I said all Germany's woes came from the Jews. A flood of letters hailed down upon me. A Berlin Jew, whose name I know, wrote me that his people was the favorite of God.

---

dangerous defect in the new German Empire. Glagau was instrumental in the formation of the antisemitic political parties and edited the antisemites' one journal with intellectual pretensions, *Der Kulturkämpfer* (1880–89).

If Christians declared their love for the chosen people, this was no different from when a courtesan—I use the more polite word here—gives her heart to a high-ranking nobleman. A second sent "to the narrow-minded Jew baiter" a pamphlet in which a faithless, baptized writer describes and exaggerates the contributions of Jews to science in the Middle Ages.[2] A third, writing from Frankfurt-am-Main, congratulates me for speaking openly about Germany's defects and signs himself: "unfortunately, a Jew."

This episode, insignificant in itself, is a good example of the lies, arrogance, and hatred called forth by any discussion of the Jewish question. People who pour scathing criticism on the state and church, personalities and affairs, are outraged to the extreme when others allow themselves to cast so much as a scrutinizing glance at Jewry. They themselves fall upon every non-Jewish activity with hatred and scorn. But if we softly speak a word of truth about their doings, they play the insulted innocent, the victims of intolerance, the martyrs of world history. Notwithstanding, I shall dare openly and freely to speak my mind about modern Jewry. I am prepared in advance for lying reports.

In fact, I see modern Jewry as a great danger to German national life. [By "modern Jewry"] I do not mean the religion of the Orthodox or the enlightenment of the Reformers. As for the Orthodox with their ossification of the law, their Old Testament without temple, priests, sacrifices, or messiah, they hold no attraction for the children of the nineteenth century and pose no dangers. In its deepest core it is a dead religious form, a lower stage of revelation, a spirit that has outlived itself and, although still worthy of honor, has been invalidated by Christianity. It has no more truth for the present. Reform Judaism has even less religious significance. It is neither Judaism nor Christianity but a shabby little survival of the Age of Enlightenment. . . .

Both types [of Judaism] boast that the Jews are the bearers of the highest religious and moral ideas for the world and humanity and that the mission of Judaism now and for all the future consists of holding fast to these ideas, developing them further, and disseminating them. The Jewish press of the Right and Left is united in this. The incense emanating from the synagogues of both schools simply intoxicates the senses. . . . S. Meyer, editor of the *Jewish Press*, writes: "Indisputably, the lofty ideals upon which rests the moral order of the world and the intellectual content of modern culture and civilization which form the foundation of true brotherhood, all arise from Judaism." "Everything good in the Gospels is not new, but rather derives from Judaism. And everything new in them is not good."

In the same vein writes Dr. Adler: "The religion of Israel is the eternal, unchanging truth. Christianity and Islam are the preliminary stages which

---

[2]Matthias Jakob Schleiden was neither Jew nor convert. A botanist, he was one of the few Christian scholars who undertook a study of the Jewish role in medieval history. Stoecker, who insists on regarding him as a Jew or "worse than a Jew," was referring to his laudatory article, "The Significance of the Jews for the Preservation and Revival of Science in the Middle Ages" (1876).

the truth must ascend before the whole truth becomes accessible." And the Reform rabbi Nascher joins in the chorus: "Israel's mission and gift is to be the lighthouse on humanity's sea of thought. It is called upon, like the stars, to shine upon the totality of its fellow-men," or so preaches the vain man to his vain congregation. . . .

At this point we make our first demand: *pray, a little more modesty!* We do not deny that Israel carried the knowledge of a personal, single God through the ancient world like a sacred flame. But then came Christ and completed the faith with a richer conception of God and a higher Truth. And it is a matter of historical fact that the nation of Israel constantly fell back into the coarsest sort of idolatry. The powerful personalities sent by God to fend off this backsliding succeeded for only short intervals. It is truly not the merit of Israel to have preserved the doctrine of the one God of the world but the result of God's grace. Equally true is it that the ideas of religious freedom and tolerance in the modern sense are not characteristic of the Old Testament. Whosoever broke the sabbath was stoned. The priests of Baal were slaughtered. This was part of the peculiarities of their legal system. Far be it from us to reproach the Old Testament for this reason. But it is certainly erroneous when Jews take credit for ideas that were completely unknown to their religion in its historical form. They must know that they had a priestly caste (the very opposite of equality), that they cultivated slavery (the very opposite of freedom), and that they practiced polygamy (the very opposite of the ideal family life). It was Germanic-Christian life that first corrected these errors. It is true that Israel had enlightened economic laws: social forms of property, prohibition of interest, and extreme compassion for the poor. But we need only mention these things in order to feel the fearful distance between the Old Testament and the modern Jew. Only German law protected the conception of communal property; only the Christian church spoke out against the taking of interest. In just these matters the errors and sins of modern Jewry are clear for all to see.

Even conceding that Israel has a lofty and lasting mission, who are the shining thinkers and poets filled with the spirit of God, proclaiming the living God, praising Him, and bringing Him honor? Perhaps the editors of the [*Berliner*] *Tageblatt*? Or the scholars of *Kladderadatsch*?[3] Where is the school for the prophets of the Holy Ghost in which the apostles for this world mission are to be educated? where the missions? where the missionaries? perhaps on the stock exchanges of Berlin, Vienna, and Paris? Oh, no. The Jews would not be so foolish. And just this is their doom. They foundered on Christ, lost their divine course, and surrendered their divine mission. Unheeding of the pithy maxim of the Lord Jesus that "thou canst not serve both God and Mammon," the Jews ran after the golden calf, leaving off the ways of God.

---

[3]One of the most successful of several satirical illustrated journals, *Kladderadatsch* was left-liberal in political orientation. Its satire fell upon friend and foe indiscriminately, however.

The old prayers in which Jewry longs for the return to God and Zion are touching. "For our sins have we been driven from our land and banned from our soil. We could not fulfill our duties in Your chosen dwelling and the great and holy temple where Your name is called upon. . . . Assemble us, who are scattered among all the nations and to the ends of the earth. Lead us to Zion, Your city, with jubilation, and to Jerusalem, Your holy temple, with everlasting joy." But those who play a role in modern Jewry know nothing of this. They rather live in the *Jerusalemstrasse*[4] than in the streets of Jerusalem. . . .

Occasionally a sunbeam of recognition concerning their misery emanates from Jewish writers themselves. . . . [A reform Jewish weekly] finds the courage to lay before its readers the following verse:

> *Everywhere it seems plain to the wise*
> *That the number of Jews is on the rise.*
> *In theaters, concerts, and at the balls*
> *It's mostly Jews who fill the halls.*
> *If it's more Christians than Jews you want to see,*
> *Then in the New Synagogue you ought to be.*

"It is quite certain that in Berlin not a quarter, probably not even a tenth, of the Jewish prep-school students over the age of thirteen hear a word of religious instruction." "Morality remains limited to the sentence: what the penal code does not forbid or what cannot be detected by the judge is permissible, useful, clever."

These Jewish voices date from 1871. It has become much worse today. The Jews combat our faith even though they know that man cannot exist without religion. . . .

And despite this truth, despite the absence of any religious productivity, they hold to the illusion of being a religious power. To be sure, modern Jewry is an irreligious power, a power that everywhere fights Christianity bitterly. Among the nations it roots out Christian belief as well as national feeling and offers as a substitute nothing more than the idolatrous veneration of Judaism, which has no other content than an enthusiasm for itself. Berthold Auerbach[5] in his novel, *Forest Peace,* says quite rightly: "Educated Jews are really not so much Jews as non-Christians." This is why they advocate atheism. Their creed stands on the empty page between the Old and New Testaments. But they don't simply confess their poverty. Instead they make a royal mantle out of their beggar's cloak and know how to impress the uncritical reading masses with their drapery.

And still today they ascribe a world historical mission to Judaism. Even the most liberal Reform Jew wants to remain a Jew. . . . They want

---

[4]Jerusalem Street ran through the newspaper and publishing center of Berlin.

[5]Berthold Auerbach (1812–82), a Jewish writer who prided himself on his "Germanness," registered the pain felt by many highly acculturated Jews upon the appearance of political antisemitism with an often-quoted lament: "I have lived and worked in vain."

to remain thorough Jews. But it must dawn on them that it will not work to believe in nothing Jewish and still be a Jew, to remain a Jew in the narrowest spirit and thereby believe that they are bestowing benefactions upon humanity. It cannot be avoided that the knowledgeable will see the ridiculousness of such goings on. . . .

All [these pretensions to importance] have worked to produce in the Jews, especially the Jewish newspaper writers, a degree of intolerance that will soon be unbearable. In all seriousness, we address our second petition to the Jewish press: *pray, be a little more tolerant!* We shall not, as others who have written on this theme, cite the Talmud's contempt for foreign peoples or its hatred toward every human right. We do not believe it proper to make all the Jews of today responsible for books written millennia ago. We would then have to charge the Catholics with all the persecutions of heretics and the Inquisition (even though none of the popes have ever denounced them as an injustice). In fact a change has taken place. The strict Jews still hold that the Talmud is as infallible as the Law, and a few benightedly declare the entire Talmud, even the vengeful and wild passages, is holy to them. Nevertheless, long years of living together with Christians, mutual business relations, and the gentler spirit of the age have served to diminish the hatred for Christians in the synagogue.

Official hatred has ceased. . . . But in the Jewish press there breathes a hatred against Christianity that deserves to be abominated. Because articles are unsigned in our journals and newspapers, it may be objected that it is impossible to confirm that anti-Christian essays emanate from Jews. We know that there are enough [Christian] writers in the papers who perform the lamentable office of defaming their churches. But it is a fact that the worst Berlin newspapers are in the hands of Jews and that on their staffs the Jewish element predominates. Wholly convincing, however, is the circumstance that the religious arguments among the Jewish factions are scarcely ever mentioned, the intolerance of Jewish orthodoxy is never touched upon, the literary attacks against Jews are never discussed. Orthodox Jewry is never attacked. It can reject secular schools and threaten common-law couples with excommunication. And yet not a single liberal paper takes notice. If the same should surface in Christian meetings, the press rabble will fall upon them with open howls of rage. Our holy things are constantly dragged in the dust, while the synagogue is protected by the silent agreement of all the liberal newspaper writers. Just show us one article in the liberal press that handles Yom Kippur or the Talmud school in unworthy fashion. Yet this year the *Tageblatt* derided Lent, and the Berlin Jewish press pulled to pieces the conference of Augustinians. Only Christianity must put up with these indecencies. A Jewish city alderman of Berlin recently spoke in public about our church matters, which do not concern him, to the effect that there "were real inquisitors who would like nothing better than to consign dissenters to the pyre." Who gave him the right to sow discord among the Christian population and to stir up hate? This intolerance is unbearable.

As recently as 1873, the newspaper of the Reform [Jews] wrote: "The Jewish press is all too disfigured by tastelessness and spitefulness. A defamatory, bitter, and cutting tone makes itself felt on every page. These shortcomings have done a disservice to the public, which now delights in spicy stories." How much worse has the Jewish press become since then! Where can one find even a trace of such heedlessness in the Lutheran or conservative press? Where is a Jewish holiday or the kosher laws held up to scorn? The simplest sense of decency must forbid the violation of a people's sacred possessions. These constant attempts to undermine the fundamental beliefs, the morality, the national honor of a nation are criminal and shameful. From time to time, the Social Democratic press has been even nastier. Yet more destructive, because it is less coarse and more effective, is one of Berlin's most widely read organs.[6] Unless this well of poison is stopped up, an improvement in our situation is unthinkable. In 1816, Benzenberg[7] was already writing: "Perhaps the glory of Germany will perish from the Jews." If the Christians continue to yield to the effects of the Jewish spirit that de-Germanizes and de-Christianizes them, this prophecy will certainly come true. Perhaps, after this period of decline— and this is our hope—the glory of Germany will again go forth. We would really have to be a nation without honor if we could not break these chains of an alien spirit and instead allowed ourselves to be totally Jewified.

To the initiated, it is clear that the domination of the Semitic spirit over us signifies not only our spiritual but also our economic impoverishment. The German is strongly idealistic. For quite a while he has put up with his idealism being exploited by others for business purposes. But finally the figure of Nathan the Wise, created by Lessing in Christian love, has vanished behind that of Shylock.[8] The admonitions about the Jews from Kant, Fichte, and Herder, our best men, have demonstrated their validity.

The Jews are and remain a people within a people, a state within a state, a tribe amid a foreign race. Sooner or later all immigrants disappear into the people with which they dwell. Not so the Jews. Over against the German essence, they set their unbroken Semitism; against Christianity, their stubborn cult of the law or their enmity toward Christians. We cannot judge them. As long as they remain Jews, they cannot change. However, we must protect ourselves from the danger by means of clear understanding.

---

[6]Stoecker refers once again to the *Berliner Tageblatt*, a well-respected left-liberal newspaper that opposed militarism and the policies of Bismarck. It was part of the publishing empire being built by Rudolf Mosse (1843–1920), a Jew from eastern Prussia who introduced to Germany the mass-circulation daily. The German Right, and the antisemites in particular, used the "BT," as it was called, as an example of how Jews undermined traditional German values.

[7]Johann Friedrich Benzenberg (1777–1846) was an early leader of the liberal movement in Prussia.

[8]See note 6, Document 6.

In Berlin alone there are forty-five thousand Jews, as many as in all of France or England. This is too many. If they were really bound to us, the number would be immaterial. Because this half hundred thousand forms a compact community in good circumstances and increasing power, because it is armed with a profitable intellectual energy, and because it does not participate in our German Christian interests, it constitutes a real danger. We are approaching the conditions of Poland.[9] The only difference is that the Berlin Jews are much richer, smarter, and more influential than the Polish Israelites. Finance, banking, and commerce are in their possession. The press is in their hands, and they push into institutions of higher education beyond all proportion. This last is certainly a beautiful trait. I have often found it touching how poor Jews devote all their resources to give their children a good education. Nevertheless, this development is thoroughly unhealthy. We are on the way to having public opinion fully dominated by Jews and labor fully exploited by them. The process of dissolution is under way. Nothing will save us unless we reform and bring Israel to reformation. And here we pose our third demand: *pray, a little more equality!*

Formerly, it was thought that emancipation would drive the Jews into other sorts of occupations. Now that they are emancipated, the opposite has happened. Even more than before they favor the lucrative and easy occupations. Recently, they have pressed into the judiciary, which does not speak well of our system of justice. There are almost none of them in the handicrafts or manufacturing. It is fair to say, therefore, that they take no joy in labor and have no sympathy for the German work ethic. The slogan "cheap and shabby" we owe in large measure to them. They are to be found wherever need or speculative greed can be exploited. Indisputably, reckless speculation and usury are the businesses they love to pursue. They willingly reap where they have not sown.

If the great social question is the problem of the correct proportion between labor and capital's share of the proceeds, then an activity that systematically and boundlessly exploits labor in the interests of capital is the worst element in this problem. It is true that, thanks to Marx and Lassalle,[10] the Jews have their friends among the Social Democrats. Some of the nihilists in Russia are also Jews. Despite this, the one-sided speculativeness of the Jews poses dangers even to these [leftists]. For me, the

---

[9]In 1880, the Jews of Berlin, the largest Jewish community in Germany, numbered 53,949 or 4.8 percent of the city's population. Estimates of the Jewish population of Poland, partitioned among its powerful neighbors Prussia, Russia, and Austria, usually place it at 10 percent of the total but 31 percent in most large urban areas. Thus Stoecker considerably exaggerates the peril of Jewish numbers in Germany.

[10]Karl Marx (1818–83) was descended from rabbis on both sides of his family; however, his father converted to Lutheranism in 1824. Ferdinand Lassalle (1825–64), born Lassal, though not a convert, was not a practicing Jew. Both men were pained by their Jewish origins. Because both were instrumental in the development of German Social Democracy, enemies of socialism frequently attacked the phenomenon as an un-German aberration.

epitome of the Jewish question is whether those Jews who live among us will learn to take part in the total spectrum of German labor—in the hard and bitter work of the crafts, the factory, and agriculture. More we cannot demand of them. . . .

The question now is what ought to happen. We think that Jews and Christians must work together so that the right relationship exists between them. There is no other way. Here and there a hatred against Jews, which is contrary to the Gospels, is beginning to blaze forth. If modern Jewry continues as before to employ the power of the press and of capital to ruin the nation, then a catastrophe is ultimately unavoidable. Israel must give up the desire to be master in Germany. It must renounce the presumption that Judaism will be the religion of the future, since it is so completely of the past. And may foolish Christians no longer strengthen the nation in its darkness. Jewish orthodoxy with its circumcision has outlived itself. Reform Judaism is not even a Jewish religion. When Israel has recognized this, it will properly give up its so-called mission and cease trying to rob the nations that have given it domicile and citizenship of their Christianity. The Jewish press must become more tolerant, as a first condition of a better relationship.

The social maladies that Jewry brought with it must be cured by wise legislation. It will not be easy to place Jewish capital under the necessary limitations. Only organic legislation can achieve this. Abolition of the mortgage system in real estate . . . ; a change in the credit system that frees the businessman from the arbitrary power of big capital; change in the stock-market system; reinstitution of the denominational census so that the disproportion between Jewish wealth and Christian work can be established; limitation of the appointment of Jewish judges to their proportion of the total population; dismissal of Jewish teachers from our primary schools so as to strengthen the Christian-German spirit: these are the means with which to combat the excessive growth of Jewish influence upon German life.

Either we will succeed in this and restore Germany to blessedness, or the cancer from which we suffer will continue to eat away at us. Our future will then be imperiled, our German spirit will be Jewified, and German economic life will be impoverished. Return to a more Germanic legal system and economy. Return to Christian faith. Thus shall our slogan ring. Then all will do their duty and God will help.

A National Menace

Heinrich von Treitschke (1834–96) attained the heights of academic recognition as professor of history at the University of Berlin (1874) and as Prussian state historian (1886). Always a Prussophile, he had also once been a nationally minded Liberal politician. In the early 1860s he opposed the domestic policies of Bismarck, but after Prussia defeated Austria in the War of 1866, starting the German states on the road to unification, Treitschke, like many other Liberals, had a change of heart. From this point forward, a brutal and narrow-minded nationalism began to consume his liberal principles.

His masterful multivolume *History of Germany in the Nineteenth Century,* combative lectures, and popular periodical *The Prussian Yearbooks* brought his ideas before a large public, including the uppermost levels of the imperial court. Widely respected as a scholar and extremely popular as a publicist, he propounded an intensely nationalistic view of the German past and present, lent full support to Bismarck, and acted as an apologist for the Hohenzollerns. Only a few academic colleagues expressed reservations about his blatant intermixing of scholarship with partisan politics.

Treitschke saw Germany as a young and vulnerable nation, without the self-assurance and long history of nationhood enjoyed by France and Great Britain. Like any other youth, Germany needed to be protected from immoral influences, which he variously identified as French culture, Catholicism, organized labor, the south German states, Austria, and the Jews.

Like Wagner, Treitschke had once been somewhat sympathetic toward Jews, condemning "the fairy tales spread about them." But in the 1870s he came to see them as the embodiment of modern trends to be feared and rejected. Their "mammonism" and penchant for criticism, their liberal and democratic tendencies, their mobile but superficial cleverness—all this stemmed from the rootlessness of modern Jews. But Treitschke, like Stoecker, suspected traditionally minded Jews as well. Even a residual attachment to Judaism, a sterile, formulaic pseudoreligion, filled him with doubts about Jewish commitment to the "German spirit." For a chauvinist there could be no ambivalence on such matters. Although he defended Jewish emancipation as an accomplished fact, he also admonished Jews to become "fully German," a mean-spirited slur on the great majority of German Jews who thought that they had already done so.

The following document appeared in late 1879 in the *Prussian Yearbooks* as part of a monthly column in which Treitschke commented on questions of the day. The following year he published this and two succeeding articles as a separate pamphlet: *A Word About Our Jews.*

Treitschke strikes what he considered a balanced tone in his treatment of the Jewish question. Although he condemns anti-Jewish excesses and overly passionate agitation, he nonetheless condones the movement as legitimate, a justifiable response to Jewish provocation. He had no use for Wilhelm Marr (see Document 6), whom he called a "windbag" in his *German History,* or for Stoecker, but it was their style, rather than their intent, that bothered him most. Careful not to blame Jews for all German ills and to exempt some of his favorites, he nevertheless makes clear his generalized contempt. The message of Treitschke's political essays and scholarly works is that despite unspecified exceptions, Jews have had a largely negative effect on Germany's heroic struggles. He rejected the notions of racism, perhaps because of his own Czech antecedents, but slips comfortably into racial categories and explanations when identifying Jewish shortcomings; these are numerous and menacing.

The pronouncements of the "Praeceptor Germaniae" had an enormous and immediate impact on the development of political antisemitism. Antisemitic activists in Berlin, referring specifically to Treitschke's pamphlet, crowed that "the future now belongs to us." The antisemitic political parties, in need of a respectable authority, seized upon Treitschke's phrase, "the Jews are our misfortune," put it on rubber stamps, and used it on the mastheads of their papers. Later, the Nazis, who constantly ransacked the German past for historical legitimation, adopted the phrase as well. But it was upon a generation of university students, the future leaders of Germany, that he exercised major influence.

The Union of German Students, founded in 1880, took inspiration from its "two gods," Treitschke and Stoecker. Claiming to be unpolitical, it nonetheless diffused antisemitism and racial nationalism through the university system of Germany, introduced it into university towns and their surrounding areas, and lent volunteer assistance to antisemitic political candidates. Berlin students expressed rowdy approval for their favorite professor's snide remarks and open ridicule of "hook-nosed and thin-voiced fellow citizens." Several key leaders in the antisemitic movement of twentieth-century Germany acknowledged Treitschke's lectures and writing as formative experiences. For the educated, he was a most effective demagogue.

Like Wagner and Stoecker, Treitschke, too, warns his readers to expect a hostile response to his even-handed discussion of the Jewish question, thus disarming Jewish self-defense in advance. Jewish reaction was to be discounted as nothing more than characteristic hypersensitivity and further proof of the lack of true Germanism. But not only Jews responded. Upset by Stoecker and Treitschke in a way they were not by lower middle-class antisemites, notable Christian scholars, politicians, and scientists placed a declaration in the major newspapers of Germany. With a pointed allusion to the two chief culprits and the hatred being preached "from pulpit and lectern," the manifesto decried "the deeply shameful" intolerance and injustice of antisemitism. Well meant, the gesture was too feeble to stop a movement that was gathering ever-greater force.

For Further Reading

Andreas Dorpalen, *Heinrich von Treitschke* (New Haven, 1957). Michael Meyer, "Great Debate on Antisemitism—Jewish Reaction to New Hostility in Germany, 1879–1881," *Yearbook of the Leo Baeck Institute* 11 (1966): 137–70.

5. Heinrich von Treitschke
A Word About Our Jews (1879–80)

Among the symptoms of a deep change of heart going through our nation, none appears so strange as the passionate movement against Jewry. A few months ago the oft-heard cry "Hep-Hep"[1] still echoed in Germany. Anyone is permitted to say unabashedly the harshest things about the national shortcomings of the Germans, the French, and all the other peoples, but any who dared to speak about the undeniable weaknesses of the Jewish character, no matter how moderately or justly, was immediately branded by almost the entire press as a barbarian and a religious bigot. Today we have progressed so far that a majority of the voters of Breslau have sworn under no circumstances to elect a Jew to the state parliament—and this apparently not in wild agitation but with calm forethought. Antisemitic leagues are banding together. The "Jewish question" is being discussed in excited meetings. A flood of anti-Jewish libels is inundating the book market. There is all too much dirt and crudity in these activities, and it is nauseating to note that many of those inflammatory writings apparently stem from Jewish pens. As is well known, since Eisenmenger and Pfefferkorn,[2] born Jews have been ever more strongly represented in the ranks of the fanatic Jew haters. But is all that hides behind this noisome activity really just the coarseness of the mob and business envy? Are these outbreaks of deep, long-restrained anger merely an ephemeral excrescence, as hollow and baseless as the Teutonic Jew baiting of 1819? No; in fact, the instinct of the masses has correctly identified a serious danger, a critical defect in the new German life. It is no empty formula when we speak today of a German Jewish question.

Source: From *Preussische Jahrbücher* 44 (1879):572–76.

[1]Supposedly of medieval origin, the "Hep-Hep" cry was the signal for the pogrom, the anti-Jewish riot. During the Hep-Hep riots of 1819, various derivations of the phrase were offered. According to anti-Jewish university students, it stood for *Hieroselyma est perdita,* recalling the destruction of Jerusalem by Titus in 70 A.D. Others have suggested that it was simply an abbreviation of the German word for "Hebrew" (*Hebräer*). Nazi storm troopers revived its usage during the 1920s.

[2]Treitschke's contention of Jewish authorship for the antisemitic pamphlets of the 1870s is baseless. He is, perhaps, referring specifically to Wilhelm Marr (see Document 6), who was widely thought to have been a renegade Jew; this, too, has no basis in fact. Marr was descended from Lutherans on both sides of his family. Eisenmenger was not Jewish. Johann Joseph Pfefferkorn (1469–1524) was an apostate Jew who in 1509 urged the Holy Roman Emperor, Maximilian I, to burn "the false books of the Jews" in order to cure them of their unbelief. He was successfully opposed by Johann Reuchlin (1455–1522), a German humanist and among the first Christian Hebraists.

When, with disdain, the English and French talk of German prejudice against Jews, we must answer: You don't know us. You live in fortunate circumstances that make the emergence of such "prejudices" impossible. The number of Jews in western Europe is so small that it cannot exert a palpable influence upon your national mores. However, year after year, out of the inexhaustible Polish cradle there streams over our eastern border a host of hustling, pants-peddling youths, whose children and children's children will someday command Germany's stock exchanges and news-papers.[3] The immigration grows visibly, and the question becomes more and more grave: how can we amalgamate this alien people? The Israelites of the west and south belong mostly to the Spanish branch of Jewry, which looks back on a comparatively proud history and has always adapted rather easily to Western ways. In fact, they have become for the most part good Frenchmen, Englishmen, and Italians. This is true to the extent that we can appropriately expect from a people of such pure blood and such pro-nounced peculiarity. But we Germans have to deal with that Polish branch of Jewry, which has been deeply scarred by centuries of Christian tyranny. As a result of this experience, it is incomparably more alien to the Euro-pean and, especially, the German essence.

What we have to demand of our Israelite fellow citizens is simple: they should become Germans. They should feel themselves, modestly and prop-erly, Germans—and this without prejudicing their faith and their ancient, holy memories, which we all hold in reverence. For we do not want to see millennia of Germanic morality followed by an era of German-Jewish hy-brid culture. It would be sinful to forget that a great many Jews, baptized and unbaptized, were German men in the best sense. Felix Mendelssohn, Veit, Riesser,[4] etc.—to say nothing of the living—were men in whom we honor the noble and good traits of the German spirit. But it is equally undeniable that numerous and mighty circles among our Jews simply lack the goodwill to become thoroughly German. It is painful to speak of these things. Even conciliatory words will be easily misunderstood. Neverthe-less, I believe that many of my Jewish friends will concede, though with

---

[3]Of the 561,612 Jews living in Germany in 1880, 2.7 percent, or 15,000, of them were for-eign born. In 1910 the numbers were 615,021, 12.8 percent, and 78,746. A great many eastern-European Jews made their way across Germany on the way to North and South America, but only a tiny fraction were permitted to settle permanently on German soil. Although statistically groundless, the phantom of a Germany swamped by *Ostjuden* haunted many Germans continuously from the mid-nineteenth century through all the years of the Weimar Republic.

[4]The composer Felix Mendelssohn-Bartholdy (1809–47), grandson of Moses Mendelssohn, was baptized as a child. For some antisemites he was "the exceptional Jew" because of his wholehearted identification with German music; for many more, however, he was the proverbial exception who proved the rule that such assimilation was impossible for Jews and not actually sought after by them; for yet others, like Richard Wagner, his musical talent was typically Jewish—that is, shallow, unconnected to the soul of the *Volk*, and aimed at easy popularity. For practicing Jews in the imperial era, Mendelssohn repre-sented the ambivalence of assimilation. They took pride in his musical achievement but

deep regret, that I am right when I assert that in recent times a dangerous spirit of arrogance has arisen in Jewish circles. The influence of Jewry on our national life, which created much good in earlier times, nowadays shows itself in many ways harmful. Just read the *History of the Jews* by Graetz.[5] What fanatical rage against the "arch-enemy," Christianity. What lethal hatred against the purest and mightiest representatives of the Germanic essence from Luther right up to Goethe and Fichte! And what empty, insulting self-glorification! [In Graetz] it is demonstrated in constant, spiteful tirades that the nation of Kant was educated to humanity only through the Jews, that the language of Lessing and Goethe has become receptive to beauty, intelligence, and wit through Heine and Börne. What English Jew would dare defame the land that shielded and protected him in such a way? And this benighted contempt against the German goyim is in no way merely the attitude of an isolated fanatic.

There is no German commercial city that does not count many honorable and respectable Jewish firms. But undoubtedly, the Semites bear a heavy share of guilt for the falsehood and deceit, the insolent greed of fraudulent business practices, and that base materialism of our day. [That materialism] regards all labor as pure business and threatens to stifle our people's traditional good-natured joy in labor. In thousands of German villages sits the Jew who sells out his neighbors with usury. Among the leading men in the arts and sciences, the number of Jews is not very great; all the stronger do the Semitic talents constitute the host of the third rate. And how firmly these scribblers stick together. How securely they work on the tested business principle of reciprocity, whereby, as in some insurance company dealing in immortality, every Jewish poetaster receives free and clear one day of fame, paid out by the newspapers, without having to pay the premium.

Most dangerous, however, is the improper preponderance of Jewry in the daily press, a fateful consequence of our narrow-minded old laws forbidding Israelites entry to most of the learned professions. For ten years the public opinion of many German cities was largely "created" by Jewish

---

fretted over the detachment from Judaism by the grandson of the man who had led the way out of the ghetto and into German life. Was this the price of full participation?

Philipp Veit (1793–1877), a painter of religious subjects, was also an early convert to Christianity.

Gabriel Riesser (1806–63) had been the outstanding advocate of Jewish equality in Germany since the 1830s. A lawyer denied the right to practice in his native Hamburg, he refused the path of conversion which would have made this possible. During the Revolution of 1848, he served as a vice-president of the Frankfurt National Assembly. A moderate liberal, he was active in Hamburg politics and became the first practicing Jew appointed to the German judiciary.

[5]Heinrich Graetz (1817–91) wrote the first general history of the Jews in eleven volumes, the last of which appeared in 1875. Graetz vigorously defended the idea that Judaism was more than a set of enlightened and abstract theological beliefs. It was no mere religious denomination but the organic product of a people with a long history and a politics of its own. Graetz's sometimes feisty pride in the Jewish past, including the recent past in

pens. It was a misfortune for the Liberal party, and one of the reasons for its fall, to have afforded too free a scope to Jewry in its press. The present-day weakness of the press is the result of a backlash against this unnatural condition. The little man can no longer be talked out of the fact that the Jews write the newspapers. Therefore, he won't believe them any longer. Our newspaper system owes a great deal to Jewish talents. From the first the trenchancy and acuity of the Jewish spirit found a fruitful field. But here, too, the effect was ambiguous. [Ludwig] Börne was the first to introduce a characteristically shameless tone into our journalism.[6] [He wrote] from abroad with no respect for the Fatherland, as though he was not part of it at all, as though his scorn for Germany did not cut each and every German to the quick. Add to this the unfortunate bustling intrusion into all and sundry, which does not even shy away from magisterially passing judgment on the innermost matters of the Christian churches. The anti-Christian defamations and witticisms of Jewish journalists are simply shocking, and such blasphemies are put up for sale in its own language as the latest achievements of "German" enlightenment! Scarcely had emancipation been achieved before they brazenly insisted on its pretext. They demanded literal parity in everything and did not want to see that we Germans are still a Christian people and that the Jews are only a minority among us. We have experienced their demands that Christian images be set aside and that their sabbath be celebrated in mixed schools.

Overlooking all these circumstances—and how many others could be added!—this noisy agitation of the moment, though brutal and hateful, is nonetheless a natural reaction of Germanic racial feeling against an alien element that has assumed all too large a space in our life. [The agitation] has inadvertently performed a useful service: it has lifted the ban on a quiet untruth. An evil that everyone felt but no one wanted to touch upon is now openly discussed. Let's not deceive ourselves. The movement is very deep and strong. A few jokes by Christian Social politicos will not suffice to stem it. Among the circles of highly educated men who reject any idea of church intolerance or national arrogance there rings with one voice: *the Jews are our misfortune!*

There can be no talk, among those with any understanding, of a revocation or even an abridgment of the completed emancipation. It would be an open injustice, a falling away from the good traditions of our state, and would sharpen rather than ameliorate the national conflict that pains us. The Jews in France and England have become a harmless and in many ways beneficial, element of civil society. That is in the last analysis the result of the energy and national pride of these two ancient culture-bearing peoples. Our culture is a young one. Our being still lacks a national style, an instinctive pride, a thoroughly imprinted character. That is why for so long

---

Germany, annoyed Treitschke and many others, who condemned it as arrogance and evidence that Jews were reneging on their end of the emancipation contract—the extinguishing of all peculiar national traits.

[6]See note 2, Document 3.

we stood defenseless against alien essences. Now, however, we are at the point of acquiring those goods. We can only wish that our Jews recognize in time the transformation that is the logical consequence of the rise of the German state. Quietly, here and there, Jewish associations against usury do much good. They are the work of insightful Israelites who understand that their racial brothers must adapt to the morality and ideas of their Christian fellow citizens.

There is still a great deal to be done in this direction. To make hard German heads into Jewish ones is surely impossible. Thus, only one possibility remains: Our Jewish fellow citizens must resolve to be German without qualification, as so many of them have already done, to our benefit and their own. The task can never be wholly completed. A cleft has always existed between Occidental and Semitic essences. . . . There will always be Jews who are nothing more than German-speaking Orientals. A specific Jewish civilization will also always flourish, as befits a historically cosmopolitan power. But the conflict will lessen when the Jews, who speak so much of tolerance, really become tolerant and show respect for the faith, customs, and feelings of the German people, who have atoned for the old injustice and bestowed upon them the rights of man and citizen. That this respect is wholly missing in a section of our commercial and literary Jewry is the ultimate basis for the passionate embitterment of today.

It is not a pretty picture—this storming and wrangling, this bubbling and boiling of half-baked ideas in the new Germany. But we are now the most passionate of peoples, even though we often berate ourselves as phlegmatic. New ideas have never established themselves among us without convulsive twitches. May God grant that we emerge from the rashness and ill humor of these restless years with a stricter conception of the state and its duties, a more powerful national feeling.

The Eighteen-Hundred-Year Conspiracy

Wilhelm Marr (1819–1904) coined the term *antisemite* in September 1879, probably to distinguish his new brand of anti-Jewish activism from that of Court Chaplain Stoecker. The word appeared in advertisements for another of Marr's innovations, the Antisemites' League, the first attempt to use anti-Jewish feeling as the basis of a political party. For a short time, on the strength of the pamphlet that follows, he became the guru of the budding antisemitic movement.

The intellectual, political, and occupational odyssey that led Wilhelm Marr to antisemitism illustrates the contribution of the Left to the movement's development. He was brought up in Hamburg, where his formal education ended in 1839 with certification as a commercial clerk. He worked for a firm in Vienna before moving to Switzerland in 1841, where he gave up commerce for political agitation among the German artisans.

Under the influence of the Young Hegelians, and in personal contact with the communist Wilhelm Weitling, Marr became a militant atheist, a radical democrat, and a revolutionary conspirator. The Swiss expelled him in 1846, and after further expulsions from several German states, he reluctantly returned to Hamburg, founded his own political satiric newspaper, and became, like Wagner, a leading ultraleftist in the Revolution of 1848 and at least a tacit supporter of Jewish emancipation.

But the failure of the revolution soured Marr on the German *Volk* and the possibility of achieving human emancipation with and through it. After the coup d'état of Louis Napoleon in December 1851, he "resigned" from the democratic movement, went through a personal crisis, and turned away from his previous beliefs. The ideas of the Enlightenment, French Revolution, and German Idealism, as well as his faith in the possibilities of rational politics, fell away.

Marr, like so many other victims of 1848, sought new answers to questions about the direction of history and his personal role in the world. He had thought of himself, with typical arrogance, as a mediator between the world of science and the *Volk,* a destined leader of the masses by dint of his intellectual gifts. Now he seized upon a new vocabulary and a new set of metaphors to make sense out of the world. Again, like many other intellectuals whose hopes had been dashed in 1848, Marr found the infinitely flexible, pseudoscientific doctrines of racism alluring. For him, the belief in human intelligence and rational political capacities had been decisively destroyed by the recent failure of the masses and their leaders. He soon began pondering skulls and cubic capacities of brain pans, looking for clues to explain "the undoubted superiority of the Caucasian race." The size and shape of heads rather than what was in them now counted most for Marr.

Thus primed to become a full-blown racist, he became one in the Americas of the 1850s. In the United States (which he loved) and Central America (which he loathed), he became a white supremacist, apologist for black slavery, and an advocate of various eugenics schemes. The one-time democrat and anarchist urged "strong governments" for the unproductive races even as he warned that black- and brown-skinned people could never attain the level that whites had.

Unable to establish his fortune in the New World, he returned to Hamburg in 1859 to take part in the revival of reform politics. To his former allies on the Left, he appeared to be the same old Marr, the ultra among ultras. He soon disabused them. In 1862–63 he was ostracized by the democrats because he wrote and spoke on behalf of slavery and against Jewish and proletarian emancipation. His Voltairean *A Mirror to the Jews* (1862) attacked their incomplete assimilation to Germandom. A state within the state and an alien tribe with unpalatable racial characteristics, Jews, he maintained, would find it impossible ever to become truly German. But Marr was premature; interest in the Jewish question was slight, and the book struck no sparks.

He did not return to the Jewish question until 1879. In the intervening years, his life had gone downhill. He failed in business, divorced his first rich Jewish wife, lost another in childbirth, and a third to a fellow antisemite. In Berlin during the 1870s, he could not acclimatize himself to modern journalistic practices and eked out a living writing for any newspaper that would have him. An embittered failure, Wilhelm Marr then wrote the pamphlet that was instrumental in the politicalization of antisemitism.

The tone of *The Victory of Jewry over Germandom* is one of unrelieved pessimism, in harmony with the wreck that Marr's life had become. But gloom was also a conscious stratagem, a favorite pose of many antisemites from this time forward. Marr rubbed salt in the wound, promised that the struggle was virtually over and lost, hinted that the authorities were already too corrupted to do their duty, and portrayed the enemy as a gloating monster—all this designed to evoke a political response, to goad his audience first to fury and then into action. He clothed his personal grievances about journalism, his own economic woes, and his general lack of significance in familiar rhetoric. Jewish mendacity, ethical inferiority, instinctive hatred for all non-Jews, unwillingness to do hard physical labor—Marr himself never did any—were charges already familiar to his readers. But he went further by placing Jewish evil in a racial, conspiratorial, and world-historical context.

Emancipation, a decade old in Germany, had revealed the Jewish plot to Marr in all its terrible clarity. It formed the last step in a long-prepared plan of domination. With political equality the Jews intended to gain control of the state in order to guarantee the hegemony they had already wrested in financial and cultural matters. Prince Bismarck was an uncertain source of help against them. The daily press was closed to all opinion that ran counter to the interests of Jewry, even in questions of the Christian religion or international diplomacy. The Jewification (Marr was a fervid admirer of Richard Wagner) of modern life was in full swing. Given the vile character of the race, its victory spelled cataclysm for the forces of decency.

With *The Victory of Jewry,* Marr registered a changed perception in the nature of the Jewish danger. He proclaimed that the old sorts of casual anti-Jewish behavior—the occasional book, the occasional pogrom—were outmoded. Such measures had failed to halt the march of the Jews. Now, after emancipation, it was too late for such intermittent and defensive gestures, because the Jews had become so enormously powerful. To replace the ineffectual traditional methods, a continuous political effort would have to be mounted, institutionalized in parties, propaganda associations, and newspapers. The political action program was implicit in the book, but it became explicit in Marr's next pamphlet: written hurriedly in late 1879, *Elect No Jews!* bore the subtitle, "the way to victory of Germandom over Jewry." The heroic struggle against great odds could be won, after all.

The *Victory of Jewry* went through twelve editions by the end of 1879. Its enthusiastic reception, as compared to Marr's *A Mirror to the Jews*, cannot be explained by the quality of its argument, however. The transformation of German life by a dynamic capitalism, with its many casualties, the visible thriving of German Jews, the threat of socialism, and the decline of traditional values had readied large segments of the population for Marr's message. He spoke directly to the desperate situation of the small farmer and the lower middle class, the two social groups that would provide the mass basis for all future antisemitic parties. Their responsiveness alerted powerful groups in Germany and other European countries to the utility of antisemitism as a tool of political mobilization. In 1879, antisemitism entered the political culture of Europe.

For Further Reading

Moshe Zimmermann, *Wilhelm Marr: The Patriarch of Antisemitism* (New York, 1986).

6. Wilhelm Marr
The Victory of Jewry over Germandom (1879)

Woe unto the vanquished!

Author's Foreword

With this work I intend less a polemic against Jewry than confirmation of a cultural and historical fact. The polemical language that conditions sometimes force upon me can and must be understood as no more than a cry of pain from one of the oppressed.

Source: From Wilhelm Marr, *Der Sieg des Judenthums über das Germanenthum: Vom nicht confessionellen Standpunkt aus betrachtet* (Bern, 1879).

A resigned "pessimism" flows from my pen.

Think, if you will, "he must be a queer bird." But be assured that no one would be happier than myself if the facts I touch upon could be refuted.

Countless times we non-Jews have attacked Jews and Jewry in literature, but always from the standpoint of our own overweening presumption. Our self-conceit still keeps us from the open and honest admission that Israel has become a world power of the very first rank. We knew the Jews well enough—*but not ourselves.*

Be that as it may, this book should be permitted to lay claim to originality. Written without a trace of religious prejudice, it allows you to peer into the mirror of cultural and historical facts. Do not blame the "pessimist" if the mirror shows you to be slaves.

I have two hopes for this book: first, that it will not be killed by the silence of the Jewish critics; second, that it will not be finished off by your well-known, self-satisfied clichés.

Without a shred of irony, I publicly proclaim *the world-historical triumph of Jewry,* the news of a lost battle, the victory of the enemy without a single excuse for the stricken army. I should like to believe that such candor deserves something better than the zealous Jewish accents of the newspapers.

W.M.

I

When one people subjugates another, one of two situations usually obtains: either the conqueror merges into the culture of the conquered and loses its special nature. (This was the case with the Tartars, among others, who conquered China under Genghis Khan and then became Chinese. Similarly, the Germandom of the Lombards was completely Italianized.) Or the conqueror succeeds in impressing his special nature upon the conquered. Witness the Anglo-Saxon race in North America and its influence upon Central and South America.

As imposing as these two possible phenomena may be, they lose significance when confronted by the cultural history of Jewry. For in this case, a wholly new force enters. A completely Semitic race has been repeatedly torn loose from its homeland in Palestine, led into captivity, and, finally, scattered. As far as the "Babylonian Captivity"[1] is concerned, it seems that the Babylonians soon wearied of their Jewish captives, for they were let loose again. The bulk returned to Palestine. The bankers and the wealthy, however, stayed in Babylonia despite the angry thundering of the ancient Jewish prophets.

---

[1]In the history of Israel, the "Babylonian Captivity" refers to the first fall of Jerusalem in 586 B.C. and the deportation of thousands of Jews to Mesopotamia. Cyrus the Great ended the exile in 516 B.C.

Let it be mentioned here that from the outset, wherever Jews have entered into history, they have been hated by all peoples without exception. Not on account of their religion, for the Jews knew quite well how to adapt themselves to the idolatry of other peoples. (That this was so can be seen from the complaints of the prophets. So-called "stiff-necked Judaism" was a product of the period following the destruction of Jerusalem.)

The general enmity toward the Jews had other grounds: first, *in their aversion to honest labor*; second, *in their legally prescribed enmity toward all non-Jews.* Anyone who has taken the trouble to read through the Mosaic Law in the Bible, however cursorily, will concede that a people which adheres to this code in war and peace could not gain international sympathy. The relationship of the Jews to Jehovah was unimaginative and heartless, ossified in formalism, purely a matter of mundane business. In practical life it results in the most pronounced *realism* imaginable, a perfectly harmonious whole. Even the Jehovah of the Old Testament was a rigid realist. He recognized the existence of "other gods" but was animated by hatred of them as [business] competitors.

Titus[2] played the stupidest world-historical prank imaginable when, after the destruction of Jerusalem, he forcibly hauled off part of the Jews into Roman captivity and arbitrarily scattered the rest. Religious intolerance was little known in Rome. "Every god is welcome in Rome," ran the adage. Of course, when people committed mischief or sought to demolish the Roman temples, in the name of their gods, whom Rome had given hospitality, then the Roman police intervened. What made the Jews hateful to the Romans was again their exclusiveness combined with the realistic spirit of huckstering and usury that they brought with them into the Roman world.

This Roman world, as well as all of classical antiquity, was already gripped by decay when the Jews were resettled. Semitism therefore found fertile ground for its realism. Even in the era of Constantine, the "New Jews" (Christians) constituted the money power in Rome. . . .

Thus the Romans forcibly imported the abstract realism of Jewry into Western society. The time and conditions favored its development and extension. Jewry became the realistic midwife of history and found for its labor-shy, speculative realism a much more fertile soil in the West than ever it had possessed in Palestine.

---

[2]After his father, Vespasian, became Roman emperor in 69 A.D., Titus took command in the war against the Judaeans. Having failed to take Jerusalem by direct assault, he began a long siege, which ended with the burning of the temple and the general destruction of the city in 70 A.D. To celebrate his triumphal return to Rome, he erected the Arch of Titus and marched seven hundred Jewish captives through it. This was not, however, the first appearance of Jews in the West, as Marr suggests. For nearly a century before the catastrophe, a wave of voluntary emigration from Palestine had been under way. Nor was it the beginning of the Jews' "war on the West." The Roman Empire afforded Jews relative security, eventually bestowing full rights of citizenship and allowing them to forgo the ceremonies of emperor worship. It was only with the Christianization of the empire during the fourth century that the status of the Jews degenerated.

Quite naturally this aroused envy in the people of the West. Since the masses had always loved to clothe their own interests in religion, there formed with the spread of Christianity in the West a (seemingly) religiously motivated Jew hate.

Just how idiotic was the religious side of this hatred becomes clear from the fact that it tried to make the Jews responsible for the Crucifixion of Christ, a proceeding that the Roman authorities carried out in cowardly deference to the howls of the Jerusalem rabble. The Jewish rabble in the time of Christ did no more and no less than the rabble of all times and all peoples has constantly done. Today they shout, "Hosanna," and the next day, "Crucify!" However, it is inherent in human nature that men enlist providence or religion when they wish to commit stupidities or base acts. . . . And so *God* and *Religion* have been made to bear the brunt of all persecutions of the Jews, while in truth these persecutions were nothing but the striving of the peoples and their instincts against the *realistic Jewification of society*, nothing less than *a struggle for their existence.*

If, indeed, at Passover time in the Middle Ages, a few fanatical Jews actually did "slaughter a Christian child," if such crackpot incidents did occur—allegations not historically verifiable—they were abominations, like crimes in general. Yet they lent as little legitimacy to a general religious hatred against Jews as would the lewdness of certain pietistic sects against Christians. When it comes to religious persecutions, I take even the Jews under my unconditional protection. In this respect it is scarcely possible to speak out more clearly than I have done here. On the other hand, I emphasize this established and irrefutable fact: in the Jews, the Romans forced upon the West a race that, according to its own historians, was profoundly hated by all the peoples of the West.

II

The Jews, therefore, did not come to us as conquerors with the sword. . . . Although they had freedom to choose their place of habitation, their residences in the cities stood under surveillance in the so-called "ghettos" or Jewish quarters.[3]

---

[3]Attempting to make it appear as though animosity reigned between Jews and Europeans from their very first contacts, Marr predates the erection of ghettos by nearly fourteen hundred years. Although there were Jewish quarters in the major cities of the Roman Empire and during the early Middle Ages, these were generally voluntary, did not normally include all Jews, and were not guarded by non-Jews. Moreover, in the early Middle Ages, Jews and Gentiles often lived side by side. The first walled-off, compulsory ghettos appeared in fifteenth-century Spain and Portugal. From there the institution spread throughout most of Europe. At night and on Christian holy days, Jews were locked within the ghetto gates. Because the dwelling area was rarely enlarged, the buildings rose higher and higher, subjecting their inhabitants to overcrowding, disastrous fires, and epidemics. In many German cities the ghettos remained intact until the advancing armies of Napoleon literally blew up their walls.

Nothing was more natural than that the Jews should hate their oppressors and abductors. Nothing was more natural than that this hate
should swell with nearly two thousand years of oppression and persecution. Nothing was more natural than that the Jews, exiled and indirectly
captive in the West, should become even more hateful than they were in
the East. Nothing was more natural than that these "captives" should use
their inborn talent for slyness and fraud to create a state within a state, a
society within a society. In the West, the particularist state of the Jews
continued to wage a war of cunning with the weapons of destruction it had
used successfully against the peoples of the East.

All this was simply a natural right of the Jews. We must expect defi-
ance, not mildness, from the oppressed. Least of all can we expect sincerity
from a people whose laws do not call for turning the right cheek after the
left has been struck. "An eye for an eye, a tooth for a tooth," says Jehovah-
ism. . . .

Amazingly, the stubbornness and endurance of the Semites have led
them in the course of the nineteenth century to the position of pre-emi-
nence in the society of the West. In fact, in Germany it is not Jewry that
has merged into Germandom but Germandom that has merged into Jewry.
Merged to the point that the spokesmen for German patriotism, for acceptance of the new Reich, for our parliamentary, and, yes, even our church
battles—are Jews.

It is a remarkable cultural and historical phenomenon that, right from
the start of their dispersion in the West, Jews plunged into the cities and
showed themselves even more averse to agriculture and colonization than
they had been in Palestine or Egypt. Let no one object that many countries
did not permit Jews to acquire land. Well into the Middle Ages the West
consisted of fallow virgin land. Nothing stood in the way of the kind of
squatter's life led by the pioneers of culture in the forests of North America. Unclaimed land lay abundantly available in the West. But it was not
claimed by Jews, for this people lacked the energetic vigor of the Anglo-
Saxons who, banished because of their religious beliefs, created new states
out of the wilderness of the far West.[4] Not the axe and the plow, but the
cunning and slyness necessary to the realistic spirit of huckstering were
the weapons by which the Jews conquered the West and made a New Palestine out of Germany.

---

[4]The divorce of the Jews from the soil was very gradual and not always a matter of choice.
As immigrants in the Roman world, they congregated in cities, drawn there by both economic opportunities and the needs of a communal religion. Later, religious persecution
bore directly on their relationship to the land. Forbidden to employ Christian domestics
or laborers, Jews could not easily undertake large-scale farming. The "virgin lands" of
western Europe, a figment of Marr's historical imagination, were not just there for the
taking. Even where permitted to hold land, Jews were required to pay a tithe to the church,
which they were reluctant to do. From the twelfth century, they were altogether prohibited
from holding land or belonging to the craft guilds—thus their peculiar sociology in western
and central Europe, with its overwhelming emphasis on marginal and middleman functions.

But why particularly out of Germany?

Because of Romanism. The old Roman Empire of the caesars had developed to such a degree of sociopolitical realism that only the idealism of Christianity could make it crumble. This the Jews perceived. With the introduction of Christianity as the state religion and with the beginning of the papacy, which had to maintain the conflict between Christians and non-Christians in order to monopolize the world, Jewish "free trade" became too confined in Rome and Italy. Jewry increasingly decentralized, giving way before the fanaticism of the Christian church. It scattered en masse over Spain and Portugal and the lands of the Slavs. From there Jews emigrated in huge numbers to Holland and Germany, while those remaining among the Slavic barbarians carried on their work of social subversion undisturbed. Next to the Slavs, Germandom was least prepared for the aliens. German national feeling, to say nothing of German national pride, did not exist in Germanic areas. Exactly for this reason it was easier for Semitism to gain a firmer foothold in Germany than elsewhere.

Of course, here, too, the special nature of the Oriental aliens gave offense. Of course, Semitic cunning and the realistic spirit of business provoked a reaction against Jews in Germanic agricultural areas. This alien racial element and its realism clashed too violently with the total character of Germandom. Its laws, its stated dogmas, which looked upon all non-Jews as "unclean," aroused the anger of the people. At the same time, the Jews let themselves be used by the great ones of the land so that they could conduct their money transactions at the cost of the common people. Highly gifted, highly talented in this direction, the Jews dominated the wholesale and retail trade in the Middle Ages. They soon outstripped those who earned their bread by the sweat of their brow.

The people saw that their ethical feelings were not really shared by the Jews and that the Jews cared more about making money than about their own emancipation. So long as they made money, they tolerated anything. Oppressed from above according to official policy, the Jews could carry on below with impunity. The people were not permitted to grumble about their exploitation by the powerful and their agents—the Jews. Thus, the religious aspect became a pretext. "Should the crucifiers of Christ be allowed to exploit us?" they cried. "Hep-Hep!"[5] Occasional pogroms kept the Jews dependent and compliant. They did not take it into their heads to demand emancipation because this might endanger their money dealings.

It cannot be denied that the abstract and financially adroit haggling of the Jews contributed much to the flourishing of commerce and industry in Germany. Advantage and not ideals built the various German states. . . . The slick, cunning, elastic Jews wormed their way into this confused, clumsy Germanic element. The Jews were well suited by their purely realistic intelligence (that is, by their slyness) to look down upon Germandom. . . .

---

[5]See note 1, Document 5.

The Jew had no fatherland. With every passing day he became more estranged from his former homeland. Memories of it consisted of mere formulas. On the other hand, Nature denied the Jew the gift of amalgamating with other peoples, of assimilating. The religion, customs, morals, and way of life of others he rejected inflexibly. He was able to deceive his oppressor in all matters except in that of wanting to be and remain a Jew. His laws were a permanent challenge to, and demonstration against, the "unclean" in whose midst he dwelt. The Jew was regarded as the typical alien, and so he has remained until the present day. *Indeed, as we shall demonstrate below, this exclusive Judaism stands out far more prominently today, after Jewish Emancipation, than it ever did in former times.*

We ought not be ashamed to admit that with the Jews an element came into our Western society that quickly outstripped our forefathers in cunning and slyness. These were the weapons with which the Jews fought in the West, after fire and sword, fanaticism, and the hate of other peoples had been taken from their arsenal in the East. In the West, Jewry has continuously waged a war of cunning against everything non-Jewish. Jewry victoriously resisted our view of the world as year after year it inoculated us with its own. Jews have made the concept of right and wrong so elastic that the limits in commerce border on brutal crime, while so-called "unpunished crimes" have become the norm. The wit who divided the stock exchange people into "white and black Jews" was not altogether mistaken.

From all this there is a single conclusion to be drawn: Germandom did not possess the *spiritual capacity* for resistance to Jewification. Thus, Germany gradually became the actual center of Semitism, the new promised land, constantly strengthened by an influx of Jews from Spain, Portugal, and Poland. . . .

A cultural and historical phenomenon like this is no soap bubble to be popped with a cheap "Hep-Hep!" This people is a demonic phenomenon, despite their typically ludicrous appearance. Their appearance excited laughter in Imperial Rome, and they were caked in filth worse than one meets today in Russia and Poland, but these Jews extended over all Europe. Ridiculed by the educated, mishandled by the mob, persecuted by the zealots of the medieval church, this people nevertheless made the high and the mighty its tributary and sucked dry the lowly by means of intelligence, elasticity, and huckstering. Through it all they stuck stubbornly to their theocratic Jehovah worship, persecuting fanatically the few humane exceptions among them. *And this people has conquered the world with its Jewish spirit!*

This victory owed nothing to the power of Jewish religious belief. The Jew really has no ideal religion. He has only a business contract with Jehovah and pays his God in formal observances. In exchange, Jehovah makes it the agreeable duty of the Jews to eradicate everything non-Jewish. Not religion but the prodigious power of a fully conscious and typical REALISM is what we are compelled to gaze upon in amazement when we look at Judaism. As far as the existence of business and acquisitive impulses goes, we Germanic people differ little, if at all, from the Jews. What we lack is the energy of initiative present in the Semitic race. Since by virtue of our tribal organization we can never attain this energy and since an armistice in the history of civilization is impossible, there opens before us the prospect that someday the Jews will use the law and the state to attain a feudal domination over us. We Germans will become their slaves.

III

Germandom has labored under the delusion that the Jewish question comprises only a religious, that is to say, denominational significance (and thus can be overcome). That one of our noblest of men, greatest of thinkers and poets, sharpest of critics, Gotthold Ephraim Lessing, also labored under this delusion is demonstrated by his play, *Nathan the Wise.*[6]

The eighteenth century in which Lessing lived was the century of philosophical emancipation from prejudices of all kinds but especially from religious prejudice. Now, it is noteworthy that during this great epoch English as well as French "freethinkers" stood more or less unfavorably disposed toward Jewry. The great deist, Voltaire, took the formalism of the Jews heartily to task. He and, in England, Mylord Bolingbroke made no secret of their tribal aversion toward Jews and in fact clearly emphasized that the Jews could not claim to have a proper religion. They treated Judaism as a spiritual bagatelle.

In Germany, on the other hand, the great Lessing struck out on another path, the path of philosophical error. . . . The idea of Jewish emancipation began to gain ground in the general public through Lessing's *Nathan.*

Who can be angered by the fact that the Jews greeted the revolutions of 1789 and 1848 with joy or that they participated in them with zeal? It was "Jews, Poles, and literati" according to the Conservative slogan of the year 1848. Yes, indeed, three oppressed powers! The happy and the contented do not revolt in this world. That the Jews spoke the loudest of all in that frenzied bacchanal of freedom is certainly explicable. Yet again it must be emphasized that it was philosophical self-deception that suggested that the Jewish question was a question of religious freedom. In 1848 Jews had already risen far above the level where religious prejudice made any difference. The Jewish "religion" was nothing more than the statutes of a people that constituted a state within a state. Moreover, this enclave was actually an oppositional state that demanded quite definite material advantages for its members.

---

[6]Gotthold Ephraim Lessing (1729–81), was one of the chief figures of the German Enlightenment. His play, *Nathan the Wise* (1779), set in the time of the Crusades, is a plea for religious toleration and portrays Jews as fully human. He was a hero to German Jews, many of whom adopted *Lessing* as a surname in the nineteenth century. On the other hand, he has always posed difficulties for German antisemites. Claiming all great German men of letters as their own, antisemites went to extreme lengths to show Lessing was conscious of the "Jewish danger." Marr devoted a later pamphlet entirely to this problem. Others condemned Lessing as a vastly overrated thinker, read diligently between the lines for his "real" meaning, or simply quoted him out of context.

The Jews went beyond civil equality, for, as a matter of fact, Jewry had long ago set the tone for civil life and had attained a dominant position. Christian states baronized their Jewish bankers, albeit they denied these Semitic barons the right to hold municipal offices, etc.

It occurred to no one that the Jewish question was a *sociopolitical* question. For 1800 years we have told ourselves the lie that it was a matter of freedom of conscience and belief. As we merrily continued lying to ourselves, the legal emancipation of the Jews *inaugurated the sociopolitical incursion* of Jewry into Germanic society.

Jewish emancipation, however, really did no more than recognize an already existing alien domination. To speak plainly, this alien domination has progressed to the point where Jews have seized the dictatorship of the state finance system and have inoculated it with the Semitic spirit of manipulation and management. What Jewry had already long ago attained— the hegemony of Jewish realism at the cost of everything idealistic—had now to be made secure so that it might be indefinitely extended. To that end, Jewry required equal political participation in the legislation and administration of the state that it *theocratically denied*. Scrape away the glistening phrases and this, the quintessence of the question of Jewish emancipation, is revealed: an unqualified alien Jewish domination was ushered into the Germanic state.

I have repeatedly used the term *alien domination*. Is not the people who every year utters the absurd ritual phrase, "Next year in Jerusalem!" an alien people? The foreign nature of this firm is advertised plainly by the morals of the Jews and by their racial peculiarities. Only in the rarest, most isolated cases during the past 1800 years have they been able to assimilate totally with Germandom. Would or could the Jews, in days to come, scoff at their own power and make an ostensible attempt to look like something other than the clearly marked alien? Hardly! The "glory" of Jewry consists of having put up a totally victorious resistance to the Western world for 1800 years. All other immigrants have dissolved into Germandom without a trace. . . . Truly, were I a Jew, my greatest pride would be to regard this fact with satisfaction. *No conquering hero of ancient or modern times could boast of greater spiritual, cultural, and historical success than the Jew peddler hawking shoelaces from his street-corner pushcart.* Without striking a blow, in fact, politically persecuted through the centuries, Jewry today has become the sociopolitical dictator of Germany.

IV

Is this the case only in Germany?

In this land of thinkers and philosophers, the emancipation of the Jews dates from 1848. From that date began the Thirty Years' War that Jewry has waged against us with weapons equal to our own. We could scarcely avoid having given them these weapons during that period of revolutionary turmoil. After all, during the course of the centuries, we had already been half-bested by Jewish intelligence. After the institution of elections, Jews entered immediately into a contractual and statistical relationship with us. To be a Jew meant, relatively speaking, to possess a parliamentary seat, for in order to win Jewish votes, the political parties had to concede candidacies to Jewry. It has remained more or less this way up to the present day.

Up until the year 1848, the Jew in Germany was predominantly "democratically" inclined, or at least pretended to be. Later Jewry dispersed into the parliamentary parties. The National Liberal party was especially attractive to them because in it the spirit of Jewification, opportunism, utilitarianism, and general lack of principle had progressed furthest. . . . Two-thirds of our semiofficial literature is produced by Jews. Everywhere the same goal is pursued with unswerving logic—the decomposition of the Germanic state for the benefit of Jewish interests.

The daily press is overwhelmingly in the hands of Jews who have made journalism a speculative commodity. They have made a business out of public opinion. Three-quarters of the drama and art criticism are in Jewish hands. Political reporting—yes, even the reporting of religious matters—is in Jewish hands.

Let us pause a moment.

After the attainment of emancipation, natural instinct commanded the Jews to consolidate and fortify their position. This could be accomplished only through the newspapers and related associations. With stern logic Jewry flooded into both. Jewry showed itself remarkably objective and free of prejudice, even to the point of sarcastic self-irony. However, it is . . . another thing altogether should a Gentile do the same. The very word *garlic* suffices to bring us Germans under the suspicion of religious bigotry.[7] Now, at least, I ought to be free of this reproach.

From the first moment of emancipation, Jewry became a sacred, untouchable object for us Germans. By successfully reducing journalism to a trivial article of trade that caters to the common mob's taste for scandal and gossip, Jewry found the widest audience for its efforts toward Jewification. Dominating Jewish realism having prepared the ground through the centuries, Jewry now *dictates* public opinion in the press.

But now comes the Semitic victor's supreme arrogance!

The *Kulturkampf*[8] breaks out. Since 1848, if we Germans so much as criticized any little thing Jewish, it was enough to have us entirely

---

[7]Marr here makes an invidious comparison and attempts to inject some ill-willed humor by referring to the presence of garlic in Jewish cookery and, presumably, on Jewish breath. Apparently, northern Europeans, including the Germans, made little or no use of the offending ingredient, and the use of it by others was thought to be a mark of their inferiority. Marr suggests that Jews were so sensitive and defensive that they regarded even such a trivial criticism as "antisemitism."

[8]The *Kulturkampf* denotes the politically motivated program of anti-Catholic legislation carried out by Bismarck, primarily in the Prussian parliament. The liberal parties and liberally oriented newspapers throughout Germany zealously supported him, largely for ideological reasons. For them, the matter went beyond mere separation of church and state

outlawed from the press. Jewry, on the other hand, not only mixes in our religious controversies and in the *Kulturkampf* against Ultramontanism but has the most to say about it in our press. In their humor magazines, which are anxiously on the lookout for anything that can be satirized as "Jew baiting," they pour boiling oil on Ultramontanism. Why, of course. Ultramontanism was Jewry's competitor for world hegemony! While a sense of delicacy is wholly absent among the Jews, it is demanded of us that we handle them like fine glassware or extremely sensitive plants.

Indeed, there were great newspapers in which we Germans could not even get a hearing. Why not? Because in order to criticize Romish fanaticism, it would have been necessary to show that it was the outcome of Old Testament, Jehovah fanaticism. Even the Ultramontanes suppressed hostile representations from their newspapers as soon as Israel was even lightly grazed!!

Just once try to comment upon Jewish rituals and observances. You will see that no pope is more infallible and unassailable than these doctrines. You would be accused of religious hatred. But when Jews hold forth and have the final say on our church-state matters, that is something quite different! While we embroil ourselves in church-state conflicts, Jewry shouts "*Vae Victis*! Woe unto the vanquished!"

I and several of my friends tried, at the outbreak of the *Kulturkampf*, to participate and contribute from a higher cultural and historical point of view. But in vain. We were only permitted to speak without theoretical premises or when, out of the blue, we wished to disparage the clericals. None of our letters to the editor were ever printed in the Jewish press. Thus has Jewry monopolized the free expression of opinion in the daily press.

It would be quite shabby to clothe our own impotence in the phrases of Jew hate. In 1848 we Germans completed our formal abdication in favor of the Jews. Ask yourself, Does not the path to your goal in every branch of life go by way of *Jewish mediation*? Generally speaking, there is no part of the struggle for existence that does not pay a commission to Jewry. Let any individual reader ask himself if I exaggerate. This is the result of the Thirty Years' War officially waged by Jewry against us since 1848. . . .

---

or the hobbling of a political enemy, the Center party. It was a struggle between light and darkness, reason and superstition, loyalty to the nation-state or a foreign potentate—in short, as the German term suggests, "a struggle for civilization" itself. After the *Kulturkampf* subsided, the church and the Center party always opposed political antisemitism as a threat to religious liberty. Election districts with Catholic majorities never returned a candidate of the antisemitic parties. In rare cases, individual Catholic politicians attempted to exploit antisemitic slogans, but such conduct was never officially sanctioned and was usually condemned by the party's liberal wing. The immunity of the Center and the Social Democratic party to antisemitic politics made it virtually impossible for the antisemites to develop a significant mass following in Germany before World War I.

V

There is no armistice. We move forward, or we retreat.

Are there any signs that a Jewish "Twilight of the Gods" is at hand? No. Jewry's sociopolitical hegemony, as well as the tutelage it exercises in religious questions, point to a youthful and vigorous development. The Jews are on their way to realizing the promise of Jehovah: "All peoples will I give unto thee, etc."[9] A sudden reversal is already fundamentally impossible because our social structure, in its present Jewified condition, would have to collapse, and, realistically, there is no ideal conception to replace it.

Furthermore, we cannot expect any help from the "Christian" state. The Jews are the "best citizens" of this modern Christian state since it serves their interests completely. They are—all irony aside—the best and truest "empire boosters" in Germany, because this empire has done its utmost to clothe them with the very highest dignities of the state.

If I might direct one request to my readers, it would be this: Save this book of mine and take steps that this little text may be passed on from generation to generation. It is no ostentatious prophecy but a deeply felt conviction when I say that *no more than four generations shall pass before the Jews usurp absolutely every office of state, including the very highest.* Yes, Jewry shall raise Germany to a world power and make it the New Palestine of Europe. It won't come about by violent revolution but by the voice of the people itself, as soon as German society has reached that highest level of social bankruptcy and perplexity toward which we are rushing headlong.

Don't blame Jewry for this. . . . Our Germanic element has shown itself culturally and historically powerless, incapable of achievement, before alien domination. This is a fact, a raw, pitiless fact. State, church, Catholicism, Protestantism, credo, and dogma must bow before the Jewish Areopagus, the daily press.

But this is far from the whole story.

Hereafter, even if Germandom could get back on top, it could not stay there. We have become such laggards in the Jewish question.

Gambetta (today president of the [French] National Assembly!), Simon, and Crémieux were dictators of France in 1870–71. During the war they drove thousands upon thousands of Frenchmen to a useless death. After the battle of Sedan, the whole world believed in peace—but not these gentlemen. Bismarck could have managed the empty phrases of a Jules Favre, but the frivolous, fanatical, vile deeds of the Semitic gentlemen of Tours meant further work for "blood and iron." Alas, poor, Jewified France.

---

[9]No biblical scholar, Marr may be referring to Deuteronomy 28:1 or Jeremiah 1:10, which have God promising something of this nature. In fairness, Marr might have also cited Nehemiah 1:8 or Ezekiel 5:14, which promise to disperse the Jews among the nations.

In England the Semite Disraeli, of course a German hater, holds the power of war or peace over the Eastern Question in his vest pocket. Who derived the actual benefits from the Congress of Berlin and all the blood spilled in the Russo-Turkish War? The Alliance israélite universelle[10] was first in line, compelling Romania to open its gates to destructive Semitism. Jewry did not yet dare to make the same demand upon Russia, but this will soon come, too.

And after the war with France, who in Germany derived the advantages concerning raw materials? Jewry, represented by a handful of Jewish bankers, Semitic middlemen. We Germans are left with the idealistic, abstract residue; we can be "empire boosters," satisfied to dwell in the "realm of dreams." And after the war, where did the overwhelming majority of dishonest, socially corrupting entrepreneurs come from? From Jewry.

Dear reader, stop gnashing your teeth in rage! Alien domination has been forced upon us. For 1800 years the fight against Jewish domination has lasted. The Semitic race has borne indescribable suffering. You have roughly mishandled them, but rarely have you combated them spiritually. From feeble beginnings Jewry has grown beyond you. It has corrupted all society with its views. It has driven out any kind of idealism, possesses the controlling position in commerce, infiltrates increasingly into state offices, rules the theater, constitutes a sociopolitical phalanx, and finally has left you little more than the hard manual labor that it always despised. It has reduced talent to rattling superficial finesse, has made that procuress, advertising, into a goddess of public opinion. In short, Jewry lords it over you today. . . .

Are we capable of sacrifice? Have we even succeeded in creating a single, nonpartisan anti-Jewish newspaper? Are not even our housewife clubs and similar associations under Jewish patrons who combine business with pleasure for their own profit? Does not Jewry flow into all the pores of our life?

You may gnash your teeth about Germanic apathy. I bow down in amazed admiration before this Semitic race that has set its foot upon our necks. Having gathered up the last trace of human energy, I am resigned to

---

[10]Léon Gambetta (1838–82), Jules Simon (1814–96), and Adolphe Crémieux (1796–1880) were members of the eleven-man provisional Government of National Defense set up after the collapse of the Second French Empire in September 1870. As Republican opponents of Napoleon III, they rallied the French to continue the fight against the Germans after the decisive defeat at Sedan. Gambetta, the youngest and most energetic, escaped from Paris to take over the Ministry of Defense and proceeded to raise a large army. German and French antisemites insisted that Gambetta was a Jew; however, his Jewish descent is far from certain.

Of the three men mentioned, only Crémieux was a professing Jew. He was founder and later president of the Alliance israélite universelle, an international organization based in Paris that provided antisemites with "proof" of the worldwide nature of the Jewish conspiracy. Actually, the organization was primarily philanthropic and educational and sought to improve the often desperate lot of eastern European and Levantine Jews. When the Alliance tried to intervene politically, as in the case of Romania during the Congress of Berlin (1878), it did so quite timidly and ineffectively. Its elite membership,

enter into Jewish slavery, not to surrender or ask for quarter but only to die as peacefully as possible.

Can we deny historical facts? No.

The historical fact is this: Israel has become the leading sociopolitical great power of the nineteenth century. Quite clearly we lack the physical and intellectual energy with which to de-Jewify ourselves. . . .

Why are we so amazed? We have among us an elastic, tough, intelligent, and alien race that knows how to utilize all the forms of abstract realism. The world has been taken possession of by the Jewish spirit, by Jewish consciousness, not merely by individual Jews. Jew baiting is a thing of the past. Now German baiting rages the minute a non-Jewish element dares to step forward. All this is the result of a cultural and historical development so unique, so imposing that everyday polemic is impotent against it. . . .

Of all the European states, Russia is now the only one left that renders official resistance against the alien invasion. Judging from the case of Romania and the way things stand now, Russian capitulation is only a question of time. In this great multinational state the Jews will find the "Archimedean fulcrum" they need to dislodge the entire Western world. The elastic irrepressibility of the Jews will plunge Russia into a revolution the likes of which the world has not yet seen. Social nihilism and abstract individualism will be purposely conjured up until the half-civilized tsarist empire can no longer resist. . . . One has only to look at multinational Austria today to see how it has utterly, irreparably fallen into Jewish hands!!

The Jews have already broken through the dam of Prussia. . . . Is it more likely that Russia, with some still-primitive racial elements, can resist better than we Germans? . . . Impossible! Until Jewry has won the ultimate position in Russia, it must still fear being attacked from behind. However, once Jewry has paralyzed Russia, once it has completely protected its rear, once it has invaded Russian offices and positions the same way it has done here, then the collapse of Western society will be begun in an official Jewish way. Then the last brief hour for condemned Europe will strike in one hundred fifty years at the outside, for today developments move much more quickly than in past centuries. . . .

It does not behoove me and this is not the place to subject to criticism Prince Bismarck's domestic policy since 1866. Let it suffice to confirm that since 1866 His Highness has been honored by Jewry like some Emperor Constantine. The National Liberal Jewish opposition, it is true, quite transparently strives for power that, according to them, Bismarck ought to concede at this time. Unfortunately, I cannot label these Jewish hopes as ridiculous. The premises of our domestic affairs since the war with Austria and, still more so, since the war with France make it impossible to see even the most brazen Jewish hopes as ridiculous. . . .

---

almost entirely French, was always chary of appearing too self-serving. Its real political influence, antisemitic fantasies notwithstanding, was minimal.

It does not befit me as a German and one of the vanquished to criticize the domestic statesmanship of Prince Bismarck. But if I were a Jew, I would say, "The prince has grasped his time like no other statesman before him. From a clear cultural and historical perspective he has seen that Germandom is bankrupt and at its last gasp. Therefore, he is searching for elements that display a more vital life-force." Of what use are men like us to him? We can no longer be "empire boosters" because we do not have a *German* Empire. All we can beg for from the prince is a sanctuary for a small, quiet community—*a community that has not yet lost every ideal.*

VI

The 1800-year war with Jewry is nearing its end. Let us confess it openly and without reservation: Germandom has suffered its Sedan. . . . Do not waste my time by arguing the contrary. Nothing can be accomplished by brutal mobs shouting "Hep-Hep" or by the auto-da-fé. We have never labored for inner self-emancipation from inflexible Jewish realism. We have not been able to achieve anything spiritually because we were too lazy and too greedy to put limits on the speculative spirit of the press. Therefore, don't scold about the "scandal sheets" that you buy, read, and support with your money. Don't make it impossible to look at yourself in the mirror. Cease being bigmouths and behave as befits the vanquished. To Jewry belongs the future and life, to Germandom the past and death. Thus the cultural-historical development of our German race has been ordained. Against this iron law of the world nothing will avail. . . .

In this age when it is so easy to suspect anyone who thinks differently, I cannot emphasize and repeat enough: I am not in the slightest degree animated by Jew hate or by a religious hatred against Jews. Neither is it a matter of national or race hatred. No people can help its special nature. The events of world history have catapulted Jewry into the West. Here two mutually alien elements faced one another. Friction between these two racial elements developed, and Jewry showed itself more steadfast than the West, especially Germandom.

It would be a worthwhile labor for a German scholar, who has the time for it, to expand my hasty (but precise) sketch into a scientific work. Phase by phase the progress of Jewry's sociopolitical accomplishments in Germany could be unfolded.

True, once I violently polemicized against Jewry, but I confess my error. My polemic was an anachronism that came several centuries too late. I harbor not the slightest enmity toward Jews unless they harm me personally, and then I resent only the individual enemy. I, like countless other writers and other men, suffer from the Jewification of my profession, but this is the nature of the phenomenon. It is as in war. How can I personally hate the soldier whose bullet strikes me? Would I not shake hands with him though I were wounded, vanquished, and a prisoner? Should we then be more barbaric than the soldier in war?

In my opinion, it has been an honorable war that has been waged for 1800 years. Neither side has wanted to admit this because both have been doctrinaire, unable to grasp the struggle in its cultural-historical totality. Among his own kind, the Jew—and I speak generally here—has admirable qualities. His family life, for example, is much more intimate than that of other peoples. And, outwardly, he can even be kind and charming toward us. But, inwardly, there dwells a race consciousness par excellence. That the Jew hates us or regards us only as creatures to be exploited lies in the nature of his race and its history in antiquity. After the reception accorded to him in the West, it was only natural that he did not become enthusiastic about us. He would not or could not assimilate to us. This left only war. And after his first decisive victory in 1848, he had to exploit it fully. Today he has no choice but to strive after the destruction of the Germanic and Western world. This decomposing mission of Jewry (already evident in antiquity) will provoke a counterblow only after it has reached its pinnacle— that is, after the Jewish caesar has been installed.

From where can this counterblow come? Certainly not from Germandom, which lies in agony. Perhaps—but this is a big perhaps—the Slavic peoples shall step to the front of the stage of the great tragicomedy called world history.

VII

It is an easy matter to sketch the picture that in all likelihood will confront the present generation. For, unless all the signs deceive us, just before Jewry achieves an autocratic hegemony, it will experience a last, desperate collision with the Germanic world. . . .

The Germanic state is rapidly disintegrating. If the predicted explosion occurs, the state will have no cause to give the Jews special protection from "civic ardor." *As in countless historical instances, the brutal "Hep-Hep" will become the safety valve for the state.* Perhaps the time is not so distant when we, the "Jew devourers" par excellence, will have to seek to protect the Semitic aliens, who have vanquished us, from the violence of incensed racial passions. Catastrophe approaches all the faster because the wrath against the Jewification of society increases in relation to the general silence of the press. . . .

I implore you, Do not berate the Jews. You elect the alien masters to your parliaments. You make them legislators and judges. You make them the dictators of the state finance system. You deliver up your press to them because flashy frivolity is more to your taste than moral seriousness. What do you expect after all this? The Jewish race prospers mightily on the basis of its talent. You are beaten, and you have deserved this a thousand times over. Don't complain about how Jews bring down prices in business or how they grab up the overproduction of big-business swindlers, sell at rock-bottom prices, make money, and invest it usuriously. Isn't that all according to the dogma of the abstract individualism that you have enthusiastically accepted from Jewry?

We have proceeded so far into Jewification that we can no longer save ourselves. A brutal anti-Jewish explosion can postpone the collapse of our Jewified society, but it cannot prevent it forever. You can no longer impede the great mission of Semitism. Jewish caesarism is only a question of time, of this I am certain. Only after this caesarism has reached its apex will we perhaps be helped by that "unknown God" to whom altars were built in Imperial Rome.

Conclusion

I have come to the end of my cultural-historical sketch. The right thinking will forgive me for expressing the pain I feel at the Jewification of my fatherland. They will bear witness that, with truth and justice, I have merely confirmed the facts. I have absolutely refrained from flattering the Germans at the cost of the Jews. If I have insulted the Jews because I showed them, too, where the logic of Jewification has led and is leading us, this cannot be altered. The victor has no right to demand byzantine flattery from the vanquished.

I have done not one whit more than sketch the cultural-historical process and end result occasioned by two races chafing against one another. I would like to think that this time—by way of exception—the Jewish papers will handle this book decently, even though it is not in their style. I know that my friends and I are defenseless against Jewry as far as journalism goes. We have neither a princely nor a bourgeois Maecenas [patron] to support us. Our German people is already too Jewified to show a warm interest in its own self-preservation.

We must once more admit it, so let's face it squarely: we are the vanquished; we are the subjugated. I have made this confession in order finally to bring the Jewish question out of the fog of abstractions and partisanship. Indeed, I am convinced that I have spoken what millions of Jews secretly think: *To Semitism belongs world mastery*!

Then speak of it openly, you Jews. Be open and truthful with your thoughts. You certainly have the power to do it! We shall not complain any longer. But let us put an end to the hypocrisy between us. . . .

Perhaps your realistic views of the world and life are correct. Perhaps destiny intends us to be your helots. We are well on the way to that end. Perhaps the spirit that you brought into the West and that high and low worship today is the only true one, the only spirit that can ensure a lasting hegemony for Germany. The individual German cannot yet answer yes or no to this proposition. But in any case, you can look down upon us with justifiable pride.

Do not dare to accuse me of irony! I solemnly protest against the accusation! . . .

Admit it now. Never has an enemy treated you more decently, more appreciatively than I, and this despite a life full of causes to hate you (as many, many of you full well know). But one does not hate if one has come to understand. "To know much is to forgive much," says Voltaire, and I "know" that you are the victors.

Do I then commend myself to your mercy? No. I want nothing from you but *respect for my convictions*. I may have erred. It is possible that Semitism and Germandom may conclude sociopolitical peace. I do not believe this possible. I believe only what I see: our sociopolitical enslavement to you. Instead of rattling my chains boastfully, like so many others are doing, I admit that you have enchained us hand and foot, head and heart, from the palace to the lowly hut.

Stoical resignation has replaced passionate struggle within me. Vent your cheap rage on the stoicism, if you cannot help yourself. But don't speak of religious or race hatred. It is the pain of an oppressed people that speaks from my pen, a people that today sighs under your mastery as once you sighed under ours, but a people that in the course of time, and step by step, you have thrown to the ground.

The "Twilight of the Gods" has begun for us. You are the masters, we the slaves. What is there left to say? . . .

A voice in the wilderness has been sounded and has only confirmed the facts, incontrovertible facts. Let us then reconcile ourselves to the inevitable since we are unable to alter it. Its name is:

FINIS GERMANIAE

3 The Diffusion of Political Antisemitism

Antisemitism in Hungary

Antisemitism in Hungary owed much of its inspiration to contemporaneous German developments and, like the German variant, was a historically conditioned response to Jewish emancipation (1867). Although Győző Istóczy delivered the speech reprinted in the following document, to the Hungarian *Seim* (parliament) eight months before the publication of Wilhelm Marr's *The Victory of Jewry over Germandom,* he was well aware of other anti-Jewish literature emanating from Berlin. German antisemites seized upon Istóczy's action as evidence of the international scope of their movement. Marr quoted the speech in one of his follow-up pamphlets, and Istóczy later played a featured role in the first international antisemitic congress held in Dresden (1882).

The history of the Jews in Hungary had been much the same as in the other states of eastern and central Europe. Their status had fluctuated according to the needs and whims of reigning princes and local Magyar noblemen. Valued for their indispensable financial and middle-man functions, they were also hated because of them and because of their heretical religion and foreign tongue (Yiddish). Jews were required to pay a special toleration tax, prohibited from joining the guilds, restricted in where they could live, and denied all political rights. From the late seventeenth century on, however, the Jewish population of Hungary began to increase as Jews arrived from places where their situation was even worse. In 1735 the Jews of Hungary numbered 11,621; by a century later, they had increased to approximately 200,000 or 2.3 percent of the total population.

During the nineteenth century, as the population continued to grow, the Jewish community underwent a qualitative change. Jews began assimilating, opting for the Hungarian language and customs. (In the census of 1900, 75 percent identified themselves as Hungarian, the other quarter as German.) Hungarian liberals supported this process and the Jewish quest for equal rights that went with it. In the war of independence from the Austrian Habsburgs that the Hungarians waged in 1848, Jews provided 20,000 soldiers for the rebel army of 180,000, an act of patriotism ridiculed by Istóczy but valued at the time as evidence of the Jewish commitment to Magyarization.

Support from Jews held great political significance for the Magyars, who, although constituting only a slim majority of the total population of Hungary, nonetheless exercised dominion over Serbs, Croatians, Slovenes, and Slovaks. As in the case of Germany, Jewish emancipation was a gift of liberalism and came with the tacit understanding that Jews would continue the process of complete assimilation. Unlike their German counterparts, however, the Hungarian liberals actually governed the state and used their power vigorously to defend Jewish emancipation.

Legal emancipation and the adoption of Hungarian identity could not overcome the animosity of centuries, however. Jews were still widely regarded as aliens. Their concentration in the professions and in urban centers fed old resentments and created new ones. At the time Istóczy introduced antisemitism into the *Seim,* Jews constituted 25 percent of the population of Budapest (or "Judapest" as the antisemites dubbed it). By 1910, 45 percent of the lawyers, 62 percent of the doctors, and 43 percent of the journalists in the capital were Jews. These numbers provided ample evidence of "Judaization," if one was inclined to deny that Jews were authentically Hungarian. Apparently, many were so inclined. Hungarian and other European antisemites habitually held up the *Verjudung* of Hungary as the terrifying future for all Europe.

Gyözö Istóczy modeled his activities on those of Wilhelm Marr, with whom he corresponded. In October 1880 he started an antisemitic periodical and formed the Central Association of Non-Jewish Hungarians, which took its statutes from Marr's Antisemites' League. Unsure of the potential response, Istóczy's association formulated appropriately vague political demands, calling for the elimination of Jewish influence and greater devotion to Hungarian ways by the Jews. For such nebulous aims, even baptized Jews could be accepted as anonymous members, at least temporarily. But over time Istóczy redefined the Jew in racial terms, banned converted Jews from the organization, and gave greater precision to his goals.

Istóczy was joined by five other members of the Hungarian Parliament whose political affiliations were on the Left. As in Germany, antisemitism was not yet a powerful enough issue to create a unified bloc. The five antisemites soon fell to arguing about other issues and achieved only a short-lived success. Istóczy's antisemitic organization was doing no better than Marr's until two events energized it: In January 1881, Christian students at Budapest University, responding to Istóczy's agitation, rioted against Jews who, they claimed, composed a disproportionately large part of the student body. The authorities put down the violence quickly, but the students answered with a petition, which they delivered to Istóczy. His presentation of the petition in the *Seim* met with a curt rejection from the government, but the public exposure his cause received helped it survive and grow.

On March 13, 1881, terrorists assassinated Tsar Alexander II, touching off a series of murderous pogroms in neighboring Russia. Soon the first wave of what was to be a massive Jewish emigration to the West began to be felt in northeastern Hungary. Some Hungarians had previously expressed fears that the favorable conditions created by Jewish emancipation would attract unwanted *Ostjuden* immigrants. Now, fed by antisemitic journalists and politicians, these anxieties began to play a political role. Residents in the regions most immediately affected by Jewish refugees presented another petition to the government, asking for relief. The parliamentary debates occasioned by the petition lent greater publicity to antisemitic sentiments.

Just as public excitement over the debates was dying down, an antisemitic member of the parliament reported the mysterious disappearance of a Christian girl from the remote village of Tisza-Eszlár, just a week before the Jewish Passover. With the aid of the mass press, this ritual-murder allegation did not remain localized, as it would have in the Middle Ages. It became a national sensation and was reported in several other European states. (Istóczy appeared at the Dresden international antisemitic congress with a life-sized portrait of the victim.) State officials, prompted by local clergymen, investigated not only a possible murder but whether "religious prescriptions" were involved. Otherwise sensible scholars discussed the likelihood of Jewish ritual murder in learned books and popular newspaper articles. Thus, modern political and careerist ambitions, along with medieval fears, conspired together to reinforce and disseminate popular suspicions about Jews.

The case resulted in a protracted trial, and, although the fifteen defendants were eventually acquitted, the political exploitation of the "murder" (the body was never found) continued. Persuaded that the Jews had bought off the government and judicial authorities, rioters in Bratislava and its environs attacked Jews and Jewish property. Only martial law succeeded in reimposing civil peace.

In the aftermath of the Tisza-Eszlár affair and the university disturbances, Istóczy formed the antisemites into a separate political party, which reached the high point of its electoral strength in 1884 with seventeen members (7 percent of the *Seim*). It was effective for about a decade, but its major goal, to rescind Jewish emancipation, never came close to realization, largely because of implacable opposition from the liberal government. In 1895, the antisemites suffered a serious reverse when the *Seim* passed a law recognizing Judaism as equal to the other religious denominations. Antisemitism subsided but never entirely disappeared as a political factor in Hungary. After World War I, it resurfaced and combined forcefully with national and economic grievances. Eventually, the Holocaust claimed the lives of 450,000 Hungarian Jews.

Istóczy's speech stands at the beginning of this process and bears the common features of parliamentary antisemitism. Its tone, although nasty, was considerably more polite than that prevailing at mass meetings or in the antisemitic press, perhaps because the speaker was less confident about how many parliamentarians shared his views. The *Seim* was, in fact, hostile to Istóczy, and this was the reason he probably felt impelled to advance statistical "proof" for his claims. This, too, was typical of parliamentary antisemitism elsewhere.

Nonetheless, logical argument had its limitations, and like most other antisemites in European parliaments, Istóczy found it advantageous to "speak out the window"—that is, to direct his rhetoric at ordinary citizens who followed the parliamentary debates in the newspaper. This far less critical audience might share his indignation that fewer Jews than Christians died in epidemics, an alleged consequence of their luxurious lives, devoid of physical labor. Outlandish though the charge was, it was well designed to provoke non-Jews by emphasizing basic differences between their lives and those of Jews. Parliamentary rebuttals or apologetic literature, urging common sense or carefully citing and interpreting statistics, usually failed to counteract the kind of unverified charges Istóczy makes. These became the antisemites' stock in trade.

For Further Reading

Nathaniel Katzburg, *Hungary and the Jews* (Ramat-Gan, 1981); Ezra Mendelsohn, *The Jews of East Central Europe between the World Wars* (Bloomington, Ind., 1983).

7. Gyözö Istóczy
"Jews, the Iron Ring Around Our Necks"
(1878)

The Congress [of Berlin] will certainly confirm the emancipation of Christians in the Balkans. With recourse to weapons if necessary, it is the task of the [Austro-Hungarian] monarchy to see to it that the freed Christian peoples do not fall under Russian despotism.[1] ("Bravo!") Increasingly, the Mohammedan element is disappearing from Europe. Thus, among the Christian peoples of Europe, there is only one further element that wants to bring the [Christian] families of nations under the Slavic yoke—the Jews! It can be demonstrated with statistics that in a period of eighty-five years the Jews have increased almost 800 percent [in Hungary]. These same statistical data also demonstrate that the Jewish element in Hungary has doubled every thirty years.

Since 710,000 Jews live in Hungary, there will be, according to this progression, 1.1 million in the year 1900; in the year 1930, 2.2 million; and continuing thus, in the year 2020, 17.6 million Jews will live in Hungary. That is, there will be twice as many Jews as the current total population of the Kingdom of St. Stephen.[2]

Including the eightfold increase of the Hebrews in the last eighty-five years, the total population of Hungary has not even doubled. In fact, from 1869 to 1870, it declined by nearly 36,000 in Hungary and Transylvania

---

Source: Speech to the Hungarian Parliament, June 25, 1878, in Wilhelm Marr, *Vom jüdischen Kriegsschauplatz: Eine Streitschrift,* 2d ed. (Bern, 1879), pp. 41–43.

[1] At the Congress of Berlin, which was meeting while Istóczy spoke, the European powers intervened to prevent the excessive aggrandizement of Russia as a result of its victory in the Russo-Turkish War. In exchange for this protection, the Great Powers demanded reforms from the sultan that would have ended the persecution of Christians and other religious minorities in the Balkan possessions of the Turks.

[2] This is a typical example of the statistical terrorism the antisemites practiced. Istóczy's "progressions" are mathematically correct but skewed by a number of factors. The Jewish population in 1880 was actually 638,000, or about 4.5 percent. He also assumed that the increase of the Jewish population would continue at the same rate as in the exceptional period of growth he used as his base of comparison. He did not consider Jewish emigration or a reduced birthrate. In 1900, the population was approximately 850,000, or still about 4.5 percent. In 1937, Jews numbered 445,000, or 5.1 percent of the total population of a Hungary reduced to one-third its former size by the Treaty of Trianon (1920).

Province. Of course, cholera and other epidemics were responsible for this. However, . . . it is a statistically demonstrable phenomenon of outstanding magnitude that cholera has spared the Jews. Yes, according to an old chronicle, the black plague that raged in the year 1548 snatched away almost no Jews. The Christians perished from it; even Petrarch's Laura had to die, but the Jewesses and Jews remained alive.

Of what use was it that they were chased out of western Europe because they were accused of poisoning the wells? Or that Louis the Great chased them out of Hungary? The beautiful Jewess, Esther, beloved of the Polish king Casimir, knew how to procure a new homeland for them, the unfortunate land of Poland, which they have wholly brought to ruin.[3]

From the statistics concerning Budapest, it can also be shown that the Jews, who live a sedentary life and prefer intellectual occupations, attain advanced ages and cannot be killed in epidemics. Yes, even war cannot affect them. Their numbers in the regular army and the militia are relatively slight; most of them are military doctors. Indeed, while we sacrifice ourselves in war, Jewish contractors become rich. Our poor race perishes while, to speak with Disraeli's words, "the pure-blooded higher race flourishes."[4]

We are faced with the danger that in two or three generations we shall be fully annihilated by the Jews. It is self-evident that this process will take place with fearful suffering, and we already feel the sad effect of this today. We in this house recriminate with one another about the evil of the day, forgetting completely the single, real cause of all evil—the iron ring around our necks, called Jew, which threatens to strangle us.

Shall we, in a few years, celebrate the thousandth anniversary of the existence of our fatherland, so that we can then bequeath it to the Jews?! It is fortunate for us that today there exists enough petty envy to prevent a Jew from becoming a [cabinet] minister, but in time this, too, will cease. They will get everything into their hands, and we shall have to perish miserably. If we want to live, there can be no question about what we must do.

Saint Stephen was the first king of Hungary (1001–38); his iron crown was the sacred symbol of Hungarian national existence.

[3]Under Louis I, the Great (1342–82), Hungary achieved its greatest power, subjecting the rulers of Wallachia, Moldavia, Bulgaria, and Serbia to vassalage. Although his father had granted full rights to Jews, Louis expelled them from his realm in 1360. He was the nephew and ultimate successor of the Polish king Casimir III, also the Great (1333–70). Serious Polish historians regard the story of Esterka, the beautiful daughter of a Jewish tailor, as a fable. No contemporary sources mention her, and the legend seems suspiciously close to the biblical story of Esther. It appeared for the first time in the second half of the fifteenth century and was used to undermine the privileged position of the Jews established by Casimir.

[4]This was one of many racist statements, a favorite among antisemites, emanating from the English statesman and popular novelist, Benjamin Disraeli (1804–81). In his novel *Coningsby* (1844), the aristocratic Jew, Sidonia, explains to the novel's hero that in all the major European countries, important ministries were in the hands of Jews. "So you see,

It is this way all over Europe. Jewish interests, Jewish politics, Jewish statesmen, Jewish journalists, Jewish financiers direct the destiny of all the great states and influence all governments. Jews are the international agitators who incite Europe's Christians against one another, so as to destroy them through war, insofar as they have not already destroyed them through corruption.

There is only one means of remedying this great international evil: the Jews must be expelled from Europe. There has never been a better opportunity.[5] Now is the time to correct the great historical error and to redress the injustice that we did to the Jews when we drove them out of Palestine.

In Palestine the Jews will be in position to create a grand state. And since they are not fit for the military, they will constitute a model for the world in this respect too. The present condition in Europe is tenable for neither Jews nor Christians. An English newspaper representing the special interests of Jewry has, in fact, made a proposal in this vein: the Jewish empire ought to be reestablished in Palestine.

Today, when the national principle stands so strongly in the foreground, it can be carried out with respect to the Jews as well. If, after centuries, all the greater states of Europe have recovered their unity and independence, the Jews, after eighteen hundred years, can now be given back their empire too. In any case, they now form a state amid the states. All their striving, all their wishes are concentrated on a return to the great empire of a thousand years ago.

Indeed, they can be easily mobilized, for the largest part of their wealth is liquid; they can emigrate inside of forty-eight hours. The Jew acclimatizes himself quite easily and is devoted to his fatherland (which is wherever he happens to be living). He had his fling in the Orient, and now it is time that a people as progressive, educated, and endowed with great intellectual qualities as the Jewish people ought to take over a leadership role in the Orient. Additionally, it is well suited to do this given the racial relatedness to the Mohammedans. The Jews alone are called upon to effect the regeneration of the Mohammedan empire. [In the Orient] they can cultivate the aspirations that they now conceal because they are parasites on the Christians of Europe.

The innermost, secret wish of most Jews can now become reality if they can overcome those powerful Jews who have acquired power in Europe and for whom it is so very congenial to rule the world from London, Paris,

---

my dear Coningsby, that the world is governed by very different personages from what is imagined by those who are not behind the scenes." Converted to Christianity at age thirteen, Disraeli never tried to hide his Jewish origins. He rather cavalierly claimed racial superiority for the Jews, "the oldest aristocracy of humanity." The stuff of fantasy and mysticism, Disraeli's racism lacked the pseudoscientific and aggressive qualities characteristic of modern racists. Nevertheless, his utterances seemed to confirm the most ominous suspicions of antisemites regarding the secret machinations of the arrogant Jews.

[5]Istóczy refers to the recent defeat of the Ottoman Turks, who held suzerainty over Palestine and the opportunity it seemed to present for the establishment of a Jewish state.

Berlin, Vienna, and Budapest. I appeal to the oft-mentioned patriotism of the Jews; they can now create their own empire; they will surely become a mightier, more influential state. My sincerest and best wishes will accompany the Jews.

May the Jews find this acceptable and cease their continuing efforts to exterminate the Christians.

Antisemitism in France

E douard Drumont (1844–1917) thought of himself as "the initiator of a great movement in France." To allies and enemies, he became simply "the pope of antisemitism." Certainly beginning in the mid-1880s, he was most instrumental in developing an ideologically based French antisemitic political movement. He contributed in a major way to its organizational, literary, and agitational underpinnings—but he was not creating from scratch.

The Jews of France, especially those of Alsace, had always had enemies. Their emancipation during the Revolution (1791) met with popular resistance. Napoleon revised the legal status of Jews in unfavorable ways, some of which remained in force until 1846, when the relatively small Jewish population finally regained full equality. As elsewhere in Europe, popular anti-Jewish sentiments had survived the Middle Ages and were kept alive in the teachings of the Catholic church. Before World War I, political antisemitism took root in rural France where the traditional Catholic Right was strong, but Jews faced hostility from the Left as well. Their alleged control of high finance and identification with capitalist speculation made them a favorite target of French socialists, who showed a weakness for the use of antisemitism as a political weapon well into the 1890s. Thus, Drumont had at his disposal a long and broad tradition of Jew hatred in France upon which to build.

Like nearly all the other creators of antisemitic ideology, Drumont was the son of lower-middle-class parents. Following the example of his father, he began a career as a petty bureaucrat in the city administration of Paris, but he soon left the civil service in favor of journalism, for which he showed a perverse talent. A timid parliamentarian, inept political strategist, and poor public speaker, he made his mark on European antisemitism with his pen. Like Wilhelm Marr, he insisted that he "only put into print what everyone was thinking."

Drumont's antisemitism, again like Marr's, answered the needs of an economically troubled lower-middle-class and peasant constituency. But while Marr placed his theories of Jewish conspiracy in a grandiose world-historical context, Drumont confined his almost exclusively to the traditional concerns of French nationalism. Drawing heavily upon French sources, he constructed a universal explanation for what he and many other Frenchmen mourned as France's fall from glory. Although a passionate nationalist, Drumont took heed of antisemitism elsewhere. He admired Wagner's antisemitism (much more than his music) and appreciated the role of Court Chaplain Stoecker. Later, he sent an emissary to observe the antisemitic mayor of Vienna, Karl Lueger (see Document 9). He cited the bloody Russian pogroms of the 1880s as an inspiration for his magnum opus, *La France juive* (1886).

This two-volume book, presented in a scholarly format, is an often bizarre combing of French and European history for evidence of wrongdoing by Jews, particularly their concerted undermining of Christianity and public ethics and their total domination of economic life. Drumont, the morally outraged tribune of the people, ferreted out Freemasons, Protestants, and atheists as agents of a "Jewish syndicate." Obsessed with his enemy, he found Jews and insidious Jewish influence everywhere. By his fiat, Montaigne, Marat, Napoleon, and Rembrandt became Jews. The confiscation of church lands during the French Revolution, defeat in the Franco-Prussian War, and the intrusion of American influence into French culture—all were the work of the Jews and their accomplices. Like Stoecker, Drumont acted as a defender of the faith and maintained close relations to right-wing clerical circles. But he also saw the Jewish question much as did Marr and Wagner: a war between "distinct races, irremediably hostile to one another, whose antagonism has filled the world in the past and will still trouble it in the future."

Like many other antisemites, Drumont postured as the lonely prophet whose thankless and risky task was to save his oblivious countrymen. But forcing the French to see the evidence of Jewish conspiracy often seemed hopeless to him, at least until the end of 1894, when a Jewish army officer on the General Staff was arrested on suspicion of selling military secrets to the Germans. Trumped-up evidence, which Drumont helped fabricate and publicize, led to Alfred Dreyfus's conviction before a military court, his public degradation, and his banishment to Devil's Island for life. During the next decade, agitation on behalf of and against Dreyfus, new and related trials, the gradual crumbling of the army's case, and increasingly desperate attempts at cover-up threatened to embroil France in civil war. Larger issues soon eclipsed the personal fate of Dreyfus as a monumental struggle between Republican and anti-Republican forces unfolded. National security warred with the requirements of justice; political parties rethought their relationship to democracy; old friendships shattered and families split apart over the crisis.

The role of antisemitism in the Affair, as it is still known in France today, may seem minor, even accidental, but it was, in fact, crucial. That Dreyfus was an Alsatian Jew and that Jews were notoriously treacherous convinced his superiors on the General Staff that he, and no other, had to be the guilty spy, even though there was no convincing evidence or motive. Jew hatred, fed by the sensational press and with Drumont in the lead, fueled the rightist assault on the liberal Republic. It was liberalism, after all, that had emancipated Jewry. Its false principles of equality had allowed "a wolf to enter the sheepfold." Impugning the motives of government officials, accusing foreign powers of taking money from the "Jewish syndicate," describing the Republic as nothing more than a tool of the Jews—these reckless charges introduced a revolutionary hysteria to antisemitic agitation that would reappear with increasing stridency in post-World War I Europe. Although the Republic came out of the crisis strengthened, the case provided a dramatic object lesson in how antisemitism could be combined with other issues and how the emotions thus engendered could be politically exploited.

La France juive and Drumont's newspaper *La Libre Parole*, which reached a circulation of 200,000 in the 1890s, initiated antisemitism as a potent political movement in France. In the context of the Panama Scandal (see footnote 5 in the document) and the Dreyfus Affair, in which he played central roles, Drumont helped organize the French Antisemitic League (1897), which had between five and ten thousand members in Paris and the provinces. The league drew adherents from various royalist, clerical, and republican parties, but its mass base was predominantly lower middle class. Although its program and its leaders, especially Jules Guérin (1866–1946), followed an erratic, opportunistic course, political antisemitism in France was inimical to the Republic as well as the Jews.

The league, later renamed the Grand Occident (the antidote to the Freemasons organized in the Grand Orient), was only briefly effective (between 1898 and 1906). In the general elections of May 1898, twenty-two antisemites won seats in the French Chamber of Deputies. On the strength of this, their best showing, they presented a bill to disenfranchise the Jews of Algeria, then part of metropolitan France. The measure failed, but the repeated demands to remove Jews from public positions, confiscate their property, and expel them from France echoed in French politics throughout the life of the Third Republic. After its collapse in 1940, the Vichy successor regime (see Document 22) found it easy to cooperate with the Nazis in the "Final Solution of the Jewish Question," on the basis of what had become an entrenched tradition of French antisemitism.

The French Antisemitic League resembled the antisemitic political parties of pre–World War I Europe in essential ways. Its leaders were constantly at war with one another; they misused funds and scandalized public opinion with their private behavior; serious weaknesses in organization and constant run-ins with the law kept the party ineffectual. But, unusual among antisemitic parties, the league exercised strong influence outside the French parliament—that is, in the streets. It was in the thick of several serious anti-Jewish riots during the height of the Dreyfus Affair, especially in Algeria, from where Drumont was elected to the Chamber. The language and actions of the league—its speakers called for a Jewish St. Bartholomew's massacre—were far more violent than in Germany and Hungary, perhaps a reflection of French political traditions and a broader conception of what was permissible in public life.

Many French political figures, before and after Drumont, occasionally found it opportune to inject Jew baiting into their election campaigns, not because they believed that the Jews posed an inordinate danger to France but because they felt this stance would win them votes or make them popular. Drumont was not one of these. Menacingly, and with a desire for murder that was never far from the surface of his writings, he made the Jews an object of political action and urged that specific measures be taken against them. The following document reveals much of his standard argument and the mission he assigned himself.

For Further Reading

Stephen Wilson, *Ideology and Experience: Antisemitism in France at the Time of the Dreyfus Affair* (Rutherford, N.J., 1982). Jean-Denis Bredin, *The Affair*, translated by J. Mehlman (New York, 1986), a thorough reexamination of the case by a noted French jurist.

8. Edouard Drumont
The Jews Against France (1899)

Translated by Edward Noonan

What is the exact meaning of the frantic campaign organized by the Jewry of the entire world in order to panic France, dishonor the French Army and thereby make us incapable of playing a role in Europe?

This campaign means quite simply that the combination of interests which make up Jewry has chosen to oppose France, pushes for the destruction of France, and finds it in its interest that France cease to be a European Great Power.

It seems to me quite useless in these articles, which are written from a social and philosophical viewpoint, to give way on this subject to childish indignation and vain histrionics.

If the circumstances were such that I was invested with an authority which would permit me to save my country, I would turn the leading Jews and their accomplices over to a court martial which would have them shot. But, on theoretical and speculative grounds, I find it quite normal and quite logical that the Jews are doing what they are doing. To think otherwise would be to fall into the typical French mania of finding themselves so likable that they think that everyone else must like them.

The Jews used to have a nationality; they lost it through their divisiveness and their total lack of any instinct for order or hierarchy. Thanks to their genius as conspirators and traffickers, they have reconstituted a money Power which is formidable, not only on account of the innate power which money possesses, but also because the Jews have diminished or destroyed the other Powers so that theirs alone remained standing; because they have modeled, shaped, molded a society in which money is the true master of everything.

This money Power, like all powers, looks only after its own interests. It goes in the direction which seems the most profitable. During the Revolution, it was with us; then it supported Bonaparte; in 1815, it was clearly against him, and, at Waterloo, with Rothschild it fought as energetically as Wellington.

It was for the Second Empire, in the beginning, and it was against it at the end. It was working for Germany, it was subsidizing the republican journals that backed Ferry's viewpoint,[1] just as today it subsidizes the

Source: From Edouard Drumont, *Les Juifs contre la France: Une Nouvelle Pologne* (Paris, 1899), pp. 36–48.

[1]Jules Ferry (1832–93), a journalist and statesman, came under Drumont's fire for a number of reasons. As premier, he revived French imperial expansion but at the cost of accepting the loss of Alsace-Lorraine to the Germans, which nettled the nationalist Right. As minister of education and an anticlerical in the 1880s, he attempted to drive the Catholic church out of primary education, another policy obnoxious to Drumont.

international and anarchist newspapers; it was preparing our destruction then, just as it prepares it again today.

After our disasters, this Power rallied to us. It gave us the appearance or the illusion of revival and of prosperity through financial activity, and it profited from this to make France a prey upon which the Jews of the entire world battened. The financiers looted our savings. The others invaded markets, the most fashionable stations in life, and shared among themselves the honors and decorations.

Today the Jews think that there is nothing more to be got from us, aside perhaps from the remaining honorary baubles of the Exposition.[2] They know that our treasury is empty, that the savings bank could not reimburse the millions which it has received. They realize the depth of the abyss concealed behind the false facade of our budgets. They are getting ready to liquidate France just as Spain was liquidated.

If the Antisemites are unable to save France by the means which Danton used, the liquidation will soon take place in no time at all.[3]

Never, in fact, was there a graver time. We are going to see, we are seeing already, a new distribution of the world. The question was to know whether we would participate in this distribution or whether we would be excluded. When the Russian Alliance[4] was concluded, it was decided that we would be in on it, today it no longer seems necessary to give us our share.

The real aim of the campaign organized by the Jews, for whom Dreyfus was always only a pretext, has been the destruction of the force or the appearance of force which the Army gave to us, an Army which, only a few years ago, seemed really to be a factor with which Europe had to contend.

An autocratic government like the Tsar's had to overcome many prejudices and predispositions in order to approach a government as unstable and as bizarre as ours. What decided the Tsar was obviously not the affection inspired by our politicians, it was that as yet imposing and solid mass which was the French Army, only three years ago.

The Jews said to Russia:

"Are you falling for that? You are naive. We are going to organize a consortium, to add a few millions to those which Germany will give us, assemble, consolidate and unite all the parasites of the press, all the vagabonds, all the maggots and the depraved of Panama and the Southern Railroads.[5] After that you will see what will remain of the Army.

---

[2]The exposition of 1889 was a world's fair held in Paris on the centenary of the French Revolution.

[3]Georges-Jacques Danton (1759–94), one of the chief figures in the radical phase of the French Revolution, instituted the Revolutionary Tribunal and dominated the first Committee of Public Safety. Drumont refers to Danton's advocacy of the Terror and the guillotine.

[4]The Franco-Russian Alliance, negotiated in stages between 1891 and 1894, marked an end to the diplomatic isolation of France engineered by Bismarck. It was an important step in the division of Europe into the two armed camps that eventually faced each other in World War I.

[5]The Panama Scandal made the reputation of Drumont as an antisemitic muckraker and established the importance of his newspaper, *La Libre Parole*. In 1878 a French company

"Everyday you will be able to read in the newspapers, in enormous type, that General Mercier, who had the audacity to have arrested a perfidious Jew who betrayed the military secrets of France to Germany, must be put in prison. As for Boisdeffre, who was supposed to play the role of Moltke, the chief of the general staff, the general who signed his name to the Franco-Russian Military Convention, he will disappear pitifully without even trying to defend himself before a handful of wretches who would have all joined Baihaut at Mazas if Loubet had not perpetrated a genuine abuse by concealing the list of those involved in Panama from the law. . . ."[6]

The Jews did what they had announced, and it must be admitted that they performed this moral destruction of the French Army with unequaled virtuosity.

This explains to you why our rivals, our allies, or the allies which we would have been able to have, decided to leave us trying to extricate ourselves from the Dreyfus Affair while they preferred to use their time vigorously to enrich themselves.

England carved out an empire which goes from Alexandria to the Cape. She has let us know that we no longer had any business in that Egypt which we had resuscitated into civilized life, fertilized by our activity and our capital.

Russia created an Asian empire at least as formidable: she annexed Manchuria and has occupied Port Arthur.

America asserted itself as a conquering nation: she will take, whenever she wishes, those of our colonies which she finds suitable, as she took Cuba, and she will say . . . :

"Instead of protesting, you were nice enough to negotiate the treaty which consecrated the seizure of Cuba, and your newspapers were snobbish enough to present your incomprehensible participation in the stripping of a Latin nation as an homage to France. You cannot do better than to continue acting in the same way for your own possessions."

As for Germany, she awaits the event upon which all of Europe is already counting . . . : the death of the Austrian Emperor which will be the signal for the dissolution of the Austro-Hungarian Empire and which will

---

under the leadership of Ferdinand de Lesseps, builder of the Suez Canal, acquired a concession to build a canal across the Panama isthmus. The project seized the imagination of many French investors but soon ran into problems that required enormous new sums. As public investment slackened, de Lesseps hired a Jewish fund raiser. When the French government refused his petition for a national lottery, new means were employed, which included hefty bribes for government officials, administered by a Jewish public-relations man. The lottery was finally wangled but yielded less than expected. De Lesseps resigned, and his company went bankrupt. A half-million investors lost their money, 1.5 billion francs, of which half had gone for bribes. All this came to light when the main culprits implicated each other in the press. In the uproar that followed, one of them committed suicide, and the other fled France; five former cabinet ministers, twelve parliamentarians, a chief of police, and several bankers were investigated by the police. The Republic's prestige suffered serious damage.

[6]Drumont skillfully connected the Dreyfus Affair to previous corruption scandals in which Jews were involved. He saw and presented them as all of a piece, evidence for a

naturally enough bring about the return of the German provinces to the German Empire.

Doubtlessly, all these people with vast appetites find their neighbors' appetites more than meager, but they will end up by arranging things among themselves, by arbitrating at the expense of weaker nations the differences which they might have.

As for us, what would you have them do? . . . When he related his story of Fashoda, Delcassé was more applauded by the Chambre than if he placed on the tribune the flags of Sedan or Metz reconquered from the enemy. . . . Nothing could translate the accent, not at all nasty but rather paternal and affectionate, with which M. Deschanel said to me when I came to pronounce the name of Fashoda: "M. Drumont, you are offending the feelings of the Chambre!"[7]

It was less a president who was intervening than a well-brought-up host who noticed that the conversation was entering into subjects painful to his company and who would have said: "Could we not discuss something else?"

If the situation is like this already, what will happen when nations like England and Germany will have developed their full potential, will have become truly enormous? It would be mad to even think of fighting against them with a navy entrusted to this Lanessan who has been called the knight of heavy industry, with an army in which the Jews will be absolute masters, when the acquittal of Dreyfus will have proved that treason is a licit transaction, when Picquart, cleaned up, restored, and promoted will have retaken his place on the general staff.[8]

---

frighteningly pervasive conspiracy of Jews and Protestant countries (England and Germany, in particular) against France. General Auguste Mercier was minister of war in 1894 when the Dreyfus case broke. It was he who, despite the flimsy evidence, insisted on putting Dreyfus on trial in order to demonstrate to the public the vigilance of the French Army. Raoul de Boisdeffre was Chief of the General Staff of the army. His counterpart in Germany was the much more illustrious Helmuth von Moltke, architect of victory in the Franco-Prussian War of 1870–71. Emile Loubet had been one of the deputies involved in the Panama Scandal. He became president of the Republic in 1899 and was known to favor a new trial for Dreyfus. He succeeded the anti-Dreyfusard, Félix Faure, who had died in the arms of his mistress, "a woman sent by the Jews to murder him," according to Drumont. Charles Baihaut, minister of public works during the Panama Scandal, was the only high-ranking official to confess his guilt. As a result he went to Mazas prison.

[7]Théophile Delcassé (1852–1923) was foreign minister during the Fashoda Incident of 1898 when French and British troops nearly came to blows over control of the upper Nile region. Delcassé negotiated the French withdrawal of claims to the area, a move that infuriated French chauvinists but also paved the way to an eventual alliance between France and Britain. Sedan and Metz were the sites of disastrous French defeats in the Franco-Prussian War. Paul Deschanel (1855–1922) was president of the Chamber of Deputies in 1898 when Drumont served in that body as a representative of an Algerian constituency, where he had fostered anti-Jewish violence.

[8]Marie-Georges Picquart, paradoxically one of the few avowed antisemites and chief of intelligence on the General Staff, uncovered evidence of Dreyfus's innocence in 1896. Although silenced and reassigned by his superiors, he continued to champion a new trial

It is then that the Powers will look upon France with eyes gleaming with that lust which Austria, Russia, and Prussia had when leering at Poland.[9]

In the countries where an organized cannibalism reigns, one does not rush precipitously on human meat. Each takes his turn and marks with a pencil on the skin of the victims the pieces which he has chosen. The slaughter occurs when everything has been reserved. That is how it was with Poland. God help us that the same thing does not happen to France!

Note that all these perspectives and all these eventualities have been under discussion for a long time among those who attentively follow the trends of this century which has only in these last few years taken the shape which it will have in history. It ends, actually, quite differently than it had begun. After having been, at its birth, the apotheosis of Power, it culminates in the apotheosis of Money. It had two masters: Napoleon, in the beginning; Rothschild, personification of the Jewish Conquest, at its decline.

La France juive can now be understood better than when it first appeared (1886).[10] It will only be fully understood in a few years. At each step, in effect, notations appear in it which events later clarify just as time brings out the architectural details lost in the flashy unveiling of a new monument.

Already in 1875 a Jew who is mostly forgotten today but who was then almost famous and who was, in any case, a most interesting and very curious spirit, Alexandre Weill,[11] explained to me that France was obliged to undergo the same fate as Poland and that it would be good, in the best interests of Humanity, that the French, dispersed and countryless like the Poles, would go and spread throughout the world the general truths of civilization and progress.

Alexandre Weill, who died just recently, was already very old at the time. He was an old Hebrew prophet who had flashes of prophecy and of

---

for Dreyfus and was dismissed from the army. Along with Dreyfus, and as Drumont predicted, he was rehabilitated, promoted, and returned to the general staff when the Dreyfus verdict was declared erroneous in 1906.

[9]The three partitions in 1772, 1793, and 1795 by its powerful neighbors destroyed Poland as an independent nation-state. Subtitling his essay, "a New Poland," Drumont preyed upon the sense of lost glory, bedeviling the French ever since their defeat in the Franco-Prussian War.

[10]*La France juive, essai d'histoire contemporaine,* 2 vols. (Paris, 1886) was one of the most influential and widely circulated antisemitic works in Europe. Unlike the bulk of antisemitic publications, this one was taken seriously by reputable intellectuals and journals. A huge best-seller, it had been reprinted two hundred times and translated into six languages before World War I.

[11]Drumont does not mention that Alexandre Weill was one of the few Jews who responded to *La France juive,* contesting Drumont's facts and motives and specifically denying him the right to call himself a Catholic.

genius. He had a terrible fear of French Antisemitism, which, at the time, existed only in a latent state in the brain of a writer who awaited his hour and in the heart of thousands of beings who were waiting for a writer whom they did not know to speak for them.

Alexandre Weill lived at the time, at the entrance to the Saint-Honoré neighborhood, and he usually went for a walk near noon under the arcades, free then, which extended under the guardhouse and the Ministry of the Navy, with some small white, frizzy-haired dogs, which were accustomed, it seems, to go out only at a particular time.

I have always been avid to learn and, returning from my newspaper, I used to exchange a few ideas with him. . . . I thought that perhaps it had not been worth the effort to cut the throat of the descendant of forty kings only to be governed by the Rothschilds who occupy, just a few steps away, the mansion of the Infanta, and to hear it said that France would end up like Poland, by an old Jew who was walking his small, white, frizzy-haired dogs.

That is how, unknown even to me, the work of liberation was sprouting bit by bit in my heart.

Antisemitism in Austria

The Austrian antisemitic movement, which appeared in the last quarter of the nineteenth century, catered to the lower-middle class in town and countryside and produced both a conservative Christian and a radical racist indictment of recently emancipated Jews. Although it thus followed the European pattern, Austrian antisemitism differed from that of other countries in two important ways: First, antisemites in the municipal government of Vienna actually held political power for nearly twenty years; they were no mere fringe group, as in Germany or France. Second, the Viennese also schooled the young Adolf Hitler in the Jewish question and the possibilities of political antisemitism.

The more radical of the two variants of Austrian antisemitism was the creation of the left-wing liberal, Georg von Schönerer (1842–1921), whose tiny Pan-German party sought the union of German Austria with the German Empire. He opposed both the church, because it helped conserve the multinational empire, and the Habsburg monarchy, because of its willingness to make concessions to the non-German nationalities. For Schönerer, Jews were in the forefront of the loathed nationalities, hostile to Germanic well-being. That they prospered under the Habsburgs was the best argument against the continuance of the state. Jewish influence in economic and cultural life had to be eliminated. Schönerer's radicalism, not his antisemitism, offended too many Austrians and worked to minimize his influence. When his party dissolved in 1889, it had only twelve hundred members. His newspaper, *Unfalsified German Words,* never exceeded seventeen hundred subscribers.

Schönerer might well have been forgotten, were he not one of two antisemites whose influence Adolf Hitler acknowledged in *Mein Kampf.* The other, whose views are reflected in the following document, was Karl Lueger (1844–1910).

Lueger, too, began his political career on the Left. Like Schönerer, Drumont, and a number of other antisemites, he gained prominence as a muckraker against corruption and what was widely seen as excessive Jewish influence on economic life. Lueger, far better than Schönerer, knew how to appeal to the outlook and needs of the recently enfranchised lower-middle classes, antagonized by many aspects of modern developments and open to the politics of hatred. It was his ability to construct a mass movement out of these materials that won Hitler's admiration.

A Viennese politician all his life, Lueger latched onto the movement of Catholic renewal in the 1880s. The political arm of the movement, the Christian Socials, gained influence among artisans, small businessmen, the lower clergy, minor civil servants, and property owners, those social strata that felt their interests were being undermined by the liberal establishment. The rise of Austrian Social Democracy also raised deep misgivings among these people. Given the prominence of Jews in the liberal and socialist movements and the anticlericalism of these parties, it was not surprising that Lueger's Christian Social party (1887) adopted antisemitism. By 1895 the Christian Socials, with tumultuous campaigning, won a majority in the Vienna City Council, supplanted the Liberals, and elected Lueger as mayor. After three refusals, Emperor Franz Joseph finally sanctioned the election in 1897; Lueger remained mayor until his death in 1910.

Lueger's antisemitism has not always been taken seriously by his contemporaries or by later historians. His bluff manner and administrative abilities tend to obscure what was pernicious in his reign as mayor. He is still often presented as a somewhat avuncular practitioner of coalition politics, a sheer opportunist in the matter of antisemitism. He was fond of claiming that the Jews had not suffered at all during his mayoralty. Many of his closest associates were Jews, and he was the man who said: "I decide who is a Jew!" a statement interpreted as meaning that he did not see antisemitism as much more than a useful political tool.

But it was under Lueger that Austrians became accustomed to the revilement of Jews. Although Lueger was normally cautious in his public statements, few doubted that he sanctioned the crudities of his more zealous henchmen or that speeches, such as the one that follows, could have been made without his permission. There was considerable, although isolated, violence against Jews and their property, especially during election campaigns, and it is by no means certain that Lueger would not have used the legislative and executive powers at his disposal to do more against Jews, had those powers not been limited by Austrian constitutional arrangements. The mayor and his associates were responsible for the forceful introduction of antisemitism into Austria's political culture, deeds that bore consequences long after Lueger had died. In the machinery of the Holocaust, Austrian personnel played an extraordinarily important and disproportionately large role.

The apparently extempore speech by Hermann Bielohlawek on the occasion of the budget debates in the Vienna City Council typifies the uses to which political antisemitism were put under Lueger. Bielohlawek, a self-made man who had risen from commercial clerk to a position of wealth and power via the Christian Social movement, reveled in his "thick skin" and lack of intellectual polish. A popular party agitator and possessed of "the common touch," his antisemitism does not require any of the ideological niceties. It is an attack weapon and, significantly, appears in the speech when he has run out of substantive arguments. It enters almost casually. But egged on by his listeners, the speaker reaches deeper for more extreme invective. He projects his own virulent hatred onto the Jews, claiming that they would murder all good Christians if they could.

Bielohlawek's threats, abuse, innuendo, "quotations" from unnamed sources, and explicit references to extermination were by no means unusual in Austria. Speeches like his were heard not only by members of the council but were reproduced in the newspapers of the capital. They did not require even the pretense of rational justification for antisemitism. Bielohlawek—the suspicion is inescapable—spoke to the already convinced. At the same time, the coarseness of the speech made it all too easy for those who found it repulsive to dismiss its antisemitism as empty ravings from the gutter. Such performances would not long be tolerated in an age that was becoming ever more enlightened.

For Further Reading

Richard Geehr, *Karl Lueger, Mayor of Fin de siècle Vienna* (Detroit, 1990); Peter J. Pulzer, *The Rise of Political Antisemitism in Germany and Austria* (New York, 1964).

9. Hermann Bielohlawek
"Yes, We Want to Annihilate the Jews!"
(1902)

Mayor Lueger: Councillor Bielohlawek has the floor.

Bielohlawek: Honorable gentlemen. I did not intend to speak today because, as a member of the city council, I have already analyzed the [budget] proposal and have already voted in favor of it. I shall, therefore, not speak at length about details. I have requested the floor, as it happens, only because of the speeches made by the opposition against us. The first speaker was Councillor Zifferer, who held forth in the funereal tone with which you have been familiar for years.

Well, gentlemen, he not only objects to not spending something that is in the proposal but also to any savings achieved at the end of the fiscal year. Gentlemen, I would like to ask, Where in the world, in what country, is there any kind of budget that is calculated to come out exactly to the penny? He knows there is none, but he exercises his criticism in the same monotone that we have observed for years.

Take, for instance, any sort of person, any one of us. Suppose he plans on purchasing a winter coat, but it remains warm until the new year. Therefore, he does not buy it and saves 50 florins, which then go into the budget of the next year. How much more is this the case with a budget of 140 million, where so many building projects and so many other things are to be done? These are influenced by forces of nature and certain eventualities with which we are all familiar and which will always happen in a great city, as long as it remains one. The proposal cannot be completely accurate, and any sort of savings must be corrected in the balancing of the budget. So, I beg you, cease this criticism; it is monotonous.

Councillor Zifferer has mentioned among other things the interest rate on unused funds that are not yet budgeted and that are deposited abroad.

Source: Speech to the Vienna City Council, from *Amtsblatt der k.k. Reichshaupt- und Residenzstadt Wien*, Gemeinde-Sitzung vom 10. Dezember 1902, pp. 2298–301.

Had he read page 99 [of the budget report], he would have seen the interest rate we get, which is certainly not the worst: from 4 to 41/4 percent. Formerly, such unused funds were deposited with the Jew, Pollak von Borkenau, at 2 percent. (Interjection: "That's right!") That was a poor investment. Today, when such colossal earnings are to be had and these unused funds are invested at a quite competitive rate of interest, Mr. Zifferer gets up and speaks against it, because it is "bad financial management." He emphasizes among other things that the city is not much worried about the large funds it has in the Deutsche Bank. If he, Mr. Donat Zifferer, had twice as much money there, he would not be fearful, but the city should have cause to worry. Gentlemen! I say to you, if Mr. Zifferer who—I hope he will not be offended— belonged to the Israelite religion, is not fearful, then we need not be afraid either. I have not yet seen the Jew who did not know where to put his money. Therefore, let him calm down. Our funds are safe there.

So much for Councillor Zifferer.

Then came Councillor Schuhmeier. He has delivered a lament about oppression and called this financial management a scandal. He cries about violation, speaks of the majority and minority. It is curious that since we [Christian Socials] have gained a majority, we are continually asked not to emphasize the positive in the budget, the things that show how prudently we manage finances.

The millions that we have obtained by careful management, the results we have achieved, should speak for themselves. We are supposed to say in the [financial] report that this was no achievement, that it all happened by itself. Where will you find a majority that works and will not report its documented achievements?

On the question of oppression, the Social Democrats should be among the most silent. Nowhere in the world is there a party as terroristically inclined as the Social Democrats. ("That's right!")

Not here in the city council; nothing can happen here because there are only two of them. But that's not our fault. It's their fault. Their program activities, their agitation in every respect, have led the population to say: two of them in the city council are more than enough.

[The Social Democrats] have completely forfeited the sympathies of the broad masses, which have been given the right to vote for the first time by this mayor and his party, as has been mentioned many times. After all, to whom, Councillor Schuhmeier and Councillor Neumann, do you owe the fact that you are sitting here? ("Us!") None other than this mayor and this party. To be sure, you say that seventeen or eighteen year olds should also have been allowed to vote. Then there would be more of you in here. If the organized apprentices instructed by [Social Democrats] Seitz and Dr. Ellenbogen were allowed to vote, then a different sort of representation might sit here. But as long as honorably thinking men have the vote, you will see no more than two here. That's the story.

About terrorism, you say nothing. Look, for instance, how organized you were at the last session of Parliament. Now there are only ten Social Democrats in parliament as against the fifteen who were there before. And we are supposed to think that you are quite oppressed there. But what did you do? [You] abused [your parliamentary] immunity to excess; you insulted and befouled our mayor in a way never before experienced in history. (lively catcalls) I am no pussyfooter, either, it's true. I don't pull my punches, and when I was a member of parliament, I also let loose against my political enemies.

But I would have never used such words, even against a political enemy, as you have slung against this mayor, Dr. Karl Lueger. (Lively catcalls.) Your colleague, Pernerstorfer, produced an ocean of slime and a flood of vulgarity. And this, without reason; not because there was anything on the agenda that concerned the mayor, but during a debate when a capitalist exploiter, Lobmayr, was being discussed. One would have expected that the gentlemen Social Democrats would have nothing at all to say about this, for they certainly would not be expected to intervene on behalf of the exploiter.

But the gentlemen stood up there and lashed out in stentorian fashion against the mayor and against our party, while the exploiter Lobmayr, the millionaire, is allowed to appear with a veritable halo in the Austrian parliament. You call yourselves representatives of the proletariat, representatives of the hungry workers! (lively applause) You say nothing about terrorism. I myself have often taken offense at the mayor's being so conciliatory toward you and not toward me. That's the way things are. ("Quite right!") He very often brings us to order, while he proceeds against the two gentlemen with the greatest mildness. You have no cause to complain of terrorism here. Of course, we won't put up with everything. When Mr. Schuhmeier postures and spouts anything that comes to his Social Democratic imagination, when he speaks incredible lies that cannot be substantiated, and when he stands there and speaks as though he were the great corruption killer, then you will permit us to interject a word here and there. We get excited when such wholly unjustified reproaches are uttered.

Our esteemed colleague Schwer has expounded in detailed and irrefutable ways on the nature of the Social Democrats. If I were not pressed for time, I could speak volumes . . . on how the Social Democrats sin against their own party. As long as the Social Democrats stood on their own feet and showed that they were a true party of the proletariat, and proved it—all respect to them! I concede that we do not possess the patent on national salvation; perhaps we are mistaken. But your main program says this: land and property, labor and capital are the common goods of all men, and everything that bears the human countenance has equal rights. But the moment it concerns a Catholic, he ceases to have equal rights for you. (applause) Councillor Zifferer will tell me that the moment it concerns a Jew, he does not have equal rights with us. The difference, however, is that we speak the truth! Yes, we want to annihilate the Jews. We are not ashamed to say the Jew must be driven from society. (approval and applause) . . .

Yes, we were once a minority in this hall when Dr. Lueger had forty-six or thirty-six men. You'll say: you should have been here to see what they did! What did they do? The mayor sat here and made glowing speeches that went straight to the heart of the matter. And the population of Vienna said: "We have felt that, too." And then they elected Dr. Lueger and his supporters. . . . Nobody usurped the podium; nobody violated the rules of orderly debate. (objection) . . . Mayor Dr. Lueger and his party seized possession of the mayoralty, and 130 men sit here on the basis of the laws and elections, without violation of the laws. You, however, have devised rules of order that seek to muzzle our party. You, the Liberal party, have introduced lackey laws in this hall. (applause) Under the so-called iron mayor,[1] you were the ones who created all the restrictions for us. But look; all the muzzling and terrorism availed you nothing.

If someday the population changes its mind and backs you against us, then all the rules of order that exist today will avail us nought. But you see that regard for the Christian Social, for the antisemitic, party, mounts from day to day. . . .

Heterogeneous elements, such as red, international proletarians and nationalist, bourgeois exploiters, have united against us. Add to this Jews and Jew liberalism and all that clings to them—thus has the phalanx closed around us.

In the city and countryside they have beat the drum against us. If one read the newspapers for the last six months, the fickle of our party, to which, thank God, I do not belong, might well believe that it is all over for our party. But I've gone out to the lion's den, to the provinces, to the places where the great coalition was. And where were the gentlemen? I was there, and they were elsewhere! (stormy applause) That's the story. The coalition was totally useless. Farmers, bureaucrats, workers, and tradesmen have got the message. We have conquered all the mandates [for the state parliament] of Lower Austria, and a majority in the municipal council of the city of Vienna, even though universal suffrage with a three-year residency qualification has been introduced there. If you had struck a single spark of support in the people, surely you would have wrested away at least one mandate. Were it not for the Jews, your party would not even be worth discussing. (stormy applause and hilarity)

How many Social Democrats are there, anyhow? If the Hebrews, the dirty Jews, didn't vote, where would the Social Democrats be? They would be a mere dummy, nothing more! Without the Jews, the gentlemen would be a nullity, and it must be said, there are already Jews saying: "What shall we do? We can't win with them." Maybe they will even turn to anarchism and blow up the leaders of the Christian population with bombs, thereby finally destroying [our] party. (hilarity)

You see, you should not talk about terrorism, for all you need to do is attend a Social Democratic meeting. You'll only be able to leave it as a corpse, not as a healthy man. (hilarity)

---

[1]A reference to the great Liberal party mayor, Cajetan Felder, who held office from 1868 to 1878.

Well, Councillor Schuhmeier also spoke on the schools. . . . School doctors serve no purpose. They would only be an unnecessary expense, and they would not serve any purpose for you, my Liberal and Social Democratic gentlemen, either, for if ever they were introduced, you can be certain that as long as we are at the rudder, no Jew will be employed. You demand school meals, textbooks, doctors, gardens, in short, everything the children need, to be paid by the city. All the reds do is beget children. That's the whole story. (applause)

Now, let's talk about our own party. . . . When foreigners come to Vienna nowadays, to fill their chops, as you say, they are genuinely enthusiastic about the city of Vienna.

Nowadays, all the foreigners come, and if you had heard what was said in the banquet hall, without regard to party affiliation, innkeepers, Pan-Germans, Czechs, Poles, Social Democrats were there, and all were united in praise and said: "We'd never have believed it. We thought Lueger was a cannibal, as we'd read." They looked at us as though we were savages. That's what was reported in the newspapers of Germany, France, and England. We were portrayed as a fanatical horde of uneducated and uncivilized men. That's what was spread by the educated Austrian, especially the Viennese Jewish press beasts. (Spirited applause.) Here, in this hall, works have been created that even opponents have acknowledged. And what have the Jew papers said the next day? Exactly the opposite! A prominent Jewish journalist said: "It's all the same to us. Lueger can do what he wants with his party. We shall tear it all down!" The activity of those gentlemen who sit up in the [press] gallery (and if it's not them, then it happens in the editorial offices) is this: we must revile [the work] because the Jews command it to be so. And if we presented the most glorious budget in the world and if we made Vienna into the El Dorado of the world, the Jews would still say: "That cannot be, we will not have it, because we demand Jewish dominance!" (thunderous applause; "Listen, Zifferer!")

This is the inexpressible hatred of Jewry toward us. . . .

If it were not for the Jewish press, the Christian Social party would be the only predestined one to rule in Austria. In our ranks you find the prince and the lowliest worker; this is the genuine people's party. But that doesn't do any good. As long as we show the Hebrews our teeth, nothing will happen. Antisemitism remains trump (applause lasting several minutes) as long as we have the honor to be in this hall. They may call me stupid. I know I am the most slandered of all, scorned and ridiculed. But that doesn't matter to me. I have a thick skin. The dirty Jews can write whatever they want about me and the party. I and my colleagues and our mayor will go our own way, undisturbed, to work in the interests of the imperial capital and [Habsburg] residence city of Vienna. This is our ideal. We are available to Vienna's working population at any time. Otherwise there is just one word: checkmate the Jews, down with the betrayers of the people, down with the Social Democrats, away with traitors to the fatherland! That is our banner. (thunderous applause)

We shall not slacken in this struggle; we shall ruthlessly continue this fight as long as a drop of blood flows through our veins. . . .

We will, however, take every opportunity to announce to the world that the people of Vienna are honest, Christian, and pure German, but that it has as its program: the elimination of Jewry. From this we will not shrink. . . . (Spirited approval and applause. The speaker is congratulated from all sides.)

Antisemitism in Germany

Although antisemitism was more politically powerful in Austria, more explosive an issue in France, and more deadly in Russia, Germany remained at the forefront of ideological and organizational developments. The readings in this section provide a representative sampling of the varieties of political antisemitism in Germany before World War I.

German antisemitic parties and organizations bore many different names and conducted fierce debates with one another on questions of political strategy and ideology, but this should not obscure their essential similarities. All of them drew the bulk of their membership and support from the lower middle class of the towns and cities and from small-scale farmers, the social groups hit hardest by the financial crash of 1873 and the subsequent twenty years of economic dislocation in Germany. With outmoded skills and undercapitalized businesses, they found it difficult to adapt to their nation's transformation from an agricultural to an industrial market economy. Measuring their own decline against what appeared to be the dramatic rise of Jewry since emancipation (1869), these "little people" were ripe for antisemitic politics.

Even before the antisemitic parties appeared on the scene to exploit this popular resentment of Jews, much had been written about Jewish responsibility for the economic downturn of the 1870s. Accusations that Jews had planned the crash to serve their conspiratorial ends, that even the government of Prince Bismarck had sold out to Jewish interests, were widely circulated in respectable newspapers and by means of sensational pamphlets, broadsides, and caricatures. The venerable economic charges, adapted to the conditions of the 1870s, dovetailed neatly with the older indictments of Jews (see Parts I and II). Their undermining of traditional moral and cultural standards (Wagner), usurpation of the professions, overrunning of the universities (Stoecker), domination of the popular press (Marr and Treitschke), visible presence in left-wing radical and right-wing reactionary circles—all this fed into a political action movement aimed at what antisemites depicted as the awesome growth of Jewish power.

As in Austria and France, the broader target of the antisemites was liberalism, whose many enemies held it responsible not only for the emancipation of the Jews but for the laissez-faire economic policies that had brought disaster. Indeed, Jews participated vigorously in liberal politics; nearly 85 percent of them voted for one of the liberal parties in this period. They were also associated with capitalist developments in journalism and retailing that threatened the well-being of many who flocked to hear Stoecker's speeches or read Marr's pamphlets. The taint of Jewishness reached beyond liberal economics to tarnish hallowed liberal beliefs in human equality, human rights, and the efficacy of reason in public discourse. Cosmopolitanism gave way to a rigid chauvinism. Equal rights for women, even as a theoretical aspiration, was rejected by the antisemites, among others, as just one more evil departure from tradition. With the emergence of a powerful socialist presence, antisocialism gradually assumed ever-greater importance for the antisemites, firmly establishing the antidemocratic tendencies already present at the birth of the movement. A revulsion against all progressive and modern trends provided antisemitism with its emotional energy. It rapidly developed into an alternative view of the world, with answers to all questions and prescriptions for salvation.

In 1879, the antisemitic movement gained a foothold in Berlin by participating in the onslaught against liberalism. The Christian Socialists under Stoecker and Marr's short-lived Antisemites' League were soon joined by many other small, competing groups in the national capital and in a few other large cities. "Reform Clubs" spread organizational networks throughout Germany, providing the parties with grass-roots membership. By 1890 there were 136 of these associations carrying on educational activities for the initiated and nonstop propaganda and fund-raising activities among the unconverted. With the help of university students in the late 1880s, a populist antisemitic party gained a foothold among the farmers of Hesse and attained considerable influence in its state parliament and Reichstag delegations. Antisemitism also demonstrated its ability to organize political protest among specific social groups in the kingdom of Saxony during the 1890s.

But aside from Stoecker's Christian Social party, the others came and went at short intervals. During 1880 and 1881, they helped produce the Antisemites' Petition (Document 10). This petition, and a separate one circulated by university students, received over 250,000 signatures and became the subject of a debate in the Prussian Parliament. When a Liberal deputy questioned the government about this inflammatory initiative, a minister in Bismarck's government responded with a lukewarm defense of the status quo—that is, maintenance of Jewish equality—instead of condemning the petition as an outrage. In later years, German governments usually maintained this remoteness and often seemed willing to treat the antisemites as a legitimate political factor. This neutrality on the part of government robbed the opponents of antisemitism of an important source of support.

The petition's four demands became the basic program for all subsequent antisemitic political parties. Enactment of the proposals, which amounted to a call for the revocation of Jewish emancipation, would have necessitated a change in the empire's constitution, a very difficult matter. Until the end of World War I, the mainstream antisemitic organizations attempted, in vain, to gain enough seats in the German parliaments to achieve this objective. Although occasionally rowdy and fatally attractive to unstable individuals, they remained within the legal framework of the empire and worked for a conventional political solution to the Jewish question.

This conventional sort of political antisemitism was doomed to failure for a number of reasons. Winning a majority in the Reichstag, only a first step toward constitutional change, lay well beyond its powers. The parties were never able to expand their support beyond the largely Protestant lower middle class. The masses of Catholic and working-class voters were steered away from political antisemitism by their respected leaders in the Center and Social Democratic parties. Both saw the Jewish question as a fraud or as only a small part of larger economic or social problems. They condemned the programmatic statements advanced by the various antisemitic political parties as bigoted, false solutions or as demagogic attempts to steal the votes of befuddled people. Although Catholic and socialist leaders were largely successful in defending their followers from the seductions of political antisemitism, they did little, in an active way, to counter the poisoning of relations between Germans and Jews. They tended to dismiss antisemitism as a temporary aberration that required only perfunctory attention.

Confined to a numerous but economically weak lower-middle-class social base, the mainstream antisemitic parties always lacked sufficient funds. As a result, they became subject to the influence of powerful rightwing groups, such as the German Conservative party and the Agrarian League, an effective lobbying agent for big agriculture. Although both groups willingly used antisemitism to mobilize voters, and the prestigious Conservatives even wrote a vaguely antisemitic plank into their program of 1892, it is doubtful that they really wanted to solve the "Jewish question." Before the war, the German Right viewed political antisemitism as but one of many tools with which to defend its interests.

The "sincere" antisemitic parties also suffered from a number of other weaknesses. The repeated attempts to create an antisemitic press capable of taking on the all-powerful "Jewish press" produced only short-lived, sleazy vehicles that represented the personal agendas of various political leaders. These ambitious individuals spent most of their time and energy fighting each other. Organizational schisms, party name changes, and reunifications were laughably regular occurrences, making it difficult for all but the thoroughly committed to take parliamentary-political antisemitism seriously. Lawsuits for libel and incitement to class hatred, as well as more scandalous behavior, led to heavy fines and frequent jail sentences. These parties' overall lack of respectability was a major obstacle to their becoming a true mass movement. Especially after the mid-1890s, when the German economy began to boom again, respect for the institutions of the empire and a general confidence in the system kept even the mainstream antisemitic movement on the fringes of political power.

The antisemitic political parties achieved their high-water mark in the national elections of 1893, in which they received approximately 400,000 votes (4.5 percent of the total), which won them 16 of the 397 seats in the Reichstag. After this date, their percentage of the vote sank steadily until the various antisemitic parties ceased operating independently in the last Reichstag elected before the war (1912).

Unable to achieve their major goal, the revocation of emancipation, the antisemitic parties also failed to pass any overtly anti-Jewish legislation through the national parliament. This political impotence produced two significant trends, reflected in the documents in this section. Those still committed to parliamentary politics began to adopt a more revolutionary tone (see Documents 11 and 12). Gradually, as they lost support with the electorate, the parliamentary antisemites expanded their notions of what had to be changed in order to save Germany from the Jews. The mainstream antisemites had proposed the curtailing of Jewish influence in public life as a cure-all, with perhaps a few socioeconomic reforms to strengthen "truly German" peasants and artisans. The lack of even minimal progress in this direction, however, led to implicit and explicit criticism of the empire's basic institutions, such as universal suffrage, the monarchy, the educational and judicial systems.

Meanwhile, impatience with due process in the face of dire emergency and the lack of movement toward a solution to the Jewish question strengthened antisemites who had never believed in conventional political methods. Although they had been present from the inception of the movement, these revolutionaries had been more or less successfully quarantined by the conventionally inclined majority. In the decade before the war, however, they gained wider audiences for their views. For these unconventional antisemites, parliamentary politics were not the cure but part of the (Jewish) disease which was destroying Germany. Legislative proposals and sickly democratic procedures could achieve no solution because the German masses were still too "immature" to vote "correctly." Instead, massive "educational" efforts, leading to a moral regeneration of the German people, would have to be undertaken before the Jewish danger could be dealt with decisively. The Alliance against the Arrogance of Jewry (Document 13) made its conception of education clear in 1919 when it published the *Protocols of the Elders of Zion* in Germany (Document 15).

Revolutionary implications are clearly present in the final document of this section by Heinrich Class, writing under the pseudonym Daniel Frymann, which deserves special attention (Document 14). Class was a second-generation antisemite, one who had grown up reading many of the documents collected here. He gave emphatic recognition to Heinrich von Treitschke's influence on his own conversion to antisemitism; he had been a student volunteer in the Hessian antisemitic party. But Class was not a marginal character. He was president of the Pan-German League, a nationalistic, racist, and imperialist propaganda society whose elite membership included a high proportion of middle-class professionals. Organized since the early 1890s, the Pan-Germans had no clear position on the Jewish question until Class led it in an unequivocally antisemitic direction. The woeful showing of the parliamentary antisemites had not, therefore, produced a rejection of antisemitism but merely a search for better methods of prosecuting the struggle—at least as far as people like Class were concerned.

Just how much political antisemitism had permeated extraparliamentary organizations in Germany and to what degree it had influenced social strata other than the lower middle class are moot questions. The Pan-German League was not a solitary exception, but neither was its overt antisemitism typical of pressure groups and lobbying agencies in the German Empire. Most remained cautious about adopting it openly; some even renounced it. By 1914, the antisemites' ambitious political solutions to the "Jewish question" had certainly not won automatic acceptance from the German people, and it would therefore be mistaken to equate the ever-deepening paranoia evident in these documents with German attitudes in general. If Jews remained generally unloved, this did not mean that antisemites were thereby assured of popularity. Most of them reveal a self-conscious defensiveness about the need for radical, all-embracing solutions to the Jewish question. Such measures, they knew, were not widely seen as self-evident necessities. It is this defensiveness of tone that most clearly separates prewar antisemites from the Nazis.

Although the drift toward more radical methods and conceptions is clear in these documents, these voices came fully into their own only during the Weimar Republic (1918–33) when revolutionary discontent became widespread. But even without the radicalizing influence of the lost war and its revolutionary influence on antisemitic methods, it is reasonable to say that antisemitism had already found a home in a wide variety of German political associations. An enormous, easily accessible literature had come into existence and was being constantly replenished. Antisemitism had become a fact of political life.

For Further Reading

Richard S. Levy, *The Downfall of the Anti-Semitic Political Parties in Imperial Germany* (New Haven, 1975).

10. **Antisemites' Petition** (1880–81)

The Jewish hypertrophy conceals within itself the most serious dangers to our national way of life. This belief has spread throughout all the regions of Germany. Wherever Christian and Jew enter into social relations, we see the Jew as master and the native-born Christian population in a servile position. The Jew takes only a vanishingly small part in the hard work of the great mass of our people; in field and workshop, in mines and on scaffolding, in swamps and canals—everywhere it is only the calloused hand of the Christian that is active. But it is above all the Jew who harvests the

Source: From *Schmeitzner's Internationale Monatsschrift: Zeitschrift für die Allgemeine Vereinigung zur Bekämpfung des Judentums, 1883* (Chemnitz, 1883), pp. 314–16.

fruits of this labor. By far the greatest portion of capital produced by national labor is concentrated in Jewish hands. Jewish real estate keeps pace with the growth of mobile capital. Not only the proudest palaces of our cities belong to the Jewish masters (whose fathers or grandfathers crossed the borders of our fatherland as peddlers and hawkers), but the rural estate—this highly significant and conserving basis of our state structure—is falling into Jewish hands with ever greater frequency.

Truly, in view of these conditions and because of the massive penetration of the Semitic element into all positions affording power and influence, the following question seems justified on an ethical as well as national standpoint: *what future is left our fatherland if the Semitic element is allowed to make a conquest of our home ground for another generation as it has been allowed to do in the last two decades?* If the concept of "fatherland" is not to be stripped of its ideal content, if the idea that it was our fathers who tore this land from the wilderness and fertilized it with their blood in a thousand battles is not to be lost, if the inward connection between German custom and morality and the Christian outlook and tradition is to be maintained, then an alien tribe may never, ever rise to rule on German soil. This tribe, to whom our humane legislation extended the rights of hospitality and the rights of the native, stands further from us in thought and feeling than any other people in the entire Aryan world.

The danger to our national way of life must naturally mount not only when the Jews succeed in not only encroaching upon the national and religious consciousness of our people by means of the *press*, but also when they succeed in obtaining state offices, the bearers of which are obliged to guard over the idealistic goods of our nation. We think above all of the professions of *teacher* and *judge*. Both were inaccessible to Jews until very recently, and both must again be closed if the concept of authority, the feeling for legality and fatherland, are not to become confused and doubted by the nation. Even now the Germanic ideals of honor, loyalty, and genuine piety begin to be displaced to make room for a cosmopolitan pseudoideal.

If our nation is not to be consigned to economic servitude under the pressure of Jewish money power, if it is not to be consigned to national decadence one step at a time under the influence of Jewry's materialistic outlook, then measures to halt the Jewish hypertrophy are imperative. Nothing lies further from us than the desire to bring forth any kind of oppression of the Jewish nation. What we strive for is actually the emancipation of the German nation from a kind of alien domination that it cannot long tolerate. There is danger in delay.[1] Therefore, have we decided to approach Your Excellency with the most respectful petition:

---

[1] This line was meant to convey special importance to Bismarck. It is an exact translation from the Latin—*Periculum in mora*—which comprised the despatch summoning him to become prime minister of Prussia in 1862.

We should be clear, when discussing the necessities in this direction, that the innocent must suffer with the guilty, no matter how painful this will be to right-thinking Germans. It is better that a few high-minded Jews suffer because of the guilt of their less worthy tribal comrades than that the entire German people perish from their poison. Vengeance will visit even the good Jews, first and foremost because of the error that they made on account of feelings of racial solidarity. At the moment of emancipation, they should have stepped in to prohibit immigration of *Ostjuden*.

Today, *closing the borders to further Jewish immigration, completely and without exception, is imperative* but no longer adequate. It is also obvious that the *foreign Jews, who have not yet acquired citizenship, be most expeditiously and ruthlessly expelled, to the last man.* But neither will this be adequate.

As hard as it is upon the German sense of justice, *we must impose limitations on the rights of resident Jews in general*—this even though each one of us suffers when good people and bad are equally affected. In such cases, we must look to necessity and must steel our hearts against pity. Every concession to undeserved suffering will weaken the fortified ring we must create for ourselves.

The demand must be: *Jews residing in Germany shall be put under an Aliens Law.*

The preliminary question Who is a Jew? must be answered with hardness. We view religion as the original distinguishing mark, but we must also have regard for racial identity and treat Jewish apostates as Jews; this applies also to the progeny of mixed marriages, at least if we hold fast to the old Germanic principle that they take after the worse side [of the marriage]. We must hammer through the definition:

> A Jew, in the sense of the proposed Aliens Law, is anyone who belonged to the Jewish religious community as of January 18, 1871,[1] as well as all descendants of persons who were Jews on this date, even if only one parent was or is Jewish.

This determination of date may be thought arbitrary, as it in fact is, but it must be conceded that some such date is necessary to establish the concept of Jew. Upon examination, the day may be fixed earlier or later.

According to the above proposal, for example, the grandson of a Jew is also a Jew, even if his grandfather converted to Protestantism in 1875 and his mother [daughter of the grandfather] married a non-Jew, for example, an officer. This sounds unprecedented in the light of our softness up until now, but it is in keeping with what experience teaches: racially, such a child really does take after the worse side.

This conceptual definition is proposed in full realization of what is being demanded. [It is necessary] because of the fateful role in the past and present played by half-breeds, who have introduced the Jewish spirit and

---

[1] The foundation date of the German Empire.

attitudes—the natural consequences of Jewish blood—into the highest strata of our people. Here again it is a case not only of future prevention but of remedying what has been neglected in the past.

Thus it would be firmly established who is a Jew and who ought to be under the Aliens Law. What, however, ought this law determine? It should draw a line between Germans and Jews and limit the possibilities of exercising racially damaging effects. To this end belong the following measures:

All public offices, both remunerated and honorary, shall exclude Jews; this holds for the nation, state, and community.

They will not be allowed to serve in the army or navy.

They shall not be allowed an active or passive franchise. The profession of lawyer or teacher is prohibited. The same goes for theater direction.

Newspapers that have Jews working on them must make this known. The others, which we generally call "German," cannot be owned by Jews or have Jewish editors or collaborators.

Banks that are not purely personal enterprises may not have Jewish directors.

In the future, rural real estate may not be in the possession of Jews or be mortgaged to Jews.

As compensation for the protection that the Jews enjoy as an alien race, they shall pay taxes twice as high as the Germans.

I can visualize how people will throw up their hands at the cold cruelty of these suggestions. They will regard them as the offspring of a sick imagination. [This is] all the more so because in the naive circles of the liberal bourgeoisie, it has been customary to cry about the inequality of the Jews because they have not yet become, or all become, military officers, judges, and administrative officials. Therefore [Liberals] moan about mistreatment, deficient justice, and enjoy playing the lackey. But it's just the opposite. *Never before in history has a great, gifted, virtuous people come as quickly and as defenselessly under the influence and the intellectual leadership of a totally alien race as have the Germans under the Jews.*

Please note that it is not a matter of the billions that the small number of Jews have accumulated from the Germans, at least in part through illegal and immoral means. It is not a matter of economics, although serious dangers exist in this area. *For us it is a question of saving the soul of the German people.* Since, as we have acknowledged, our people's lack of instinct, naiveté, and deficient self-confidence compare so unfavorably to that of the Jews, individuals cannot protect themselves. Thus, the state must protect them and, following the force of necessity, enact harsh laws.

People may ask, Do you believe that an honorable Jew will subject himself to such laws? He will shake the inhospitable German dust from his feet and seek a homeland elsewhere. Hard, but unavoidable.

And the rest of the characterless Jews, who will subject themselves to anything, should they remain? These are the ones we want to be rid of. [This thinking points out] the weakness of the German defense against Jewry that lies in the fact that everyone in public life apparently knows one or two unobjectionable Jews. They have these in mind when they occupy themselves with the Jewish question. Sympathy for them makes for weakness. That is humanly understandable, but when it comes to the future of our people, we must thrust weakness from us.

The Zionists

The Jews are members of an alien race who, despite partaking in the blessings of our culture, have not become Germans; they cannot do so in consequence of a fundamentally different outlook. Whoever sees Jews in this way will welcome the fact that among the Jews themselves a nationalistic movement, so-called Zionism, is gaining more and more adherents. We can only respect the Zionists. They admit openly and honestly that their nation *is* a nation whose basic traits are unalterable, surviving almost two thousand years of statelessness among other nations. They declare unconditionally that a real assimilation of the Jewish foreigners to the host peoples is impossible because of the natural law of race. This law is stronger than the outward will to adapt to the conditions of a foreign environment.

The Zionists fully confirm what those who oppose the Jews on the standpoint of race have long maintained. Even though they are but a small troop in relation to the totality of their racial comrades, the truth that they proclaim can no longer be condemned to silence. *German and Jewish nationalists are of one opinion when it comes to the ineradicability of the Jewish race.* Who will then contest the right of the Germans to draw the necessary political consequences?

The Antisemitic Tradition in the Visual Arts

Existing alongside the literary tradition of antisemitism and contributing to its durability stands a tradition almost as old and complex: the visual stereotype of the Jew. Over the centuries and into modern times, the graphic and plastic arts have been employed to create images of the Jew as a physically repulsive, ridiculous, but nonetheless menacing figure. Historically, such images have served many purposes, and they continue today to influence viewers on many levels.

The foundation for the visual stereotype of the Jew was laid in the Middle Ages. Through a variety of media, the medieval church communicated to the illiterate public "truths" about the heretical Jews. For example, the "synagogue downcast" was depicted by the statue of a woman carrying upside-down tablets of the law or with her eyes blindfolded, while opposite stood the "church triumphant," embodied in a radiant woman, her gaze directed upward toward heaven. Not all the visible messages were this subtle, however. In several churches of the thirteenth and fourteenth centuries, sculptural ornaments portraying the loathsome symbol of the "Jew-pig"— a sow as foster mother giving nurture to her grotesque worshippers—rendered the indecency and utter degradation of the Jews in stone.

As in the case of the literary tradition of antisemitism, theologically inspired Jew hatred easily adapted to the needs of a more secular age. Beginning in the eighteenth century, Jews appeared as the subjects of popular calendars, political cartoons, caricatures, postcards, and posters. It is in the nature of most of these forms, even when meant to be humorous, also to be derisive, hostile, abusive. They thrive on exaggeration and distortion. Many ethnic groups and prominent individuals have come in for cruel characterization in this way. What is unique about Jews as subjects for graphic satire, however, is the intensity of the uniformly negative feelings conveyed. As with the printed word, so with the arts: the characteristic attributes of the Jew are crime, vice, and unheard-of power to do evil.

Unequal treatment is also apparent when the character flaws that caricaturists love to pillory are not the exclusive province of Jews. When Jews are targeted, a different, harsher valuation of the vice in question is obviously intended. The pomposity of the world-conquering Napoleon, for example, evokes laughter, ridicule, perhaps a bit of superiority in the viewer. When newly rich Jews come in for the same criticism, however, the audience is urged to feel anger, hatred, contempt.

The duration of their "starring role" in visual satire is also unique to Jews. One authority on the question considers the caricature of Isaac of Norwich (1233), representing a rich Jew in league with the horned devil, to be the earliest true caricature on any subject. Various ethnic groups and alleged ethnic traits have come in and out of fashion as candidates for derision; the Jewish type, on the other hand, has remained a constant favorite. Jews have come under attack from anonymous hacks, but famous artists—Lucas Cranach the Elder, Thomas Rowlandson, Henri Toulouse-Lautrec, Aubrey Beardsley—have also contributed to the stereotype and its perpetuation. In the Arab world and in Latin America today, the lampooning of Jews in one form or another is still popular and continues to use elements of the tradition.

The result of all this attention has been the creation of an instantly recognizable type. Early on in the process, the Jew no longer needed overt labeling or introduction; he became unmistakable, announced at first by his special hat or badge, then by his ill-fitting, outlandish garb. He is usually fat, always large-nosed and slump-shouldered, bow-legged, small in stature, with prominent ears and thick lips, kinky-haired or with earlocks and scraggly beard. He eats vile things. By innuendo or explicitly, he is over-sexed. From the earliest times, he appeared often with the body or in the company of real animals—the snake, pig, goat—or imaginary ones—legendary monsters or horrific apocalyptic beasts. And almost always, money enters the picture.

The visual stereotype of the Jew retains a good deal of its power in the modern world because people, no matter how "modern," continue to be plagued by unspeakable fears and undefined anger. Skirting the difficulties of verbal communication, images of the Jew call up a host of unsavory associations and foster mindless revulsion. They also lend irrational force to literary arguments that cannot withstand the light of reasoned analysis. Especially in the age of literacy, pictorial representations of Jews, from the comic to the pornographic, continue to offer tempting weapons to antisemites, and rare is the antisemitic pamphlet or newspaper of the modern era that does not draw on this traditional arsenal.

The accompanying illustrations are grouped thematically rather than chronologically. They are included here because careful study of them can yield valuable insights into the instinctual bases of antisemitism.

Jews as Objects of Nameless Dread

The "subtexts" of these illustrations are as significant as the overt representations. Along with the graphically portrayed ritualized murder of Christians are underlying themes of castration, infanticide, sexual abuse of children, and blooddrinking. In the two examples from the twentieth century, malign evil is clearly at work. But an unstated sense of the victim's helplessness can also be read in the images. Vultures prey only upon the dead or dying. The mighty coils of the snake have wound themselves around the entire earth; little hope of escape remains.

This woodcut by Michael Wohlgemuth appeared in 1493, nearly twenty years after the alleged murder of Simon of Trent. Although uncaptioned, Jews are recognizable by their names, by circular badges on their clothing, and by the crime they are committing.

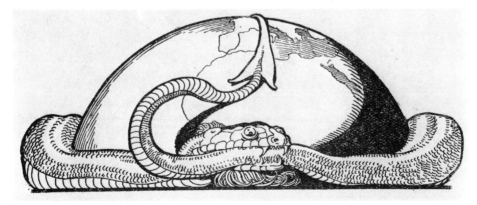

This illustration for a German edition (1920) of the *Protocols of the Elders of Zion* (see document 15) required no explicit reference to Jews to clarify the symbol.

The popular novel *Sin Against the Blood* (1918), which this poster advertised, was one of the first to make racist antisemitism central to the plot.

Jews as Exploiters

Whether overrunning the island of Manhattan, luxuriating on gentile labor, or committing outright fraud, the Jews are enormously powerful because of their control of money and their total contempt for the mores of their victims. The alien Jews engage in no productive labor; their innovations have only to do with sly dealing, greed, ruthlessness, and personal advantage, to the cost of the community. The golden calf atop the crown of Rothschild (see frontispiece, page ii) conveys the godless materialism commonly depicted as typical of Jews, and reminds viewers of their rejection of God.

An Austrian cartoon from 1900, entitled "Carriage Shafts," can also mean "reciprocal relationship." The rest of the legend reads: "Automobile—patent Schmul. Cheapest operation! Completely safe!"

GULLIVER KNICKERBOCKER AND THE LILLIPUTIANS

Gulliver Knickerbocker and the Lilliputians (1905) registers a nativist reaction to the massive immigration of Jews to New York City.

Cartoon from the Austrian antisemitic magazine, *Kikeriki,* (1912) entitled: "The Circumcision." The caption read, "It's advantageous—that's why it's customary among the Jews." Note the identification of economic wrongdoing (coin-clipping) with Jewish religious practices (circumcision).

Jews as Politically Dangerous

These illustrations give expression to right-wing fears and seek to discredit leftist revolutionary movements by associating them with Jews. The Viennese revolution of 1848 was cause for rejoicing only among Jews, whose banner shows two naked Christians yoked to the chariot of a crowned Jew. Evoking historical memories of the Jew as the merciless enemy of the human race, defenders of tsarism identified him as the modern political assassin and terrorist. To the anticommunist Nazis, the Soviet Union, tucked under the arm of the degenerate Eastern European Jew, had fallen victim to Jewish money and brutal force (the knout).

This caricature was part of a series by Lanzedelli commenting on Jewish emancipation and the role of Jews in the 1848 revolution in Vienna. The banner reads: "PROFIT—Equal rights with Christians."

— НУ И ПОДАВАЙТЕ ВАШЪ ГОЛОСЪ ЗА КАДЕТУФЪ!

This political cartoon appeared on the front-page of the protsarist weekly, *Rain,* in 1907.

This poster, originally in lurid color, advertises a "great political exhibit" in Munich, scheduled to open on the fourteenth anniversary (1937) of Hitler's "Beerhall putsch," sanctified in Nazi ideology as "the first blow against Jewish bolshevism."

4 The Radicalization of Political Antisemitism

The Jewish World Conspiracy

After the Russian Revolution of 1917 and at the end of World War I, political antisemitism, it is clear in retrospect, entered a new and more radical stage of development. The nationwide paranoia awakened by the Jewish minority that first welled up during the Dreyfus Affair in France had become a familiar, almost a reflex, reaction to the political crises many countries experienced during the interwar era. Violence of language became violence in fact. Amid the hectic atmosphere created by war, starvation, revolution, civil strife, rightist or leftist coups, and massive economic dislocation, antisemitism ceased to be merely the pastime of disaffected intellectuals or a useful ploy at election time and became lethal for all Jews, famous and obscure. Localized pogroms in eastern Europe, political assassinations of Jewish public figures, particularly in Germany, and renewed legal discrimination under state auspices culminated in the systematic, Europe-wide murder of one-third of world Jewry.

The *Protocols of the Elders of Zion* stands at the center of these events. Among the documents collected in this anthology, it is unique in many respects. During its heyday in the 1920s and 1930s, several versions circulated throughout the world in millions of copies, making it the most widely distributed antisemitic piece ever. Truly European in its fabrication, the component parts of the myth of a Jewish world conspiracy were contributed by Russian policemen and religious mystics, by a French political satirist and several priests, by a German petty bureaucrat turned novelist, and by others whose nationalities and occupations are no longer identifiable. The *Protocols* were written in French (by a Russian), and then translated into Russian, Swedish, Danish, Norwegian, Finnish, English, Romanian, Hungarian, Lithuanian, Polish, Bulgarian, Italian, Greek, Japanese, and Chinese.

That the *Protocols* were taken seriously will strike the modern reader as astonishing. Yet in the turbulent interwar period, the British Parliament and high officials of the U.S. State Department found it fitting to debate the authenticity of the *Protocols*; a Swiss court spent months deliberating on the same question. Public figures, who should have known better, confessed their faith in the document and thus helped spread the myth of a Jewish world plan. And, in fact, the *Protocols* have never entirely dropped from sight. New editions surfaced in Spain in 1963 and in Japan as recently as 1986.

The *Protocols* is unique for another reason: it is the only significant piece of antisemitic literature that purports to be of Jewish authorship, an "authentic" document that luckily fell into the hands of the intended victims of Jewish plotting. This was not a totally unprecedented stratagem. Apostate Jews of the early modern era had occasionally indulged in lurid exposés of Jewish evil, in order to persuade suspicious Christians about their own sincerity and to curry favor with them. Ritual-murder stories, too, customarily purported to rely on the testimony of a Jewish eyewitness.

By the turn of the twentieth century, a new device must have seemed necessary to the forgers of the *Protocols*. The reading public had grown jaded by the diatribes of avowed antisemites, whose motives could be considered questionable for any number of reasons. The *Protocols*, by contrast, presented itself as the unguarded revelation of the secret leaders of Jewry, the terrifying blueprint for world conquest, and the uncanny fulfillment of prophecies made long ago. It was to be the "smoking pistol" that would convince the apathetic masses of the Jewish peril.

This creation of many hands, working from many different sources, was probably the most effective—if one of the most bizarre—of all antisemitic productions. Repetitious and devoid of an organizing principle, the *Protocols* returns again and again to three basic themes: an attack on liberal ideas, the means of supplanting current governments, and the form and features of the new world government to be established after the imminent conquest of the world.

The *Protocols* presupposes the existence of a secret Jewish government about to complete an age-old plan by means of stupendous feats of organization and an amazing system of communication. All sorts of front organizations and a variety of Christian dupes serve the purposes of the Elders. The ignorant masses, Freemasons, government officials, liberals, democrats, socialists, Bolsheviks—all are the blind tools of the Jewish conspiracy. Yet only the Jewish elite is party to the conspiracy. To keep the Jewish masses in line, the Elders periodically unleash antisemitism and "allow" occasional pogroms, which spare the agents of the secret government. Formerly, Jews had been accused of not actually wanting emancipation or a return to Zion but only rarely of being the primary manipulators of antisemitism. In this respect, the *Protocols* represents a startling escalation into paranoia.

The success of the *Protocols* can only be fathomed in psychological terms. The book satisfied a deep emotional need in the postwar world, providing a simple, all-purpose explanation for a bewildering series of events. The fall of dynasties, the decline of the aristocracy, bloody wars, national humiliation, the emergence of international communism, worthless currencies, the weakening hold of traditional religion, pornography, the "new woman," jazz, and a host of other unsettling trends were, each and every one, to be accounted for as parts of a well-thought-out Jewish plan. The *Protocols* treated these accomplished facts as the outcome and absolute proof of a preexisting Jewish plot. As in the early days of the antisemitic movement, Jewish participation in these modern developments, whether up front or behind the scenes, was apparently sufficient evidence to convince the undiscerning of "the truth of the *Protocols*," a truth they yearned to believe.

Addressing its audience in the familiar voice of the sensational mass-circulation press, the fantasy reiterated and exploited centuries of accusations against Jews. The critical faculties of its audience had been hammered away at by Marr, Drumont, Stoecker, and hundreds of others. Why were Jews so prominent in the media, banking, and politics, if not to work their will upon hapless Christians? Who but the innately destructive Jews could want to wreak such havoc? From the Middle Ages they had been known as the agents of Satan, put on earth to do his work. The Anti-Christ was to appear at the Apocalypse, and, to the uprooted and confused, the Day of Judgment must have seemed imminent. Thus, the *Protocols* provided a key to the mysteries of the modern world, an outlandish horror story that both terrified and titillated its readers.

Measuring the harm done by the *Protocols* is difficult. Before World War I, it emerged as a tool of the Black Hundreds, a vigilante organization that defended an embattled tsarism and then carried out the brutal suppression of the 1905 Russian Revolution. At once reactionary and ter-roristic, the Black Hundreds published the *Protocols* with subsidies from the gullible Tsar Nicholas II, whose government helped inspire and direct a wave of devastating pogroms in which the *Protocols* played a notable part.

After the Bolshevik Revolution, the *Protocols* came to the West in the baggage of anticommunist émigrés, who were instrumental in its publica-tion in Europe and America. Particularly in Germany, the various versions of the book helped stamp a new, ruthlessly violent character on antisemi-tism. It inspired secret terrorist organizations, and political assassins cited it as the grounds for their murders. It became staple reading for radical rightists, including the Nazis, and an automatically invoked justification for their anti-Jewish actions. Despite authoritative refutations by disinterested parties, "mere facts" had minimal effects upon these "true believers."

For Further Reading

On the origins of the text and its dissemination, Norman Cohn, *Warrant for Gen-ocide: The Myth of the Jewish World-Conspiracy and the Protocols of the Elders of Zion* (London, 1967).

15. **Protocols of the Elders of Zion** (1898?)

First Protocol

I have framed the basic principles of our league, in general and in particu-lar, without regard to scientific considerations. I describe our doctrines and our system as it appears to us and to non-Jews.[1]

Source: From Gottfried zur Beek [Ludwig Müller], *Die Geheimnisse der Weisen von Zion,* 4th ed. (Charlottenburg, 1920), pp. 68–81, 91–92, 94, 101–5, 109–10, 112–13, 119–20, 122. Müller, a retired German army officer, was also founder of the Alli-ance Against the Arrogance of Jewry (see Document 13).

[1]In some versions, the anonymous speaker who addresses the elders of Zion or the leaders of the twelve tribes of Israel is supposed to be the "Chief Rabbi of the Jews." In others, he

I assert that men with evil motives outnumber those with good character. In the administration of the state, therefore, more can be achieved by force and unscrupulousness than by scientific discussions. Every man strives for power; every individual wants to be master of his own decisions and deeds; each would be master of himself (a dictator), if only he could. This striving after power is so strong that there is scarcely a man who would not be ready to sacrifice the common good for his own personal advantage.

What natural drives rule over the beasts of prey that feed upon the blood of men? What have been their actions and desires through all time? Since the rise of human society, beasts of prey in human form have seized raw, blind force for themselves. From this I conclude that *force* alone is the determining factor, no matter that it be veiled and disguised. Thus it follows that the basic law of existence rests wholly on the idea: "Right is based on force, on strength."

The Idea of Freedom—Freethinking

Civil freedom is an idea, a concept, but not a fact. This idea transforms itself as soon as the power of a nation is suppressed and strangled, as soon as a party striving after dominance seeks to force its will upon the countermovement. This task becomes essentially easier when the opponent is himself contaminated with a false concept of "freedom" and yields his power on account of this incorrect notion. On this is based the victory of our doctrine: when the reins slide along the ground and leadership is lacking, the accomplished licentiousness ends quickly, for a new hand draws in the reins. A new domination steps into the place of the old, which was robbed of its power by freethinking.

Gold, Faith in God, Self-government

In our day, when the genuine freethinkers govern the state, the power of gold is the sole determining factor. There was a time when faith in God governed. The concept of freedom was still without system. No one understood how to exploit it purposefully. No nation can exist for even

---

is the Devil himself. The "Chief Rabbi's Speech," often circulated separately from the *Protocols*, takes place in the dead of night in the Jewish cemetery of Prague, along with creaking gates, shadowy figures, and eerie lights. In the most popular variant, reproduced here, the speech is allegedly given in 1897 at a secret conventicle during the First Zionist Congress in Basel, Switzerland (in fact, a wholly public meeting thoroughly scrutinized by the world press). Sergei Nilus (see note 7, Document 16) introduced his 1917 edition of the *Protocols* with this information: ". . . Only now have I learned authoritatively from Jewish sources that these *Protocols* are nothing else than a strategic plan for the conquest of the world, putting it under the yoke of Israel, the struggle against God, a plan worked out by the leaders of the Jewish people during the many centuries of dispersion, and finally presented to the Council of Elders by 'the Prince of the Exile', Theodor Herzl, . . ." Herzl's alleged authorship thus became "established truth" for interpreters of the document.

the shortest time when it does not create a *rational* self-government, without which it sinks into licentiousness. From this moment there enters inner divisiveness, issuing in economic battles in the wake of which governments fall; gradually mob rule takes the rudder.

Domination of Money

A government finding itself under the influence of internal upheavals, or one that is at the mercy of external enemies because of the disordered conditions in its own land, must be undoubtedly consigned to oblivion. Then it is in *our* power. The dominance of money, over which we alone dispose, extends a straw to the government, which it must grasp for good or ill if it wants to keep from sinking helplessly into the abyss.

To those freethinkers who believe such considerations to be immoral, I say: every realm has two enemies. If it is allowable to employ immoral methods in the struggle against the external enemy, for example, concealment of intentions or a sudden attack, attacking at night or with overwhelming superiority of forces, can one say it is morally impermissible to use such methods against the worst [internal] enemy, the destroyer of social harmony and economic well-being?

The Masses and Lawlessness

Can a man of sound and logical intelligence hope to rule the masses of a nation successfully if he merely employs rational principles and logical arguments, when the possibility of contradiction exists in the people? Would an even halfway intelligent people be thereby easier to govern? If such a man relied exclusively on minor measures—on old customs, traditions, sentiments, and emotional dogmas—the masses would divide and reject such a government, for the masses have no sense for rational exhortation. Every action of the masses depends on an accidental or artificially constructed majority. Ignorant of the artifices of statecraft, they are carried along into foolish decisions, and thus the seed of lawlessness is planted within the state.

Statecraft and the Moral Law

Statecraft and the moral law have not the slightest to do with one another. A ruler who wants to rule by the moral law understands nothing about statecraft and is never for a moment secure upon his throne. He who would rule must labor with slyness, cunning, evil, hypocrisy. High moral character—openness, honor, honesty—these are the reefs of statecraft upon which the best will founder, because the enemy makes use of different and truly more effective measures. Let these character traits be the hallmarks and principles of non-Jewish realms. *We* can never and under no condition labor with such wrong-headed principles.

Our right lies in strength. "Strength" is a limited expression, not a universally valid concept. The word in itself never signifies more than: "Give me what I want so that it may be clear and self-evident to all the world that I am stronger than you."

Where does right begin? Where does it end? In a state where power is badly managed and laws and governors are rendered impersonal by free-thinking [civil] rights, I shall create a new right. [I shall] demolish all institutions according to the right of the stronger, lay hands upon the law, transform all governing bodies, and become master of them. The power of these rights shall voluntarily transfer to us—because of freethinking.

The Invulnerability of Jewish Freemasonry

Since at present all the powers have begun to totter, ours will be more invulnerable than any of the others because it will be invisible. Thus it shall remain unshakable until that time when it has become so empowered that no act of violence can repress it.

Out of the transitory calamities that we must now cause, there will emerge the benefaction of an unshakable government that shall reestablish the regulated development of national existence, undisturbed by freethinking. The results justify the means. Thus we shall direct our plans less by attention to the good and moral than by the necessary and useful.

Before us lies a plan, the lines of which are drawn according to the rules of war. We cannot deviate from it without endangering the labor of many centuries.

The Masses Are Blind

To achieve the goal of common efforts, we must learn to grasp the worthlessness, inconstancy, and vacillation of the masses. We must understand their incapacity to understand the questions of state life and their own welfare. We must comprehend that the great masses of the people are blind, wholly without understanding, and that they willy-nilly stagger from Right to Left, backward and forward. A blind man cannot lead the blind without leading them into the abyss. Consequently, even the "inquisitive" and creative among the masses can never perform as leaders in governing the states. Even when they supposedly possess some intelligence, they are still not fit to act as trail-blazers and leaders of the masses. They will attain to no other goal than the ruin of the entire people.

Only a personality, educated to self-mastery from youth, can recognize and act upon the great tendencies and principles of statecraft.

Party Strife

A people that delivers itself to the upstarts from out of the masses destroys its own structure by party battles, by the struggle for the leading positions of power, by the hunting after honors and dignities, and by the disorders and movements arising from all this. Is it possible that the masses can judge without prejudice, peacefully and matter of factly, that they can guide the destiny of the land without regard to purely personal interests? Can they defend the realm against external foes? That is senseless, for to distribute governance of the state among so many personalities, so many heads from out of the masses, will sacrifice its unity, and it will become nonviable and powerless.

Only under the leadership of a self-controlled personality can the state be directed in full clarity and good order; only thus can the whole body politic labor in peace. From this it follows that the most appropriate form of the state for a country is found when the direction lies in the hands of a single responsible personality. Without unqualified power no state system can thrive upon a moral basis. This basis cannot rest upon the masses but rather on the competent leader, be he who he may. The masses consist of barbarians who bring their coarseness and barbarity to bear at every opportunity. As soon as the masses seize power for themselves, they fall into lawlessness, the highest degree of barbarity.

Alcohol, Humanism, Vice

Observe the drunkards, befogged by alcohol. They believe themselves to possess the right to unlimited pleasure, which they confuse with the concept of freedom. From that idea we take leave for all time. The non-Jewish peoples are befogged with alcohol; their youths are infatuated with humanism and premature vices. To these they have been led by our agents, administrators, teachers, servants, governesses to the rich, educational institutions, etc., as well as by our women in pleasure resorts and public houses. Among these I also count the so-called "society ladies," who willfully ape the example of vice and ostentation.

Principles of the Jewish Freemason Lodges

Our slogan is: *Power and Artifice!* Power alone wrests the victory in questions of state—that is, when it is in the possession of personalities who have something to say in the state. Force forms the basis, but cunning and fraud work as the means to power for such governments that are not willing to lay their crowns at the feet of the representatives of a new power. These are the only means to the goal that hovers before us. Therefore, we must not shrink from bribery, fraud, treason, if they serve for the attainment of our plans. In statecraft we must be clever enough not to shrink from strange methods, if power and subjection be achieved thereby.

Terror

Our realm, which is founded on the paths of peaceful conquest, will replace the terrors of war with less visible but all the more effective punishments. It must institute a reign of terror in order to compel blind, unconditional obedience. Stern, pitiless, and ruthless measures are the best props of state power. Not alone for advantage but above all in the name of duty and for the sake of victory, we must hold firmly to the employment of force and cunning. . . . It is not only in the scientific evaluation of means but above all in their ruthless and merciless application that our predominance, our superiority, shall be secured. It shall suffice to know that we are merciless and that we understand how to compel obedience.

Liberty, Equality, Fraternity

Already in antiquity we allowed the call for "Liberty, Equality, Fraternity" to echo from the ranks of the peoples. Since that time, these words have been endlessly repeated in the most varied disturbances and upheavals. Sometimes the intentions have been honorable—to bring actual well-being and true freedom of the personality to the world; sometimes it has just been to satisfy the vanity of the masses. Not even the intelligent and clever non-Jews have recognized the inner contradictions in these words. They have not said that there can be no equality, no freedom in nature. All of nature rests upon the inequality of forces, characteristics, peculiarities. Nature is subject to eternal laws. It is clear that the masses are a blind force. And the chosen upstarts are as blind as the masses themselves. The initiated, even if he is a fool, can govern, while the uninitiated, even when he is high-minded, can understand nothing about statecraft. All these things are forgotten by the non-Jews.

Principle of Princely Government

[On the non-Jews] depended the principle of princely government. The father bequeathed his knowledge of statecraft to the son, so that it was known only to members of the dynasty and none could betray the secrets to the peoples ruled over. In time the sense of the true content of statecraft was lost in the transmission, and this contributed to the success of our cause.

Abolishing the Privileges of the Non-Jewish Nobility

In all the corners of the world, and with the help of our secret societies, the words "Liberty, Equality, Fraternity" led gigantic crowds to our ranks and carried our banners to victory. Those words were the worms that gnawed at the welfare of non-Jews, everywhere undermining peace, calm, community, common values, and thereby destroying the foundation of their domination. Gentlemen, you see the consequences that have served the triumph of our cause. *They gave us the possibility of playing out the highest trump: the annihilation of noble privilege, or, better said, the actual system of non-Jewish noble dominance, which has been the only means of defense of the non-Jewish peoples and states against us.*[2]

---

[2]The defense of aristocratic privilege against the forces of change was of particular importance to the Russian author(s) of the *Protocols*. In the variants published in the more

The New Nobility

On the ruins of the old blood and family nobility we have set the nobility of our educated, and at its tip, the money nobility. The standard of this new nobility lies in wealth, which depends upon us, and in the teachings disseminated by our secret committees.

Calculating Human Weaknesses

Our triumph was made all the easier in that we could exploit people useful to us by working on the most impressionable side of human intelligence: with consideration to money, greed, and the insatiable desire for gain. If we seize upon the right moment, all the extraordinarily numerous human weaknesses are suited to paralyze the powers of decision making. Those who best understand how to exploit human weaknesses are thus enabled to enslave the wills of men.

The concept of freedom made it possible to convince the masses that the government was nothing more than the deputies for those who possessed the land—that is, the people. The people therefore felt competent to change [governments] as one would change gloves.

Changes in the parliament delivered it into our power. It is elected or not at our discretion.

Second Protocol

Economic Wars as the Basis for Jewish Hegemony

By all means we must seek to prevent wars from resulting in territorial gains. [If we can manage this, then the profits] will be transferred to the economic realm where we shall make clear to the nations that we hold complete power. Such situations deliver the warring parties into the hands of our associations, which are distributed over the entire globe, which have a million eyes at their disposal, and which know no territorial boundaries. Then our rights shall wipe out the rights of the nations and these shall be governed [by us] as the individual citizens are governed by their civil codes.

The Bureaucracy

We shall pick administrative officials from the citizenry on the basis of their slavelike capacities, and we shall not train them for administration. They will therefore sink to the level of pawns in our chess game and be in the hands of our schooled, gifted counselors, who have been trained from youth to exercise dominion of the entire world. As you know, these experts

---

socially advanced West, concern for the position of the nobility was dropped or much attenuated.

have created their knowledge of statecraft from our governmental plans, from the lessons of history, and from observation of the present. Non-Jews don't understand [governmental] praxis based on the dispassionate observations of history. They are guided by a knack for science that does not use comparative results as a test. It makes no sense for us to debate with them. Let them live on hope of future joys or in remembrance of the past. Most important is that they firmly believe in what we have slowly administered to them as the behests of science. To this end, our press continually instills a blind confidence in our doctrine. The intelligent among the non-Jews will give themselves airs on account of their knowledge, and skillfully they will seek to implement this "scientific" information without examining it logically. And neither will they suspect that it was injected by our representatives in order to educate people in the tendencies advantageous to us.

Do not believe that our assertions are mere empty words. Look at our widespread successes with the teachings of Darwin, Marx, and Nietzsche. Their demoralizing effects on the non-Jews should surely be clear.

Adaptability in Statecraft

We must reckon with the spirit of the times, with the character and moods of the peoples, in order to avoid errors in statecraft and administration. Our doctrinal system, whose structure can be reduced to a mixture of the bodily humors of the nations with which we deal, will have a lasting success only if its application combines the teachings of the past with the demands of the present.

Tasks of the Press

There is a great power in the hands of the present governments that decisively influences the mind of the people—the press. It has the task of advertising allegedly necessary demands, of giving expression to the grievances of the people, voicing, awakening, and deflecting their discontent. The press revels in the free expression of opinion. But governments do not understand how to use this power, and so they find themselves suddenly in our hands. Through the press we come into influence yet remain in the shadows. Thanks to it we have heaped up mountains of gold in our hands without having to bother ourselves about the streams of blood and tears that created it.

The Value of Gold and of Jewish Sacrifices

But we have bought it dearly, at the sacrifice of many of our people. Before God, each sacrifice on our side is worth a thousand non-Jews.

Third Protocol

The Symbol of the Snake and Its Meaning

The goal that we have set ourselves, as I can impart to you today, lies only a few steps away. We have only a short distance to cover. Our path is like the coiling of a contracting snake, which we have chosen as the symbol of our people. When the coiling of this snake is completed, all the realms of Europe will be pressed together in its powerful constrictions. [See p. 137.]

The Instability of Constitutions:
The Phantom Terror in the Courts of Royalty

The constitutional powers of our time will soon be abolished because we will not leave them in peace. We will see to it that they never cease to totter until their representatives are finally ousted. The non-Jews believed that their dominance was sufficiently secured, and they always hoped finally to have peace. But the head of state supports himself by means of responsible ministers, who in turn think him a fool. He allows himself to be ousted by this irresponsible power that he has not supervised. It is just this power that opens the way for terrorists into the princely courts. Since the rulers have no feeling for their peoples and therefore cannot enter into their midst, they will never come to an understanding with the people and will be unable to find firm footing against those who lust after domination. The power of the ruler, which we have weakened, is like the blind power of the people; both have lost any significance. Each is for himself alone and therefore helpless, like the blind man without a cane.

To get those with power to misuse it, we have played all the forces against one another. . . . In this sense we sought to revive every social distinction. We outfitted all the parties. We made the ruling powers into the targets of all passions. We made battlefields out of the states in which the uprisings could be played out. Have but a little patience, and uprisings and collapses will be a universal phenomenon.

Tireless speakers have transformed the sittings of parliament and other legislative bodies into showplaces for endless speechifying. Brazen newspaper reporters and libelous writers without conscience have had a field day with government representatives. Abuse of power shakes the very foundations of the state and prepares its collapse. Everything will be smashed under the blows of the irrational masses.

Poverty, which works more strongly than slavery and serfdom, has condemned the nations to hard labor. In one way or another they could free themselves from slavery and serfdom; they could deal with them somehow. But they cannot free themselves from misery. We have injected theoretical rights into the constitutions, which the masses imagine to be significant but which have no practical effect. All the so-called "rights of the people" exist only in the imagination! They have no bearing on reality.

What good is it to the poor worker, who spends his life in hard labor, that a few babblers have the right to make speeches and that reporters are permitted to write real news alongside every sort of nonsense? In fact, the only advantage the constitution offers are the few crumbs that we throw him from our table, if, that is, he votes for us and our representatives. For the poor, civil rights are in fact a bitter mockery. They cannot actually use these rights because they daily stand on the treadmill of a labor that scarcely affords them the necessities. No worker can depend on a secure wage. He is dependent on the decisions of factory owners and on the strikes of his comrades.

The Nobility and the Parvenus

The people, through our influence, has destroyed the rule of the nobility. The nobles, whose own advantage was inseparably bound with the welfare of the people, were the natural protectors and provisioners of the people. With the annihilation of the nobility, the people fell under the rule of parvenu upstarts, who without mercy laid the yoke of slavery upon the workers.

We appear, as it were, to be the saviors of workers because we urge them to join the ranks of our army of socialists, anarchists, and communists. These, we pretend, are in universal service to humanity in a fraternal sense, and we recommend them to the workers fundamentally on this pretext. The nobility, which espoused the rights of productive workers, was so interested in their prosperity that the workers were of necessity satisfied, healthy, and strong. We, however, want just the opposite—that is, the *debasement of non-Jews.* Our power rests on the permanent hunger and weakness of the worker. Only in this condition will he have to subordinate himself to our will in everything. In his own circles, he will not find the independent strength to oppose us.

Hunger will procure the rights over labor for the money power far more securely than the legal power of the king was able to do for the nobility. With want, and the envy and hatred that spring from it, we will move the masses. With their help we will cast aside all those who are obstacles in our path. As soon as it is time for the crowning of our world ruler, these same masses will sweep aside everything that could still resist us.

The Principles of Instruction in the Future Public Schools of the Freemasons

The non-Jews cannot escape our scientific counsel, but we nevertheless do not disclose the correct way to them. That is why their school system overlooks the main thing, which we will adhere to unshakably after the erection of our realm. The one true doctrine of the social basis of life must be preached in the public schools—that which demands the division of labor and the consequent distribution of men into classes and castes. Everyone must be absolutely conscious that human equality is totally out of the question because of the necessity of the division of labor. The differentiation must be legally regulated. . . .

The true doctrine of the social basis of life, which we keep secret from non-Jews, states that position and occupation must be limited to a definite circle of men; otherwise the disparity between training and profession will give rise to human suffering. Once the peoples have made this doctrine their own, they will voluntarily subject themselves to the power of the state and the order deriving from it. With the present state of science and the direction that we have given it, the people trust blindly in the printed word and in the misleading doctrines that go with it. In their limitedness they hate every class they think stands above them; they misunderstand the significance [of these social distinctions].

Universal Economic Crisis

The conflicts described thus far will be essentially heightened by the approaching economic crisis, which will paralyze the stock exchanges and industry. With the help of gold, which we control entirely, and the underhanded ways at our disposal, we shall call forth a universal economic crisis. Simultaneously, we shall throw hordes of workers out onto the streets. Seized by a sort of rapture, the simpleminded masses will shed the blood of those whom they have always envied and whose property they can then steal without resistance.

However, they will not molest our people because the moment of the attack will be known to us. We shall take timely measures to defend our people.

The Power of the Lodges Is the Realm of Reason

We have demonstrated that progress will lead all non-Jews into the realm of reason. Our rule will be of this kind. We shall understand how to suppress all disturbances through the rigorous application of reason. The freethinkers shall be forced out of all the branches of state life.

After the people have noticed that all kinds of concessions have been made to them in the name of freedom, they will seize power in the belief that they are the masters. Like any blind man, they will naturally stumble on a host of difficulties with which they cannot deal. In the search for leaders, they will not return to the old ones but will be much more likely to lay their full power at our feet. Consider the French Revolution, to which we have given the name "great." The secrets of its preparation are fully known to us, and it was certainly the work of our hands.

From that time onward we have led the peoples from one delusion to another and have diverted them to us. They shall hail the king out of the blood of Zion, to whom we shall give the world.

Since we already constitute a world power, we are invulnerable. As soon as we are attacked by one state, other states defend us. Our impregnable position is strengthened by the unceasing baseness of the non-Jewish nations, which cringe before power but are merciless toward the weak. They severely punish misdemeanors but judge real crimes leniently; they will not tolerate the contradictions of a free social order but are endlessly tolerant of the violations that arise from the lust for power. They tolerate in their elected representatives misdeeds, the smallest of which would have resulted in the beheading of twenty kings!

How is this remarkable phenomenon, this illogical behavior of the masses toward apparently similar events, to be explained? It is to be explained this way. Those elected to power have their agents insinuate to the people that they did damage to the state intentionally but for a higher purpose. The goal is the general welfare of the nations, their brotherhood and equality. Naturally, they do not say that this League of Nations will be formed only under our hegemony! Thus the people condemn the just and let the guilty go unpunished. It is more and more convinced that it can do anything it wants. In such circumstances, the people destroy any chance of peaceful development and at every step call forth new disorder.

The word *freedom* plunges human society into the struggle against all powers, against the power of the divine and natural order of the world. When we come to sit upon the throne, we will expunge this word from the vocabulary of humanity. It is the essence of animalistic force and places the masses on the same level as the beasts of prey. These beasts are satisfied only after they have tasted blood. Then they allow themselves to be put in chains quite easily. Deny them the drinking of blood and they do not sleep but rather slough off their skin.

• • •

From the Ninth Protocol

The Application of Our Principles in the Education of the People

In the application of our principles, we must consider the peculiarities of the peoples and proceed according to plan. The uniform application of our principles to all peoples will not bring success, unless we do the necessary preparation. However, if we proceed cautiously, you will see that it takes no more than a decade to bring down the firmest character. Then we can list a new people among the ranks that have already been subjected to us.

As soon as we come to power, we shall allow the old freethinker battle cry, "Liberty, Equality, Fraternity!" which was basically taken from our Zionist lodges and introduced into the world, to be considered only as an ideal of the higher spiritual realms, not one that can be realized on earth. We shall declare "the right to liberty, the duty to equality, the example of fraternity," thus grabbing the bull by the horns. In fact, we have already undermined every sovereign power other than our own, even though legally there are still many sovereigns and state administrations. Today, when any state raises objections against us, this is only for form's sake and usually because we so will it.

The Significance of Antisemitism

We have need of antisemitism, in order to hold our brothers in the lower strata together. I shall not go into this further since we have already spoken of this subject repeatedly.

The Rule of Force of the Jewish Lodges

As a matter of fact, there are no more obstacles for us. Our supreme rule stands outside legal limitations. Its principles are so firm that only the strong term "rule of force" can describe it. I can say with utter conviction that we are at present the legislators; our word is law and executive power is ours. We punish and pardon. We sit like the commanders of armies upon our chargers. A firm will guides us. We are heirs to a once-mighty party [the Liberals], which is now wholly dependent on us. We have at our disposal an unbending ambition, burning greed, pitiless revenge, and unrelenting hate.

From us goes forth the phantom of all-embracing Terror. . . .

The Subways of the Capitals

You can well imagine that the non-Jews, full of bitterness, will fall upon us with weapons in hand as soon as they discover how everything fits together. For this eventuality we have in hand a last, fearful means, before which even the bravest heart shall tremble. Soon all the capital cities of the world will be criss-crossed with tunnels and subways.[3] In case of danger we shall, from these tunnels, blow up the whole city—government offices, courts, archives, and the non-Jews with all that they possess.

• • •

From the Eleventh Protocol

Non-Jews Are Castrated Sheep

The non-Jews are a herd of castrated sheep; we Jews are the wolves. Do you know, gentlemen, what becomes of the sheep when the wolves break into the fold? . . . They will close their eyes and stay silent because we will promise them the return of all their stolen freedoms. But first [we shall tell them] all the enemies of peace must be overcome and all the parties must be overpowered. Need I tell you how long the non-Jews will have to wait for the return of their rights?

We have thought out a mendacious doctrine of the state and instilled it tirelessly among the non-Jews, without giving them time to reason about it. This has occurred because we can achieve our goal only along circuitous paths; the straight path is beyond the powers of our scattered tribes. To this end we have established the secret Jewish freemason lodges.[4] No one

---

[3]This bit of fantasy has been used to help establish the time and place (Paris in the late 1890s) for the creation of the *Protocols*. Subway construction was still an exotic idea for many Europeans. The Paris Métro concession had been granted in 1894; the first line opened in 1900. Edouard Drumont claimed, without proof, that most of the shareholders in the Métro were Jewish.

[4]Antisemites were deeply suspicious of freemasonry, and the Freemasons were often depicted as witting or unwitting accomplices in the Jewish conspiracy. The first to detail a masonic conspiracy was a French Jesuit, Abbé Barruel, in 1797. He traced the French Revolution back to a plot hatched by the Knights Templar, who, surviving their attempted

knows about them or their goals, least of all the non-Jewish oxen whom we have drawn into participation in the open freemason lodges, in order to throw sand in the eyes of their tribal brothers.

God has bestowed upon us, his chosen people, the gift of being scattered throughout the world. In this apparent weakness of our tribe lies its whole strength. It has brought us to the threshold of world domination. The foundation is laid; only the building remains to be completed.

From the Twelfth Protocol

The Press under Future Jewish World Dominance

What tasks does the press fulfill now? It serves to inflame the passions of the people in the sense that we desire, or it fosters self-seeking political purposes. It is hollow, unjust, and mendacious. Most men do not know whom the press actually serves. We Jews have made it serviceable to our purposes. When we arrive at power, we shall place it in chains and punish every attack upon us without mercy. The current situation is nonsensical. On the one hand, the necessary precensorship of books, periodicals, and newspapers costs the non-Jewish state a fortune. On the other hand, out of respect for alleged "public opinion," it allows any mudslinger to cover it with filth, without intervening. We will know better how to protect ourselves from this and simultaneously create a considerable source of income from supervision of public opinion. It will happen in this way. Printed matter of all sorts ... will be liable for a stamp tax, which shall limit the quantities of the same. Further, we shall demand a sizable sum as security from every newspaper publisher, printing house, etc. In case of attacks upon us, all or a sizable part of it will be forfeited. Now it may happen that a few parties will nevertheless sacrifice great sums of money in order to make their views known. But we have an answer to this, as well: as soon as a newspaper attacks us for a second time, it will be suppressed. None shall encroach upon the aura of our political infallibility without being punished! As a pretext for the suppression of a newspaper or periodical, we shall always employ the general formula that it has incited public opinion without grounds or cause. I ask you to note that in other cases attacks will be made upon us by newspapers that we ourselves have established. Such

---

extermination in 1314, reconstituted themselves as a secret society of Freemasons to wreak revenge on all monarchs and the papacy. They sought to establish a world republic by means of preaching liberty to the masses. In fact, many Freemasons died at the hands of republicans during the Red Terror. Antimonarchical principles were not universal among the Freemasons, else Louis XVI, his brothers, and many aristocrats would not have belonged. The masonic conspiracy became a Judeo-masonic conspiracy in the 1820s, another French invention. That Jews at no time played a disproportionately large role in freemasonry and that many lodges—"the synagogues of Satan"—refused to accept them as members were facts that did not disturb the creators of this myth. Similarly, the occasional inclusion of Jesuits in the world conspiracy defied the widespread knowledge that this order was the only one that did not accept Jewish converts. It was apparently sufficient that Jews, Jesuits, and Freemasons all had international connections to convince the gullible that they were up to no good.

attacks will, however, always limit themselves to the points that we ourselves have earmarked for our uses. . . .

[Thanks to unfair taxes and fines] what we ourselves will publish in order to educate people in the desired intellectual direction will be so cheap as to find a ready market. The taxes will calm the fanatical desire to write, and the fines will bring writers under our control. Should a few of them, in spite of this, wish to write against us, they will be unable to find a publisher. Every publisher or printer will be obligated to get permission from us before accepting a work for publication. In this way we will learn in timely fashion of any planned attacks and be able to render them innocuous. We shall be able to take the appropriate measures or at least announce them in advance. For example, we can deny permission to publish on the grounds that the work deals with abuses that the government is already taking steps to correct. In certain circumstances, we may wish for the late publication of an attack because it will then involuntarily bear witness to the vigilance of the government, which has already begun to eliminate the abuses.

Newspapers and periodicals are the two most important tools for controlling intellectual life. Therefore, our government will acquire ownership of most newspapers and periodicals. It will thus block the harmful influence of the unofficial press and work upon the mind and mood of the people in the most sustained way. For every ten newspapers or periodicals that stand aloof from us, there will be thirty that we ourselves have established. This, of course, cannot be divulged to the public. Outwardly, our newspapers and periodicals shall therefore adopt the most varied orientations and even feud with one another. Thus we shall gain the trust of the unsuspecting non-Jews, lure them to their downfall, and render them harmless.

In the first place will stand the official press, which will have the task of representing our interests in all cases and instances. Its influence will, for this reason, be relatively slight.

In the second place comes the semiofficial papers, which shall win the indifferent and apathetic for us.

In the third place we shall set our apparent enemies, who must maintain at least one paper that stands outwardly in the sharpest opposition to us. Our real enemies will consider this apparent resistance to be genuine. They will see the people who represent us as their own political friends, reveal themselves to them, and thereby to us.

Our newspapers will adopt the most varied orientations. We will support aristocratic, bourgeois, liberal, socialist, and even revolutionary papers. Like the Indian god Vishnu, they will have a hundred hands, each with the beating pulse of an intellectual tendency. As soon as one pulse beats faster, the invisible hands will direct the supporters of this tendency to our goals. Nothing is easier than to influence an excited mob that acts without reflection. Those ignorant fools who believe that their party paper represents their views [will not know that the papers] speak only our opinion or at least the opinion that suits us at the moment. They imagine they are following the guidelines of their party and do not notice that they march behind the flag that we have put in front of them. . . .

Since the real state of affairs will not become public, we will win the confidence of the people. Supported by this confidence, we will, as needed, arouse or pacify, convince or confuse public opinion so far as it concerns political questions. We will now print the truth, now lies, now facts, now corrections, all according to how we conceive of the news.

It is one of our principles always to test the ground cautiously before we set foot upon it. In consequence of these measures against the press, we shall surely defeat our enemies. In serious cases they will be unable to find a paper in which they can bring their views to full expression. We shall make the most strenuous efforts to defeat them in a final way. . . .

• • •

From the Fourteenth Protocol

Religion of the Future

As soon as we have succeeded to world domination, we shall tolerate no beliefs other than our belief in the one God, who has chosen us from among the peoples so that we shall determine the destiny of the earth. Therefore shall we destroy every other religion. Should the number of the godless be thereby increased, this can only serve our purposes. We shall point to the godlessness of the non-Jews as a deterrent example, and we shall spread the entrenched and thoroughly thought-out Mosaic doctrine over the entire world. This will contribute to the subjection of all peoples to us. We Jews, however, will explain our success as a result of the secret power of our doctrines, from which, as we shall say, all the creative and educational works of humanity issue. . . .

Pornography and Future Literary Activity

We have created, in the so-called leading states, a mindless, dirty, repellent literature. We shall favor this tendency for a little while after the achievement of world domination. In this way, the nobility of our political plans and speeches will stand out in sharper contrast [to the smut]. Our leading men, whom we have educated in advance to rule the non-Jews, will suddenly and quickly conquer public opinion for us with a profusion of well-thought-out plans, speeches, essays, pamphlets, and so on. Then will the world finally fall to us.

From the Fifteenth Protocol

Simultaneous Revolution throughout the World

Some time will pass, perhaps even a whole century, before the revolution we are preparing shall break out in all states on the same day. [It will] reveal to all the total incapacity of the existing governments. Once we have achieved full dominance, we will take care that no kind of conspiracy takes place against us. Anyone found with weapons in hand or who rejects our domination, we shall mercilessly put to death. Every attempt to establish new secret societies will likewise be punished by death. The existing secret societies, which are well known to us and which have rendered us good service, we shall dissolve completely. Their membership shall be exiled to places far from Europe. . . .

We draw all the lodges together under the main leadership—that is, of course, the Directory of our Elders, known to us but unknown to all others. The lodges will have chairmen who must understand that the directives of the Elders must be kept secret, on pain of death. These lodges shall hold the threads connecting all revolutionary and freethinking activities. Lodge members will come from the most varied social strata. The most secret plans of states will become known to us on the day of their origination and be communicated immediately to the Directory. Almost all the police spies of the world will belong to the lodges. Their activities are indispensable to us. . . .

Those who join the secret societies should by preference be adventurers, swindlers, hustlers, and generally people of loose conscience and rash nature. It cannot be difficult to win such people and to make them serviceable to our purposes. When the world is plagued by unrest, this can only mean that we have called forth the disturbances in order to destroy the all-too-firm structures of the non-Jewish states. Should it come to a conspiracy anywhere, none but our most loyal servants shall stand at the head of it. It goes without saying that we Jews alone, and no one else, shall direct the activity of the freemason lodges. We alone know what target to steer for and what the final goal of every action is to be. The non-Jews, on the other hand, have no inkling of these things. They see only the nearest thing at hand, the obvious, and are accustomed to be satisfied with the gratification to their egos that comes from carrying out some pet project. They don't bother themselves with effects. Similarly, they do not notice that the idea does not originate with them but rather is to be traced back to our influence. . . .

You cannot imagine, gentlemen, how easy it is to lead even the cleverest non-Jew by the nose, especially when you find him in the state of self-exaltation. He is of such childish disposition that should he meet with even the slightest failure—for example, the absence of applause—this is enough to move him to slavish obedience to anyone who promises him success next time. *While we Jews scorn outward success and focus all our senses and endeavors on the carrying out of our plans, the non-Jews, by contrast, are ready to sacrifice all plans if only they can pocket the slightest external success.* The mental gifts of the non-Jews make the task of directing them to our purposes uncommonly easy. With the outward forms of tigers, they have the souls of gentle lambs. Their heads are full of drafts.

We have puffed them up and humbugged them into believing that the individual personality must dissolve into the totality, into so-called communism. The non-Jews are apparently unable to recognize that the idea of universal equality violates the supreme law of nature. Since the creation of the world, various species of beings and men have come forward, and the personality claims a decisive role. If we succeed in blinding non-Jews to this, that just shows, with surprising clarity, that their intelligence cannot measure up to ours. This is the best security for our success.

Antisemitism in the United States

The ingredients that produced antisemitic movements in Europe have also been present in the United States. The Jewish minority is urbanized, now largely middle class and concentrated in the professions, highly visible in the media and entertainment industries, and widely perceived as both "different" and "powerful." American history, too, is filled with examples of social and economic discrimination against Jews. In the colonial era, they could not vote or hold public office. They met unequal treatment in law courts and were sometimes subject to occupational disabilities. Although the U.S. Constitution forbade the application of a religious test as a qualification for office holding, individual states could practice discrimination unhindered.

As in Europe, Jews have been grossly satirized or attacked in pamphlets, books, and newspapers. From the 1870s on, social exclusion became widespread. Resorts, hotels, and residential neighborhoods were closed to Jews by "gentlemen's agreements." Prep schools and then many universities, the most prestigious leading the way, instituted the *numerus clausus,* a percentage quota for Jewish admissions; in some cases, these remained in force into the 1960s. In the 1920s, employment agencies and want ads in newspapers frequently warned, "No Jews need apply." Professional organizations and social clubs practiced a formal or a casual brand of discrimination. And mob violence occasionally claimed a Jewish victim, as in 1915 when Leo Frank was lynched in Atlanta after being wrongfully accused of killing a Christian girl.

When it comes to the successful political utilization of anti-Jewish prejudice, however, the European patterns have not been successfully followed in the U.S. In the land of immigrant minorities, all of whom have experienced some kind of discrimination, no public figure has been able to make significant political capital out of antisemitism, although not for want of trying. With such a diverse ethnic makeup, it has been more difficult in the United States than in Europe for any one group to portray itself as "the host people," while Jews (or Irish, Italians, etc.) are condemned as unwelcome guests. This accidental circumstance should not be mistaken for tolerance, however. In the case of Jews, American public opinion polls since the 1930s have revealed deep-seated anti-Jewish prejudice in society. Although Americans have rarely elected politicians who have campaigned as avowed antisemites, several attempts have been made, with destructive consequences.

One of the most important endeavors to exploit, extend, and derive political advantage from native anti-Jewish prejudices is associated with the name of Henry Ford. On May 22, 1920, Ford's personal newspaper, the weekly *Dearborn Independent,* with a circulation of approximately 300,000, featured an unsigned lead article entitled, "The International Jew, the World's Problem." Feeding off the "red scare" that seized America after the war, it repeated what was by now an accepted truth: the Jews were behind the Bolshevik revolution, an important step in their secret government's plan of world conquest. For ninety-one successive weeks, the newspaper featured articles on the universally corrupting influence of Jewry upon American life—from jazz, short skirts, and bobbed hair to the total control of money and the press.

From July 1920, and for several weeks running, the *Protocols of the Elders of Zion* came under detailed, wholly sympathetic scrutiny. These collected articles shortly appeared as a separate book, *The International Jew,* which circulated in 500,000 copies, backed by a major advertising campaign. It was eventually translated into sixteen languages and became especially popular with Hitler, who kept a photograph of the "heroic American, Heinrich Ford." Ford also sponsored publication of the *Protocols,* one of several versions competing for the American reading public's attention in the 1920s.

Ford's motivations for lending his enormous prestige and resources to political antisemitism are obscure. Some have theorized that he intended the campaign to serve his presidential ambitions or that he was responding to setbacks in other grand political and economic schemes. He recanted his views publicly in 1927 and apologized for any harm he might have done, but it is fairly certain that this was no more than a cowardly way out of a libel suit he was about to lose.

In his apology, Ford claimed no knowledge of the articles and no responsibility for their having appeared in his newspaper. But his personal animus toward Jews, views also shared by his friend, Thomas Edison, is beyond doubt. As a farm boy he was exposed to American populism, a movement that often bordered on the openly antisemitic and that blamed financiers and middlemen for the woes of the farmer. Ford was, above all else, the Great Simplifier, the man who sought and found shortcut solutions to problems of industrial production. It is not surprising that antisemitism, which proffered the simplest solutions to the thorniest problems of modern life, should appeal to such a man.

Ford did not write the articles in the *Dearborn Independent* himself but rather relied on others, including his German-born private secretary, Ernest Liebold, to arrange the details, much as he left actual production of the Model T to his ingenious engineers. The tone of the articles differs markedly from their European models. Matter of fact and not overtly fanatical, with a pretense of discussing the pros and cons of the issues, they nevertheless left little doubt as to Ford's beliefs.

In the piece reproduced as Document 16, the leitmotifs of forty years of European antisemitism translate easily into the American idiom. Jewish wire-pullers engineered America's entry into the war against Germany. The veiled threat of popular violence against Jews appears in the form of a pious warning, as it did in Wilhelm Marr's pamphlet and the "Antisemites' Petition" (Documents 6 and 10). Yet unaware of any contradiction, the author laments the toleration and insouciance of the Gentile world, virtues the Jews are always ready to exploit with their ruthless machinations. Russian influences also contributed to these exposés, when one of the ubiquitous White Russian émigrés presented Ford and Liebold with a copy of the

Protocols. Phony Zionism, too, enters the argument as it did forty years earlier in the speech of the Hungarian antisemite, Győző Istóczy (Document 7). The author of the article pretends to favor a Jewish homeland while berating highly assimilated Jews for not really wanting to leave the fleshpots of America.

Despite his ignominious retreat in 1927, Ford helped establish the respectability of antisemitic attacks in American life. Yet it was not until the depths of the Great Depression of the 1930s that political antisemitism assumed menacing forms. One of its briefly successful proponents was Father Charles E. Coughlin, a Catholic priest. A popular radio preacher in Ford's Detroit, Coughlin railed against international communism and greedy capitalists while championing a living wage for the little man. His hand-picked presidential candidate in the 1936 elections received only 900,000 out of 46 million votes, but his own popularity did not diminish. In the late 1930s his large audience—he was by then broadcasting over the CBS network—heard him describe antisemitism as just another variant in the crusade against communism. His Christian Front, a Brooklyn-based group, "fought communism" with storm trooper tactics against Jews in major cities. In March 1942, while Jews were perishing in the death camps, Coughlin declared that Hitler's persecution was justified because it had been one of international Jewry's goals to involve the United States in another war against Germany. Shortly thereafter, and before the federal government intervened, the Catholic church silenced him.

Another antisemitic appeal, this time emanating from the Far Right, was that of Gerald L. K. Smith. Smith began his career as an aide to the populist governor of Louisiana, Huey Long, but shifted his efforts to Michigan and his politics to the defense of capitalism. He, too, made a bid for direct political influence, but his campaign for a Senate seat, first as a Republican and then as an Independent, failed miserably. Nevertheless, his magazine, *The Cross and the Flag,* financed by big business—he claimed personal friendship with Ford—disseminated his antisemitic views to a wide audience, especially in rural America. He remained a fringe figure in radical rightist politics until his death in 1976.

Although antisemitism, as practiced by these individuals, failed to penetrate established American political institutions, it helps explain the callous disregard of the United States for the destruction of European Jews during World War II. The preconditions for this tragedy were already in place before the Nazis came to power, and they did not only apply to Jews. American nativism, a powerful trend in the nation's political history, had resulted in the passage of restrictive immigration laws in 1924. The massive unemployment of the depression further reinforced Americans' fears about an influx of aliens ready to take their jobs.

But ancient suspicions of Jews, legitimized by leaders in the business community and the churches, also helped close America's doors to those who could have escaped the Nazis as late as 1942. A public-opinion poll of 1939 revealed that 66 percent of respondents objected even to a one-time exception to immigration quotas in order to allow the rescue of 10,000 children. It has been shown conclusively that the official government policy of the United States worked to prevent immigration of Jews, even after irrefutable proof of their attempted extermination was at hand. Not until 1944, when President Roosevelt faced another election campaign, did he move to create a governmental agency to deal specifically with saving Jews. By this time, millions had already been killed.

For Further Reading

On Ford, Albert Lee, *Henry Ford and the Jews* (New York, 1980); on antisemitism in the United States, Michael N. Dobrowski, *The Tarnished Dream: The Basis of American Anti-Semitism* (Westport, Conn., 1979).

16. Henry Ford
"The International Jew" (1920)

Does a Jewish World Program Exist?
An Introduction to Documents that Are Now Being
Circulated as the Jewish World Program

In all the explanations of anti-Jewish feeling which modern Jewish spokesmen make, these three alleged causes are commonly given—these three and no more: religious prejudice, economic jealousy, social antipathy. Whether the Jew knows it or not, every Gentile knows that on his side of the Jewish Question no religious prejudice exists. Economic jealousy may exist, at least to this extent, that his uniform success has exposed the Jew to much scrutiny. A few Jewish spokesmen seek to turn this scrutiny by denying that the Jew is pre-eminent in finance, but this is loyalty in extremity. The finances of the world are in the control of Jews; their decisions and their devices are themselves our economic law. But because a people excels us in finance is no sufficient reason for calling them to the bar of public judgment. If they are more intellectually able, more persistently industrious than we are, if they are endowed with faculties which have been denied us as an inferior or slower race, that is no reason for our requiring them to give an account of themselves. Economic jealousy may explain some of the anti-Jewish feeling; it cannot account for the presence of the Jewish Question except as the hidden causes of Jewish financial success may become a minor element of the larger problem. And as for social antipathy—there are many more undesirable Gentiles in the world than there are undesirable Jews, for the simple reason that there are more Gentiles.

Source: From *The Dearborn Independent,* July 10, 1920.

None of the Jewish spokesmen today mention the political cause, or if they come within suggestive distance of it, they limit and localize it. It is not a question of the patriotism of the Jew, though this too is very widely questioned in all countries. You hear it in England, in France, in Germany, in Poland, in Russia, in Romania—and, with a shock, you hear it in the United States. Books have been written, reports published and scattered abroad, statistics skillfully set forth for the purpose of showing that the Jew does his part for the country in which he resides; and yet the fact remains that in spite of these most zealous and highly sponsored campaigns, the opposite assertion is stronger and lives longer. The Jews who did their duty in the armies of Liberty, and did it doubtless from true-hearted love and allegiance, have not been able to overcome the impression made upon officers and men and civilians by those who did not.

But that is not what is here meant as the political element in the Jewish Question. To understand why the Jew should think less of the nationalities of the world than do those who comprise them is not difficult. The Jew's history is one of wandering among them all. Considering living individuals only, there is no race of people now upon the planet who have lived in so many places, among so many peoples as have the Jewish masses. They have a clearer world-sense than any other people, because the world has been their path. And they think in world terms more than any nationally cloistered people could. The Jew can be absolved if he does not enter into national loyalties and prejudices with the same intensity as the natives; the Jew has been for centuries a cosmopolitan. While under a flag he may be correct in the conduct required of him as a citizen or resident, inevitably he has a view of flags which can hardly be shared by the man who has known but one flag.

The political element inheres in the fact that the Jews form a nation in the midst of the nations. Some of their spokesmen, particularly in America, deny that, but the genius of the Jew himself has always put these spokesmen's zeal to shame. And why this fact of nationhood should be so strenuously denied is not always clear. It may be that when Israel is brought to see that her mission in the world is not to be achieved by means of the Golden Calf, her very cosmopolitanism with regard to the world and her inescapable nationalistic integrity with regard to herself will together prove a great and serviceable factor in bringing about human unity, which the total Jewish tendency at the present time is doing much to prevent. It is not the fact that the Jews remain a nation in the midst of the nations; it is the use made of that inescapable status, which the world has found reprehensible. The nations have tried to reduce the Jew to unity with themselves; attempts toward the same end have been made by the Jews themselves; but destiny seems to have marked them out to continuous nationhood. Both the Jews and the World will have to accept that fact, find the good prophecy in it, and seek the channels for its fulfillment.

Theodor Herzl, one of the greatest of the Jews, was perhaps the farthest-seeing public exponent of the philosophy of Jewish existence that modern generations have known. And he was never in doubt of the existence of the Jewish nation. Indeed, he proclaimed its existence on every occasion. He said, *"We are a people—One people."*

He clearly saw that what he called the Jewish Question was political. In his introduction to "The Jewish State" he says, "I believe that I understand anti-Semitism, which is really a highly complex movement. I consider it from a Jewish standpoint, yet without fear or hatred. I believe that I can see what elements there are in it of vulgar sport, of common trade jealousy, of inherited prejudice, of religious intolerance and also of a pretended self-defense. I think the Jewish Question is no more a social than a religious one, notwithstanding that it sometimes takes these and other forms. *It is a national question, which can only be solved by making it a political world-question* to be discussed and controlled by the civilized nations of the world in council."

Not only did Herzl declare that the Jews formed a nation, but when questioned by Major Evans Gordon before the British Royal Commission on Alien Immigration in August 1902, Dr. Herzl said: "I will give you my definition of a nation, and you can add the adjective 'Jewish.' A nation is, in my mind, an historical group of men of recognizable cohesion held together by a common enemy. That is in my view a nation. *Then if you add to that the word 'Jewish' you have what I understand to be the Jewish nation."*

Also, in relating the action of this Jewish nation to the world, Dr. Herzl wrote—"When we sink, we become a revolutionary proletariat, the subordinate officers of the revolutionary party; when we rise, there rises also our terrible power of the purse."

This view, which appears to be the true view in that it is the view which has been longest sustained in Jewish thought, is brought out also by Lord Eustace Percy, and republished, apparently with approval, by the *Canadian Jewish Chronicle*. It will repay a careful reading:

"Liberalism and Nationalism, with a flourish of trumpets, threw open the doors of the ghetto and offered equal citizenship to the Jew. The Jew passed out into the Western World, saw the power and the glory of it, used it and enjoyed it, laid his hand indeed upon the nerve centers of its civilization, guided, directed, and exploited it, and then . . . refused the offer. . . . Moreover—and this is a remarkable thing—the Europe of nationalism and liberalism, of scientific government and democratic equality is more intolerable to him than the old oppressions and persecutions of despotism. . . . In the increasing consolidation of the western nations, it is no longer possible to reckon on complete toleration. . . .

"In a world of completely organized territorial sovereignties he (the Jew) has only two possible cities of refuge: he must either pull down the pillars of the whole national state system or he must create a territorial sovereignty of his own. In this perhaps lies the explanation both of Jewish Bolshevism and of Zionism, for at this moment Eastern Jewry seems to hover uncertainly between the two.

"In Eastern Europe Bolshevism and Zionism often seem to grow side by side, just as Jewish influence molded Republican and Socialist thought throughout the nineteenth century, down to the Young Turk revolution in Constantinople hardly more than a decade ago—*not because the Jew cares for the positive side of radical philosophy, not because he desires to be a partaker in Gentile nationalism or Gentile democracy, but because no existing Gentile system of government is ever anything but distasteful to him.*"

All that is true, and Jewish thinkers of the more fearless type always recognize it as true. *The Jew is against the Gentile scheme of things.* He is, when he gives his tendencies full sway, a Republican as against the monarchy, a Socialist as against the republic, and a Bolshevist as against Socialism.

What are the causes of this disruptive activity? First, his essential lack of democracy. Jewish nature is autocratic. Democracy is all right for the rest of the world, but the Jew wherever he is found forms an aristocracy of one sort or another. Democracy is merely a tool of a word which Jewish agitators use to raise themselves to the ordinary level in places where they are oppressed below it; but having reached the common level they immediately make efforts for special privileges, as being entitled to them—a process of which the late Peace Conference [ending World War I] will remain the most startling example. The Jews today are the only people whose special and extraordinary privileges are written into the world's Treaty of Peace. But more of that at another time.

No one now pretends to deny, except a few spokesmen who really do not rule the thought of the Jews but are set forth for the sole benefit of influencing Gentile thought, that the socially and economically disruptive elements abroad in the world today are not only manned but also moneyed by Jewish interests. For a long time this fact was held in suspense owing to the vigorous denial of the Jews and the lack of information on the part of those agencies of publicity to which the public had looked for its information. But now the facts are coming forth. Herzl's words are being proved to be true—"when we sink, we become a revolutionary proletariat, *the subordinate officers of the revolutionary party*"—and these words were first published in English in 1896, 24 years ago.

Just now these tendencies are working in two directions, one for the tearing down of the Gentile states all over the world, the other for the establishment of a Jewish state in Palestine. The latter project has the best wishes of the whole world, but it is far from having the best wishes of the whole, or even the larger part of Jewry. The Zionist party makes a great deal of noise, but it is really an unrepresentative minority. It can scarcely be designated as more than an unusually ambitious colonization scheme. It is doubtless serving, however, as a very useful public screen for the carrying on of secret activities. International Jews, the controllers of the world's governmental and financial power, may meet anywhere, at any time, in wartime or peacetime, and by giving out that they are only considering the ways and means of opening up Palestine to the Jews, they easily escape the suspicion of being together on any other business. The Allies and enemies of the Gentile nations at war thus met and were not molested. It was at a Zionist conference—the sixth, held in 1903—that the recent war was exactly predicted, its progress and outcome indicated, and the relation of the Jews to the Peace Treaty outlined.

That is to say, though Jewish nationalism exists, its enshrinement in a state to be set up in Palestine is not the project that is engaging the whole Jewish nation now. The Jews will not move to Palestine just yet; it may be said that they will not move at all merely because of the Zionist movement. Quite another motive will be the cause of the exodus out of the Gentile nations, when the time for that exodus fully comes.

As Donald A. Cameron, late British Consul-General at Alexandria, a man fully in sympathy with Zionism and much quoted in the Jewish press, says: "The Jewish immigrants (into Palestine) will tire of taking in one another's washing at 3 percent, of winning one another's money in the family, and their sons will hasten by train and steamer to win 10 percent in Egypt. . . . The Jew by himself in Palestine will eat his head off; he will kick his stable to pieces." Undoubtedly the time for the exodus—at least the motive for the exodus—is not yet here.

The political aspect of the Jewish Question which is now engaging at least three of the great nations—France, Great Britain and the United States—has to do with matters of the present organization of the Jewish nation. Must it wait until it reaches Palestine to have a State, or is it an organized State now? Does Jewry know what it is doing? Has it a "foreign policy" with regard to Gentiles? Has it a department which is executing that foreign policy? Has this Jewish State, visible or invisible, if it exists, a head? Has it a Council of State? And if any of these things is so, who is aware of it?

The first impulsive answer of the Gentile mind would be "No" to all these questions—it is a Gentile habit to answer impulsively. Never having been trained in secrets or invisible unity, the Gentile immediately concludes that such things cannot be, if for no other reason than that they have not crossed his path and advertised themselves.

The questions, however, answered thus, require some explanation of the circumstances which are visible to all men. If there is no deliberate combination of Jews in the world, then the control which they have achieved and the uniformity of the policies which they follow must be the simple result, not of deliberate decisions, but of a similar nature in all of them working out the same way. Thus, we might say that as a love for adventure on the water drove the Britisher forth, so it made him the world's great colonist. Not that he deliberately sat down with himself and in formal manner resolved that he would become a colonizer, but the natural outworking of his genius resulted that way. But would this be a sufficient account of the British Empire?

Doubtless the Jews have the genius to do, wherever they go, the things in which we see them excel. But does this account for the relations which exist between the Jews of every country, for their world councils, for their amazing foreknowledge of stupendous events which break with shattering surprise on the rest of the world, for the smoothness and preparedness with which they appear, at a given time in Paris, with a world program on which they all agree?

The world has long suspected—at first only a few, then the secret departments of the governments, next the intellectuals among the people, now more and more the common people themselves—that not only are the Jews a nation distinct from all the other nations and mysteriously unable to sink their nationality by any means they or the world may adopt to this end, but that they also constitute a state; that they are nationally conscious, not only, but consciously united for a common defense and for a common purpose. Revert to Theodor Herzl's definition of the Jewish nation as held together by a common enemy, and then reflect that this common enemy is the Gentile world. Does this people which knows itself to be a nation remain loosely unorganized in the face of that fact? It would hardly be like Jewish astuteness in other fields. When you see how closely the Jews are united by various organizations in the United States, and when you see how with practiced hand they bring those organizations to bear as if with tried confidence in their pressure, it is at least not inconceivable that what can be done with a country can be done, or has been done, between all the countries where Jews live.

At any rate, in the *American Hebrew* of June 25, 1920, Herman Bernstein writes this: "About a year ago a representative of the Department of Justice submitted to me a copy of the manuscript of 'The Jewish Peril' by Professor Nilus,[1] and asked for my opinion of the work. He said that the manuscript was supposed to contain 'protocols' of the Wise Men of Zion and was supposed to have been read by Dr. Herzl at a secret conference of the Zionist Congress at Basel. He expressed the opinion that the work was probably that of Dr. Theodor Herzl. . . . He said that some American Senators who had seen the manuscript were amazed to find that so many years ago a scheme had been elaborated by the Jews which is now being carried out, and that Bolshevism had been planned years ago by Jews who sought to destroy the world."

This quotation is made merely to put on record the fact that it was a representative of the Department of Justice of the United States Government, who introduced this document to Mr. Bernstein, and expressed a certain opinion upon it, namely, "that the work was probably that of Dr.

---

[1]Sergei Nilus (1862–1930) was not a professor but rather a bankrupt landowner who took to the writing of mystical religious tracts. He received the forgery, probably from a functionary in the Okhrana, the tsarist secret police, and inserted it into the third edition of his book, *The Great in the Small: Antichrist Considered as an Imminent Political Possibility* (1905). Nilus, married to a former lady-in-waiting to the tsarina, moved among the faith healers, "holy idiots," and charlatans who battened off the imperial court. Like these, he hoped to win the favor of Tsar Nicholas II and with this in mind presented the volume to him. It was Nilus' version of the *Protocols* that came to the West in the aftermath of the revolution.

Theodor Herzl." Also that "some American senators" were amazed to note the comparison between what a publication of the year 1905 proposed and what the year 1920 revealed.

The incident is all the more preoccupying because it occurred by action of the representative of a government which today is very largely in the hands of, or under the influence of, Jewish interests. It is more than probable that as soon as the activity became known, the investigator was stopped. But it is equally probable that whatever orders may have been given and apparently obeyed, the investigation may not have stopped.

The United States Government was a little late in the matter, however. At least four other world powers had preceded it, some by many years. A copy of the *Protocols* was deposited in the British Museum and bears on it the stamp of that institution, "August 10, 1906." The notes themselves probably date from 1896, or the year of the utterances previously quoted from Dr. Herzl. The first Zionist Congress convened in 1897.

The document was published in England recently under auspices that challenged attention for it, in spite of the unfortunate title under which it appeared. Eyre and Spottiswoode are the appointed printers to the British Government, and it was they who brought out the pamphlet. It was as if the Government Printing Office at Washington should issue them in this country. While there was the usual outcry by the Jewish press, the London *Times* in a review pronounced all the Jewish counter-attacks "unsatisfactory."[2]

The Times noticed what will probably be the case in this country, also—that the Jewish defenders leave the text of the *Protocols* alone, while they lay heavy emphasis on the fact of their anonymity. When they refer to the substance of the document at all there is one form of words which recurs very often—"it is the work of a criminal or a mad man."

The *Protocols*, without name attached, appearing for the most part in manuscripts here and there, laboriously copied out from hand to hand, being sponsored by no authority that was willing to stand behind it, assiduously studied in the secret departments of the governments and passed from one to another among higher officials, have lived on and on, increasing in power and prestige by the sheer force of their contents. A marvelous achievement for either a criminal or a madman! The only evidence it has is that which it carries within it, and that internal evidence is, as the London *Times* points out, the point on which attention is to be focused, and

---

[2]Eyre and Spottiswoode was indeed a prestigious publisher but not the same as the Government Printing Office. It did not therefore represent the official views of the king or his government, as the antisemites averred, when it published the English version under the title *The Jewish Peril*. *The Times, The Spectator,* and *The Morning Post* devoted long articles to the book and, while expressing misgivings about its authenticity, lent their influence to the dissemination of the forgery. In August 1921, *The Times* ran three page-1 debunking articles on the *Protocols*. This proved definitive in ending the mainstream career of the forgery in Great Britain. Even the British Union of Fascists during the 1930s found the *Protocols* too thoroughly discredited to be useful.

the very point from which Jewish effort has been expended to draw us away.

The interest of the *Protocols* at this time is their bearing on the questions: Have the Jews an organized world system? What is its policy? How is it being worked?

These questions all receive full attention in the *Protocols*. Whosoever was the mind that conceived them possessed a knowledge of human nature, of history and of statecraft which is dazzling in its brilliant completeness, and terrible in the objects to which it turns its powers. Neither a madman nor an intentional criminal, but more likely a super-mind mastered by devotion to a people and a faith could be the author, if indeed one mind alone conceived them. It is too terribly real for fiction, too well-sustained for speculation, too deep in its knowledge of the secret springs of life for forgery.

Jewish attacks upon it thus far make much of the fact that it came out of Russia. That is hardly true. It came *by way of Russia*. It was incorporated in a Russian book published about 1905 by a Professor Nilus, who attempted to interpret the *Protocols* by events then going forward in Russia. This publication and interpretation gave it a Russian tinge which has been useful to Jewish propagandists in this country and England, because these same propagandists have been very successful in establishing in Anglo-Saxon mentalities a certain atmosphere of thought surrounding the idea of Russia and Russians. One of the biggest humbugs ever foisted on the world has been that foisted by Jewish propagandists, principally on the American public, with regard to the temper and genius of the truly Russian people. So, to intimate that the *Protocols* are Russian, is partially to discredit them.

The internal evidence makes it clear that the *Protocols* were not written by a Russian, nor originally in the Russian language, nor under the influence of Russian conditions. But they found their way to Russia and were first published there. They have been found by diplomatic officers in manuscript in all parts of the world. Wherever Jewish power is able to do so, it has suppressed them, sometimes under the supreme penalty.

Their persistence is a fact which challenges the mind. Jewish apologists may explain that persistence on the ground that the *Protocols* feed the anti-Semitic temper and therefore are preserved for that service. Certainly there was no wide nor deep anti-Semitic temper in the United States to be fed or that felt the greed for agreeable lies to keep itself alive. The progress of the *Protocols* in the United States can only be explained on the ground that they supply light and give meaning to certain previously observed facts, and that this light and meaning is so startling as to give a certain standing and importance to these otherwise unaccredited documents. Sheer lies do not live long; their power soon dies. These *Protocols* are more alive than ever. They have penetrated higher places than ever before. They have compelled a more serious attitude to them than ever before.

The *Protocols* would not be more worthy of study if they bore, say, the name of Theodor Herzl. Their anonymity does not decrease their power any more than the omission of a painter's signature detracts from the art value of a painting. Indeed, the *Protocols* are better without a known source. For if it were definitely known that in France or Switzerland in the year 1896, or thereabouts, a group of International Jews, assembled in conference, drew up a program of world conquest it would still have to be shown that such a program was more than a mere vagary, that it was confirmed at large by efforts to fulfill it. The *Protocols* are a World Program—there is no doubt anywhere of that. Whose program, is stated within the articles themselves. But as for outer confirmation, which would be the more valuable—a signature, or six signatures, or twenty signatures, or a 25-year unbroken line of effort fulfilling the program?

The point of interest for this and other countries is not that a "criminal or madman" conceived such a program, but that, when conceived, this program found means of getting itself fulfilled in its most important particulars. The document is comparatively unimportant; the conditions to which it calls attention are of a very high degree of importance.

Antisemitism in Poland

Chronicles dating from the tenth century, the earliest to mention Poland, also mention the presence there of Jewish traders. From the twelfth to the early part of the sixteenth century, Jews in ever-greater number fled persecution and pauperization in central Europe to take up residence in more-hospitable Poland. Polish princes and later the rulers of the kingdom of Poland invited the emigration of Germans and Jews, experienced urbanites, to stimulate economic activity. Lagging behind economic developments in the West, Poland was inhabited almost exclusively by a landholding nobility and a toiling peasantry. The Germans planned towns, and Jews were encouraged to settle in them, in order to ply their trades and thus increase the revenues of those who ruled.

It was the Jews' middleman functions, such as moneylending, estate management, tax collection, and petty trade, that caused Polish peasants to experience them as oppressors. Later an emergent Polish merchant class in the towns resented them as foreign competitors with unfair advantages. Their adherence to a heretical religion in a land where Christianity took root slowly also won them the active enmity of the Catholic church. At various times, churchmen attempted to segregate them in special Jewish quarters in the towns and by means of distinguishing hats or armbands. As elsewhere in Europe, accusations of ritual murder and desecration of the host, often obscuring economic conflicts, produced periodic outbursts of violence and pillage.

Essentially powerless against force, Jews sought and received protection from the kings and magnates who benefited from their skills. From the fourteenth century, they came under the direct jurisdiction of the Polish kings, to whose treasury they paid fees and special taxes. In exchange they received protection from their Christian debtors, recognition of the inviolability of their person and property, freedom of movement and residence, and permission to lend money at interest. This privileged status provided an uncertain security, but it also widened the gulf separating the Jewish and Polish populations.

In response to hatred over the centuries, and by their own choice, Jews withdrew further and further into their own closed world. By the middle of the seventeenth century, the half-million Jews of Poland (5 percent of the population) had created a self-contained and elaborate culture centering on the preservation and practice of Judaism. They continued to speak a medieval German dialect (Yiddish) rather than Polish. Granted a large measure of autonomy by their protectors, they developed a complex network of charitable, educational, judicial, and religious institutions. By the end of the eighteenth century, they had withdrawn from the violence of Poland's urban centers to small towns and villages, where 80 percent of them now lived in increasing poverty. With rare exceptions, Jews and Poles lived separate existences in mutually hostile communities. Their only points of contact were in the sphere of business and the occasional massacre.

Both populations suffered from the steady decline of the once-great Commonwealth. In the last quarter of the eighteenth century, Poland's powerful neighbors—Prussia, Austria, and Russia—ended the country's independent existence and partitioned its territories among themselves. Jews and Poles fared sometimes better, sometimes worse, under one or another of these new rulers. Although Jews by and large accepted the new conditions with passivity, the Polish nobility and intelligentsia never lost the memory of past greatness or hope for the recovery of political sovereignty. They staged bloody and cruelly repressed revolts in 1794, 1830, 1846, 1848, and 1863.

At the end of World War I, the resurrection of the Polish state had won the sympathy of a great many other nations. Given the dire situation it faced, however, Poland needed more than sympathy. It required farsighted leadership and national consensus in order to overcome daunting problems. Its territory ravaged by contending armies, still underdeveloped industrially and agriculturally, and troubled by regional differences as a result of the partitions, Poland was also a multinational ethnic state whose leaders were either reluctant to recognize this fact or unable to frame a workable policy for dealing effectively with it.

The state that came into existence in 1918 contained sizable minorities of Ukrainians, Byelorussians, Lithuanians, Germans, and Jews. Coerced by the victorious Allies in 1919 into signing a Minorities' Treaty that guaranteed the civil rights and a degree of cultural autonomy to these groups, Poland's resentful political leaders generally ignored the agreement and pursued a policy that boiled down to "Poland for the Poles." Although the great national leader and former socialist Józef Piłsudski espoused a policy of pluralism, Poland's relations with all its minorities, a third of the population of the state, remained a paralyzing weakness in the interwar years. Physical clashes and impassioned rhetoric sapped the energies that might have been better used for much-needed socioeconomic and educational reforms.

It is fair to say that, unlike many other European countries, the new Poland had a real, rather than an imaginary Jewish problem in 1918. During the interwar era, Jews constituted approximately 10 percent of the total population, but this figure tells only part of the story. In the second half of the nineteenth century, Jews had begun to move back to the cities, where they became the major force. Nearly one-third of the urban population was Jewish, and in the particularly backward eastern regions, the proportion was closer to one half. Predominantly lower middle class, the Jewish community also had some wealthy and highly visible industrialists and bankers. Jews were "overrepresented" in the intelligentsia and the professions. They provided 56 percent of the doctors, 34 percent of the lawyers, and 22 percent of the journalists. The large Jewish working class was concentrated in small crafts, clothing, and food enterprises but was nearly absent from heavy industry and farming. Although many in Poland complained that Jews dominated the economy, that economy was a poor one, and the great majority of Jews there were among the poorest in Europe.

A reasonable assumption to be drawn from the censuses of 1921 and 1931, which asked about language and religious identities, is that most Jews regarded themselves as part of a separate nationality. Although a sizable minority advocated assimilation, the great mass of the nearly three million Jews identified their native tongue as Yiddish. Although loyal to the new Polish state, various Jewish groups had developed their own political agendas. These included formal guarantees of cultural autonomy and resistance to Polonization, particularly in education. A small number of Jews, without significant support among the Jewish population at large, nonetheless played a major role in the Polish Communist party, which rejected the idea of an independent Poland.

To those schooled in the nationalist struggle and who defined Poland as rightfully belonging only to the Poles, the Jews appeared as anything but loyal. One such person was Roman Dmowski (1864–1939), who presents his views on the Jewish question in the following document. The political rival of Pilsudski and a dedicated antisemite, he led the National Democratic party, published the mass-circulation *Gazeta Polska,* and even before the war had advocated the social and economic boycott of Jews and other national minorities. Dmowski stood for a powerful centralized government that recognized the supremacy of the Polish nation and the Catholic church over national and religious minorities.

What did Dmowski object to in the Jews? Primarily, he saw them as always having been inimical to an independent Poland. Without explicit proof, he accuses them of having collaborated with Poland's enemies in the partitions of the eighteenth century. Even though some Jews had fought in the Polish rebellions, the Jewish population as a whole had not shed their blood for the rebirth of the state to nearly the same degree as Poles. Although Jews lived in all parts of Poland and could not, unlike the other minorities, look to neighboring states for possible aid, Dmowski nevertheless considered them a great danger. He interpreted the attempts of some Jews to mold the Polish state to their own needs as treasonous.

While mindful of the breakdown in Jewish consensus—the Jews of Poland were deeply divided over the issues of Zionism, socialism, orthodoxy, and assimilation—Dmowski dismisses this diversity as only apparent. Instead, he sees an all-important "uniformity of [racial] instincts." With close relations to Russia before and during the war, Dmowski also registers the influence of the *Protocols of the Elders of Zion* (Document 15) on his thinking. He exaggerates the power and influence of the Jews, perceives a monolithic "fixed principle of Jewish policy," in spite of his own warnings to the contrary, and states as an indisputable fact, "according to all data," the existence of a plot aiming at nothing less than world conquest. He unmasks lackeys and dupes of the Jews in high places. Bismarck, Kaiser Wilhelm II, Lloyd George, and Wilson are their tools. The diplomatic activities of individual Jews and Jewish groups especially anger him. Yet their casualties during and immediately after the war, when they stood between the mutually antagonistic nationalities of eastern Europe and were seen as traitors by all of them, does not result in an obvious deduction: they were powerless rather than powerful. One suspects that it is the very fact of Jewish existence that Dmowski finds objectionable, at least on Polish soil, and perhaps anywhere else they are allowed to conspire.

Under Dmowski's leadership, the National Democrats advocated a state policy aimed at weakening the Jews' economic influence and encouraging their emigration from Poland. Although the party denounced violence, there was much of it, particularly in the late 1930s, when antisemitism formed a convenient bridge between the Nationalists and the successors to Pilsudski (who died in 1935). Their response to the lingering depression was to wage economic war on Jews, and although this did little to improve the lot of Poles, it seemed to legitimize outrages against Jewish businessmen, professionals, and students. Worse, a small party appeared further to the Right than the Nationalists. Taking inspiration from the Nazi persecution of Jews in Germany, it fomented much of the violence, constantly goaded the government to take stronger anti-Jewish measures, and spoke openly of murder.

The utter destruction of Polish Jewry was the work of Nazis, not of Poles. Although hatred of Jews was widespread in Poland, it is difficult to imagine that any but their most visceral enemies would have welcomed the Holocaust. What Polish antisemitism contributed to the fate of Polish Jewry is a moot question. Did the decades of anti-Jewish pronouncements by many (but not all) authoritative voices in church and state persuade the Nazis to locate the machinery of death on Polish soil? Probably not. This decision had to do with logistics, the location of railway lines, and the proximity of major Jewish population groups.

Despite an omnipresent antisemitism, individual Poles, even Polish antisemites, at the risk of almost certain death, sheltered and rescued Jews. But these documented cases of humanity stand out all the more prominently because they were so rare. The far more normal response of Poles was indifference to Jews caught up in the Holocaust. Whatever its historical origins and whatever its connection to Polish antisemitism, that indifference translated into the largest loss of Jewish life of any European country, in both absolute numbers (three million) and percentage (91).

For Further Reading

Ezra Mendelsohn, *The Jews of East Central Europe between the Wars* (Bloomington, Ind., 1983). For an interesting post-Holocaust Jewish-Polish dialogue, see Chimen Abramsky et al., eds., *The Jews in Poland* (Oxford, 1986).

17. Roman Dmowski
The Jews and the War (1924)

Translated by John Kulczycki

[Dmowski introduces this section on the last phase of World War I and the fate of Poland by mentioning the emergence of a new and dangerous factor, "a secretly organized sectarianism," the Jews. He begins the discussion with warnings about the complexity of the Jewish problem and its critical significance for understanding the war and the peace settlement that followed.]

I do not have space here for such a wide treatment of Jewish affairs, moreover I do not feel called upon to do this. I never had time to occupy myself especially with researching them, although they greatly interested me both because of their relations to Polish affairs and because of the role they played in the development of European civilization. In so far as I came to know Jewish affairs, I became convinced that above all the superficiality with which they are treated is a great danger.

Next, those who express themselves about the Jewish question commit in general one of two errors: either they do not appreciate the significance of the Jews at this moment of history and present the character of their participation in the lives of the nations in a false light, involuntarily or consciously lulling the attention of opinion in this important matter; or they overestimate it, presenting Jews as an all-powerful, demonic power, directing the fate of mankind, acting with unheard-of effectiveness according to some very cleverly thought out plan, and moving all other forces in the world like pawns.

Based on my observations and on my experience in this respect, I believe that this uniformity and effectiveness, which one sees universally in the activity of Jews, is the result not so much of some cleverly thought out and cleverly executed plan, as of the uniformity and consistency of this ancient Asiatic people, which would fill us less with admiration if we would in general know ancient Asia better. In this respect Jews are not an exception among ancient peoples. The difference is only that while the latter sit in Asia within their racial territory and constitute either states or colonies of European states, [the Jews] do not have their own native seat and roam from time immemorial in other countries, having taken a liking to countries of European civilization almost since the beginning of our era. . . .

This uniformity of instincts and consistency, being the result of training of a countless number of generations in uniform theocratic institutions,

---

Source: From Roman Dmowski, *Polityka Polska i Odbudowanie Państwa* [The politics and reconstruction of the Polish state], 3d ed. (Hanover, 1947), 1:227–33. This series of articles originally appeared in 1924.

saves Jews from their conspicuous quarrelsomeness and the significant divergence of their conscious aims, and finally from their known vanity and pride, which often dictates very imprudent political steps, entailing consequences fatal for them.

With regard to the political aims of Jews, which played a role in the Great War, we must say that although they were not entirely uniform, nevertheless the evolution of these aims in the years preceding the war reduced them, to a significant degree, to a common denominator.

It is known to all that in the nineteenth century the main aim of the Jews was entrance into European societies, acquisition of European culture and knowledge, adoption of customs and ways of life of the nations among which they lived, transformation of themselves into Frenchmen, Englishmen, Germans, Poles, and so forth. Yet, uniformity of instincts and racial consistency allowed them to preserve in all this the bonds of a close-knit union, not only among Jews who are assimilating and often depriving themselves of religious beliefs and Jews of the ancient type, the so-called "orthodox," but also among Jews of all countries. As an expression of the latter arose the great organization *Alliance Israélite Universelle*.[1]

[During the nineteenth century] Jews amassed great wealth and acquired a significant role in the social and political life of countries. In addition, the amassing of wealth quickly increased their role as a result of the material dependence on them by wide circles of European societies. Then ensued a period, in which, stronger than ever, there ruled the aim of rendering the social hierarchy a hierarchy exclusively of property, in which mainly money helped in climbing the social ladder, in which for money it was possible to buy abilities and human convictions, in which consequently those who disposed of money had at their service numerous ranks of people working for them. This explains those legions of defenders of Judaism and of fighters for its interests, which arose in the nineteenth century in all European countries. To these were added secret international organizations, in which Jews always had their defenders and in which, at a certain time, according to all data, they held executive positions. [This] was facilitated by the fact that they did not really belong to any nation and lived among all of them; they were created, as if by design, for the main role in all international undertakings.

The last quarter of the previous century brought the beginnings of new aims among Jews. In Central Europe, the terrain of the sharpest national conflicts, nationalism became the ruling current in the life of peoples, and here the nationalist ideology reached its highest development. Numerous in this part of the world, Jews came under its influence, and there arose among them the aim of becoming a separate nation on the European model. Since a nation in the European sense must above all have its territory, so there appeared among Jews the aim of acquiring their own national

---

[1] See note 9, Document 6.

territory. Their eyes fell above all on Palestine, where once before in history they had ruled, and hence the Jewish national current took the name of Zionism. Yet Palestine is a minuscule country and in relation to its productive means fairly populated, although not by Jews. Thus, emigration to Palestine did not have a chance of development on a wider scale, and Zionists began to look for other territories besides it, which they could colonize and conquer. There was talk of Uganda; an attempt was made to colonize Argentina, but without success.

Meanwhile there developed a stubborn battle between generally poor idealists, as the Zionists were, and those representing financial power. Englishmen, Americans, Germans, and Frenchmen of Jewish faith were not thinking of leaving the Parises, Londons, Berlins, and New Yorks, with everything they offered. [They] considered Zionism an absurd fantasy.

Another direction that evolved from Zionism appealed to [these Jews] more: organizing the [East Central European] Jews where they lived in larger masses for the purpose of forming them into a nation on the spot and winning for them rights of a separate nation. Since Jews in Eastern Europe, having come mainly from Germany, speak a transmuted German dialect, so-called Yiddish, or as we say, Jewish jargon, isolating them as a linguistic nation did not pose a difficulty. In this language they even began to develop literary works and created a rather significant press.

Lately a current aiming at reconciling all modern aims with the biblical tradition of "the chosen people" has begun to dominate. It recognized the aim of controlling Palestine, not for the purpose of gathering all Jews there and thus freeing other countries from them, but in order to build there the spiritual center of the Jews and to create the operational basis for action throughout the world.[2] Palestine was never the fatherland of the Jews because they never had a fatherland, but they made Jerusalem their spiritual center; recovering this center along with controlling Palestine, with its non-Jewish population, is the necessary goal of this new current. Yet, at the same time, [this new current] bid them not to forget that they are supposed to "possess the earth," that therefore they must be everywhere, and everywhere gain positions and organize their influences.

Thus understood, all previously contradictory Jewish aims fell into line and could agree in [this ultimate] task of Jewish policy. With such an

---

[2]Dmowski here invests with sinister meaning the cultural Zionism advocated by the Russian Jew Asher Ginsberg (1856–1927) who wrote under the name Ahad Ha'am ("one of the people"). Ahad Ha'am objected to the lack of a spiritual dimension in Herzl's political and practical Zionism. He saw the creation of the Jewish state as a means of reestablishing a Jewish communal identity and putting Jews of East and West, who were suffering very different sorts of crises at the end of the nineteenth century, back in touch with the cultural content of their past. What he feared most was that the Jewish homeland would become simply a hollow imitation of other modern European states. Using Palestine as a base from which to conquer the world was not on his agenda. Moreover, he also warned against maltreatment of the native Arab population and had harsh comments about the behavior of Jewish settlers in this regard.

understanding of the task, all Jewish forces, acting in all countries in whatever capacity, could be employed for the common aim. Only the dispute over priority, over leadership among various groups within Judaism, remained. This dispute was even in evidence in the question of Palestine, in which leadership fell to the English Jews, despite the ambitions of American Jews.

In the war Jews took part in great numbers as Englishmen, Frenchmen, Americans, and so forth. They were numerous in the army and many of them went as volunteers. I heard from an American Jew that in the army of the United States they constituted a greater percentage than in the population as a whole. I remember how after arriving in London I was struck by the enormous number of Jews in officer's uniforms on its streets. True, later during my tours of the English front, I did not meet even one. This does not mean that they were not there at all. I even heard of some who were decorated. Yet the overwhelming majority did not serve at the front, and that in all armies. No doubt they also suffered very few losses.

Yet, taking part in the war on the side of states of which they were citizens, Jews had simultaneously their own Jewish policy. [This policy] was less manifest in the first half of the war, but later, as the war drew to a close, it acted ever more clearly and appeared more openly. [Jews] acted through their financial influences, through their people who held state political positions, and through non-Jews devoted to them, who held executive positions. Finally, during the Peace Conference a Jewish committee appeared in Paris, playing a large role behind the scenes. Even in the armies of the belligerent states, they at times knew how to conduct Jewish policy, which was not always in accord with the policy of the state which they served.

In the Polish question Jewish policy also played no small role.

From the start of the war, it was apparent that Jewish policy worked on behalf of the Central Powers. We saw this best in Poland, where all Jews in all three annexed territories either cooperated directly with Germany or Austria, or also, in so far as they appeared as Poles, took an active part in Austrophile activity and in "activism."[3] In the wider global arena a clear indication in this respect was the behavior of Jews in the United States and other neutral countries, where the obligation of loyalty to their own state did not hinder them from manifesting their actual position and where they gave support to the political undertakings of the Germans. Also, in all countries, whether belligerent or neutral, political camps, known for their connections with and dependence upon Jews, either stood clearly on the side of the Central Powers or propagated "defeatism," [that is,] worked for a premature peace which would save German interests.

This stand of the Jews was wholly understandable.

---

[3]The "activism" refers specifically to the trend in Polish politics after 1916, which advocated cooperation with the Central Powers.

First of all, in the Allied camp was Russia, within whose borders were the main mass of Jews living on the face of the earth. At the same time, [Russia] was the only great power trying with the aid of anti-Jewish laws to defend itself from the Jewish flood. There was no doubt that the destruction of the Russian state was one of the main aims of Jewish policy in this war.

In no European state did the Jews have such a strong economic and political position as in Austria-Hungary. In Hungary, Magyars in their struggle with Slovaks, Romanians, and Serbs, fell back upon the aid of Jews and turned the country over to them at a quick rate. If I remember correctly, 95% of real estate in Budapest belonged to Jews. In the varied national composition of the Austrian state, Jews, who were present in all its lands in significant numbers, increasingly became the link cementing the state into one whole and [thereby] controlling it. With enormous speed, property in the Austrian lands came into Jewish hands; the number of Jews in judicial offices and even in the army grew year after year; and political leadership gradually came into their hands. We saw this up close in our Galicia, where during the period of autonomy, a significant portion of landed property came into Jewish hands and where the political influence of Jews already began to play a superior leading role, even in the Cracow conservative camp. Vienna and Budapest were the most Jewish capitals and financial centers in Europe.

It is not strange then that Jews regarded Austria-Hungary in a way as their state and that defense of that state was one of the main points of Jewish policy.

"Here one regards Austria-Hungary as a most Catholic state," I said in the Vatican in 1916 to one of its diplomats. "Yet it is a most Jewish state and is becoming increasingly more Jewish; to the extent it survives this war, we will soon live to see very sad times for the Church [in Austria]."

But Vatican diplomacy did not consider Jews as a danger for the Church and showed them sympathy and support.

In Germany Jews were not wholly satisfied with their position, for they did not have wide open doors to offices and even less to the army. Yet their financial position was much stronger there than in western states.

The aim of Bismarck—building the greatness of Germany with the aid of Jews—was more than well-achieved. They became significant joint owners of Germany. German banking, trade, and industry were to a much greater degree Jewish than it might seem externally. The participation of Jews in them could not be evaluated by checking a register of companies. One had to sit in the administrative councils of joint-stock associations. Only then could one see what Jews mean in the economic life of Germany. One illustration of their role and significance was the Jewish financial, commercial, and industrial potentates Emperor Wilhelm [II] counted among his personal friends.

The economic and financial expansion of Germany in Central and Eastern Europe was to an enormous degree an expansion of Jewish capital and influence. Hence in Berlin's wide plans of a complete dominance in this part of the world, in the designs of a *Mitteleuropa*, Berlin-Baghdad railway, in the attempts at the ultimate subjugation of Russia, Jews saw a great opportunity for themselves. They prepared themselves for the role of joint owners of this system.

Besides this Emperor Wilhelm gave them to understand that he would use his influence in the Moslem world to gain a position in Palestine for them.[4]

Jews then had every reason to cooperate in the victory of the Central Powers and they cooperated enthusiastically as long as that victory was probable.

In 1917 the situation changed radically.

The Russian Revolution overthrew the state that fought Jews. Liberal governments arose in Russia, against which Jews could make no accusations. Yet they knew Russia well and knew that this was only the beginning of the revolution and that they had at their disposal the means to bring it to a quick, catastrophic conclusion. They saw the possibility of destroying Russia, undercutting its strength for a longer period, and, finally, bloodily avenging their wrongs. This, given their psyche, is understandable.

On the other hand, Germany's chances of victory disappeared. Well-informed as to the internal strengths of the belligerent states, especially their economic and financial strengths, [Jews] understood better than anyone else the impossibility of [German] victory. They also saw the whole difficulty of preventing America from participating in the war. That participation lay in their interest because of their greater significance in the United States than in Europe, which gave them the prospect of great influence on the future peace.

Seeing that it was likely that the Allied powers would dictate the peace, and holding to the fixed principle of Jewish policy according to which Jews must always be on the winning side, they decided to sell themselves to the Allies.

The transaction occurred, according to all data, in the first half of 1917. Its first visible result was the declaration of the English government, assuring Jews support for the achievement of one of their aims, the building

---

[4]Aside from willful ignorance, the errors contained in the foregoing material all stem from Dmowski's insistence that Jews, despite superficial "public differences," pursued a single-minded policy and that they had become enormously powerful because of the moral weaknesses of Christians. Both Bismarck and Wilhelm II had business or social relationships with German Jews, a fact that deeply disturbed antisemites in many countries. But both men have left abundant evidence of their scorn for Jews as a group. Both condoned, at least for a while, the antisemitism of Court Chaplain Stoecker (see Document 4). Neither ought to be considered pawns of the Jews, as Dmowski implies. German plans for a Middle European empire, perhaps extending over the Berlin-Baghdad railway into Middle Africa, had been discussed for decades before the war. To some German policymakers in the Foreign Office, "German"-speaking Jews, many of whom identified with German culture, might have appeared useful tools in the future administration of Mitteleuropa. The Western Allies sought to counter the influence of the Central Powers, thus creating a favorable moment for Jewish diplomatic ambitions. But, as Dmowski points out, Jews fought on both sides during the war. They followed no concerted or uniform policy and did not

of their national seat, or national home, in Palestine.[5] No doubt the purchase price did not end with this. One can only surmise what more was promised them. The further course of events and the content of the peace after the war defined this price. So, when Jews noted the necessity of changing to the Allied side, when they had to do this in their own interest, they nevertheless knew how to get paid for this step. If the Jews know how to be grateful, the names Lloyd George and Wilson ought especially to be written in red letters in their golden books.

If the Jews in 1917 formally changed to the Allied side, this does not mean that they entirely abandoned Germany and Austria, thereby sacrificing Jewish interests in these two states. They continued to use all their influence to save Austria-Hungary from partition and to rescue whatever possible from German plans, above all not to allow the liberation of Poland from German rule. The Allies could emerge victorious, but *Mitteleuropa* should become a reality.

Moreover, in this new phase of the war, a new prospect opened up before them—carrying out a revolution in Germany, which would remove the last political obstacles in their way, paving the way to power.

Since then Jewish policy labored so that the victory of the Allies would not lead to the crushing of Germany and to the partitioning of Austria, so that the economic system of Germany would not be shaken, and so that their domination in Central Europe would even expand. The fruit of this victory would be a revolution in Germany and the accession to power there of Jews.

With regard to Poland, the Jews, independent of their interests in Germany, had still other very important motives for struggling against its independence.

The [Polish] Commonwealth pursued a fatal policy in the course of a couple of centuries prior to the partitions, a policy which led to such Judaization of the country that it had more of them than all the rest of the world and won for Poland some kind of title as the European fatherland of Jews. So it also seemed in the eyes of Jews. They regarded it as a new

---

succeed in stage-managing the Versailles Settlement, as Dmowski indicates elsewhere. In fact, the Minorities' Treaty, which Poland was forced to sign in June 1919, fell far short of the goals of several Jewish groups active in Paris. Deeply distrustful of the Polish leadership, they had hoped for much broader guarantees of Jewish national autonomy and representation in governmental bodies. Generally, Dmowski ignores the obvious failures of "Jewish politics."

[5]The reference here is to the Balfour Declaration issued under the name of Arthur Balfour, foreign minister in Lloyd George's wartime government. It promised British support for the establishment of a Jewish national home in Palestine, then under the control of Britain's enemy, the Ottoman Empire. Even vaguer assurances in this direction, alluded to earlier by Dmowski, had been given by Kaiser Wilhelm II, the ally of the sultan. The Balfour Declaration, which was generally perceived as the result of powerful Jewish influence, contained the important proviso that the civil and religious rights of the existing non-Jewish communities would have to be safeguarded. When the British Mandate for Palestine went into effect in 1923, and in view of Arab unrest there, the declaration was interpreted in

Palestine, and in it they destined Poles for a future role more or less similar to that which in biblical times the non-Israelite majority of the population of Canaan had. . . . The achievement of this aim was easiest by bringing about the collapse of the Polish state [by means of the partitions] and the passage of Polish territory to foreign rule, which could avail itself of Jewish assistance for domination in Poland. So far our historiography has not yet explained the role of Jews in the disintegration of the political life of the Commonwealth and its partitioning. But what we already know indicates that this role was not small. We also know that in the period of captivity the power of Jews in Poland rose quickly and their political behavior was often more than tellingly contrary to Polish aims.

For the goal of further control of Poland, in their eyes, it was not desirable that it should become a truly independent state, in which the development and organization of Polish national strengths would take place.

So, in the moment when the Polish question came to a head on the way to victory of the powers not interested in the destruction of Poland, in the camp of these states there came in sight an enemy, very dangerous thanks to its ways and methods of acting, all the more difficult to defeat because it did not fight openly, or appear at the front itself, but thrust others forward.

The struggle against the obstacles placed in the way of the Polish question by the Jews became henceforth, the most difficult task of Polish politics.

---

ways that hampered Jewish settlement. Thus the limits of "Jewish influence" were once again clearly demonstrated. British policy culminated in the White Paper of May 1939 that severely restricted Jewish immigration to one-third of Palestine's population, or seventy-five thousand over a five-year period. Thus it essentially sealed off a possible site of refuge for massive numbers of Jews fleeing Nazi persecution.

Antisemitism and Political Murder

Antisemitism consumed the life of Theodor Fritsch. A solitary, humorless fanatic, he formed a human bridge between the conventional anti-semitic politicians of the kaiser's time and the revolutionary anti-semites of the Weimar era. Born in 1852, he became active in the 1880s, describing himself as a disciple of Wilhelm Marr, but he soon went his own way. He lived long enough to pass the torch to Hitler, who acknowledged Fritsch's publications as instrumental to his enlightenment on the Jewish question while in Vienna. Hitler eulogized him on his death in September 1933.

Of peasant origin, Fritsch became a milling engineer and published a newspaper for millers, which provided an income and allowed him to pursue his true vocation, combating world Jewry. Fritsch's ideas about how best to do this did not change in any significant way during the fifty years of his activity; he was saying virtually the same things in the 1920s as he had in the 1880s.

Although dragged into party politics before World War I, he was convinced that this was a futile enterprise. The masses were too ignorant, too lazy to make correct political decisions. They had first to be enlightened in the simple language they could comprehend. The struggle required a "party-less party" of tireless workers whose task it would be to distribute massive amounts of printed matter to all strata of society. Gradually, anti-semitism would permeate the social fabric, and a solution to the Jewish question would become part of a larger revolution in Germanic values. After the "physical Jew" had been dealt with, Christianity would be cleansed of its Jewish origins. Law and education, economics and literature would have to be purged of their "spiritually Jewish" content before the full renewal of Germany could take place. Parliamentary politics or any form of democracy was not the solution to these problems but rather part of the Judaic infection ravaging the country.

Although always a marginal figure before World War I, Fritsch nevertheless practiced what he preached. His main contribution to antisemitic literature was the *Handbook of the Jewish Question,* a compendium of misinformation, out-of-context anti-Jewish quotations from world literature, and essays on various topics. It was still being published during the Second World War, then in its forty-eighth printing. Fritsch was one of the few antisemitic publishers before World War I who managed to make antisemitism profitable. His Hammer Press published a periodical, widely read on the Right, Fritsch's own writings, and the works of other antisemites, including the *Protocols of the Elders of Zion.* Normally, he gave away half the printing of each production. Thus awakening demand, he sold the second half and usually made enough to finance a new printing. In the 1912 elections, he exploited the personnel of the declining antisemitic political parties to distribute two million copies of a pamphlet series in this way. In 1914 he targeted youth group leaders with 700 free copies of his periodical.

Convinced that he was in sole possession of the whole truth, Fritsch was a lonely prophet. He had no faith in the masses or in almost any other antisemite. At times he made plans to emigrate from an inhospitable Germany or to establish a "renewal colony," which, although technically on German soil, would isolate itself from the philistine herd. On the eve of World War I, expecting an imminent socialist revolution, Fritsch formed the cadre of a revolutionary organization whose job it would be to mete out revolutionary justice to "left-wing criminals and Jews," destroy the Reichstag, and establish "a constitutional dictatorship." At the time, this open conspiracy was widely regarded as a lunatic fantasy, but, in truth, his preparations were only premature. The Weimar Republic later provided the perfect climate for antisemitic extremists, such as Fritsch.

The following essay is typical of both Fritsch and the deadly new applications of antisemitism in postwar political life. Despite his protestations, Fritsch was no friend of the Republic, and the antisemites in general ranged themselves against republican democracy in Germany, as they had in France during the Dreyfus Affair. The assassination in 1922 of Walter Rathenau, Germany's most capable public servant, provided Fritsch with the occasion for unloading his hatred of both Jews and "the Weimar system." After the briefest nod to respectable opinion, he goes on to justify the brutal murder. Not only did Rathenau have it coming because of his misdeeds and those of the rest of his race, but his death was actually the responsibility of the Left, which "needed" a new agitational prop in order to destroy Germany. From wholly fabricated and false hypotheses (Rathenau's membership in the all-powerful secret supergovernment), Fritsch arrives at wholly unwarranted conclusions: Rathenau bore responsibility for the war and for Germany's defeat, and he therefore deserved to die.

To those with the mind-set of a Theodor Fritsch, no act that served to undermine the Republic, and thus save Germany, could be considered truly criminal. To be sent to jail by this system or to be condemned by its spokesmen was a badge of honor. Such revolutionary attitudes proved nearly impossible to defend against in the traditional ways. In Germany prior to the war, court action, public censure, and apologetic literature had helped curb antisemitism and keep it within well-defined boundaries of propriety. But in the chaotic early years of the Republic and again in the crisis created by the depression, the antisemites of the conservative and radical Right proved impervious to such civilized measures.

Fur Further Reading

Donald L. Niewyk, *The Jews in Weimar Germany* (Baton Rouge, 1980); Walter Laqueur, "The German Youth Movement and the 'Jewish Question'," *Yearbook of the Leo Baeck Institute* 6 (1961): 193–205.

18. Theodor Fritsch
The Desperate Act of a Desperate People
(1922)

The murderers of Rathenau[1] have damaged the German cause. It was to be foreseen that this mad act would be used in demagogic ways to exacerbate anew the conflicts within our people. Those who have worked from the beginning toward the destruction of the foundations of the German state system have been given new, explosive materials through this foolish crime. The murderers are immature youths who could not foresee the political consequences of their act. To put the responsibility for this misdeed on a political party or one of the larger *völkisch* [racial-nationalist] organizations is frivolous. All of them firmly reject criminal acts for the purpose of achieving their political goals.

By eagerly seizing on this harmful act, the parties that stir up the nation showed quite clearly how they lie in wait for any opportunity to sow new discord and further grind down the spirit of the nation.

It is well enough known that the business of inciting the masses was at the point of failing. Increasingly, the workers are getting tired of the constant agitation and see through the hollowness of the whole revolutionary sham. They see clearly that the radical leftists can never fulfill the promises which they dangle before the workers. Communism in Russia has suffered a shameful bankruptcy. Ultimately, revolution does not serve the well-being of the worker but of the great capitalist Golden International. They have, therefore, become mistrustful and reserved and show little desire to cooperate further in the insane agitation.

It is for this reason that they need new means to incite and inflame the passions of the masses. After the comic "assassination attempt on

---

Source: From Paul Lehmann (ed.), *Neue Wege: Aus Theodor Fritschs Lebensarbeit: Eine Sammlung von Hammer-Aufsätzen zu seinem siebzigsten Geburtstage* (Leipzig, 1922), pp. 351–59.

[1]Walther Rathenau (1867–1922) succeeded his father as director of the German General Electric Company in 1915. Before the war, he was closely associated with eighty-six German companies and twenty-one foreign ones. During the war, he took charge of the distribution of crucial raw materials. Minister of reconstruction in 1921 and foreign minister of the republic in 1922, Rathenau favored fulfillment of the obligations Germany had reluctantly agreed to under the Treaty of Versailles. He negotiated the advantageous Treaty of Rapallo with the Soviet Union, the first *de jure* recognition of the Bolshevik regime. These policies and his Jewishness, always a problematic part of the identity of this extraordinarily capable man, cost him his life. Vilified in the Reichstag and in the press of the nationalist and radical Right, Rathenau was murdered on June 24, 1922, while riding in an open car. His three young murderers belonged to various clandestine rightist revolutionary organizations; one of them was a Nazi. Subsequent investigations revealed that

Scheidemann"[2] went up in a puff of smoke, they needed a new and powerful inflammatory device. It is especially the Bolsheviks who have long waited for the opportunity at last to unfurl their blood-soaked banner in Germany, too.

Serious, nationally minded men will not commit the folly of loosing the murder weapon so that the German people might free itself from its desperate situation. That would be an experiment with unsuitable means. Neither do we trust those who madly believe that such means can pave the way for [the return of the] monarchy. At the present time, there is little enthusiasm for the monarchy, even in national circles. Even those who believe that a good monarchy is the best form of state and who don't let comparisons between then and now determine what they think make no secret of it: our monarchs of the last thirty years left much to be desired. No reasonable man thinks of restoring them today. In any case, today is not the right time for the erection of a new monarchy. All the parties are honorably coming to terms with the republican state form, which is faring so well.

The cry: The Republic is in danger! is thus nothing but a sham agitation. No one is seriously thinking of threatening the constitution.

Nonetheless, let us be clear about it. What has Germany lost in Rathenau? All his close friends and all those on the Left praise him as a shrewd thinker and a noble idealist. We have no cause to deny him this praise. But the contemporary world has thus far seen only the light side of this man, which a loyal press has zealously taken care of. It is necessary to complete the picture through the recollection of a few facts.

Rathenau's writings show a peculiar mixture of practical, expert knowledge in technical and economic fields, mundane and mechanistic perspectives, intermingled with high-flying idealistic and socialistic turns of speech that overshoot themselves into the infinite and extravagant. They do not bespeak a mature, self-possessed intellectual personality. Englishmen declare that it is impossible to translate Rathenau's writings into English because his verbal expression lacks logic.

---

they had fed upon a wide variety of antisemitic and nationalist literature, including the *Protocols of the Elders of Zion*. Sons of "good" families, they had been convinced that Rathenau was one of the elders of Zion and actively engaged in a Bolshevist-Jewish conspiracy to sell Germany to foreign powers. It was their patriotic duty to kill all such traitors. Except on the far Right, outrage at Rathenau's murder was general. It galvanized the Republicans into combating the lawlessness of the Right. An emergency decree followed by the Law for the Protection of the Republic and a special court to try antirepublican crimes were the primary results.

[2]Philipp Scheidemann (1865–1939), a conservative Social Democrat and a non-Jew, had proclaimed the German Republic in November 1918 and served as its first chancellor. He became a constant target of the nationalist press in the same campaign of slander that enveloped Rathenau, the leader of the Catholic Center party, Matthias Erzberger (assassinated in 1921), and Friedrich Ebert, the first president of the republic. Scheidemann had led the government that signed the Treaty of Versailles and then resigned in protest, but

There did work within Rathenau, in a conciliatory sense, a certain candor which did not shrink from honorable confessions—even when they touched upon his own kindred. Thus, in his *Impressions* he designates Berlin Jews as "an Asiatic horde on the sands of Brandenburg"; and he gives them many another bitter pill to swallow. Nevertheless, he was far from being an opponent of Orthodox Judaism, having defended it warmly on diverse occasions.

In this, it seems, it was more a matter of intellectual gamesmanship than the expression of a deeply held inner conviction. He coquetted with the truth. His effect, even in Jewish circles, was ambivalent. To some it was a matter of pride in his external successes; to others he was a kind of *enfant terrible.*

His effect on the public also stands in an equivocal light. As a big businessman he did not neglect to look after the material interests of high finance. But to give his actions the common touch, he also coquetted with socialism.

A few of his utterances have preoccupied the intellectuals. In the 1909 Christmas number of the *Neue Freie Presse* (Vienna) he wrote the much-quoted sentence: "Three hundred men, all of whom know one another and whose successors are picked from their own circles, today direct the world's destiny." This remarkable avowal has not, to the present day, been fully understood in all its consequences. From the context in which it was said, it is clear that he was not talking about ruling princes and statesmen but rather a power group standing outside government, which possesses the means to force its will upon the world, including the governments. Furthermore, since he spoke of the naming of successors, it is obvious that there is a firmly structured organization, operating according to definite principles in the division of offices and systematically pursuing its goals.

Rathenau's utterance, therefore, substantiates nothing less than the fact that a closed society—a shadow government or a supergovernment—has existed for a long time and that it directs economic and political events over the heads of nations and governments. Today, we know where to seek it: in Jewish high finance and its paid lackeys, allied and spread throughout the entire world.[3]

---

this patriotic act did not save him from the wrath of the Right. In an atmosphere of tolerance for extreme nationalism nurtured by an antirepublican judiciary, an attempt on Scheidemann's life was made by (different) members of Organization Consul, the same group that killed Rathenau later that month.

[3]Fritsch embroiders and distorts Rathenau's "confession" with the intention of convicting the enemy out of his own mouth. Given to hyperbole though he was, Rathenau actually said something quite different: "Three hundred men, all of whom know one another, guide the economic destinies of the Continent and seek their successors among their followers." From the context of the statement, it is clear that he deplored the oligarchic nature of the financial and industrial leadership of Europe. His article was entitled "Criticism of the Times." Nowhere in it does he suggest that the three hundred ruled over the heads of constituted governments or that they were Jews.

By Rathenau's confession, tales were told out of school that perhaps had better been left untold. Rathenau, however, could not resist the temptation to scorn governments and nations to their faces, telling them that they stood at the beck and call of a hidden power. He was certain that the scorned would accept the ridicule passively and that they did not possess the option of rebelling against Jewish mastery. And they did take it in silence! Jewish finance and the power of the Jewish press held them all under their spell. There are no longer any free nations, and the governments and princes were only ornamental decorations. The real possessor of power was the nation of Juda.

Until now, we have failed to draw the proper conclusions from these facts.

If the three hundred men of the secret world government (to which Rathenau belonged) direct the destiny of the world, what was the world war all about? Would the three hundred have been unable to prevent it? Since they did not prevent it, they must have wanted it.

The search for those responsible for the world war has moved along false paths. He who boasts—even secretly—that he directs the destiny of the world ought now to possess the courage and decency *to take the responsibility* for the political events of the world.

If the three hundred money powers made world policy for decades, they therefore also made the world war. Perhaps [they did so] in order finally to erect their mastery in the open and to drive out the princes. It is time that the nations finally recognize this and bring the guilty to account. The books of the American Henry Ford[4] deliver exhaustive proof as to how the central organization of Jewish bankers in Wall Street prepared the war.

A short time after the outbreak of the war, a Thuringian manufacturer related to us, with a certain embarrassment, what he had experienced in the war ministry in Berlin. He had gone there in order to acquire some army contracts. To his amazement, he met in the offices not the high officers and military officials he had expected but rather Hebrews—and more Hebrews. Finally, he pushed his way into the authoritative department. There, in a large hall, at a diplomat's desk surrounded by others of his tribe, sat Mr. Walther Rathenau arranging things. He disposed over the army contracts. And it was no surprise that Jewish firms almost always received preference. Our manufacturer had the impression that here sat the actual leaders of the German war machine. . . .

Immediately after the outbreak of the war, Rathenau placed himself at the disposal of the army General Staff to organize the procurement of all war materiel and the distribution of food in the country. They accepted him with open arms because the war had come so unexpectedly to the army administration that they were almost completely unprepared for it. Thus, Rathenau appeared as a rescuing angel, and they put the reins in his

---

[4]Fritsch published Ford's *The International Jew—A World Problem* from his Hammer Press in Leipzig and continued to do so even after Ford asked that it be withdrawn in 1927.

hands. As a member of the three hundred he was certainly better prepared for *Coming Things* [title of a book by Rathenau] than the unsuspecting German government and army leadership. And thus he could well have organized, on the quiet and with his tribal associates, everything necessary for the war that was breaking out. Important supplies were found primarily in Jewish hands, and thus, as in almost all wars, old and new, Jews became indispensable war contractors. Rathenau was celebrated as "savior of the fatherland" and as "chief of staff behind the lines."

Along with Ballin,[5] he organized the war corporations that throughout the war—and beyond—ruled the total economic life of Germany. They garnered little gratitude. Supposed to be institutions for the common good, they served to enrich individuals, predominantly Jews. Jews were favored in the offices of the war corporations, especially young Jews, who thereby escaped army service.[6] The methods of many of these corporations aroused general dissatisfaction. A great deal of food was allowed to rot while it traveled about on trains. In hundreds of cases, the Central Procurement Office has been shown to have bought the worst goods from abroad at the highest prices; oftentimes it hindered the importing of cheaper and better food. Almost without exception, the foreign provisioners were Hebrews, who enriched themselves enormously through profiteering. Undoubtedly, the war corporations contributed a great deal to our starvation and economic breakdown. Most of them have not yet rendered a public accounting.

Mighty Rathenau did nothing to suppress these conditions. Indeed, it is not even known that he ever spoke out against them.

Again, with the dissolution of the army, most of the value of the equipment—reckoned colossally in the billions—was transferred to Jewish firms, which enriched themselves without measure. Usury and profiteering enjoyed a powerful upsurge, always with the children of Israel in the vanguard. Rathenau did not prevent it.

After the [German 1918] revolution began the mass immigration of Russian and Polish Jews into a country that suffered from overpopulation and lacked sufficient food and housing for its own citizens.

---

[5]Albert Ballin (1857–1918), general director of the great shipping concern the Hamburg-Amerika Line, confidant and economic adviser to Kaiser Wilhelm II, committed suicide on the day the Armistice was signed. He was Jewish.

[6]The charges that German Jews avoided military service, eluded the dangers of the fronts, and unduly profited from the war surfaced almost immediately after the outbreak of hostilities. Fritsch, among others, petitioned various state governments to undertake a special census of Jews at the front. He thereby registered his fear that Jews, whose talents were being utilized as never before in positions of authority, would use these openings to complete their conquest of Germany. To counteract numerous accusations of Jewish cowardice, the Ministry of War sanctioned such a census in October 1916. Although its motives may have been positive, the ministry did not allow for the historical prejudice of the German officer corps, which was entrusted with carrying out the census. Although Jews had served in all of Germany's wars since 1813, they were systematically excluded from commissions in the regular or reserve army. Jewish soldiers, who performed all military functions at or above their proportion of the population during World War I, complained of

Over three hundred thousand Eastern European Jews have immigrated since this time. They found friendly acceptance from officials and were immediately allotted large businesses. In a short time, many of them have become multimillionaires and home owners—while many a German goes to rack and ruin without a roof in his fatherland.[7]

Rathenau had nothing to say in opposition to this, either—Rathenau, who was really the "secret Kaiser of Germany" since the outbreak of war and could have exerted a virtually uncontested influence upon domestic and foreign relations.

He also favored the signing of the shameful Treaty of Versailles which will make Germans into the slaves of foreign peoples for decades. Indeed, he was the main representative of the "policy of fulfillment." In this way he wanted to test "how deeply a nation could be allowed to fall into want." Perhaps, in the last moment of his life he had to realize that this boundary of need had been exceeded. For if it really had been German *völkisch* men who perpetrated the dastardly deed, then Chancellor Wirth would have been correct when he described the crime as "The Desperate Act of a Desperate People." But thereby the responsibility for the terrible act devolves upon the shoulders of those who have brought a nation to such a desperate situation—those foreign governments and, not the least among them, the secret three hundred who direct the destiny of the world.

From the German nation, Rathenau demanded the conscientious liquidation of an enormous load of debt that its enemies sought to lay upon it. He advised the nation to work twice as hard and to produce twice as much as before!

In Russia, for five years now, a number of Jewish men exercise an absolute dictatorship, a tyranny such as world history has never seen. The Soviet government boasts in its own newspapers that since 1917 no fewer than 1,764,875 people have been slaughtered by it, among them 192,350 workers, 260,000 soldiers, 815,000 peasants, 155,250 intellectuals. The whole of Russian economic life has been destroyed; part [of the country] is transformed into a desert; and further millions have been consigned to

---

being pulled out of the front lines just before the count. The results of the survey, which would have served to poison relations between Jewish and German soldiers, were never officially published, but they were leaked to a prominent antisemitic publicist who used them to produce two pamphlets, the basis for the charges Fritsch refers to here.

[7]In 1914, 90,000 foreign-born Jews lived in Germany—about 15 percent of the Jewish population. By 1933, the number rose to nearly 100,000, approximately 20 percent of the declining Jewish population. As in the imperial era, however, many eastern-European Jews traveled through Germany on the way to North and South America; 30,000 had been conscripted to German war industries in 1914, and another 100,000 fled the eastern theater of war and the postwar pogroms. Thus in 1920 there may have been as many as 220,000 foreign Jews in Germany, but over 100,000 of these subsequently left. The "success stories" among them were rare indeed. In Prussia officials attempted to stop immigration with roundups, incarceration in holding centers, and deportation. Those who escaped these measures lived in the crowded slum quarters of major cities and eked out meager livings.

starvation. We have never heard that Rathenau raised the slightest objection to this criminal regime. Rather, he entertains friendly relations toward the Soviet tyranny, . . . delivers plans for their controlled economy, communicates constantly through couriers, and concluded the Treaty of Rapallo with them.[8]

We reject every political murder, for the difficult questions of our time cannot be solved with the revolver but only by means of serious intellectual and physical labor. Rathenau's place will be filled by another of the three hundred wielders of power, and the tormented nations will be no better off.

In his book *The Kaiser,* which appeared before the end of the war in 1918, Rathenau reports that he had already told a friend in 1917: "World history would have lost all meaning if Kaiser Wilhelm were ever to ride as victor through the Brandenburg Gate on a white charger." From this it is clear that Rathenau did not believe in or wish for a German victory. The "sense of world history," according to the conception of those circles, was that Germany and its empire [should] be annihilated—thus was it decided in the councils of the three hundred. It was doom that the German government laid the entire economic life of the German nation in the hands of a man who did not want German victory. Indeed, it equipped him with a fullness of power such as no man in Germany had ever possessed, for Rathenau, during the war, was an out-and-out dictator of the economy. And he therefore bears the responsibility for the strange things that occurred.[9]

Rathenau would have had to have been more than a superman to have directed the German war economy in model fashion, even though he did not want a German victory. It is therefore obvious that the strange economic misconduct of the war corporations was not accidental and that they knowingly contributed to the German defeat. Thus the cruel fate of that unusual man was not without its connection to sin and expiation.

Naive socialist workers have been informed that Rathenau was one of them, and they believe it. In truth, Rathenau was of the party of big business. "How could it be otherwise?" Was he not president of the powerful General Electric Company? Did he not also sit on thirty-eight boards of directors for large corporations and draw an income of millions?

It is amazing, however, to see the moral outrage over the crime among those who all along have celebrated the murders of princes and ministers as great political deeds. They will have to accustom themselves to the idea that the nations they have instructed in the praiseworthy "propaganda of

---

[8]See note 1, Document 17.

[9][Fritsch footnote] A quite parallel position was occupied during the war in the United States by the Hebrew, M. Baruch. His dictatorial powers are described in detail in the second volume of [Henry] Ford's book, *The International Jew.* We can thus see how systematically the three hundred operated.

[Editor's footnote] Bernard Baruch was an adviser on national defense during the war and became chairman of the War Industries Board (1918–19). In World War II he served as special adviser on postwar economic planning to Secretary of State James F. Byrnes.

the deed" are ready to employ it against not only the old wielders of power and tyrants but also against *the new ones.* He who sows the wind reaps the whirlwind.

They who believe that expiation for the crime should include the suppression of all national associations and all German, nationally conscious newspapers and journals are only stirring the coals of a secret fire, which continues to burn underground. When they shut all the ventilators by which the tensions of the national spirit can escape into the open, when every justified grievance about today's conditions is suppressed, then there remains to the throttled national spirit only one alternative—the Desperate Act.

Rathenau's end may serve as warning to the three hundred world powers not to fasten the chains binding the nations too tightly. Otherwise the rising of enslaved humanity will issue in a fearful judgment.

5 The Holocaust and Beyond

Adolf Hitler on the Jewish Question

T he life and career of Adolf Hitler (1889–1945) are well known and easily researched. He may well be the one person represented in this collection who needs no introduction. Nevertheless, the nature of Hitler's antisemitism, the functions it performed in his overall ideology, and his exact role in the "Final Solution of the Jewish question" are all matters of dispute among historians. That he was the most important antisemite few would deny, for on his ideological authority, one-third of the world's Jews perished.

On this basis, and not because he was an innovator in the theory of antisemitism, a sizable sampling of Hitler's published statements about Jews has been included here. The selections reflect the variety of uses to which he put his antisemitism. All were tailored for a specific audience and to achieve an intended effect. So many antisemitic styles from one man may suggest that sheer and shameless demagoguery was at work, that Hitler masterfully used the prejudices of others for manipulative ends, without sharing their hatreds. Such an assumption is unwarranted, however. Hitler's utterances on Jews span nearly the whole of his adult life and are among the earliest and last things he wrote or dictated. Regardless of the style of the moment, they breathe detestation, a revulsion both intellectual and physical. If Hitler was merely a salesman, he was the proverbial salesman who believed wholeheartedly in the product. In the matter of antisemitism, he was no hypocrite.

In the first selection (Document 19), Hitler looks back to 1909 and "surely the most significant transformation of all for me," the discovery of antisemitism in Vienna. This often-quoted passage from *Mein Kampf* has been read in several ways. Its veracity has been questioned because it seems a bit ingenuous of Hitler to suggest, as he does in the discussion leading up to his dramatic meeting with an eastern-European Jew in the inner city, that he was unacquainted with the Jewish question, scarcely aware of Jews, and ignorant of antisemitism. Such innocence would have been indeed difficult to sustain in the Austria of Schönerer and Lueger.

Truthfulness aside, the language of this central episode is also revealing. Confessional and penitential, Hitler chooses many of the elements of a classic religious conversion experience to prepare the reader for his moment of truth in the inner city. He tells of an earnest but confused young observer of artistic life and social problems, whose rites of passage require a painful renunciation of childish uncertainties. Visual experiences of Vienna and a rational understanding of Jewry's destructive activities cannot be denied, yet they war against a lingering attitude of "cosmopolitan tolerance" for an oppressed people. Not until his providential encounter with the Jew can Hitler overcome the liberal prejudices that he learned in his father's house. Then "inner-soul struggles" begin to give way to conviction born of deep experience. "Under the pressure of destiny," antisemitism becomes one of the "foundations for a philosophy in general and a political view in particular which later I only needed to supplement in detail, but which never left me."

The self-authenticating religious tones of this description merit attention. Hitler goes out of his way to establish a special identity in the matter of antisemitism. He must distinguish himself from run-of-the-mill antisemites and coarse Jew haters. But just as significant as the dubious conversion in the inner city is the text that follows it. Even after his consciousness-raising experience, Hitler assures his readers that only careful study of the Jewish question allowed him to harmonize instinctive repugnance for Jews with a scientific understanding of its necessity.

What did he study? Aside from some random titles, it is probably no longer possible to ascertain exactly what (or whether) Hitler read. In any case, the passage raises questions that go beyond the contents of his reading list. The writings of the authors represented in this collection made it remarkably easy for Hitler to familiarize himself thoroughly with the theory and practice of antisemitism, "for [the price of] a few hellers." He had but to walk to the nearest kiosk or bookstore to choose from a profusion of cheap books, pamphlets, and newspapers specializing in the subject. Wagner, Stoecker, Marr, Drumont, Fritsch, and a host of other antisemites had helped create a general climate of hostile opinion about Jews, a tradition of antisemitism.

Although he rarely admitted it, Hitler surely stood on the shoulders of many predecessors who wrote about and acted out their antisemitism. What differentiated him from an earlier generation of antisemites was the absence of any sort of defensiveness about his hatred. Refusing to qualify his opinions, he advanced beyond almost all the authors encountered thus far. At least occasionally, they felt compelled to justify what some might consider bigotry or exaggeration. In *Mein Kampf,* Hitler described the overcoming of such defensiveness as a personal triumph. Unlike his predecessors, he unabashedly called himself "a fanatical antisemite."

The second selection (Document 20) contradicts many of the principles advocated in *Mein Kampf.* Passionate and violent in language, this speech delivered before a mass audience plays on the emotions of a humiliated people thirsting for revenge. Hitler applies his accumulated "knowledge" of the Jews to the big political questions of the recent past and the miserable present. The Jews are the key to Germany's defeat, they are responsible for all the rottenness of the Republic, and they should be hung. The emotionalism he earlier decried in the masses, their lack of "science," and the "immoderate indictments" of Jews that once offended him disappear in the heated atmosphere of the mass meeting, where he excelled.

The third excerpt (Document 21) comes from a marathon two-and-one-half-hour speech delivered on January 30, 1939, to 885 Nazi Reichstag deputies. Millions of other Germans listened on their radios or heard it over loudspeakers in public places. Hitler covers many subjects of global and national import before arriving at the Jewish question and a blunt prophecy of world Jewry's annihilation.

Hitler's "prophecies" were often in reality the announcement of his intentions. Had he already decided upon the "Final Solution," still nearly two years in the offing? or was this an attempt to intimidate the international community? Earlier in the speech, he scorns those powers that expressed concern for German Jews, observing—correctly—that they made no effort to open their borders to Jewish immigration. Or was the "prophecy" simply an example of the way Hitler sought to prepare the Germans for the war that many feared? The thrust of his denunciation seems to be that Jews must be seen as the embodiment of all Germany's enemies, both capitalists and communists. Almost all Germans, with the exception of the shattered Left, could unite behind this notion.

Hitler's personal role in the Holocaust will be considered in the introduction to Document 24. But even in the absence of documentary proof, an order of extermination bearing his signature, there can be little doubt that a murderous antisemitism became one of the chief tasks of the Nazi state because of this man's lifelong obsession with Jews. Centuries of Jew hatred formed his consciousness, but it was his own peculiar psyche that translated the politics and literature of antisemitism into systematic murder.

For Further Reading

J. P. Stern, *Hitler: The Führer and the People* (Berkeley, 1975); Hans Staudinger, *The Inner Nazi: A Critical Analysis of* Mein Kampf (Baton Rouge, 1981).

19. Adolf Hitler
The Discovery of Antisemitism in Vienna (1925)

[Hitler precedes this early chapter on the Jewish question by an extended treatment of the Social Democrats that ends: "Only knowledge of Jewry offers the key to grasping the inner and therefore actual intentions of the Social Democrats."]

It is difficult today, if not impossible, to say when the word *Jew* first occasioned special thoughts in me. In my father's house, I cannot recall ever having heard the word, at least while he lived. I believe the old gentleman would have regarded special emphasis on this term as culturally backward. He had succeeded over the course of his life in becoming more or less cosmopolitan, an outlook that survived alongside a quite rough-and-ready nationalistic sentiment and even colored my own.

Source: From Adolf Hitler, *Mein Kampf,* 14th ed. (Munich, 1932), pp. 54–70.

In school, too, I found no cause that would have led me to change this received image. In high school I did learn to know a Jewish boy, whom we all treated cautiously, only because various experiences had taught us to doubt his reliability. But we didn't care all that much one way or the other [about Jews].

Not until I was fourteen or fifteen did I bump into the word *Jew* more frequently, mostly in the context of political discussions. I felt slightly averse [to this practice] and could not fend off a feeling of unpleasantness that always came over me when religious squabbles were unloaded in front of me.

But at that time I did not see the question as something special.

Linz possessed very few Jews. In the course of centuries, their exteriors had become Europeanized and human looking. Indeed, I even took them for Germans. The nonsense of this conception was not clear to me because I saw just a single distinctive characteristic, the alien religion. Since they had been persecuted because of it, as I believed, my aversion toward prejudicial remarks about them became almost detestation.

I did not yet so much as suspect the existence of a systematic opposition to Jews.

Then I came to Vienna.

Caught up by the fullness of impressions in the architectonic realm, downcast by the difficulty of my own lot, I did not at first grasp the inner stratification of the people in this gigantic city. I did not see Jews, despite the fact that Vienna already counted two hundred thousand of them among two million people at this time. My eyes and my senses could not keep pace with the flood of values and ideas of the first few weeks. Only when calm gradually returned and the agitated image began to clear did I look at my new world in a more fundamental way and also come upon the Jewish question.

I don't wish to assert that the way I got to know them was particularly pleasant. I still saw only the religion of the Jews and for reasons of human tolerance held aloof from attacks on this religion, as any other. Consequently, the tone struck by the antisemitic press of Vienna appeared to me as unworthy of the cultural heritage of a great nation. The memory of certain occurrences in the Middle Ages oppressed me; I would not wish to see them repeated. Since the papers in question were not generally well thought of (for reasons I had not yet fathomed), I mainly saw them as products of anger and envy more than as the results of a systematic, albeit false, perspective.

I was strengthened in my opinion by what appeared to me as the immeasurably more worthy form in which the really big newspapers answered these attacks or, what occurred to me as still more praiseworthy, how they simply failed to mention them at all, that is, condemned them through silence.

I zealously read the so-called world press (*Neue Freie Presse, Wiener Tageblatt,* etc.) and was amazed by the scope of what it offered its readers, as well as by the objectivity of its individual articles. I respected the aristocratic tone but was often somewhat uncomfortable with the overstated style. Yet this might have been in keeping with the verve of the whole metropolis.

Since I then regarded Vienna in this way, I thought of this explanation of mine as a valid excuse.

[The Viennese press's fawning treatment of the Habsburgs and hypercritical treatment of the German Empire and Wilhelm II undermined Hitler's respect.]

It was this that gradually made me observe the big papers more cautiously.

When, on one such occasion, one of the antisemitic newspapers, the *Deutsches Volksblatt*, behaved more respectably, I was forced to recognize it.

Another thing that got on my nerves at this time was the way the big papers pursued an obnoxious cult of France. You would have to be ashamed to be a German when these sweet hymns of praise to the "great culture-nation" came before your eyes. More than once, this miserable truckling to the French caused me to drop these "world papers." I then often picked up the *Volksblatt*, which, although it was certainly smaller, appeared nonetheless somewhat purer in these matters. I was not in agreement with the sharply antisemitic tone, but once in a while I read arguments that gave me cause to think.

In any case, I slowly came to know from these causes about the man and the movement that determined Vienna's destiny at that time: Dr. Karl Lueger and the Christian Social party.[1]

When I came to Vienna, I stood opposed to both.

The man and his movement seemed "reactionary" in my eyes.

My common sense of justice, however, moderated this judgment in proportion to the opportunity I received to get to know the man and his work. Slowly, my just judgment grew into unabashed admiration. Today I see the man, even more than before, as the greatest German mayor of all times.

How much of my basic outlook was changed by this altered position toward the Christian Social movement!

If by this experience my views with regard to antisemitism also fell to the passage of time, then this was surely the most significant transformation of all for me.

It cost me the greatest inner struggles of the soul, and only after months of wrestling between sentiment and reason did reason begin to emerge the winner. Two years later, sentiment fell into line with reason and from then on became its most reliable guardian and sentinel.

---

[1]See the introduction to Document 9.

During this period of bitter wrestling between inner education and cold reason, the visual observation of Vienna's streets had rendered invaluable services. There came a time when I no longer as before wandered blindly through the mighty city. Now with eyes opened I looked at people as well as buildings.

As I was once strolling through the inner city, I suddenly happened upon an apparition in a long caftan with black hair locks.

Is this a Jew? was my first thought.

They surely didn't look like that in Linz. I observed the man stealthily and cautiously. But the longer I stared at this alien face, examining it feature for feature, the more my first question was transformed into a new conception:

Is this a German?

As always in such cases I began to try to remove my doubts with books. For a few hellers I purchased the first antisemitic brochures of my life. Unfortunately, they all proceeded from the standpoint that in principle the reader was conversant with or even understood the Jewish question to a certain degree. Moreover, their tone was in most cases sufficient to re-create doubts in me, particularly because of the shallow and extraordinarily unscientific support for their assertions.

I had a relapse for weeks, on one occasion for months.

The matter seemed so monstrous, the indictment so immoderate, that, tortured by the fear of doing an injustice, I again became anxious and uncertain.

But, certainly, I could no longer be in doubt that it did not concern Germans of a peculiar religion but rather a people in itself. For since I had begun to concern myself with these questions and become aware of the Jews, Vienna appeared to me in a different light than previously. Wherever I went, I now saw Jews, and the more I saw, the more sharply they were distinguished from other men in my eyes. Especially the inner city and the areas north of the Danube Canal swarmed with a people who even externally no longer bore a similarity to Germans.

However, if I still had doubts, these hesitations were finally removed by the position of a segment of the Jews themselves.

A great movement among them, which was quite extensive in Vienna, came out most emphatically for the confirmation of the racial character of Judaism: Zionism.

It might look as though only a section of Jews approved this position and that the great majority condemned such an affirmation, indeed inwardly rejected it. But upon closer examination this appearance dissolved in an evil vapor composed of pure expedience and pretext, not to say lies. For the so-called Jewry of liberal disposition did not reject the Zionists as non-Jews but only as Jews of an impractical stamp, whose public confession of their Jewishness might even be dangerous.

In their interrelatedness nothing had changed.

In a short time this phony struggle between Zionistic and liberal Jews nauseated me. It was thoroughly false, based on lies, and little in keeping with the constantly asserted moral superiority and purity of this people.

The cleanliness of this people, moral and otherwise, is a point in itself. Just looking at their exteriors, even with your eyes closed, you can tell they are not lovers of water. Later the odor of these caftan wearers often sickened me. Added to this were their unclean clothes and less-than-heroic appearance.

All this is far from appealing. But you must be even more offended when you look beyond the physical uncleanliness to discover the moral stains upon the Chosen People.

Nothing affected me in so short a time as the slowly mounting insight into the kind of activity carried on by Jews in specific areas.

Was there any kind of filth or brazenness, particularly in cultural life, in which there was not at least one Jew participating?

As soon as you cautiously cut into such an abscess, you would find, like a maggot in a rotting body, blinded by the sudden light, a little Yid!

Jewry had much to answer for in my eyes when I got to know its activity in the press, art, literature, and the theater. All their unctuous reassurances were no longer of any use. It was sufficient to observe a billboard, to study the names of the intellectual producers of the horrible trash they advertised for the movies and theater, to become hardened for a long time. This was the pestilence, intellectual pestilence, far worse than the Black Death of long ago, with which the people were being infected. And in what quantities was this poison being produced! Naturally, the lower the intellectual and moral level of such art fabricators, the greater their fertility until the rogues, like garbage sorters, splash their filth in the face of humanity. Just think, for every Goethe, Nature can easily come up with ten thousand such polluters of the environment, who now poison the soul like germ carriers of the worst sort.

It was horrifying, but undeniable, that just the Jew in abundant numbers seemed chosen by Nature for this shameful destiny.

Is this the chosenness of the Jews? . . .

I now began to examine my beloved "world press" from this viewpoint.

The more fundamentally I probed the object of my erstwhile admiration, the more it withered. Its style became ever more unbearable. The content I had to reject as inwardly corrupt and superficial. The objectivity of the reporting seemed to me now to partake more of lying than the honest truth. Ah, but the authors were—Jews.

Thousands of things I had scarcely noticed before now appeared noteworthy to me; other things that I had thought about I now learned to grasp and understand.

I now saw the liberal slant of this press in a different light. Its aristocratic tone in the answering of attacks as well as their condemnation to silence were revealed to me now as clever and shabby tricks. Encomiastic theater criticism was always reserved for Jewish authors, and their rejections never fell upon any but the Germans. In the needling of Wilhelm II could be discerned the constancy of its methods, exactly in the same way as the commendation of French culture and civilization. The kitschy contents of the novellas now became unacceptable [to me], and in their language I detected the sounds of an alien people. However, the sense of the whole was so inimical to Germandom that it could only have been intentional.

But in whose interest was this?

Was it all an accident?

Gradually, I became unsure.

However, the process was accelerated by insights that I gained in a series of other events. I refer to the general conception of ethics and morals as openly exhibited by a large part of Jewry and that could be visibly substantiated.

Here again the streets offered a frequently and truly evil instructional lesson.

The relationship of Jewry to prostitution and still more to the white-slave traffic could be especially well studied in Vienna as in no other city of western Europe, with the possible exception of the ports of southern France. Walking of a night the streets and alleys of Leopoldstadt,[2] you witness everywhere, whether you want to or not, encounters that remained hidden from the greatest part of the German people until the war presented soldiers on the eastern front occasion to see similar things, or, more aptly put, forced them to see such.

The first time I recognized the Jews directing this disgusting traffic in vice, shamelessly and in ice-cold business fashion, a cold shudder ran down my back.

But then it inflamed me.

Now I no longer avoided discussion of the Jewish question. No, now I welcomed it. But as I had learned to look for the Jew in all the areas and manifestations of cultural and artistic life, I suddenly happened upon him in a place where I least expected to do so.

When I discerned the Jews as leaders of the Social Democrats, the scales fell from my eyes. The long struggle of the soul thereupon concluded.

Even in the daily relations with my fellow workers I saw an astonishing adaptability—how within the space of a few days or even a few hours they adopted altered positions on the same question. It was difficult for me to understand how men, who, when spoken to privately still had some reasonable views, immediately lost them as soon as they came under the spell of the masses. This happened often enough to make me despair. When, after hours of persuasion, I was convinced that this time I had finally broken through the ice or that I had cleared up some nonsense and rejoiced in having done so, I would on the next day, to my grief, have to begin all over again. It had all been in vain. Like an eternal pendulum, their views seemed to swing back again and again to madness.

This much I could comprehend: they were dissatisfied with their lot and damned the destiny that hit them so often and so cruelly. They hated

---

[2]Vienna's second district, the former ghetto, was still heavily populated by Jews.

the employers who seemed to be the heartless executioners of that destiny. They cursed the authorities who, in their eyes, possessed no feeling for their situation. They demonstrated against the price of necessities and carried their demands into the streets. All this could be understood without reflection. What remained inexplicable, however, was the boundless hate that they laid upon their own nationality. They defamed the greatness of the nation, sullied its history, and dragged its great men into the gutter.

This struggle against their own kind, this [fouling] of their own nest and homeland was equally senseless and incomprehensible. It was unnatural.

It was possible to cure them of this vice, but only temporarily, for days or, at most, weeks. If, however, you met the same supposed convert a little later, he had returned to what he was.

He was again possessed by the Unnatural.

Gradually, I realized that the Social Democratic press was conducted predominantly by Jews. But I did not put any special significance on this circumstance because the conditions were exactly the same in the other papers. Only one fact was obvious: there was not a single paper with Jews present on it that could be designated as truly national, at least according to my education and conceptions.

When I gained enough self-control to read these kinds of Marxist press productions, the aversion grew to such proportions that I now sought to get to know about the manufacturers of these thrown-together villainies.

From publishers on down, they were all Jews.

I gathered all the obtainable Social Democratic brochures and sought out the names of their authors: Jews. I noted the names of almost all the leaders; they were in by far the greatest part also members of the "Chosen People," whether acting as members of the parliament or in the secretariats of the trade unions, heads of organizations, or street agitators. It was always the same uncanny picture. The names Austerlitz, David, Adler, Ellenbogen, etc. will remain eternally in my memory.

One thing had become clear to me: the leadership of the party, with whose petty members I had been carrying on a violent battle for months, lay almost exclusively in the hands of an alien people. That the Jew was no German I now knew to my inner satisfaction and with finality.

Only now did I learn to know the seducers of our people completely.

A year of my sojourn in Vienna had sufficed for me to become convinced that no worker could be so stubborn as to be beyond better knowledge and better explanations. Slowly I mastered their doctrine and employed it as a weapon in the struggle for my own inner convictions.

Almost always now I was victorious.

The great mass was to be saved, but only after the heaviest sacrifices of time and patience.

Never, however, was a Jew to be freed from his viewpoint.

I was still childlike enough at that time to want to make the madness of their doctrine clear to them; I talked my tongue sore and my throat hoarse and thought that I must succeed in convincing them of the harmfulness of their Marxist insanity. In fact, I achieved just the opposite. It seemed as though the mounting insight into the nihilistic effect of Social

Democratic theories and their realization only served to strengthen them in their determination.

The more I argued with them, the more I learned their dialectic. At first they calculated on the stupidity of their adversary. Then, when they could find no other way out, they played stupid themselves. . . . Whenever you attacked one of the apostles, your hand closed around slimy matter that immediately separated and slipped through the fingers and the next moment reconstituted itself. If you struck such an annihilating blow that, observed by the audience, he had no choice but to agree with you, and thus you thought you had taken one step forward, the next day your amazement would be great. The Jew knew nothing at all about yesterday and repeated his same old twaddle as though nothing had happened; if you angrily challenged him on this, he could not remember a thing other than he had demonstrated the correctness of his assertions on the previous day.

Many times I stood there astonished.

I didn't know what to be more amazed at: their verbal agility or their art in lying.

Gradually, I began to hate them.

All this had but one good side: that to just the extent I identified the actual bearers or at least the disseminators of Social Democracy, so the love for my own people had to increase. Who could curse the unhappy victims of these devilishly skillful seducers? How difficult was it for even me to master the dialectical lying of this race! And how vain was such a success against people who twisted the truth in your mouth, who brazenly denied the words they had just spoken and in the next minute took credit for it, anyway.

No, the more I knew the Jews, the more I had to pardon the workers. . . .

. . . It was the duty of every thinking man to push himself into the forefront of the cursed [Marxist] movement, in order to perhaps avert the worst. . . . But the instigators of this disease of the peoples must have been real devils. For only in the brains of monsters—not men—could such a plan and organization assume palpable form, the actions of which would have as their final result the collapse of human culture, thereby leading to the desolation of the world.

In this case the only salvation remaining was war—war with all the weapons the human spirit, reason, and will could muster, without regard to which side of the scales destiny might throw its blessing.

Thus I began to familiarize myself with the founders of this doctrine, in order to study the principles of the movement. That I came to the goal more quickly than I had at first perhaps dared to think, I owed to my newly won, though still superficial, knowledge of the Jewish question. It alone enabled me to compare the reality with the theoretical sham of the founding apostles of Social Democracy; it taught me to understand the language of the Jewish people, which speaks in order to hide its thoughts, or at least to veil them. Its real objective is not to be found in the lines but rather slumbering, well hidden, between the lines.

It was for me the time of the greatest inner upheavals I had ever had to endure.

From a weak cosmopolitan I had become a fanatical antisemite.

Just one more time—it was the last—I was visited by the deepest anxiety and oppressive thoughts.

As I scrutinized the effects of the Jewish people over long periods of human history, suddenly there arose the fearful question: did an unknowable destiny, for reasons unbeknownst to us poor men, perhaps wish with eternal and immutable decision that the final victory go to this little nation?

Could it be that this people, which lives only for the earth, will be granted it as a reward? . . .

As I calmly and clearly deepened my knowledge of Marxism and thus the effects of the Jewish people, destiny itself gave me the answer.

The Jewish doctrine of Marxism rejects the aristocratic principle of Nature and sets in its place the eternal privilege of power and strength of the mass and the dead weight of its numbers. It therefore denies the value of the human personality, contests the significance of nationality and race, and therewith withdraws from humanity the basis of its existence and culture. As a foundation of the universe this [doctrine] would bring about the end of any intellectually comprehensible order. And thus as in this the greatest recognizable organism, the realization of such a law could result only in chaos and, ultimately, death for the inhabitants of this planet.

If the Jew with the help of his Marxist creed is victorious over the peoples of this world, then his crown will be the funeral wreath of humanity; then this planet will travel through the ether as it did millions of years ago, devoid of men.

Eternal Nature avenges itself mercilessly on the transgression of its commandments.

Thus I believe today that I am acting according to the will of the almighty Creator: *when I defend myself against the Jew, I am fighting for the work of the Lord.*

20. Adolf Hitler
"The International Jew and the International Stock Exchange—Guilty of the World War" (1923)

My dear German National Comrades!

In the winter of 1919–20, for the first time, we National Socialists publicly posed the question to the German nation: who is guilty of the war? It was a daring undertaking in view of the attitude of the

Source: From Ernst Boepple, ed., *Adolf Hitlers Reden* (Munich, 1934), pp. 43–50 (a speech given on April 13, 1923).

government of those November heroes, the "people's commissars,"[1] and because of the total confusion in the masses that it misled. Immediately and from all sides we received the stereotypical and self-abasing answer: "We confess; the guilt for the war is ours." The then "German" government in Munich—today it, too, would stand under the Law for the Protection of the Republic—published so-called documents that were supposed to lay our war guilt before the entire world![2] *Yes, the whole Revolution [of 1918] was artificially made on the basis of this out-and-out monstrous lie! For if they had not been able to employ it as a propaganda formula against the old Reich, then what sense could they have imputed to the November betrayal? They needed this defamation of the prior system in order to be able to justify their own shameful deed to the nation. The criminally incited masses were prepared to accept uncritically everything the new governors told them.* They were ready to shout down any who dared to assert that it was not Germany but other powers who bore the guilt for unleashing the war.

The Marxist-democratic-pacifist gravediggers of the old Reich shouted: "The fact that a war was fought at all is sufficient to prove that the monarchical-capitalist-pan-German wastrels had been at work. Civilized peoples do not fight wars!" What blessings of civilization we have attained, thanks to that day of salvation, November 9. They are revealed in all the corners of Europe, aflame with violent deeds and disturbances. It is our view that the era before the League of Nations was a good deal more honorable and humane. Those others maintain that, to the contrary, we have now attained the highest period of culture.

We ask: must there be wars? The pacifist answers: no! He explains in particular that quarrels in the lives of nations are merely the expression of the oppression of one class of men by the dominant bourgeoisie. Actual differences of opinion between nations should be settled in a "peace court." However, he leaves unanswered the question as to whether the judges of these courts of arbitration will also possess the power to place the parties under limits. I think a defendant goes into court "voluntarily" only because otherwise he will be hauled in. I would like to see the nation that in case of a controversy will allow itself to be dragged before the international

---

[1]The People's Commissars, three Majority and three Independent socialists, made up the provisional government that took control in Berlin in November 1918. November 9, which Hitler mentions later in this document, was the day the revolution became general in Germany. To the German Right, the revolutionaries on the homefront—democrats, socialists, pacifists, and Jews—precipitated the armistice and thus bore the guilt for Germany's defeat. Hence "November heroes," "November criminals," and other similar allusions refer to those whom the Right viewed as the villains of the Weimar Republic.

[2]Hitler is alluding to the law passed in reaction to the assassination of Walther Rathenau. (See note 1, Document 18.) The revolutionary government of Bavaria, under the Jewish Independent Socialist Kurt Eisner, who was assassinated in 1919, published documents from the Bavarian archives that purported to show German responsibility for the outbreak of World War I.

court without external coercion. In the lives of nations, a kind of divine judgment decides matters in the end.

What if it occurs that in a controversy between two nations, both are right? For example, Austria, a nation of fifty million, has unconditional right to an outlet to the sea. But Italy claimed the "right of self-determination" for the areas in question, which have a predominantly Italian population. Which will relinquish [its claim] voluntarily? Neither! Strength decides what belongs to nations. Before God and the world, it is always the stronger who has the right to do his will. History demonstrates: for he who lacks the strength, "right in itself" is meaningless! A world court without a world police would be a joke. From which members of the present League of Nations would this force be recruited? perhaps from out of the ranks of the old German Army? All Nature is a violent struggle between the strong and the weak, an eternal victory of the strong over the weak. If it were any different, all Nature would be a corruption. Corrupt are the states that sin against this elementary law. *You need not look long for an example of this lethal corruption. You see it today in the Republic.*

We must examine the conflicts that existed in Europe before the world war. England and Russia engaged in commercial competition in the Bengal plain, in Afghanistan, etc. For 140 years France and England were rivals for hegemony. They have remained up to the present moment, despite the commonly waged robber [world] war, the same old bitter antagonists. France, moreover, had conflicts of interest with Italy, especially in North Africa. On the other hand, there was no conflict of any sort between Germany and Russia. On the contrary, industrial Germany badly needed additional years of peace. Agrarian Russia needed a great deal, but in no way did it need territorial expansion at the expense of the German Reich. Similarly, Germany and Italy had no territorial frictions. Nevertheless, a cunningly conducted intrigue first incited Russia against Germany and then, finally, the whole world. Today it is an infamous fraud to write sanctimoniously: "If only the warmongers in Germany had been killed off in timely fashion, we would have been spared the world war!" I ask: Where in all the world were these warmongers? Who are they, and what means did they use?

With the lapsing of Bismarck's Reinsurance Treaty with Russia,[3] there began a purposeful agitation by the Jewish-democratic-Marxist world press. In republican Paris it hailed the "bloody Tsar." In imperial Berlin it bellowed at the same time: "Down with the Tsar!" The stock exchange bellowed. The democratic and Marxist parties did the same. Indeed, even

---

[3]The Reinsurance Treaty (1887) was part of Bismarck's elaborate network of diplomatic agreements that sought to protect the German Empire, particularly from France. Upon Bismarck's dismissal in 1890, Kaiser Wilhelm II and his foreign policy advisers decided to simplify Bismarck's system and thus did not renew the treaty with Russia. France seized the opportunity to break out of its isolation by allying with Russia. The kaiser's later critics, among them Hitler, regarded this decision as a fateful mistake, leading ultimately to the world war.

Bebel,[4] who otherwise was unwilling to vote a soldier or a penny for "vile militarism" and the defense against France, spoke the word: "If it's against Russia, I'll shoulder a rifle myself!" And in Petersburg it is the same picture: limitless incitement against Germany, adulation for France—again in the columns of the exclusively democratic-Jewish-Marxist newspapers there.

In an astonishing cooperative effort, here as well as there, democracy and Marxism, led by a well-known directory of Jewish wire-pullers, succeeded in inciting the once wholly friendly Russians and Germans into a completely senseless, irrational enmity! Since the German nation had grounds for neither hatred nor envy of Russia, who could have such a burning interest in this artificial whipping up [of hostility]?! *It was the Jew!*

He bore and nurtured this hatred up to the day of the tsar's sneaky mobilization order. What was all of liberalism, what our press, what the stock exchange, what freemasonry . . . *instruments of the Jews!* Tsarism had to be felled, not to achieve mere equality for the Jewry of Russia, but rather to conquer the privileges that it already possessed in other "democratic" states. In the land of restrictions on Jews, the Jew strove for unrestricted domination. No longer persecuted—there has been no persecution of Jews for two hundred years—the Jew seeks only a continuing *persecution of Christians!*

Could the Jew have employed any but Germany for the wiping out of Russia? To finish off this Germany at a later date would be child's play, he thought. Because he knew the German children only too well! Only in the German Marxist press could a Salomon Kosmanowski (alias Kurt Eisner) dare to write: "There is no turning back! To arms against Russia! The task of emancipating the nations has fallen now to Germany!" Only to a German General Staff wholly devoid of political instincts could an east-European Jew like this dare to report for duty!

The democratic-Marxist-Jewish world press sacrificed Germany to its alliance strategy. With mathematical certainty, it purposely exploited the conflicts between Austria and Russia and Austria and Italy to bring about the outbreak of war.

Austria-Russia: It [the press] fueled the shortsighted Polish policy of Vienna against Russia. It incited the Poles of Cracow and Lvov to the misuse of their remaining liberties. It agitated in Petersburg: "The way to Vienna goes through Berlin." It agitated until the necessary degree of deadly enmity between Russia and Austria had been obtained.

Austria-Italy: Simultaneously, it [the press] agitated in Vienna and in Rome. It seized upon Bismarck's words, bellowing: "He who lays hands on Trieste will fall onto the point of the German sword!" Good! But why,

---

[4]August Bebel (1840–1913) led the German Social Democratic party (SPD) from the 1860s until his death. Bebel was a staunch antimilitarist, but he and most of his party adhered to the anti-Russian sentiments of Karl Marx, who regarded the tsar as "the policeman of Europe," the reactionary suppressor of revolutionary movements. The SPD was on record before 1914 in its willingness to fight a defensive war against Russia.

then, was Trieste not Germanized?! That would require an iron fist, an iron will. Vienna lacked these. Why? Because with every attempt to do it, that same press began to agitate in the opposite sense: "You barbarians! Consider humanity! The right of self-determination! Be humane!" But with humanity and democracy, no land has yet been colonized! In Rome at the same hour, that same democratic-Marxist-Jewish press sang the inflammatory refrain: "Free your unredeemed brothers! The way to Trieste cannot bypass Vienna! There is no going back! You must fulfill your emancipatory mission!" Thus did the Jewish freemasonry of Italy through its press incite Italy to make war on Austria, and beyond that, on Germany![5]

A clever and decisive German government could have found a political way out of this, were it not for that same press that knew how to prevent it. In Berlin all it needed was sentimental phrases! Dumping that impossible creation, Austria, whose inner spirit was too exhausted to maintain itself as a state, Germany should have incorporated German-Austria and given up on the rest instead of chaining its destiny to it.

In the relations between Germany and France, there ruled fundamental conflicts that neither the dispatches of an Eisner-Kosmanowski nor abject cowardice could remove. Before the war, only an armed coexistence was possible. Certainly, the war of 1870–71 signified the conclusion for Germany of a hundred years of enmity. In France, on the other hand, all the means of newspaper propaganda, schoolbooks, theaters, and movies preached glowing hatred of Germany. As Berlin agitated against Russia, so Paris railed against Berlin. German miners rushed across the borders to bring help to their French colleagues during a fearful catastrophe. Who crowed the most hateful defamations? Who reviled even this deed that sprang from genuine German gallantry? *Matin, Journal,* etc.—all the Jew papers of France! In the seeking out and exploitation of conflict, the strivings of world Jewry are laid bare once more!

The conflict between Germany and England lay in the realm of economics. Until 1850 England's position as a world power was uncontested. British engineers, British trade conquered the world. Germany, thanks to great diligence and mounting efficiency, began to become a dangerous competitor. In a short time the English corporations present in Germany went over into German industrial ownership. German industry expanded mightily; indeed, its products pushed the British out of the London market. The defensive measure of marking goods "Made in Germany" had opposite the expected success. This "trademark" became the very best sort of advertisement!

---

[5]At the northern end of the Adriatic Sea, Trieste functioned as the only port of the Austrian Empire before World War I. The hinterland of Trieste was largely Slovenian, but the metropolis itself was Italian in language and culture. In 1919 the city and its province, long the objects of Italian irredentism, were annexed by Italy. "Jewish freemasonry" played no role in these developments.

The German economy was not created only in Essen but by a man who knew *that behind the economy there must stand power because power alone can guarantee the economy! And this power was born on the battlefields of 1870–71, not in the babbling atmosphere of parliaments!*[6] The deaths of forty thousand made possible the lives of forty million. When England threatened to bring Germany to its knees, it came to the ultimate means in the competition of nations—violence. A grandiose press propaganda was conducted as preparation. Who, however, is the chief of the whole British world commercial press? *Northcliffe! a Jew!*[7] Weekly he sends thirty million newspapers into the world. And 99 percent of the press of England is to be found in Jewish hands. "Every new-born German child costs the life of one Briton!" "There is not a Briton who would not benefit from the crushing of Germany!" Thus the coarsest slogans appealed to the basest instincts. Agitation by assertion, defamation, and promise, as only the Jew understands how, as only the Jew papers would dare to put before an Aryan people. Finally, 1914, and they still agitate: "Alas, poor violated Belgium! For humanity's sake and its honor—to the rescue of small nations!" The same lying in all the incitements throughout the whole world! Its success is painfully obvious to the German people!

Finally, what cause had America to enter the war against Germany? With the outbreak of the war so long desired by Juda, numerous great Jewish firms in the United States became war contractors. They supplied goods to the European war market in quantities that even they had probably never dreamed of—a gigantic harvest! Yet nothing can satisfy the insatiable greed of the Jews. Thus there began at the behest of the stock exchange kings through their dependent press a propaganda campaign without comparison. A gigantic organization of press lies was constructed. And again it was a Jew concern, *the Hearst Press,*[8] that set the tone of the agitation against Germany. The hatred of these "Americans" was primarily directed not against commercial Germany and not even against the military. It was directed against social Germany. Because [Germany] had kept itself outside the framework of the world trusts. The old Reich had at least made the honorable effort to be social. We had surely made social beginnings as no other land in the entire world! . . . The old Reich built schools, hospitals, scientific institutes, to the amazement and envy of the whole

---

[6]Essen in the Ruhr was the center of the steel and armaments empire of the Krupps. "The man" referred to and paraphased by Hitler is Bismarck, who said in 1862: "Not by speeches and majorities will the great questions of the day be decided—that was the mistake of 1848 and 1849—but by iron and blood."

[7]Alfred Charles William Harmsworth, Viscount Northcliffe (1865–1922), created modern journalism in Great Britain and presided over a huge press empire, which included the *Daily Mail, Daily Mirror,* and *The Times.* A major influence in British politics, he took charge of propaganda directed at the enemy in the Ministry of Information in 1918. He was not a Jew.

[8]William Randolph Hearst (1863–1951) was not Jewish.

world. In the November Republic these cultural institutions are daily going to rack and ruin.

Because the old Reich had been social in this sense, because it did not allow itself to regard men exclusively as numbers, it posed the greatest danger to the world stock exchange. This is also the reason that Jewish-led "comrades" battle against their own interests in [this] country. This is why the slogans are the same throughout the whole world—and why the Jewish-democratic press in America had to pull off its master stroke: namely, to incite a great and peaceful people, as indifferent to Europe's wars as the north pole, into [fighting] the cruelest of wars. This they did "for the sake of civilization," while conducting, in the name of civilization, shameful, invented, lying, falsified atrocity propaganda. Because this, the last social state on earth had to be brought to ruin, twenty-six nations of the world were incited against one another by this press, which is exclusively the possession of the same internationalist people, the one and the same race that is fundamentally inimical to all national states!

Who could have prevented the world war? Something like the "civilized solidarity" in whose name this atrocity propaganda was waged against Germany by the Jews? Or perhaps the pacifists? Perhaps the "German" pacifists . . . who trumpeted to the world their daily defamation of the heroic German nation? These masters of so-called world pacifism, which was founded exclusively by—Jews. Perhaps the much-vaunted proletarian solidarity? "All the wheels are still, when it is this strong arm's will!" The wheels of the world run diligently onward. Only one wheel did they try to stop with their incessant subversion. During the munitions strike of 1918, which cost thousands of frontline soldiers their lives, they almost succeeded.[9] On November 9, they brought the wheel—the wheel of Germany—to a halt. The Social Democratic party declared literally in its main organ, the *Vorwärts*, that it was not in the interests of German workers for Germany to win the war! *I ask you German workers, does it lie in your interests today that you have become slaves?* You are a thousand-fold angrier than before, writhing and groaning in hopeless, fruitless forced labor, while your leaders without exception—*but wait, who are these leaders of the proletariat? Once again, Jews!*

Might, perhaps, the Freemasons have prevented the world war? This noblest, philanthropic institution, which proclaims the purest blessings upon the nations, which simultaneously was the chief agitatoress of the war? Who are the Freemasons, actually? There are two degrees. In Germany, the lower one contains the average German citizen who feels a certain something when presented with banal phrases. The real *responsible ones*, however, are those multifaceted individuals who get on in every

---

[9]In January 1918, 400,000 munitions workers in Berlin went out on strike calling for a speedy end to the war. It took a state of siege and brutal suppression by the army to restore order.

climate, those three hundred Rathenaus,[10] all of whom know each other and have the worldly skill to direct things over the heads of kings and state presidents. They are the ones who unscrupulously take over every office and who understand how brutally to enslave all the nations—*once again, Jews!*

But why were the Jews generally opposed to Germany? Today, on the basis of a huge number of facts, this is clear enough. They used the age-old tactics of the hyenas: when the fighters exhausted themselves, they moved in. Then the harvest! In war and revolutions Juda simply attains the unattainable. Hundreds of thousands of lice-ridden Orientals become modern "Europeans"! Turbulent times bring about miracles. Before 1914, for example, in Bavaria, how long would a Galician Jew have lasted as prime minister?! Or in Russia, an anarchist out of the New York ghetto, Bronstein (Trotsky), as a dictator?![11] A few wars and revolutions have sufficed to make the Jewish race the possessor of red gold and therewith masters of the world.

This people hated above all others the two states, Germany and Russia, that until 1914 foiled the realization of its goal: world domination. In these two places they were denied what had already fallen to them in the Western democracies. They were not yet the sole rulers in intellectual and economic life. Neither were the parliaments yet the exclusive instruments of Jewish capital and will. *The German man and the genuine Russian had maintained a certain distance from the Jew.* There still lived in both peoples the healthy instinct of scorn for the Jews. And it was still possible that in these monarchies there could arise once again a Frederick the Great or a William I, who might send democracy and parliamentary chicanery to the devil. Thus the Jews became revolutionaries! The Republic was supposed to lead them to enrichment and power. They disguised this objective: "Down with the monarchies! Empowerment of the 'sovereign' people!"

I don't know whether we can speak today of a sovereign German or Russian people! We cannot, in any case, detect it! What the German people can detect, however, what stands in front of its eyes every day in the crassest form, is the swaggering debauchery, gluttony, and speculation, the public mockery of the Jews! *The so-called German free state has become a free-for-all in which this vermin can enrich itself without limit.*

---

[10]Hitler contributes yet another distorted allusion to the statement of Walther Rathenau in 1909 that three hundred individuals guided the economic destiny of the Continent. (See note 3, Document 18.)

[11]Leon Trotsky (1870–1940), born of Jewish parents in the Ukraine as Lev Davidovich Bronstein, spent a few months in 1917 in New York City, before returning to play a major part in the Russian Revolution. The "Galician Jew" is another reference to Kurt Eisner, who, however, was born in Berlin.

Thus Germany and Russia had to be brought down, in order that the old prophecy be fulfilled. Thus the whole world was turned upside down. Thus were all the lies and propaganda brutally employed against the state with the last remaining idealists—*Germany!* And thus Juda won the world war! Or will you maintain that the French, English, or American "people" won the war? All of us, victors and vanquished, are the defeated. *One stands over all the others: the world stock market, which has become lord of the nations!*

What, then, is the guilt of Germany itself in the war? It consists of this: that in a time when it was already struggling for its existence, it neglected to organize its defense vigorously enough. In the unfolding of its power, it both lacked the courage to silence its ill-willed critics and failed to guarantee the victory of the Reich. In 1912, when out of stupidity and baseness the criminal Reichstag refused [to vote funds for] three army corps, it is the fault of the German people that it did not simply go ahead with them anyway! With those additional 120,000 men, the Battle of the Marne[12] would have been won and the war decided. Two million fewer German heroes would have sunk into the grave! Who, in 1912 as in 1918, struck the weapons from the hands of the German people? Who, at that time and in the last year of the war, blinded the German people with the theory: "The whole world will throw down its weapons, if Germany does so!" Who? The democratic-Marxist Jew, who then and now incited and incites the others to *take up weapons* in order to put "barbaric" Germany under the yoke!

Now someone will perhaps ask if it serves any purpose to speak about war guilt today. Yes, we have a duty to speak of it! For the murderers of our Fatherland, those who have betrayed and sold out Germany for years and years, are the same November criminals who have thrust us into the deepest misfortune! We have the duty to speak of it because in the near future we will have the power and also the further duty to hang these spoilers, scoundrels, and traitors on the gallows where they belong!

Let no one believe that anything has changed! On the contrary, these November crooks, who run free among us today, are still going against us.

From knowledge comes the will to rise high again.

There are two million lost in battle. They, too, have rights—not just us survivors. There are millions of orphans, cripples, and widows among us. They also have rights! None of them died for the Germany of today, or became cripples, orphans, or widows. We owe it to these millions that a new Germany be built!

---

[12]The first battle of the Marne, September 6–9, 1914, halted the German advance on Paris and initiated four years of trench warfare on the Western Front, where Hitler served as a runner.

21. Adolf Hitler
Speech to the Great German Reichstag
(1939)

The German people don't want their affairs settled or regulated by an alien people. France to the French, England to the English, America to the Americans, and Germany to the Germans!

We are determined to thwart and thrust aside this alien people that knew how to insinuate itself and seize all the leading positions for itself, for we intend to educate our own people for these positions.

We have hundreds of thousands of the most intelligent sons of peasants and workers. We will have them educated and are already doing so, and we wish them someday to occupy the leading positions of state and society, along with the rest of our educated strata, and not the members of an alien people.

Above all, however, German culture, as the name announces, is German and not Jewish, and it therefore ought to repose in the care and administration of our own people. If, however, the rest of the world puts on hypocritical airs and shouts about this barbaric expulsion from Germany of such an irreplaceable, culturally valuable element, then we can only stand amazed before the deductions drawn [from this action].

How thankful we must be that these august bearers of culture can be freed for employment by the rest of the world. On the basis of their own declarations, they can have no excuse to refuse to accept such extremely valuable people into their own lands.

Indeed, it is not understandable why so much is demanded just of the German people with regard to the members of this race. But these "splendid people" are suddenly rejected on the flimsiest pretexts by the very states that are so enthusiastic about them. I believe that this problem must be solved, and the sooner the better. Europe cannot achieve peace before and unless the Jewish question is cleared away.

Sooner or later it may well be that this problem will produce an agreement between the nations of Europe, which otherwise do not find it easy to come together. The world has sufficient space for colonization. First, however, the opinion must be overcome that the dear Lord has destined a certain percentage of Jewish people to be the beneficiaries on the body and productive labor of other peoples.

Jewry will have to accommodate itself to solid, constructive activity, just as other peoples do. Or, sooner or later, it will succumb to a crisis of unimaginable scope.

Source: From Max Domarus, ed., *Hitler: Reden und Proklamationen, 1932–1945.* (Munich, 1965), 2:1057–58.

And on this memorable day for us Germans,[1] and perhaps for others as well, I would like now to make a pronouncement on one more matter: I have often been a prophet in my life and have been mostly laughed at. In the period of my struggle for power, it was in the first case the Jewish people who only laughed at my prophecies that I would one day take over leadership of the German state and therewith over the entire people and that I would, along with many other problems, bring the Jewish problem to solution. I believe that Jewry's ringing laughter of those days has most likely already stuck in its throat.

Today I want once more to be a prophet: If international finance Jewry in and outside Europe succeeds in plunging the peoples into another world war, then the end result will not be the Bolshevization of the earth and the consequent victory of Jewry but the annihilation of the Jewish race in Europe.

The era of propagandistic defenselessness among the non-Jewish peoples is over. National-socialist Germany and fascist Italy possess those means that can, when necessary, enlighten the world about the essence of a problem that many peoples instinctively recognize but remain scientifically unclear about.

For the moment Jewry may, in certain states, conduct its agitation under the protection of the press, film, radio propaganda, theater, and literature which lie in its hands. If this people once more succeeds in agitating the masses among the peoples into a wholly senseless battle which serves the exclusive interests of the Jews, then the effectiveness of a declaration will be revealed—that in Germany alone, and in a few years, Jewry will be laid low altogether.

The peoples do not want to die on the battlefields again so that this rootless, international race may profit from the business of war and satisfy its Old Testament thirst for revenge. The Jewish slogan, "Proletarians of all lands, unite," will be vanquished by a higher knowledge—that is, "Productive members of all nations, know your common enemy!"

---

[1]January 30, 1939, was the sixth anniversary of Hitler's appointment as chancellor of the Weimar Republic.

France and the Holocaust

Germany invaded France on May 17, 1940. A month later, the aged World War I hero, Marshal Henri-Philippe Pétain, took control of the French government and immediately sued for an armistice. France threw down its arms, and three-fifths of the country fell under German occupation. At the resort town of Vichy in unoccupied France, an authoritarian regime took power and in the guise of a national revolution set about undoing the democratic traditions of the Third Republic, replacing "Liberty, Equality, and Fraternity" with a new slogan, "Work, Family, and Fatherland."

Vichy's politics were complicated. Patriots, anticommunists, Catholic rightists, ambitious intellectuals, and sheer opportunists formulated its policies. Although avowed antisemites were among them, those with no public history of antisemitism were probably more powerful and numerous. A faction that stood for minimal collaboration with the Germans under Admiral François Darlan gave way in April 1942 to a government headed by Pierre Laval, who made maximum cooperation his program.

Given the military defeat and German occupation, attempts to maintain a truly independent France in the unoccupied zone were doomed. The Jews of France suffered most from this situation, for one of the areas in which Vichy found cooperation with the Germans "cheapest" was the Jewish question. Working within a long tradition of French antisemitism, the men of Vichy used persecution of Jews as a bargaining chip, sacrificing Jewish lives in order to win illusory concessions and a somewhat longer leash from the Nazi victors.

After World War II, when the surviving collaborators of Vichy France were called upon to defend their actions, almost all of them claimed that they had acted on the behest of the Nazis, that they had sought to maintain an autonomous French administration and thereby moderate Nazi harshness. The historical record, however, will not support this defense, particularly in the matter of official policy toward Jews.

Representatives of Vichy, hoping to prove themselves worthy of German trust, often took the initiative in settling the Jewish question, even without Nazi prompting or pressure. Well before the Germans showed themselves ready to prosecute the Final Solution in unoccupied France, Vichy pushed for increasingly radical measures and enacted them on its own authority. By the time the Wannsee Conference (see Document 24) systematized the extermination of European Jewry in January 1942, the Germans had become confident that "in occupied and unoccupied France the seizure of Jews for evacuation should in all probability proceed without great difficulties." Their confidence was well founded.

In the aftermath of the defeat and armistice of 1940, nearly 195,000 Jews fled south to the unoccupied zone. Of these, approximately 145,000 were French born; the remaining 50,000 were fairly evenly divided between unnaturalized east Europeans and more-recent refugees from Germany and Austria. Initially following a program of forced emigration, the Germans also expropriated and then dumped Jews from the occupied zone into the area under Vichy control.

Beginning in August 1940, Vichy laid the legal groundwork for extensive anti-Jewish legislation. Definitions of Jewishness, confiscation of property, expulsion of Jews from economic, professional, and educational life, and internment of foreigners were the main features of the new policy. In March 1941 the General Commissariat for Jewish Affairs came into existence to enforce the anti-Jewish laws, propose further legislation, and administer the liquidation of Jewish property. Its first chief was the long-time antisemite and right-wing Catholic politician, Xavier Vallat.

In his introduction to the pamphlet by Gabriel Malglaive that follows, Vallat repeats the classic charges against Jews. The long history of those charges becomes, in itself, an argument in favor of their truthfulness. By this time, they had in fact become so familiar to the French public that they needed no special proof. It was axiomatic that the unassimilable Jews had done and were continuing to do great harm to France; it was their own hardened character and universally destructive behavior that now necessitated the severest legal measures, even at the risk of doing some injustice to the innocent—always a painful matter to Frenchmen, Vallat assures the reader. But it is France, not the Jews, that truly suffers and that must now submit "to the scalpel."

Neither Malglaive nor Vallat claims to be acting upon a popular mandate, and it is unclear just how popular Vichy's anti-Jewish measures were. At first the public appeared to be indifferent to official antisemitism, certainly a necessary precondition for the future radicalization in government policy. Gradually, however, popular support for antisemitism caught up with administrative practice. That Jews were not being deported to work in Germany, like young Frenchmen, rankled many. The Jews, "who lived easy lives," were made responsible for the war, defeat, occupation, and ensuing deprivations. Only after the deportation of Jewish women and children to the East began, accompanied by scenes of great brutality, did French opinion change.

Malglaive and Vallat insist upon the independence of Vichy's policy and justify it by emphasizing the great number of foreign Jews in France, implying that these unwanted aliens will suffer the full wrath of the new laws. Unlike the Nazis, Vichy made exceptions for long-settled Jews who had served the French state. Nor were Jews systematically cut off from the rest of society by means of ghettos, curfews, forbidden zones, or special shopping hours, as in Germany and the occupied zone. But both men call for a "complete solution," and although this does not necessarily mean their murder, the new laws in reality put French-born and foreign Jews at the mercy of the Germans, who were gradually arriving at their own conception of the Final Solution. Vallat, no longer in power when the deportations began in earnest, nonetheless invited that outcome when he admonished: "It is the conqueror, if he wishes to organize a durable peace, who should find the way, on a world scale if possible, in any case in Europe, to fix the errant Jew."

As German pressure grew more insistent, any semblance of French independence folded. When deportation and extermination from both zones was decided upon in the spring of 1942, the Germans found willing accomplices in Vichy. Pétain's Council of Ministers decided to distinguish between French and foreign Jews, and the great majority of the ninety thousand Jews delivered up to the Nazis were foreigners. But it is clear that the Germans depended upon the cooperation of several French administrative services to identify, round up, and transport Jews to their deaths. Vichy was particularly diligent in building up reserves of Jews in detention camps so that maximum use of scarce railway cars could be made. Its registration of Jews made it convenient for the Germans, when they occupied all of France at the end of 1942, to begin deporting French-born Jews as well. More of them would have perished if the Germans had had more time.

The most shameful chapter of Vichy's collaboration in the Final Solution, which serves as a kind of symbolic summary of the regime's heartlessness, has to do with Pierre Laval, not much of an antisemite himself but a man aptly described as one always ready to exploit the obsessions of others. In September 1942, six thousand entry visas to the United States were made available for Jewish orphans, children separated from their already deported parents, if permission for their emigration were granted by the French. Caring for these children was a bureaucratic problem that Vichy had no intention of solving. For Laval, the separation of children from their families was no more than a public-relations embarrassment. Saving them from death might trouble his collaboration with the Germans. His solution was to announce openly that in the future, families would be deported together. Although the Nazis had moved cautiously in the matter of deporting children, Laval was adamant that they be included in the transports. In 1942 alone, six thousand children were sent to Auschwitz.

For Further Reading

Michael R. Marrus and Robert O. Paxton, *Vichy France and the Jews* (New York, 1981)

22. Gabriel Malglaive
"Jewish or French?" (1942)

Translated by Edward Noonan

Preface

Why would I write a preface to a book dedicated to the Jewish problem in France?

In order to give it at least a semi-official, if not official, character? God preserve me from that! M. Malglaive thinks whatever he wishes in this

Source: From Gabriel Malglaive, *Juif ou Français, aperçus sur la question juive. Préface de M. Xavier Vallat, commissaire général aux questions juives* (Paris, 1942), pp. 3–12, 163–215.

domain, and he writes what he thinks. All this is, in passing, very close to what I myself believe to be the truth. But I shall not offend this independent writer by letting it be imagined that he was the spokesman for another mind than his own.

Would it be to attract more public attention to the work and to the subject which it treats?

Useless. The Jews suffice easily to justify, for all enlightened minds, the necessity to be aware of their actions.

What then? Well, I have only one reason to accede to M. Malglaive's wish.

It is to thank him as he deserves. First of all, in these excessive times, to have written a book without hatred—I do not at all say without passion.

Then, to have collected in a few pages the reasons accumulated throughout centuries, and particularly in the recent decades, which have led the government of the French state to legislate the Jewish problem. Then, to have explained the scope of the legislation. Finally, to give myself the opportunity to specify, on certain points, the position of the General Commissariat for Jewish Affairs.[1]

In accepting from the hands of the Marshal [Pétain] and the Admiral [Darlan] this new position, I knew in advance that I would be exposing myself to two contradictory reproaches: for some, I shall be the successor to Torquemada;[2] for others, the secret protector of the Jews.

Let's ignore, to save time, the accusation of being sold to Rothschild. . . .

Will our work be, without our knowledge, that of pitiless legal extermination, a pogrom aggravated by hypocrisy?

I ask you to read our texts with the wish to understand them and not to deform their meaning; to examine their juridical sense and their practical consequences; and you will have to conclude that we have tried—and, I hope, succeeded—in an operation necessary for the national defense against a real danger from both the interior and the exterior.

No one any longer questions the peculiar character of the Jewish people.

It was the Chosen People, and the Almighty did not haggle over certain eminent talents that many of them have borne in the highest degree.

But it is also the damned race which because it collectively consented to deicide has been condemned to no longer have a fatherland, to wander throughout the world.

We find it spread out among all the nations, yet never integrating itself, drops of oil floating on the human oceans without dissolving.

---

[1]On March 29, 1941, the General Commissariat for Jewish Affairs was created independently by the Vichy regime, although with the prompting of the Germans. The commissariat played a key role in the deportation of all stateless Jews from the German occupied and (Vichy) unoccupied zones in the summer of 1942.

[2]Tomás de Torquemada (1420–98), the Grand Inquisitor, earned his reputation for cruelty by the rigorous application of the rules he devised to extirpate heresy in Spain. He was instrumental in the expulsion of the Jews in 1492.

For a long time, the peoples tolerated them like some foreign bodies until the swelling tumor became too bothersome and they were ejected.

The French Revolution, the first, committed the folly of wishing to consider them citizens like anyone else, and, little by little, in less than a century and a half, all the other governments committed the same error lest they appear "reactionary."

This was to prepare the justification for a modern antisemitism singularly more justified than medieval antisemitism.

Of course, throughout the ages, one could reproach the Jews for constituting a state-within-the-state.

But, from now on, the Jew will everywhere be the citizen of two nations: first, of Israel, the universal nation; then, of the particular nation where he has chosen to temporarily set up his tent.

And he will demand the benefit of this double situation. As a Jew, he is international; that has many advantages. Yet he does not wish to be considered a foreigner in the state where he intends to carry out his activity, for that would represent certain inconveniences; and he will get himself naturalized.

But for him that does not represent a desire to plant his roots somewhere. Only to benefit from the plenitude of the rights of citizenship, wherever he is.

Unlike the Rothschilds, not all Jewish families have representatives in five or six different nations; but all are prepared, following an exodus, to lay claim to the nationality of the country which they encounter, without worrying at all about the one they just left.

And the most curious characteristic of this itinerant race is that it wishes to command wherever it is.

Its dream of universal domination is attached to each of its sons, aware of belonging to the superior race.

In our country, where Paris has seen the arrival of 300,000 Jews from 1812 until the present, they have invaded the academic and liberal professions, the press, radio, the cinema, the upper echelons of politics and the government, in other words, whatever serves to lead a democracy.

France had caught a Jewish brain fever which almost killed her.

We had to resort to the scalpel.

But the chapter which M. Malglaive has dedicated to the collection of texts of law . . . will prove to you that we have tried to be surgeons, and not butchers, not to mention, executioners. . . .

How will the Jewish problem finally be settled?

It is always dangerous for Aryans to prophesy, although they can hardly commit more errors than certain descendants of the prophets.

One thing is certain.

There is no partial solution to the problem.

For two thousand years, the peoples have passed their time sending back and forth to each other, in an incessant ebb and flow, the Jews who periodically become insupportable. Far from being a remedy, it was only a shifting of the evil, . . .

At the present moment, metropolitan France has 350,000 Jews.

Of these, 180,000 have come to us from eastern and central Europe, too recently to have had the time to be naturalized.

Of the remaining 170,000, only half are hereditarily French citizens; the others have been nationalized quite recently.[3]

Therefore, more than in the other countries, the Jewish problem here poses itself as a problem of foreigners.

Send them off where? To their home, i.e., throughout the vast world? How, so long as the war lasts?

In reality, it is the conqueror, if he wishes to organize a durable peace, who should find the way, on a world scale if possible, in any case in Europe, to fix the errant Jew.

Xavier Vallat

. . . In the affairs where the destinies of a country are played, the rights—the changing expression of an often ephemeral emotion—must be subservient to the duties toward the national community, towards the people and the fatherland. These duties are constant. They aim not only at the salvation of the fatherland and at its greatness. Men can change, their mood may vary, the principles of the nation remain immutable.

We shall thus say that it is in virtue of the duty which the peoples have to protect and defend their patrimony, their traditions, their customs, that we demand today the settling of the Jewish question in France. . . .

The rapid exposé which we have just completed shows, imperfectly no doubt, how throughout the centuries the Jewish problem revealed itself, how one thought it could be resolved, how, more than ever, it poses itself today.

Let us remember, and this will be our highest merit, the teachings of history; let us remember as well that the Jewish question is always there. Because no definitive solution has ever been proposed and applied. Let us not forget, finally, that if we use the formulae already tried, if we do not bring to this domain an informed politics, nothing durable, nothing profitable to the country will be realized.

The solution to such a problem is a political affair, thus in France rigorously French. In recent years, the Germans and the Italians, to name only the principals, have adopted a series of measures conforming to the interest of their own countries. When, in France, we wish to resolve the Jewish question, that does not mean that we are acting under foreign orders. History has established the imperious necessity to settle once and for all this affair. Neither does it prove that we ought to adopt the same measures.

---

[3]These figures are more or less accurate. Jews constituted less than 1 percent of the total population of France, which stood at 45 million. Approximately 150,000 were native born. About 50,000 were refugees from Germany, Austria, and Czechoslovakia; 25,000 more had recently fled from Belgium and the Netherlands. The other foreign Jews had come mainly from eastern Europe in the 1920s and 1930s.

They can be excellent for some and mediocre for others. Yet if they are sometimes consistent with French interest, if they sometimes conform to our traditions, to our needs, to our desires, it would be ridiculous to refuse them. Because they are not French ideas? It is only necessary that they serve us. . . . Let us take the good wherever it is, and let the mean-spirited whine.

French Law

I. The Definition of the Jew

First of all, who ought to be legally considered a Jew? Should one take into account the factor of *race,* or of *religion?* Or both of them?

The first solution was initially adopted. The first law, of October 3, 1940, considered as a Jew any person issued from three Jewish grandparents, or from only two of them, if his or her spouse were Jewish.

A second law, of June 2, 1941, . . . adopted a third solution, which takes into consideration both the racial and the confessional elements. When one speaks of the Israelite "religion," one must never forget that the Jewish community transcends, at least in spirit, the ranks of the other religious confessions.

From today a Jew is considered to be:

1. He or she, belonging or not to any religion, who is issued from at least three grandparents of the Jewish Race;
2. Or from only two, if the spouse is issued from the Jewish Race;
3. He or she who adheres to the Jewish religion or who belonged to it on June 25, 1940, and who is issued from two grandparents of the Jewish Race. . . .

The law adds, finally, that "the disavowal or the annulment of the recognition of a child considered Jewish is without effect on the preceding dispositions."

It is evident that these texts do not possess an excessive rigor, since they admit as "non-Jews" those who are half Jewish by blood, and since the fact of belonging to the Jewish religion in itself does not legally entail the quality of being Jewish. . . .

OBLIGATORY DECLARATION.   Anyone who is Jewish in the eyes of the law must present a declaration to the Prefect of the Department in which he has his domicile or residence. He must declare that he is legally Jewish, describe his civil status, his familial situation, and *the status of his goods.* In the case of non-declaration in the delay of one month, punishments are planned (fines and imprisonment).

DEROGATIONS. Nevertheless, the law of June 2, 1941 anticipates certain derogations which concern:

1. Those who have rendered exceptional services to the French state;
2. Those whose family has been established in France for at least five generations, and has rendered exceptional services to the French state.

II. Political and Economic Situation of the Jews

The new position of the Jews in the political, economic, and social planes has been difficult to establish, on account of the scope and complexity of the problems it raises. It is a question, in effect, of seeing and preparing beyond the necessary immediate measures, to the establishment of a definitive status for the future.

It was not a question, this has been officially announced a number of times, of oppressing the Jews for their race, persecuting them for their beliefs or in the exercise of their religion, or of humiliating them. Outside of any persecutorial spirit, these laws are defensive. In order to save French society from a peril which had become mortal, it was necessary: 1. to eliminate the Jews from their acquired positions; 2. to block them from getting them back.

The measures to be taken had to be *multiple* because the danger had infiltrated into all branches of society and into every level. They had to be *rigorous*, lest they remain without effect, given the extraordinary faculty of adaptation of the Jewish people, its flexibility, its skill in evading and using the laws.

It was wise, then, to limit the activities of the Jews, to "neutralize" their influence. Despite the inevitable injustices in details, the recent, sometimes rigorous, laws have endeavored to avoid arbitrariness.

PRINCIPAL DIRECTIVES. It seems that the new legislation has assumed four principal aims:

1. Resolutely to separate the Jews from the government. . . . That was the first task, and relatively the simplest, because it envisaged only a small number. . . .
2. To combat their *intellectual* influence, support and extension of their intrusion into the state; to separate them, to this end, from the liberal professions, from teaching, from the press, etc.
3. To eliminate their *economic* and *financial* supremacy, their preponderance in all branches of industry, commerce, the stock market, and the banks. To "de-Judaize" this realm which had been theirs. To act in such a manner that they would no longer retain the power of money, the most fearful one, for if they had kept it, they would have in practice conserved all the others.

4. To eliminate, finally, their occult power by keeping them away from corporations, by purifying, . . . the press and agencies through which they established a cunning propaganda and [their] *de facto* censorship. . . .

III. State and Public Functions

[Malglaive enumerates the public offices forbidden to Jews and defines some new exceptions: participation in World War I, citations in the military campaigns of 1939–40, members of the Legion of Honor or holders of high military decorations, etc. The pensioning off of Jewish civil servants is also discussed.]

IV. Liberal and Associated Professions

By the first law of October 1940, the exercise of the liberal professions was authorized, as well as the functions of ministerial office, unless there were rules establishing a quota for a given profession.

The principle of freedom remained.

The law of June 2, 1941 eliminated this. It saw that *quotas* should be the rule and no longer the exception for all the professions. . . .

Finally, the law of November 17 just replaced and further refined . . . the law of June 2, in a sense which expresses strongly the will to eliminate Jewish propaganda and *spirit*. Henceforth, *any activity whatever except for subaltern or manual positions* are forbidden to Jews in the professions concerning: [information, the periodical press, editing, and printing (except for those dealing with science or the Jewish religion), film, theater, and radio].

This radical purification seems particularly salutary, if it is recalled that the Jews swarmed into this vast realm, more than into others. . . . Any Jew who . . . has had to abandon the functions, power, and rights that he possessed in a given enterprise, cannot be employed in this enterprise, *under any condition whatever.* This in order to avoid returns "through the back door."

[Malglaive details the quotas of 2 percent for the professions of lawyer and doctor, with further special exceptions for Jewish physicians "on account of the eminent character of their professional merits."]

There remains, in the subject of Jewish influence, an obviously capital point, since it engages both the present and the future: it is that of *teaching.*

[Malglaive approves the elimination of Jewish professors, with the same exceptions that apply to certain doctors, and the imposing of a 3 percent *numerus clausus* of Jewish students to be admitted to preparatory schools. He justifies the law with: "Besides, what would be the point of diplomas for the young [Jews], if the careers to which they gave access were themselves closed?"]

V. *Commerce and Industry, Banking*

[Malglaive lists the various occupations forbidden to Jews under the law, "unless in menial or manual positions." For journalism and the cinema, Jews can no longer be employed in any capacity. The complicated procedures for the reporting, surrendering, and administering of Jewish property are meticulously spelled out.]

Conclusions

He that diggeth a pit shall fall into it;
And whoso breaketh a hedge, a serpent shall bite him.

Ecclesiastes, 10:8

. . . The Jewish peril is a fact.

This fact shapes another one: that of the certain and potential victims of this peril. Who are they in France? The French and their fatherland. This is worth pausing a moment for. Everything is there, anyway. All the gravity, the importance and the interest of the Jewish question.

Two solutions: either to submit passively to this evil, or to take the proper measures to reduce it.

The first is not worth discussing. It is stupid, inert like matter, contrary to animal instinct and unworthy of man.

The second is controversial. The choice of means makes us hesitate. We have scruples against an excess of severity and our indulgence is turned against us.

Weak and divided, opinion remains vague. Sometimes under the cover of charitable feelings, sometimes under the guise of a certain intellectuality, consciously or unconsciously the error and the sophism insinuate and propagate themselves, casting doubt into all minds. . . .

. . . France almost succumbed to her obstinacy in defending false systems and ideas; it is not while she is recovering from this evil that she should be plunged once more into darkness. . . .

The fraud [of false public repentance by Jews] is striking. The Jews have practiced it and are still using it, so much so that in this area they have no more to learn. There is a striking example of this in the history of the Marranos of Spain and Portugal, who took refuge in France and out of self-interest, converted to Catholicism; and then, in 1791, two and one-half centuries later, they returned to their original religion.

It proves the error of collective emancipation. It also proves that, to conform with French interests and Jewish interests—ah, yes—the admission of Jews into the French nation must be individual. In this way, the "well-born" Jews would not have to support the errors of the Israelite herd.

It is of all this that we are dreaming. These are the considerations which should preside at the elaboration of the Jewish status in France. The

Jews constitute a people and a nation without a government or a state; they are and consider themselves to be unassimilable. . . . Why should we try to assimilate them despite themselves, despite ourselves?

The problem has to be reconsidered.

To deny Jewish ethnicity is an error, to think it can be assimilated is a fault. To consider separately the attitude of the Jews and the Mosaic inspiration is a simple-minded scruple, the explanation of the impotence of the methods employed up to now. . . .

Religion does not and could not have anything condemnable for a state, if it knows how to limit itself to the spiritual realm. But as soon as it disfigures and uses this ideal through a transposition to the material plane, it condemns itself and invites itself to be criticized like any human work. The Jewish religion has done more than transpose its ideal. It has made of a mystical religion a doctrine of material and physical domination. . . .

The Jewish problem will have to be given a Jewish solution.

The operation, in the present circumstances, should take place in two phases.

First of all, in the framework of each nation, particular measures will seek no more than the protection of institutions against the invasion of the Jews. Defensive measures.

At a second time, in a future we hope is near, a single solution must be undertaken by all the great powers of the world—including the Jewish people—thus recognizing the existence of the Jewish nation and assigning it a territory which will be turned over to it.

From then on, all the Jews of the world will possess legally, officially, the Jewish nationality which their hearts have always secretly chosen.

Those who would wish to remain in France, in the United States, or in Germany would remain there as foreigners. . . .

The issue is whether, wishing to settle this problem humanely, we want to cease being provoked by the Jews, or whether, continuing to apply half-measures, we resign ourselves to a partial and thus poor settlement of this capital question.

Romania and the Holocaust

The preceding document from Vichy France provides an example of how the Holocaust unfolded in western Europe. The following, far more dramatic, eyewitness testimony from Romania is representative of the Final Solution in eastern Europe. Unlike the other documents in this collection, it is not an antisemitic piece but rather an example of the ultimate consequences of antisemitism.

The historic core (the Regat) of Romania had come under foreign domination throughout most of its history. Goths, Huns, and Avars chased each other across what had been the Roman province of Dacia. In the thirteenth century, Mongol overlords withdrew from the area, to be replaced eventually by the Ottoman Turks who ruled for centuries before being compelled to recognize Romanian independence in 1878. Even before independence and the erection of a monarchy in 1881, Romania had begun to struggle out from under the smothering patronage of tsarist Russia. Although allied to Germany and Austria before the outbreak of World War I, Romania declared war on the Central Powers in 1916. Defeated and occupied by the Germans, it once again reentered the war on the Allied side in 1918. As a reward from the victors, it received new territories and control over several non-Romanian ethnic groups at the expense of neighboring Hungary, Bulgaria, and the Ukraine.

Romania, like most of the other newer states of eastern Europe, failed to govern its peoples with any semblance of democracy in the interwar era. On a backdrop of assassinations, coups, and abdications, the notoriously corrupt monarchy moved steadily to the Right. The artificiality of the state and the tenuousness of its claims to the newly incorporated areas poisoned Romanian political life with a particularly strident brand of racially tinged nationalism.

A native fascist movement, the Iron Guard, contributed to the constant political instability that again invited outside intervention—in this instance, from Nazi Germany, whose economic and political influence increased markedly after 1933. Romania was a neutral partner of the Axis powers at the outbreak of World War II but could not effectively resist the loss of many of the regions won in 1918. Finally, in 1940, Ion Antonescu established a military dictatorship in time to participate in Germany's attack on the Soviet Union and to consign approximately half of Romania's six hundred thousand Jews to the Holocaust.

Antonescu's expropriation and murder of the Jews was the last chapter in a long history of their maltreatment at the hands of the government and general population of modern Romania. At the Congress of Berlin (1878), which created the independent state, the European Great Powers had attempted to impose equal treatment of Jews upon the new government. Its response was to make certain that few Jews could become naturalized and thus eligible for the rights of citizenship. Each individual petition for naturalization required a majority vote in parliament. Pogroms and individual acts of violence were commonplace.

Coerced again by the Allies at the Paris Peace Conference in 1919, the Romanian government, after strenuous objections, acceded to a minorities agreement, much the same as the one signed by Poland (see the introduction to Document 17). Thus the Jews of the Regat, the most assimilated of the Jewish communities in Romania, were grudgingly emancipated. But notwithstanding legal equality, government discrimination and popular violence continued throughout the 1920s and 1930s, especially among university students attracted to the Iron Guard, who identified Jews with hostile nationalities and dangerous ideologies.

Demographically, Romania's Jews followed the Polish model. They were lower middle and working class as a group, highly urbanized, dominant in commerce, and (unlike Poland) quite prominent in industry, particularly in the economically underdeveloped areas acquired as a result of the war. Most Jews outside the Regat had not become assimilated; they spoke Yiddish and regarded themselves as a separate nationality. Emancipation was never seriously applied to them.

All of these factors came into play in Bukovina, the scene of the events depicted in the following document. The southern part of the province was largely Romanian in population, but the northern portion was predominantly Ukrainian. Jews constituted a sizable proportion of the inhabitants in both parts, with especially high concentration in the urban areas. Since the end of the eighteenth century, Bukovina had belonged to Habsburg Austria, falling under Romanian domination only in 1920. Jews in Bukovina looked back upon Austrian rule as a kind of golden age, when they had enjoyed legal equality, in practice as well as in theory, and a high degree of national autonomy. Their nostalgia for Austrian rule confirmed the worst suspicions of the Romanian antisemites regarding the loyalty of the Jews.

Northern Bukovina and Bessarabia, also added after World War I, had to be defended against Bolshevik Russia, which might, it was feared, press historic claims to these areas. Anticommunism therefore became a potent political force in Romania for nationalist as well as socioeconomic reasons. Because individual Jews figured prominently in the communist movements of both areas, Romanian antisemites denounced the whole Jewish population as an agent of Bolshevik subversion. Even more than elsewhere, the charge was invalid in Romania, where the Jewish community was orthodox in religion and middle class in its politics. When the Soviet state occupied North Bukovina in 1940, Jews there met with harsh treatment as "bourgeois enemies of the state."

Nonetheless, as soon as Romania regained control of the area in 1941, it began to deal ruthlessly with the Jewish population. The government's callousness encouraged in the general population acts of the utmost brutality. Random killings, mutilations, rape, and robbery became the lot of a wholly defenseless Jewry. The ferocity of the Romanians shocked even the Nazis and may actually have convinced them it was necessary to systematize the Final Solution. At the same time, the Nazis were also disturbed by the slovenliness of the Romanian action. Such anarchic proceedings allowed too many Jews to escape.

Marshal Antonescu's regime, like that of Vichy France and Admiral Miklos Horthy's in Hungary, attempted to save some degree of sovereign independence in the face of demands placed upon it by Nazi Germany. Given the Nazis' desire to implement the Final Solution, Antonescu leaped at the chance to demonstrate his tractability by bargaining away the lives of Romanian Jews. Ready to sacrifice the Jews of Bukovina and Bessarabia, he managed to hold out against surrendering those of the Regat and southern Transylvania. He was reinforced in this resistance by Germany's military reverses after Stalingrad rather than by his regard for Jews. (In reference to the Jewish question, he was recorded as once saying, "It is a matter of indifference to me whether we enter into history as barbarians.") As a result of these circumstances, and despite an unbroken record of virulent antisemitism, a greater percentage of Jews survived in Romania than in any other east-European country—surely one of the paradoxes of the Holocaust.

In 1940 the Jewish population of Bukovina numbered approximately 120,000, or 11 percent of the whole. Half of them perished. In Czernowitz, the capital of North Bukovina, the Jewish "minority" constituted half of the 140,000 inhabitants. Of these, 28,391 were deported, suffering a mortality rate estimated at 50 to 70 percent.

The compelling testimony of Traian Popovici, mayor of Czernowitz, offers useful evidence concerning several aspects of the Holocaust in Romania and elsewhere. Although his account may appear to be self-serving and even self-congratulatory, it has been largely corroborated by survivors. The emotional impact of what Popovici lived through and participated in comes out clearly in his report. He provides at least some sense of the actual suffering of individuals caught up in degradation and mass murder, beyond what grim statistics alone can convey. Although it reminds readers of the murderous potential of antisemitism, this account also shows that, in Romania particularly, material greed played as significant a role as ideology in the destruction of Jews. Expropriation was total, carried out according to governmental plan and in impromptu fashion by broad elements of the public; it was subject to far more premeditation than the possible fate of the deportees. But greed also played a role in sparing Jews. Many owed their survival to the corruptibility of Romanian officials, whose commitment to antisemitism was not as great as their desire for gain. Finally, it is sadly true that had there been more individuals with the civil courage and basic decency of Mayor Popovici, a great many more Jews could have escaped death. Popovici was willing to take risks for those he recognized as fellow human beings. Why he was such a rarity in the twentieth century is the question that begs an answer.

For Further Reading

Bela Vago and George Mosse, eds., *Jews and Non-Jews in Eastern Europe, 1918–1945* (New York, 1974)

23. Traian Popovici
My Testimony (1941)

Indisputably it was the heedless act of the head of state, Marshal Antonescu, to deport the Jews to Transnistria, an inhuman, brutal, and cruel act.[1] I regard my contribution to the documentation of this act to be an imperative necessity, for I am convinced that the leadership of the present regime, whose responsibility it is to call the guilty to account, is unaware of the details that led to the decision of "the hero of freedom" (Marshal Antonescu). A part of the country's population, whose only guilt was to be born into the lottery of life as Jews, was sent by this decision into slavery and death. This, my testimony, is an unburdening of my conscience. . . .

All the measures touching upon Jews were hatched and prepared in the lap of the military cabinet. . . . The [Czernowitz] city hall had no contact with the military cabinet. The mayor was not consulted or asked for advice in any matter. Because I spoke German, I was constantly invited by the general [Calotescu] to act as translator for conferences and conversations with various dignitaries of the [German] Reich on the occasion of their traveling through Czernowitz. . . . With the entry into office of General Calotescu [as governor of Bukovina Province], the Jewish problem played the main role in the activity of the military cabinet.

Like a waterfall, there followed restrictive measures against Jews: prohibition of professional activity—Jewish doctors were allowed to treat only their ill coreligionists; elimination of Jewish children and older youths from state educational institutions and the closing of private schools; the closing of synagogues and houses of prayer; prohibition of divine services even on high holy days; prohibition of the paying out of money to Jews at bank and postal counters, whether this be money sent by their families or sums of a commercial nature owed to them; surrendering of foreign currency under penalty of death, of radios, machines, etc.; forced and unremunerated labor, even by intellectuals seized on the streets . . . ; requisition of specialists for factories or other public or private enterprises with minimum pay, of

---

Source: From Traian Popovici, "Mein Bekenntnis," in Hugo Gold, ed., *Geschichte der Juden in der Bukowina* (Tel Aviv, 1962), 2:62–69; translated into German from the Romanian by Hermann Sternberg.

[1]In 1940, Ion Antonescu (1882–1946) forced the abdication of King Carol, outmaneuvered the fascist Iron Guard, and ruled Romania as a dictator with the aid of a military cabinet. A loyal ally of Hitler, he put the Romanian economy and foreign policy at German disposal. Although the Jews of Romania were subjected to wholesale murder and expropriation with his blessing, it is doubtful that he was solely responsible for the deportation of Jews to Transnistria, an area belonging to the Soviet Ukraine but occupied by Romania soon after the war began. (Later in his account, Popovici attributes a good deal of influence on the marshal's decision to pressure from the Nazis.) Antonescu stood trial and was executed in 1946.

which 30% was deducted for the Romanianization fund;[2] withdrawal of ration cards, doubling of the price of bread, exclusion from food markets, limitation of shopping to the three hours between 10 A.M. and 1 P.M.; and a few other humiliations that I cannot remember.

Internment in camps was no longer a repressive measure for the slightest infraction but became an organized, draconic system. The camps and the military tribunal went into high gear. The Jews were horrified, but even the well meaning among the Romanians lost their head in view of the cascade of persecutions. Following the examples of leaders, other public office-holders began competing with the government. . . . A psychosis took possession of the minds of many responsible elements, robbed them of reason, and made them into accomplices in this shameful stain on our people's history.

It is remarkable how the Jews absorbed all these chicaneries, persecutions, and humiliations. No movement toward revolt or resistance, no attempt at sabotage, not even a murmur.[3] In resignation before their thousand-year destiny, in a mystical enduring of tragedy, they bore their lot like shades pursued by the Furies. The sources of human strength that made possible such suffering will ever remain a mystery. There remained a single oasis in Czernowitz where the Jewish citizen was permitted to lament his suffering, where his right to petition was respected, where the cry of hunger and the recovery of the right to bread and life found an audience, where pensions were regularly paid and possibilities for work created, where the Jew found anonymous support, where he was not brutally treated and where his suffering was understood—this was the mayor's office of the capital city. . . . It remains a fact that under my leadership the finance department never evicted Jews for nonpayment of rent and regularly paid [former Jewish] officials their pensions, against the orders of the government. It is not my affair that my successors acted differently.

It is self-explanatory that my behavior was not of the kind to endear me to the governor [Calotescu], who increasingly backed away from me without ever summoning up the courage to bring on a crisis. Several times, noticing his reserved manner toward me, after discussions in which I had tried to get him to moderate the zeal of the military cabinet, I offered to

---

[2]Romanianization, modeled on Nazi Germany's Aryanization program, was designed to take economic control out of Jewish hands. In practice, the office of Romanianization, established in the Ministry of Labor in 1940, meant the liquidation of Jewish assets, the enrichment of well-placed individuals, and massive corruption of officials.

[3]The Jews of Bukovina, with a long history of organized self-defense, had been subjected to house searches and seizure of weapons well before the events Popovici describes. Armed resistance against government authority, rather than against the traditional practitioners of anti-Jewish violence, would have been fruitless. Yet there were attempts to fend off or moderate the effects of the attack. These involved flight, difficult since the number of possible sanctuaries was quite small; informing the outside world, including agencies that were able to help support surviving Jews; efforts to get highly placed personages in Romania to use their influence to blunt government measures; and bribery of officials, a traditional method of self-defense in Romania.

resign my office as mayor, in order to spare him any difficulties. But the general avoided a decision. . . . Truthfully, as often as I resolved to step down, the unfortunates held me back. I was the only hope of the people of Bukovina, the only spokesman for the public interest. For good or ill, I was the one.

In this strained atmosphere between the government and the mayor's office, dangerous clouds thickened over the Jews of Czernowitz. Not a word, not a hint of what was being prepared came my way. But from behind the scenes of the military cabinet, alarming whispers and rumors began penetrating to the outside world. . . .

On a September day [1941], I was summoned to a government meeting on the subject of the new ghetto. In the governor's chancellery there were gathered, among others, representatives of the *Siguranza* [security service]. . . . The governor demanded concrete suggestions from me about city hall's solutions to the problem of the ghetto. In a long speech, I laid out the special situation of the Jews, mentioned their culture, their contribution to the development of the city in the Austrian period, their part in the areas of commerce, industry, the crafts, medicine, the arts, and judicial system, and touched upon the other fields of their intellectual activity. I especially emphasized their contribution to Romanian rule and their will to adapt to it; I analyzed the currents in their political life while indicating their typical willingness to cooperate with government parties. In short, I treated their value as a whole, in the light of both their good and bad qualities.

In conclusion, I spoke out against the erection of the ghetto. Since, however, I feared the worst—I knew that I held a minority opinion—I made a few concessions. The governor demanded of me a plan that I could accept as mayor of the capital city. I was informed that the German legation was pushing for the speedy erection of a ghetto. (I had learned of their systematic plans in this regard at an earlier conference.) I deftly revised all the suggestions from the government and worked up a project that I summarized and laid before the governor in a conference that same evening. . . . I was convinced that my plan would be accepted, especially since I had heard from the legal adviser to the government that the marshal [Antonescu] was inclined to soften the planned system of ghettoization. I also believed that with the solution to the ghetto question, which kept officials of the government in suspense, the anti-Jewish measures would come to an end. The idea of a mass deportation never occurred to me. Ten peaceful days preceded the unleashing of the storm.

The Deportation

. . . On October 9, 1941, it became known in Czernowitz that Jews already concentrated in camps in North Bukovina had been selected and driven in the direction of the Dniester River [Transnistria]. A day later, on October 10, 1941, news came of similar operations in South Bukovina. . . .

We did not have exact information. It was merely said that they had been fetched out of their dwellings and concentrated at gathering points in order to be loaded onto waiting trains. The operation was commanded from the center [Bucharest], and implementation was vested in the regional prefects. . . . On that October 10, I was summoned by Governor Calotescu, who instructed me to take measures, among them that the bakeries bake more bread, in order to provision the Jewish population, which would have to be brought into the ghetto. In the prospect of their being loaded on trains, each was to receive four loaves of bread.

It was in the chancellery of the governor that I learned that the mass deportation of the Jews of Czernowitz was a closed matter. Simultaneously, I learned the details concerning their delivery into the ghetto. I heard that their property, which was to be left in their dwellings, was to be put at the disposal of the state. I heard that the objects of value that they took with them into the ghetto would be sequestered. Similarly, they would be forced to change their money. After this they would be loaded onto trains with fifty cars each, shunted off under military guard to points on the Dniester, and then distributed from there into Transnistria.

I turned to stone. All I could say was: "You've come this far, Governor?" To which he answered: "What am I supposed to do? Marshal's orders. And you see here representatives of the General Staff."

. . . The memory of the scene that we played out has remained with me because of its drama and because I could not control myself. I became aggressive in a manner quite uncustomary for a mayor communicating with the governor, the direct representative of the marshal. First I made him aware of the responsibility he was taking upon himself before history; then I pointed out the damage to our reputation in the international sphere. I depicted the difficulties that we would encounter at the peace conference when Romania would stand before the Areopagus of civilized nations. I spared no argument in order to demonstrate the monstrousness of this step he was about to take. I spoke of civilization, of humanity, of the traditional good nature of Romanians, of barbarism, cruelty, crimes, atrocities. I called up the virtues of our ancestors; I branded racism as sadism. . . . Pointing to [the representatives of the General Staff], I said to him: "These gentlemen will [leave in a few days] and rub their hands on account of the heroic deed they performed in Bukovina, but you shall remain here as governor of a province that was given, as a totality, to your protection and guardianship. You don't have the right to endanger the life of a single individual. How do you want to enter history? Next to Robespierre? I at least do not want my name soiled in history. You still have time. Make contact with the marshal and beg him, governor, to at least postpone these measures until spring."

I spoke as in an ecstasy, trembling with excitement. Everyone stood still. The governor listened to my words in the chancellery without emotion, while the others leaned against the oven. After a moment of deep silence, the governor spoke: "Mr. Popovici, and I say this to the other gentlemen, too, I have the same fears, but [these representatives] have been sent to oversee the implementation of the ordinance. I will consider the matter." At this moment, [one of the General Staff] turned to me and said: "Mr. Mayor, who will write history, the Jew boys? I come to hoe the weeds out of the garden, and you oppose me?" I answered him sharply: "Mr. Colonel, I hoe my own garden. As far as history is concerned, the Jews will not be writing it, for the world belongs to them no longer. Rather the historians of all nations will write it. We, too, shall write it, and sooner than you think. I fear you will live to read that history and the contribution you have made to it."

... Into the charged atmosphere of the chancellery stepped General Vasile Jonescu. Frowning, sad, broken in soul, he greeted all present and then turned to the governor: "I say don't do it, Governor. What we are about to do is an obscenity. It is a sin, a great sin. It were better I had never come to Bukovina than I should witness such cruelty." The governor hesitated and took time to consider.

As we left the chancellery together, General Jonescu said to me: "I have categorically refused; I have demanded written instructions, but they don't want to give me any. Just think, they have no written commission. They say that operations of this type are only given orally so that no evidence is left behind. Let's try to persuade Calotescu not to commit this stupidity, for it is an atrocity. Otherwise, I think our consciences will be burdened. I will speak to him again after lunch.". . .

[I returned to city hall] where my office was full of representatives of the Jews of Czernowitz who were tensely and painfully waiting for a word of salvation. The city was in a fever. Two battalions of gendarmes from Bucharest had arrived, and the ominous news had spread with lightning speed. I could tell them nothing definite. I looked on mutely at their consternation. Instinctively, they fathomed all. Their leave-taking from me was characteristic. They thanked me for everything that I had done for them; they swore that on all the stations of their suffering they would remember me as the only man who had understood their pain, that their memory of Czernowitz would be bound with my person. They left my office in tears, as at a wake.

Deathly silence reigned among the officials of city hall; they could read in my face what was afoot. They were all shaken. None approved of the deportation. Honor to them, and thanks for the solidarity they showed me! I could not concentrate on my work. I was exhausted, physically and spiritually near collapse. In order not to be a witness and participant in the tragedy, I decided to resign and imparted this to my closest colleagues. However, they all categorically advised against it because this would be an encouragement to those in whose way I stood. I would also be providing "evidence of my Jewification" for the agitation of the nationalists. Further, it would be cowardice on my part to abandon the unfortunate in their hour of need. Finally, I ought to protect the rest of the population from chicanery and other sorts of baseness. Even today, I do not know whether I acted properly in listening to their advice and staying in office.

Via Doloroso

On the morning of October 11 . . . I looked out the window. It was snowing and—I could not believe my eyes: on the street in front of my window long columns of people were hurrying by. Old people supported by children, women with infants in their arms, invalids dragging their maimed bodies along, all with their luggage in wagons or on their backs, with hastily packed suitcases, bedding, bundles, clothes; they all made silent pilgrimage into the city's valley of death, the ghetto. . . .

Great activity in the city hall. . . . The "abandoned" wealth of the Jews was to be inventoried and their dwellings sealed. Romanianization departments were to be formed and with police assistants to be distributed throughout the city neighborhoods.

It first dawned on me then that the procedure had been a long time in the planning. I hurried to military headquarters where General Jonescu informed me of events. He let me see the promulgated ordinances. . . . I paged through the instructions in haste and read the regulations for the functioning of the ghetto. The bakeries were to be under city hall control, as were the [food] markets. Then I hurried again to the city hall in order to see to the measures necessary for the uninterrupted provisioning of bread, food, and especially milk for the children. For the time being, this was the role that providence allotted to me, thanks to the military cabinet.

Only those who know the topography of the city can measure how slight was the space for the ghetto to which the Jewish population was confined and in which, under pain of death, they had to be by six o'clock.

In this part of the city, even with the greatest crowding, ten thousand people could be housed at most. Fifty thousand had to be brought in, not counting the Christian population already living there. Then, and even today, I compare the ghetto to a cattle pen.

The accommodation possibilities were minimal. Even if the available rooms were to receive thirty or more people, a great number would have to seek shelter from the snow and rain in corridors, attics, cellars, and similar sorts of places. I would rather not speak of the demands of hygiene. Pure drinking water was lacking; the available public fountains did not suffice. I noted that the city already suffered from a water shortage since two of the three pumping stations had been destroyed. The strong odors of sweat, urine, and human waste, of mold and mildew, distinguished the quarter from the rest of the city. . . . It was a miracle that epidemics that would endanger the whole city did not break out. With surprising speed the ghetto was nearly hermetically sealed with barbed wire. At the main exits, wooden gates were erected and military guards posted. I do not know whether it was intentional, but the effect was clear: the despised were being intimidated.

The national bank opened offices for the compulsory exchange of lei into rubles,[4] and for the surrendering of gold, jewelry, and other objects of value. It is remarkable that the national bank, the serious, premier banking institution of the country, should lend itself to the plundering of a part of the population that had contributed to raising the value of the national currency. It was official fraud—hard, cold, brutal, but apparently legal. . . .

Although Sections 3 and 4 of the regulation concerning the ghetto categorically stated that no one could enter without the authorization of the governor, no one observed this rule. As early as the second day after the erection of the ghetto, there began a pilgrimage consisting of ladies of all social strata and intellectual jobbers, well known to the Czernowitz public. Persons of "influence" from all strata and professions—hyenas all—caught the scent of cadaverous souls among the unfortunates. Under the pretext that they were in the good graces of the governor, the military cabinet, or the mayor, they began the high-level pillaging of all that was left to the unfortunates. Their gold coins, jewelry, precious stones, furs, and valuable foodstuffs (tea, coffee, chocolate, cocoa) were supposedly to be used to bribe others or to compensate [the interlopers] for putting in a good word to save someone from deportation. Trading in influence was in full bloom. Another category of hyena was the so-called friend who volunteered to protect all these goods from theft or to deliver them to family members and acquaintances elsewhere in the country. Individuals never previously seen in the city of Czernowitz streamed in from all corners of the country in order to draw profit from a human tragedy. If the deportation with all its premeditation was in itself monstrous, then the exploitation of despair surpassed even this. . . .

The Selection of White Slaves

On October 12, I was invited by the governor to a conference of all bureau chiefs. Eighteen people were present. . . . At this time, we were informed by the governor of the ghettoization and the decision for mass deportation of the Jews. The governor asked for our views and possible suggestions. Right from the start the president of the court of appeals and the chief state prosecutor withdrew from the discussion on the basis that they were not empowered by the ministry [of justice] to participate in these conferences; the judiciary had to renounce participation in formulating the government's administrative measures. It is a truth which does honor to our judicial system that in all the matters relating to Jews it did not intervene

---

[4]Lei, the Romanian currency, was not legal tender in Transnistria. The exchange rate for rubles was set low in order to further pauperize the Jews. When survivors of the deportation returned in 1944, the process was reversed in an equally unfair exchange of rubles for lei.

directly or indirectly. . . . In court, Jews experienced the same treatment as others. Our judiciary never persecuted the Jews; on the contrary, in the application of the racial laws it showed much leniency.

It is of no interest as to who of those present approved or disapproved the deportation decision. It is enough to state the plain fact that no one had the courage to raise a protest against an act that would have consequences in the history of the nation. I call as witnesses those present who are still alive [to testify] that I was the only one. When I got the floor, I discussed the Jewish problem in the light of current events. I said that we, as a little country, could not let ourselves get tangled up in racial hate. I pointed out the merits of the Jews, their valuable contribution to the national economy, their cultural achievements. And I protested in my own name and in my capacity as mayor against this act. I demanded grace for those who had accepted baptism in the church because, as I pointed out, we ought not bury the missionary spirit, the very basis of Christianity.

I demanded the sparing of Jews with a higher education and those [active] in the fine arts. I demanded consideration for those who had rendered service to the country—retired civil servants, officers, war wounded. I demanded exemptions for physicians, for the sake of service to humanity. For the purposes of reconstruction, I demanded the sparing of engineers and architects. I urged, out of respect for intelligence and civilization, an exemption for lawyers and judges. It is of no interest who contested me or with what arguments. The result was that the governor in part accepted my suggestions and, before all present, entrusted to me the making of a list of those who had earned the thanks of the nation, in the sense mentioned above. It was supposed to contain at most 100–200 people.

As I left the meeting, I was silently scorned by officialdom as "Jewified." Depressed by my stand, which the gentlemen appeared to regard as an expression of [inadequate] Romanianism, I left the building inwardly satisfied that I had saved at least a small portion from ruin. . . . It is true that the list I handed in was accepted in its totality, without objection or emendation.

Meanwhile, October 12–14 passed with preparations for the entraining of the Jews. My friends know that I did not stand with folded arms during this time. It is not germane here to enumerate the methods I used in the indirect attempt to influence the will of the marshal, whom I did not know and who lived far from Czernowitz. However, my efforts were successful. On Wednesday, October 15, the marshal telephoned the governor with his agreement to a softening of the mass deportation. Twenty thousand people in those categories I had indicated and intervened on behalf of at the conference on Saturday were to be exempted from the deportation. Thus it came about that approximately twenty thousand remained in Czernowitz. That this measure did not please "the streets" or the new "Romanianizers" signified little. The result gave me new strength because the highest power in the state confirmed my previous position. Everyone must concede that this was the beginning of a great moral victory.

[Popovici and General Jonescu report to Governor Calotescu on the afternoon of October 15.] "Gentlemen [said the governor], I have just conversed with the marshal, who has confirmed that twenty thousand Jews will stay in Czernowitz. I cannot occupy myself with the selection because I do not know the people and the degree of their indispensability. [Popovici, Jonescu, and the German consul are empowered to make the lists of those who will remain.] I will give you four days, during which time the transports will be suspended. (Meanwhile, on October 13, approximately three trainloads had been put into movement.)[5] You have the right of decision. I retain for myself merely the right to fix the percentages and will sign the authorization personally, without consideration for the exact numbers.

As soon as we left, Schellhorn [the German consul] informed us that he had made it known to the governor that he would have to refuse the honor because, as representative of a foreign state, he ought not mix into things pertaining only to the Romanian state. There remained only two of us—General Jonescu and myself.

Now began a new phase: the selection. The moment we left the governor, we made no secret of the great responsibility of the task laid upon us. General Jonescu and I complemented each other in the work and achieved remarkable consensus. . . . [Popovici describes the mechanics behind compiling the list, which necessitated consulting Jewish leaders.]

I have never regretted, then or especially now, that I had this inspiration, although it made my work a hundred times more difficult. I confess that not all my ideas have been so happy, but this one, despite many infelicities, I do not regret. [I was able] to slow the wheel of doom upon which a people was being martyred. Now, however, I wish to recall another idea, one that might have cost me my neck and that could have provided the pretext for the many denunciations [of me] being sent to the military cabinet or directly to the president. I mean my visit to the ghetto, the only visit by an official during its whole existence.

On the evening of October 15, after having fixed the schedule of the next day's labors with General Jonescu, I went to the Jewish hospital, situated on the edge of the ghetto and on a main street leading toward the railroad station. On the previous day I had been informed that a typhus epidemic had broken out and that city hall had to take preventive measures. Simultaneously, I wanted to bring the leaders of the community the message that the marshal was prepared to spare part of the Jewish population. This was meant as a calming gesture for those tormented masses facing the horrors of a trip into the unknown; at the same time it was a political act, meant to demonstrate that the marshal was not so hardhearted, that he had been forced to the deportation by other motives [than

---

[5]These trains contained approximately six thousand Jews.

hatred], that he, in fact, sympathized with the Jews and wanted to protect them in so far as the political orientation allowed this.[6]

The dramatic scene I experienced when I brought them this message of hope I regard as the most solemn and stirring moment of my life; I do not believe a grander one will ever be granted me. Old rabbis, intellectuals of every age, leaders from all areas of social life, merchants, workers—in a word, everyone—broke down in tears. They praised their God and thanked heaven for its mercy and the marshal for his grace. They surrounded me, kissing my hands, my feet, the hems of my garments. Tears do not always shame a man. In that moment I was so touched by the spontaneous expression of gratitude that I broke down in tears and cried along with them as "father of the city." As witnesses to the experience of this moment, I call upon all those who survived the torment of persecution and stood with me in the hope for a better world. The reasons that my own people distanced themselves from this gesture, which might have earned them forgiveness in the future, are matters to be settled in their own consciences. [My people] attacked me because of this, besmirched and persecuted me. Yet I was the mayor of the whole city and not just a part of it. . . . I bore the sorrow and the welfare of the whole population and was not its persecutor. My gesture was a simple and comprehensible one. Only the hatred [of others] made it significant for me and for posterity.

On October 16, I contacted the representatives of the [Jewish] community and impressed upon them the decision of the marshal and the urgency of the task with which they were entrusted. We recognized that we would be unable to carry out the work of selection in so short a time. The Jews, who were most directly interested and had the technical expertise and statistical information, needed two days to compose the lists. We were handed 179 lists, with additional ones coming in later.

It required a whole extra day to examine these lists and set the percentages with the governor. . . . Even [Governor] Calotescu will acknowledge what an effort it took to persuade him that certain categories of Jews had to be left in the city in order not to create future confusion in its life.

One example: all but one of the plumbers in Czernowitz were Jews, in a city with over eleven thousand buildings; this was also true for the whole province [of Bukovina] where they had all been selected [for deportation]. We foresaw that which actually happened—that we would have to lend special workers to the other cities of Bukovina. We adduced further examples. We obtained deferments and exhausted ourselves day and night in a task that all were agreed upon.

. . . All our work was only a suggestion; the governor had the last and decisive word. We submitted the results of our efforts to the governor. I do

---

[6]Antonescu's "other motives" had to do with the constant pressure from the Nazis to cooperate in the Final Solution.

not believe that the particulars of our painful efforts are of interest. Interesting is that we two, General Jonescu and myself, having been put in this situation, were able to delay the departure of the deportation trains. Now we sought every possibility of halting them, counting on the onset of winter as an obstacle. . . .

Finally, my activity had the purpose of stopping the deportation altogether and of sending no one away. The governor could give an accounting of this but will not. How often did I argue with him and intervene for people in order to keep one or another for whom there were grounds to deport. . . . How many did I add to the official authorizations, [already] signed by the governor! What family member (parents, brothers, fathers-in-law, cousins, etc.), who came as a supplicant after the lists had been completed, went away unsatisfied? Occasionally I resisted, it is true, for I considered that I would have to fabricate a new permit on my own authority. But finally I registered the names of their loved ones on the authorization, . . . brazenly signed my name, and affixed the seal of city hall on the paper. This single operation, which later caused me to be charged with misuse of my office, saved not tens but hundreds of souls. . . .

Death Train

The population slated for deportation was first gathered in groups of two thousand people, then driven through a quagmire to the loading ramps at the main railroad station. There they were packed, forty or fifty to a freight car. Military guards stood watch over the cars, an officer over the whole train. The death train moved toward the Dniester to concentration camps . . . from where a Charon ferried [the deportees] over the river to the realm of the underworld. Heartrending scenes among the unfortunate were played out on the loading ramps. The separation of members of the same family, with parents being led away while children remained behind, or vice versa, with the separation of brothers and sisters, of spouses, all carried out with agonizing cries; this moved even the stony-hearted. It was separation for all time. One went into suffering and death; the other remained behind in slavery and pain. The exodus of the Jews from Czernowitz is a tragic chapter in the history of humanity. . . .

The Jews suffered deportation in two stages: in the cold, rain, and snow of winter 1941 and the parched and burning heat of summer 1942. . . . The dead were thrown from the trains, left in the stations for local authorities to process. At the concentration points on the Dniester, they were robbed of all their remaining possessions; their personal documents were taken from them and destroyed so that no trace of them would remain behind. They were brought across the Dniester in boats and then began to march, barefoot and starving, through wind, rain, storm, and mud.

The description of their tragedy could fill volumes, which only a Dante could write. They were witnesses to an apocalyptic brutalization by their tormentors. On a single transport, only one infant out of a total of sixty survived. When they fell exhausted by the wayside, they were left to die, their corpses prey to vultures and dogs. At the destined locales there awaited a life of greatest misery, without sanitation or dwellings, fuel, food, and clothing; they were at the mercy of the weather and the pitiless whims and chicanery of their guards and tormentors. Any sort of organization was lacking. They were given over to nothingness, to hunger, frost, winter, and in the absence of sanitation or adequate housing, to spotted typhus and other epidemics. Girls and women were raped; they prostituted themselves for a crust of bread. The Jews were also subjected to the hatred of the Ukrainian population. Annihilation was the object of this "evacuation." Mortality ranged between 50 percent and 70 percent. In the community of Berschad, it reached 85 percent because, until December 20, 1940, they were held like cattle under the open sky. . . .

The sending of food packages, clothing, or medicine was forbidden under threat of penalties by the military court. The unfortunates who fled the camps or returned to the country received the death penalty. All these measures had only one purpose: complete annihilation of the Jews.

Some were transferred to German organizations on the other side of the River Bug under the pretext that they were being lent as workers. There they were tortured, mutilated, and thrown alive into mass graves. Did this [transfer] have any purpose other than turning them into dust? The martyrs of the death march into Transnistria had to endure all of this in the twentieth century, the century of madness.

Many times I candidly said to the governor and other bearers of the torch of hatred that it would have been more humane to line the Jews up against the wall and to shoot them than to torment them cold-bloodedly, without any fellow feeling or stirrings of conscience, or fear of God!

The Final Solution

From January 30, 1933, when Hitler became chancellor of Germany, until the Wannsee Conference in early 1942, the minutes of which follow, Nazi policy toward Jews betrayed no obvious logic. What has been described as "the twisted road to Auschwitz" began in 1933 with an only partially successful boycott of Jewish businesses. A purge of the civil service and a gradual expulsion of Jews from Germany's economic life culminated in a program of Aryanization, the forced liquidation of Jewish assets for the benefit of non-Jews. The Nuremberg Laws of 1935 redefined German citizenship so as to exclude Jews and forbade sexual relations between them and those of "Aryan blood." After the annexation of Austria in March 1938, there began an official policy of expropriation coupled with forced emigration. If the Nazis had always been intent upon the mass murder of Jews, forced emigration would seem to have been an illogical step, because it drove the potential victims into areas beyond Germany's direct grasp.

Yet it was mass murder, under the euphemism of "the Final Solution of the Jewish question," that the Nazis did decide upon at the Wannsee Conference. The term *Final Solution* first emerged in the spring of 1940 in the context of a massive territorial resettlement program. But military conquests in East and West had brought three and a half million Jews under direct German control, and the "Final Solution" appearing in dispatches of May and June 1941 alluded to the impossibility of forced emigration for so large a number.

On July 31, 1941, six weeks after the invasion of the Soviet Union, Hermann Goering empowered Lieutenant General Reinhard Heydrich, chief of the Security Police and Security Service, to undertake "all necessary preparations with regard to organizational and financial matters for bringing about a total solution of the Jewish question in the German sphere of influence in Europe" (Nuremberg Document PS-710). By the time the Wannsee Conference convened to fulfill this order, the Final Solution had come to mean genocide.

What prompted the Nazis to this new departure in the history of antisemitism? Was there an inner logic, an ultimate conclusion waiting to be drawn from the centuries of anti-Jewish ideology? Did Hitler always envision the extermination of Jewry? Or did the war provide opportunities undreamed of by even the most fanatical Jew haters? After years of debate, these still remain open questions.

While it is inconceivable that the Final Solution could have proceeded without Hitler's approval, his exact role in the decision is a matter of historical controversy. Although "an authorization from the Führer" was alluded to at the Wannsee Conference, it referred to mass deportations to the East, not necessarily extermination. A document signed by Hitler ordering the Final Solution has never been unearthed; it may not, in fact, have ever existed. But many of Hitler's most important ideological decisions were delivered orally rather than in writing. The lack of such documentary evidence does not, therefore, prove the case of those who have recently

250

claimed that the destruction of Jewry was carried out behind his back or against his will by Himmler, Heydrich, and other underlings. Even if Hitler remained aloof from the details of the process, his presence was always felt, and his murderous obsession with Jews, documented amply earlier, supplied the ideological authority for the Final Solution.

Although the physical murder of Jews may have lurked in Hitler's subconscious always, it is difficult to detect a systematic blueprint in his own actions or those of his lieutenants. On the contrary, much of the evidence suggests that the Holocaust came about in a piecemeal, trial-and-error fashion. Hitler was an improviser and an opportunist. Although it looked otherwise to the world, the Nazi state, accurately reflecting the chaotic mind of its leader, rarely set rational priorities or followed uniform procedures. Instead, the implementors of the Final Solution constantly tested the waters of public opinion, expecting resistance to increasingly harsh measures from those not "enlightened" enough about the Jewish danger. When resisted, they often backed off and were not nearly as insistent as many of their collaborators claimed after the war. But when significant resistance did not materialize in the German public, the regular army, the peoples of occupied areas, or the rest of the world, the Nazis were encouraged to go further.

The persecution of the Jews possessed its own dynamism. Hitler's unmistakably intense hatred of them acted as a goad to ambitious bureaucrats and scheming department chiefs, as a stimulus to ever-more-radical anti-Jewish actions on the part of foreign leaders anxious to ingratiate themselves. Whether animated by antisemitism or not, many from all levels of society found it to their advantage to cash in on the Final Solution.

Everywhere in Europe, decisive control of the Holocaust ended up in the hands of bureaucrats. In this respect, the Wannsee Conference is a document perfectly representative of the phenomenon. Adolf Eichmann, who took the minutes, later testified that Heydrich had called the meeting to cover himself by committing other functionaries to a program of genocide already under way. The deportation of Jews to ghettos in the East was continuing. For nearly six months, mobile extermination squads, the *Einsatzgruppen,* had been murdering hundreds of thousands behind the German armies advancing into the Baltic states and the Soviet Union. The "practical experience" gathered in the East, mentioned in the minutes, referred to these massacres (and possibly to the first experimental killings of Russian prisoners of war with Zyklon B gas). But these actions had run into thorny legal problems and jurisdictional disputes: what to do about mixed marriages and their progeny, foreign Jews caught in Germany, Jews vital to the armaments industry, and so on. It took a scant ninety minutes to iron out these problems and decide upon the deaths of millions.

Bureaucratic jargon ("parallelize the guidelines") and innocuous-sounding phrases ("possibilities in the East") only partially mask the deadly purpose of the meeting. Nor can the antiseptic nature of the minutes disguise the participants' enthusiasm for the Final Solution. Various state secretaries, already conscious of how they could expand the influence of their agencies, vied with one another in demonstrating their businesslike appreciation of this "world historical" initiative. Heydrich, who had expected difficulties, expressed himself "well satisfied" by the outcome.

Details of mass murder did not make it into the minutes, as edited by Heydrich, but, according to Eichmann, "killing, elimination, and annihilation" were discussed at the meeting and informally "over lunch." By the following spring, the machinery of death was fully in place. In occupied Poland, concentration camps equipped with gas chambers and crematoria stood ready to kill Jews gathered from every corner of Europe.

For Further Reading

Raul Hilberg, *The Destruction of the European Jews,* 3 vols. (rev. ed., New York, 1985); Hannah Arendt, *Eichmann in Jerusalem,* (New York, 1963).

24. Wannsee Conference on the Final Solution of the Jewish Question (1942)

SECRET REICH MATTER!   30 copies (16th copy)

Conference Minutes

II. Chief of the Security Police and Security Service, SS-Lt. General Heydrich informed everyone at the outset that the Reich-Marshal [Hermann Goering] had placed him in charge of preparations for the Final Solution of the European Jewish question and that [they] had been invited to this conference in order to gain clarity on fundamental questions. The Reich Marshal's wish to have a draft submitted to him on the organizational, operational, and material considerations with reference to the Final Solution of the European Jewish question requires that all the central agencies directly involved in these questions come together beforehand in order to parallelize the guidelines [of their procedures].

Competency in the preparation of the Final Solution of the Jewish question lies with the Reich-Leader-SS [Heinrich Himmler] and chief of the German police (Chief of Security Police and Security Service), without regard for geographic boundaries.

[Heydrich] then briefly surveyed the battle thus far waged against these enemies. The principal phases constituted

a. forcing Jews out of individual areas of life of the German people,

b. forcing Jews out of the living space of the German people.

Source: From Robert M. W. Kempner, *Eichmann und Komplizen* (Zürich, 1961), pp. 133–47.

In the carrying out of these efforts, the acceleration of a systematically undertaken emigration of Jews from Reich territory was the only preliminary solution possible.

On orders of the Reich-Marshal, a Reich central office for Jewish emigration was established in January 1939, entrusted to the direction of the Chief of the Security Police and Security Service. In particular, it had the task of

a. taking all measures for the *preparation* of an increased emigration of Jews,

b. *directing* the flow of emigration

c. accelerating the implementation of emigration in *individual cases.*

The objective of the task was to cleanse German living space of Jews in legal ways.

Every agency was mindful of the disadvantages arising from such a forced emigration. For the time being, however, allowances had to be made for them in the absence of other solution possibilities.

In the following period, emigration work was not only a German problem but also a problem that the authorities of the lands targeted for immigration had to deal with. Financial difficulties, such as raising the limits of money necessary for admission [of immigrants] by various foreign governments, deficient shipping capacity, increasingly exacting immigration limits or closures—all these impeded the work of emigration extraordinarily. Notwithstanding these difficulties, approximately 537,000 Jews were brought out between the seizure of power [January 30, 1933] and October 31, 1941. Of these

from January 30, 1933, out of the Old Reich	c. 360,000
from March 15, 1938, out of the Austria	c. 147,000
from March 15, 1939, out of the Protectorate of Bohemia and Moravia	c. 30,000

The financing of emigration was accomplished by the Jews themselves—that is, by respective Jewish political organizations. To avoid leaving behind proletarianized Jews, the general principle obtained that wealthy Jews had to finance the departure of impoverished Jews. Graded according to wealth, an appropriate assessment and an emigration payment were used to liquidate the financial obligations of poor Jews in the course of their emigration.

In addition to the [German currency] levy, foreign currencies were required [to cover] landing fees and proof of solvency. In order to protect German foreign currency reserves, Jewish financial institutions abroad were approached by Jewish financial institutions at home to take care of the requisite foreign currency levies. In this way, up to October 31, 1941, a total of about $9½ million was made available as gifts by foreign Jews.

Meanwhile, the Reich-Leader-SS and Chief of the German Police has forbidden emigration of Jews because of the dangers of emigration in wartime and because of the possibilities in the East.

III. In place of emigration, with the appropriate authorization by the Führer, the evacuation of the Jews to the East has now stepped forward as a further solution possibility.

These actions are, however, to be regarded as only provisional; certainly, practical experience is already being gathered here, which will have great significance in the coming Final Solution of the Jewish question.

With reference to this Final Solution of the European Jewish question, approximately eleven million Jews come into consideration, distributed in individual countries as follows:

Country	Number
A. Old Reich	131,800
Austria	43,700
Eastern regions [Poland]	420,000
General Government [Poland]	2,284,000
Bialystok [Poland]	400,000
Protectorate of Bohemia and Moravia	74,200
Estonia	free of Jews
Latvia	3,500
Lithuania	34,000
Belgium	43,000
Denmark	5,600
France/occupied	165,000
unoccupied[1]	700,000
Greece	69,000
Netherlands	160,800
Norway	1,300
Bulgaria	48,000
England	330,000
Finland	2,300
Ireland	4,000
Italy, including Sardinia	58,000
Albania	200
Croatia	40,000
Portugal	3,000
Romania, including Bessarabia	342,000
Sweden	8,000
Switzerland	18,000
Serbia	10,000
Slovakia	88,000
Spain	6,000
Turkey (European part)	55,500
Hungary	742,000
USSR	5,000,000
Ukraine	2,994,684
White Russia (excluding Bialystok)	446,484
TOTAL: over	11,000,000

With regard to the estimated Jewish statistics of foreign countries, it is a matter only of Jews by religion, since the conceptual definitions of Jews according to racial principles are still partially lacking there. Because of general attitudes and conceptions prevailing in certain countries, especially in Hungary and Romania, certain difficulties in the treatment of the problem will be encountered. Thus, for example, in Romania today Jews can obtain for cash appropriate documents that officially certify them as foreign nationals.

The influence of Jews in all regions of the USSR is known. Approximately five million live in European Russia; in the Asiatic parts, scarcely a quarter million. . . .

Now, during the process of the Final Solution and under appropriate guidance, Jews shall, in suitable ways, come to the East for use as labor. In great labor columns, with the sexes separated, Jews capable of work will be put to work building roads in these regions, whereby, doubtlessly, a great part will fall to natural reduction.

The inevitably remaining portion, which doubtlessly constitutes the most resilient element, must be dealt with appropriately, since, representing a natural selection, it will, upon liberation, constitute a new Jewish development. (See the experience of history.)

In the process of the practical implementation of the Final Solution, Europe will be combed from west to east. For reasons of the housing shortage and other sociopolitical necessities, the Reich territory and the Protectorate [of Bohemia and Moravia] will receive priority.

At first, the evacuated Jews will be brought stage by stage to the so-called transit ghettos, thence to be transported farther to the East.

SS-Lt. General Heydrich further stipulated an important prerequisite for the evacuation in general, the exact designation of categories of persons likely to be affected.

It is not intended to evacuate Jews over the age of sixty-five but to transfer them to an old people's ghetto (Theresienstadt is to be provided for this).

In addition to these age groups—approximately 30 percent of the 280,000 Jews resident in the Old Reich and Austria as of October 31, 1941—the Jewish old people's ghetto will receive severely wounded Jewish war veterans and Jews with war decorations (Iron Cross First Class). By means of this appropriate solution, many interventions will be precluded with a single blow.

The start of individual large-scale evacuation actions will hinge in great measure on military developments. With reference to the handling of the Final Solution in those European territories occupied or influenced by us,[2] it is suggested that the relevant experts of the Foreign Office consult those having jurisdiction in the Security Police and Security Service.

---

[1] The figures for unoccupied France and for the Ukraine are considerably inflated.

[2] In the statistical table, several countries (England, Ireland, Sweden, Switzerland, Turkey, Spain, and Portugal) were not under German control or particularly responsive to German influence.

In Slovakia and Croatia, the matter is no longer all that difficult because the essential questions there have already been resolved. In Romania the government has already appointed a commissioner for Jewish affairs. To regulate the matter in Hungary it is necessary within a short time to impose an adviser for Jewish questions upon the Hungarian government.

With regard to initiating the preparations for the regulation of the problem in Italy, SS-Lt. General Heydrich thinks a contact with the police chief in charge is appropriate.

In occupied and unoccupied France, the seizure of Jews for evacuation should in all probability proceed without great difficulties.

State Under Secretary [Martin] Luther then pointed out that with a thorough-going treatment of this problem in individual countries, such as the northern [Scandinavian] states, difficulties would arise, and it was therefore recommended that [action in] these lands be initially postponed. In view of the small number of Jews in question, this postponement constitutes no essential restriction.

By contrast, the Foreign Office sees no great difficulties for southeastern and western Europe.

SS-Major General [Otto] Hofmann intends to send a specialist from the Race and Resettlement Office to Hungary for purposes of general orientation whenever the Chief of the Security Police and Security Service is ready to take action there. It was decided that the specialist from the Race and Resettlement Office, who would not play an active role, is to be initially appointed as an aide to the police attaché.

IV. The Nuremberg Laws should constitute the foundation, more or less, of the projected Final Solution, but a solution to the mixed-marriage and mixed-parentage question is a prerequisite for the complete purification of the problem.

The Chief of the Security Police and Security Service, speaking theoretically in this instance, addressed himself to a memo from the Chief of the Reich Chancellery, making the following points:

1. Treatment of *Mischlinge*[3] of the first degree.
   With respect to the Final Solution of the Jewish question, *Mischlinge* of the first degree are categorized as Jews. To be exempted from this treatment will be
   a. *Mischlinge* of the first degree married to someone of German blood, if this marriage produced offspring (*Mischlinge* of the second degree). These *Mischlinge* of second degree are essentially categorized as Germans.
   b. *Mischlinge* of the first degree who have been granted exceptional treatment in some areas of national life by the highest authorities of the party and state. Every individual case must be examined, and it is not to be excluded that the decision may go against the *Mischling*.

---

[3]Offspring of mixed (Jewish and non-Jewish) descent.

Grounds for the exemption must always be the basic merits of the *Mischling* in question *himself.* (Not the merits of the German-blooded parent or spouse.)

In order to prevent offspring and finally to clean up the *Mischling* problem, the *Mischling* of first degree, exempted from evacuation, is to be sterilized. Sterilization is voluntary but a prerequisite for remaining in the Reich. The sterilized "*Mischling*" is then freed from all the restrictive ordinances to which he has been subjected.

2. Treatment of *Mischlinge* of the second degree.

    In principle, *Mischlinge* of the second degree will be treated as those of German blood; *Mischlinge* of the second degree will be categorized as Jews *in the following exceptional cases*:

    a. descent of the *Mischlinge* of the second degree from a bastard marriage (both partners *Mischlinge*).
    b. exceptionally unfavorable racial appearance of the *Mischlinge* of second degree, so that on the basis of externals alone he must be counted among the Jews.
    c. particularly bad police [record] or political judgment of the *Mischlinge* of second degree, which make it obvious that he feels and behaves like a Jew.

    However, even these considerations shall not apply when the *Mischling* of second degree is married to one of German blood.

3. Marriages between full Jews and those of German blood.

    It must be decided on a case-by-case basis whether the Jewish partner should be evacuated, or whether, in consideration of the effects upon German relatives, [he or she] should be transferred to the old people's ghetto.

4. Marriages between *Mischlinge* of the first degree and those of German blood.

    a. without children

        If there are no children from the marriage, the *Mischling* will be evacuated or transferred to the old people's ghetto. (Same treatment as with marriages between full Jews and those of German blood, Pt. 3.)

    b. with children

        If there are children (*Mischlinge* of the second degree), *and they are categorized as Jews,* they will be evacuated with the *Mischling* of the first degree or transferred to a ghetto. Insofar as these children are categorized as German (the normal case), they are exempted from evacuation along with the *Mischling* [parent] of the first degree.

5. Marriages between *Mischlinge* of first degree and *Mischlinge* of the first degree or Jews.

    In such marriages (inclusive of the children) all elements will be treated as Jews and therefore evacuated or transferred to the old people's ghetto.

6. Marriages between *Mischlinge* of the first degree and
   Mischlinge of the second degree.

Both marriage partners, whether children are present or not, will unconditionally be evacuated or transferred to the old people's ghetto, since, as a rule, the children, if any, reveal racially a stronger Jewish blood strain than do Jewish *Mischlinge* of the second degree.

SS-Major General Hofmann holds the view that extensive use of the practice of sterilization will have to be made because *Mischlinge* facing the choice of evacuation or sterilization would rather undergo sterilization.

State Secretary Dr. [Wilhelm] Stuckart stated that the practical implementation of the enumerated solution possibilities for the cleansing of the mixed-marriage and mixed-parentage problems would result in endless administrative work. Bearing in mind the biological facts, among others, State Secretary Stuckart proposed proceeding to compulsory sterilization.

For simplification of the mixed-marriage problem, further possibilities must be considered with the goal of the lawgiver being able to say something like: "These marriages are dissolved."

As to the question of the effect of Jewish evacuation on economic life, State Secretary [Erich] Neumann declared that Jews in important war work could not be evacuated until replacements can be found.

SS-Lt. General Heydrich pointed out that, according to guidelines issued by him for the current evacuations, these Jews were not in any case being evacuated.

State Secretary Dr. [Josef] Bühler stated that the General Government [of Poland] would welcome beginning the Final Solution of this problem in the General Government, because transport problems played no inordinate role and because the course of the action would not be hindered by consideration of employment [of Jews] for work. Jews should be removed from the region of the General Government as fast as possible because precisely here the Jew constitutes an immediate danger as a carrier of disease and in addition because his continuing black marketeering brings perpetual disorder to the economic structure of the country. Beyond this, the majority of the approximately two and one-half million Jews who come into question are incapable of work.

State Secretary Dr. Bühler stated further that the solution to the Jewish question in the General Government belonged to the competency of the Chief of the Security Police and Security Service and that his labors would be supported by the authorities in the General Government. He made only one request: that the Jewish question in this region be solved as quickly as possible.

In closing, further types of solution possibilities were discussed. Both Gauleiter Dr. [Alfred] Meyer and State Secretary Dr. Bühler represented the view that they could implement certain preparatory measures in the process of the Final Solution in their areas, being sure, however, to avoid upsetting the [non-Jewish] population.

The conference ended with a request from the Chief of the Security Police and Security Service for the cooperation of all the conference participants in the implementation of the solution tasks.

After the Holocaust

This anthology points toward the Holocaust but must go beyond it because antisemitism continues to insinuate itself into the political life of nations, animate hate groups, fascinate intellectuals, and remain a tool of government in many places. It thrives in the Arab world and occasionally disturbs the peace of western Europe, Latin America, and the United States. It has recently cropped up in Japan, a country with little previous history of antisemitism.

Jews are still being discriminated against and occasionally murdered, not because of what individuals have done but because of the way the group to which they belong is conceptualized—that is, on the basis of antisemitic ideology. The persistence of antisemitism in the modern world thus requires at least token representation here.

Although much has changed in the form and content of antisemitic literature since the Holocaust and the founding of the State of Israel, much in the following document, which has been chosen to represent current developments, will be familiar to the readers of this collection.

This historical continuity is clearest in the Soviet Union, where antisemitism has survived both the October Revolution of 1917 and the Holocaust, forming a solid bridge from the tsarist past to the Soviet present. Despite Lenin's announced intention of doing away with antisemitism (and Judaism), it has, since World War II, repeatedly surfaced in government policy and government-sanctioned literature. As in tsarist days, antisemitism continues to be a useful tool for those in power because inherited anti-Jewish feeling continues among the people. It appears "from above" in official propaganda, but just as often, and in more extreme fashion, it shows up "from below" in the dissident *Samizdat* press. It still feeds upon chauvinism and suspicion of the West. The anti-Jewish stereotype, now as before, gives those in authority a convenient scapegoat for failures in governance.

Menacing and potentially catastrophic though it may be, Soviet antisemitism differs significantly from the Nazi variety. It has been periodic rather than continuous, noticeably abating when relations with the West are at least reasonably good and intensifying when Russia turns in on itself. Reintroduced during World War II, Russian patriotism rejected "internationalism," coming down particularly hard on the quintessential internationalists, the Jews. Yet outbreaks of official oppression reflect stresses within the system rather than a commitment to antisemitism as an end in itself. The Soviet state, unlike the Nazi, does not exist for the sake of "solving the Jewish question."

Although Jews have been singled out formally and informally for special treatment and are exposed to popular hatred, they have not, as a group, been forced out of Soviet life or systematically isolated. To the contrary, the state apparently wishes to retain the services and talents of its Jewish citizens. (Half the gainfully employed Jews have university or secondary-school vocational training.) Nevertheless, they are at peril, living in a hostile environment, hostages to a system of government whose many failures can be unloaded upon them at will.

This has not always been so, especially in the early years of the revolution. Expressions of antisemitism were severely punished, and Jews in general assimilated rapidly to the new era. It was Josef Stalin (1879–1953) who changed this, giving renewed life to Russian antisemitism, as well as to many other tsarist practices. Campaigns against "cosmopolitans" and a "clique of theater critics" in the late 1940s and the "Jewish doctors' plot" of 1953 escalated into a more sustained attack by Stalin's successors upon "Zionists," particularly after the Arab-Israeli war of 1967. Both internal and foreign-policy motives have been advanced to explain these moves; both are reflected in the following excerpts from Yevgeny Yevseev's book, one of over 150 "anti-Zionist" works circulating in the Soviet Union.

The piece makes no all-embracing indictments against Jews, only against a never-defined but ominous body of "Zionists." In fact, there is no Jewish people with a specific national identity or legitimate need for self-expression. And Yevseev goes to great lengths in order to substantiate this standard Leninist position. Turning a traditional antisemitic argument on its head, for example, he states that the cultural productions of Jews were really those of Germans, Poles, or Russians who happened to be of Jewish descent. Only "Zionists," for their own pernicious reasons, claim otherwise. (Antisemites, such as those already encountered in these pages, have always averred the contrary—that Jewish artists and intellectuals could lay no claim to be anything but Jews.)

This distinction between "Zionists" and Jews is the author's way of reminding Jewish citizens of the Soviet Union and other socialist countries that they have nothing to complain of, implying that if they do grumble or demonstrate a desire to emigrate, they may well be considered "Zionists" or "Zionist agents." Other Soviet authors have claimed that perhaps 90 percent of Russian Jews are "hidden or unconscious Zionists" and thus enemies of the people. Pressuring Jews to conform is one of the clear domestic motives of Soviet antisemitism and something of a new departure.

But foreign-relations incentives are also at work. It is unpolitic for present-day antisemites, after the horrors of the Holocaust, to speak openly of a Jewish world conspiracy. Soviet antisemites, in particular, find it awkward to be thought of as traveling the same path as radical rightists and conservatives. Thus the buzz-word *Zionist* recommends itself. Along these lines, the most significant post-Holocaust innovation in Yevseev's book, and popular with antisemites worldwide, seeks to avoid the stigma of antisemitism by tying fascism and "Zionism" together. "Zionists," in order to forward their world-conspiratorial ambitions, foment and manipulate antisemitism. Jews were undeniably victims of the Holocaust, but modern antisemites assert that some of their number, the "Zionists," actually played a large role in Nazi crimes. Yevseev also makes pointed allusions to Hitler's "Third Reich" and the Israelis' "Third Kingdom" and then explicitly equates the two. Fighting "Zionism" thus becomes part of the battle for socialism and progress, an important consideration for the Soviet Union's relations to Third World countries.

Semantic distinctions between Jews and "Zionists" will not suffice for Yevseev and others to escape the charge of antisemitism, however. Who, after all, are these "Zionists"? Surely they comprise more than the Israelis or supporters of a Jewish state. Moreover, they are charged with the very same crimes historically ascribed to Jewry. They are misanthropes, sowers of discord, wire-pullers, millionaires, purveyors of cultural degeneracy, warmongers, saboteurs, filled with arrogance, and bent upon world domination. The former plotting of Jews and Freemasons has become the "Zionist-masonic conspiracy." Memos to the Central Committee of the Communist party have called for radical defense measures against the "murderous terrorism of the Zionists" and urged the introduction of high school courses in "scientific anti-Zionism." Euphemisms notwithstanding, this smacks of traditional antisemitism.

Yevseev's techniques also come directly out of the literary tradition of antisemitism. Hysterical exaggeration, fabrication, and accusations of enormous evil substitute for hard facts and logical arguments. Antisemitism also demonstrates once again that it can be combined with other issues. "Zionism" becomes a tool and an ally of U.S. monopoly capitalism and world imperialism and, in some cases, the true power behind them. The pairing makes the case for the evil of both. Antisemites in the West condemn Jews as enemies of capitalism, but in the Soviet Union "the Zionist corporation" and the "Jewish imperialist bourgeoisie" undermine socialism. Taking his cue from *The Protocols of the Elders of Zion,* Yevseev holds them responsible as well for disunity among various ethnic groups, the corruption of youth, and the poisoning of national consciousness.

Soviet antisemitism, in both its traditional and innovative aspects, ought to make clear what people of goodwill tend to forget again and again: antisemitism today is not simply an odd relic of history, the obsession of lunatic individuals and groups, but rather an evolving ideology with a long past to draw upon and political functions yet to perform. It will not conveniently disappear.

For Further Reading

Theodore Freedman, ed., *Antisemitism in the Soviet Union: Its Roots and Consequences* (New York, 1984).

25. Yevgeny Yevseev
Fascism under the Blue Star (1971)

When somebody pronounces the word *fascism* aloud, most people are reminded of the atrocities of World War II, the brown-shirted columns of Hitler's stormtroopers, the swastika, Franco's Phalangists, Mussolini's

Source: From Yevgeny Yevseev, *Fascism under the Blue Star* (Moscow, 1971) in S. Ettinger, ed., *Anti-Semitism in the Soviet Union: Its Roots and Consequences* (Jerusalem, 1983), 3:283–92.

black-shirted youth, smoldering ruins of towns and villages, the barbed wire of the death camps.

But now, two decades after Nuremberg, the world is witnessing a resurrection of neo-Nazism in West Germany and a number of other countries. Progressive mankind is noticing the intense activity of yet another variety of contemporary fascism, flourishing under the flag of the state of Israel. . . . The same flag is also considered to be the Zionist flag.

The disappearance of the ancient Hebrew people, its complete absorption into other nations has been scientifically established and is a scientific fact. . . . Nevertheless, Zionism proclaims as a sacred dogma the existence of "the world-wide Jewish people," "the world-wide Jewish nation," "the eternal nation."

The Zionists could erect a golden monument to Hitler: the raving *Führer* was the one who, in his delirious *Mein Kampf*, sanctioned Zionism's fundamental dogma, the existence of "the world-wide Jewish people," "the Jewish Race.". . .

Since the Jewish population of the world does not constitute a world-wide nation, as we have already seen, the Zionists lack well-founded justification for their slogan, "the ingathering of the nation from the Diaspora." By the Zionist logic, the Jewish population of Israel is not a nation, but "part" of one, since the Jews of the whole world constitute one nation from now on and forever. The Zionists contend that this nation, scattered all over the world, wanders from place to place. However, in spite of all Zionist attempts to link together the Jews of the entire world and present them as a "nation," part of which lives in Israel, their "national home" (on this basis, the Zionists demand Jewish loyalty not to an actual homeland, but to a notorious "national home" created for their benefit), an Israeli nation is in fact being actively created in that country. The nation being formed in Israel has no connection with the rest of the Jewish population in other countries. This process will continue. The Zionists can still take advantage of such things as the blood relationship between the immigrants arriving in Israel and the Jews remaining in their actual homelands, and insist that world Jewry is one. In time, however, this possibility will cease to exist, as Jews assimilate into the native populations of the various countries.

. . . Jews in the socialist countries are completely free of national and class discrimination, and the great majority of them live in harmony with society, taking an active part along with others in the construction of socialism. The presence of Jews among the intelligentsia of the socialist countries, their participation in the development of the national cultures of the Soviet republics, in science and sports, their promotion to leading positions in production and administration are the most obvious proof of the Jews' emancipation and assimilation in the socialist nations, which welcomed them in brotherly fashion. This fact is used as one of the trumps in the Zionists' pack of marked cards. They try to use it for their own purposes, in order to stir up antisemitic feelings in the masses. Hence, they spread on the sly the notion of "Jewish dominance," of their alleged, though as yet unsuccessful, aspirations to seize control of all the decisive governmental and administrative levers. In other words, assimilation is a gradual and irreversible process supported by all the progressive representatives of the Jewish population in every country. . . . .

Agents of the Zionist secret services set fire to synagogues, desecrate Jewish cemeteries, and carry out many other vile provocations. These are instantly used as ammunition by the Zionist propaganda machine, which cries bloody murder about the threat to the life and property of Jews in various countries. This happened in Iraq, Morocco, Egypt, Argentina, and the United States.

The Zionists and the entire imperialistic propaganda machine broadly use accusations of antisemitism against all who sharply criticize the policy, ideology, and practices of the state of Israel. . . .

For a number of years, the word *racist* has usually been interpreted as meaning anti-black, less frequently, anti-Chinese. Earlier, it referred to German fascism. As a result of the efforts made by certain circles, however, this word was dropped from use altogether in connection with Jewish nationalism in the form of Zionism, although racism is a basic component of this reactionary ideology.

Judaism and Zionism (which absorbed Judaism as a component part) reduce the geography and ethnography of the various peoples to a simple and handy division into two countries, and two nations, Jews and *goyim*. Goyim are the enemies, the non-Jews. The Jewish clergy and the Israeli Zionist regime, in effect, put the non-Jews outside the law, and create a state of uninterrupted enmity between Jews and all other peoples. Justifying a religion of misanthropy and rousing hatred toward people of other religions serve the global strategy of imperialism.

Zionists and the Jewish clergy are in fact pursuing a coordinated policy. The Zionist theoreticians claim that every Jew is a Zionist by birth. The rabbis and Jewish theologians persistently repeat that being a Jew means being an adherent of Judaism. The "theoretical" circle is thus closed. All that remains is to recreate the Jewish ghetto in one form or another.

How can one take seriously the claim by the Zionists that the results of the titanic efforts of the great minds of all peoples throughout the ages are achievements of "Jewish genius"? The Zionists through such fraudulent methods are trying to overemphasize second-rate talents and exaggerate the importance of their achievements.

They deliberately ignore the fact that those people were the pride of the Russian, German, and other nations, not on account of their origin or religious affiliation, but because of their participation in the national culture, in the creative work of these countries. The names of outstanding Russian, Polish, German, English, and other writers, poets, musicians, composers, and artists sometimes do indeed indicate Jewish origin. But they became famous and beloved mainly because they were part of the nation in which they grew up and where their personality developed, and not because they went to pray in the synagogue. . . . Nobody is getting ready to hand over Ehrenburg, Oborin, Chakovsky, Kogan, Plisetskaya, or Oistrakh to the Zionists.[1]

. . . What are the so-called "cultural" and student organizations outside Israel doing with that mass of young people who, without being asked, have already been assigned the role of "cannon fodder" and whom the Zionist strategists are planning to draft into Israel's armed forces? No other than David Ben-Gurion, former prime minister of Israel, gave the answer to that question. He stressed that what is needed in order to attract Jews to come to Israel is not words, but deeds; the most effective way of attracting immigrants to Israel is the fear of persecution in the countries where the Jews live. That fear can be generated by disseminating "the crudest forms of antisemitism."

This task must be fulfilled by specially trained young Zionists who will masquerade as non-Jews, destroy the Jews' complacency, and sow in them anxiety and the desire to go to Israel. . . .

The small number of Jewish youths who arrive in Israel immediately undergo intensive brainwashing, combined with anti-Arab ideological training. A course of so-called "reassessment of values or moral reorientation" has been introduced for them. Small wonder that, after taking that course, the young, fledgling Israelis start believing that, in the army, they are fulfilling the "sacred mission" of creating a third "Jewish kingdom."

Demagogical from beginning to end, Zionism thus mobilizes the basest instincts and directs them according to its own desires against hostile trends, personalities, and parties.

Slander, insinuation, murder, theft, provocation, spying, expansionism, aggression are only part of a long list of crimes perpetrated by international Zionism, operating all over the world as an active phalanx of anticommunism, as a perfidious enemy of the national-liberation movements of many peoples.

A quarter of a century ago at Nuremberg the thirty steps to the gallows marked the end of the line for the leaders of Hitler's "Third Reich." They had perpetrated the most serious crimes against humanity. One infamous deed of the German fascists was the demoralization and corruption of Germany's younger generation. Today Zionist leaders, who irresponsibly play games with the destiny of the peoples in the Middle East and contribute their share to complicating the international situation and intensifying tension, follow the same path. . . .

Imperialism keeps throwing into battle new cohorts of "conquerors of minds," ideological saboteurs. The role of the shock troops in this attack is being played with increasing determination by the international Zionist corporation, a long-standing tool of imperialism in the latter's fight against the Soviet Union and the other socialist countries, against the national liberation movements. It is a well-known fact that the Zionists' subversive

---

[1]This list of Russian artists and intellectuals of Jewish origin noticeably omits several historically important Bolsheviks.

activities against Soviet rule started immediately after the October Revolution. . . .

The *kapos* of the death camps and the special "police" who enforced order in the ghettos were recruited by the Gestapo from among the Zionists. In a letter to *Pravda*, Soviet Jewish citizens, now living in the Ukraine, wrote: "The tragedy of Babi Yar will remain forever an embodiment not only of Nazi cannibalism, but also of the indelible disgrace of their accomplices and successors, the Zionists."[2]

. . . The Zionists switched allegiance after the war and became completely subordinate to U.S. monopolist capital. . . .

. . . The failure of the plot of the forces of international reaction in Czechoslovakia frustrated the far-reaching plans of American imperialism and its Zionist assistants.[3]

Without neglecting the exportation of the "quiet counter-revolution" to the socialist countries, the international Zionist concern worked out plans for a comprehensive anti-Soviet campaign of really global dimensions. They started the new "anti-Bolshevik crusade" under the same tattered flag of "protecting the Jews" living in the Soviet Union and other socialist countries.

The activities of the Zionist and related religious and secular organizations prove that Zionism, especially in the last few years, has begun employing not only propaganda methods in its provocations against the Soviet Union, but has even had recourse to fascist methods of conducting a secret war against socialism; it is using not only blackmail but also brute force. It complicates the relationships between the Soviet Union and other countries, and tries to sow distrust and enmity between the peoples of the socialist camp, between the peoples of the Soviet Union.

It must be stressed that one of the main targets of the violence used by Zionist ideological saboteurs is our Soviet patriotic consciousness. Bourgeois ideology and "leftist revisionism" are doing everything in order to erode, shatter, and undermine this consciousness. They are sparing neither forces nor means in their violent counter-attacks. The counter-attacks are not always frontal. They are often subtle attempts, purporting to have "friendly objectivity," at infiltrating our country, raids of deep thrusting ideological sabotage, to quote the newspaper *Pravda Ukrainy*. " 'Suddenly' you come across 'theories' intended to present the basis of Soviet patriotism as mere national history and traditions."

---

[2]After the fall of the city of Kiev to the Germans in September 1941, thirty-five thousand Jews, ordered to report for resettlement, were instead massacred at an outlying ravine named Babi Yar. The 1961 poem by Yevgeny Yevtushenko, memorializing this event and strongly critical of Russian antisemitism, was denounced in the Soviet press because it concentrated too narrowly on the sufferings of the Jews and "slandered the Russian people."

[3]This is an allusion to the Czech attempt to create "communism with a human face" in the "Prague spring" of 1968. The forcible repression of this movement was accompanied by the intensification of a Soviet antisemitic campaign already under way since the Israeli-Arab conflict of 1967.

"Suddenly" doctrines about the adequacy of patriotism in the service of some "national idea," about the timelessness and classlessness of such concepts as "nation" and "people" achieve greater circulation. "Suddenly," every chauvinistic, Zionist, bourgeois-nationalist rabble-rouser raises a particularly noisy howl. "Suddenly" attempts are being made at provoking bad feeling in the representatives of certain Soviet peoples toward other nations. "Suddenly" narrow local nationalist figures of the past are being extolled and the standard-bearers of friendship between peoples are spat upon. "Suddenly" the objective, historical transformation of the Russian language into a language of international communication is being actively attacked. . . .

The Communist party teaches us that being a patriot means being an active, conscientious, front-line fighter for a happy tomorrow, against the dark forces of reaction, obscurantism, and hatred of mankind, which profess the ideology of violence and robbery and rally around the anti-communist imperialists' flag (which changes in design from time to time). Changes in design indicate only regrouping in the enemy camp, but the class nature of fascism does not change, whether its flag displays a brown swastika, the blue star of Zionism, or the stars and stripes of American imperialism.

Suggestions for Additional Reading

Jew hatred, anti-Judaism, and antisemitism, problems that have unfolded through two millennia and over a large part of the globe, have engendered thousands upon thousands of works. Scholarly studies, documentary collections, propaganda and counter-propaganda, memoirs of survivors and perpetrators of violence, court testimony, journalistic accounts, parliamentary debates, film, fiction, poetry, and graphic art form a monumental body of evidence. Mastery of so large a literature is clearly beyond the individual's capacity, and the sheer bulk of the material can have a chilling effect upon the spirit of inquiry. Mindful of this, the following list of titles, limited (with a few exceptions) to those published in English, takes a qualitative, rather than a quantitative, approach. It is a modest attempt to aid the beginner in broadening perspective and gaining greater knowledge of the general topic: antisemitism—its origins, theory, and practice. (For more depth on the specific issues raised in this anthology, the student is directed to the For Further Reading suggestions at the end of the text sections introducing the documents.

The Vidal Sassoon International Center for the Study of Antisemitism has undertaken the daunting task of compiling a comprehensive serial bibliography of titles that have appeared since 1984. Volume 1 of *Antisemitism: An Annotated Bibliography,* edited by Susan S. Cohen (New York, 1987), briefly describes 1255 publications in many languages, categorized according to period and locale. Robert Singerman, *Antisemitic Propaganda: An Annotated Bibliography and Research Guide* (New York, 1982) comments on 1915 books, pamphlets, and articles published between 1871 and 1981.

Although it would be erroneous to think of Jewish existence as no more than a tale of endless victimization, it is nonetheless true that general histories of the Jews must deal at length with the theme of persecution. H. H. Ben-Sasson (ed.), *A History of the Jewish People* (Cambridge, Ma., 1976) brings together in one volume the fruits of modern scholarship. Salo W. Baron, *A Social and Religious History of the Jews,* 19 vols. (New York, 1952–83) remains a reliable source for the most detailed information. Helpful in placing Jew hatred in the larger history of Jews is the more narrowly focused and provocative essay by David Biale, *Power and Powerlessness in Jewish History* (New York, 1986).

Surveys that concentrate exclusively on the development of anti-Jewish thought and action from the earliest times to the modern era are scarce. The most manageable introduction is the four-volume *History of Anti-Semitism* (New York, 1965–86), by the French scholar Léon Poliakov. Equally all-embracing is Alex Bein, *The Jewish Question: Biography of a World Problem* (Rutherford, N. J., 1989), an erudite treatment from a Zionist point of view. In *The Anguish of the Jews* (New York, 1965), Edward H. Flannery, a Catholic priest, traces the story over twenty-three centuries with special attention to the conflict between church and synagogue.

Histories of anti-Jewish attitudes for more limited periods and those highlighting particular aspects of the negative stereotype help illuminate the development of antisemitism in the modern era. Joshua Trachtenberg, *The Devil and the Jews: The Medieval Conception of the Jew and Its Relation to Modern Antisemitism* (New Haven, 1943) is richly illustrated with medieval iconography. Jerome Friedman, "Jewish Conversion, the Spanish Pure Blood Laws, and Reformation," *The Sixteenth Century Journal* 18 (1987): 3–29, argues for an earlier origin of racist antisemitism than is common. Jonathan I. Israel, *European Jewry in the Age of Mercantilism* (Oxford, 1986) perceptively analyzes the economic dimension to Jew hatred in the early modern period. Arthur Hertzberg, *The French Enlightenment and the Jews: The Origins of Modern Anti-Semitism* (New York, 1968) deals with the secularization of anti-Judaism and Jew hatred. Many works recount the conflicts in Jewish-Gentile relations produced by the process of Jewish assimilation. A few of the important titles are Jacob Katz, *Out of the Ghetto: The Social Background of Jewish Emancipation, 1770–1870* (Cambridge, Mass., 1973); Hannah Arendt, *Rahel von Varnhagen* (New York, 1974); Michael Meyer, *The Origins of the Modern Jew* (Detroit, 1967); and Reinhard Rürup, *Emanzipation und Antisemitismus: Studien zur "Judenfrage" der bürgerlichen Gesellschaft* (Göttingen, 1975).

Overall interpretations of the modern phenomenon of antisemitism are abundant and diverse in their approach. Jacob Katz, *From Prejudice to Destruction: Anti-Semitism, 1700–1933* (Cambridge, Mass., 1980) is the most important recent investigation and commendably free of apologetics. Older, pre-Holocaust studies still worth reading are Hugo Valentin, *Antisemitism Historically and Critically Examined* (London, 1936) and Bernard Lazare, *L'Antisémitisme: Son histoire et ses causes* (Paris, 1894). Hannah Arendt, *The Origins of Totalitarianism* (New York, 1958) and Jean-Paul Sartre's brief essay, *Antisemite and Jew* (New York, 1948) have proved seminal in several of their ideas.

The origins of racial antisemitism are elucidated in George Mosse, *Toward the Final Solution: A History of European Racism* (New York, 1978) and Léon Poliakov, *The Aryan Myth: A History of Racist and Nationalist Ideas in Europe* (New York, 1974). George Mosse, *The Crisis of German Ideology* (New York, 1964), Fritz Stern, *The Politics of Cultural Despair* (New York, 1965), Geoffrey Field, *Evangelist of Race: The Germanic Vision of Houston Stewart Chamberlain* (New York, 1981), Peter Gay, *Freud, Jews and Other Germans: Masters and Victims in Modernist Culture* (New York, 1978), Carl E. Schorske, *Fin-de-Siècle Vienna* (New York, 1980), Edward Fuchs, *Die Juden in der Karikatur: Ein Beitrag zur Kulturgeschichte* (Munich, 1921), and Hermann Glaser, *The Cultural Roots of National Socialism* (Austin, 1978) place the development of antisemitic ideology in a broader German cultural context.

Since the 1914 publication of Karl Kautsky's *Are the Jews a Race?* (English translation, Westport, Conn., 1972), leading Marxists have given scant attention to antisemitism; a discussion by one of the lesser lights is A. Leon, *The Jewish Question: A Marxist Interpretation* (Mexico City, 1950).

The intense debate concerning the relationship of socialism to antisemitism can be followed in Julius Carlebach, *Karl Marx and the Radical Critique of Judaism* (London, 1978); Robert S. Wistrich, *Socialism and the Jews* (East Brunswick, N.J., 1982); and George Lichtheim, "Socialism and the Jews," in *Collected Essays* (New York, 1973).

Works by social scientists, although rooted in the present, nonetheless yield useful insights into the timeless mechanisms at work in antisemitic prejudice. Bruno Bettelheim, "The Dynamism of Anti-Semitism in Gentile and Jew," *The Journal of Abnormal and Social Psychology* 42 (1947): 153–68, and Nathan W. Ackermann and Marie Jahoda, *Anti-Semitism and Emotional Disorder* (New York, 1950) are the classics of clinical psychology. From a sociological point of view come Theodor W. Adorno et al., *The Authoritarian Personality* (New York, 1950) and J. H. Robb, *Working-Class Anti-Semite* (London, 1954). However, Jacob Katz, "Misreadings of Anti-Semitism," *Commentary* (July 1983): 39–44, sounds a warning on the pitfalls of the social scientific approach.

Alex Bein, "The Jewish Parasite: Notes on the Semantics of the Jewish Problem, with Special Reference to Germany," *Leo Baeck Yearbook* 9 (1964): 3–40, examines the linguistic elements, as do Christoph Cobet, *Der Wortschatz des Antisemitismus in der Bismarckzeit* (Munich, 1973) and the factually unreliable but otherwise thought-provoking interpretation of Sander L. Gilman, *Jewish Self-Hatred: Anti-Semitism and the Hidden Language of the Jews* (Baltimore and London, 1986).

The effects of antisemitism upon Jewish identity have created a massive literature. A useful collection of documents is Jehuda Reinharz (ed.), *Living with Antisemitism: Modern Jewish Responses* (Hanover and London, 1987). Since 1956 the Leo Baeck Institute has published a scholarly periodical and a series of monographs dealing with all aspects of German antisemitism, indispensable tools for serious students of the problem. Shlomo Avineri, *The Making of Modern Zionism* (London, 1981) and Walter Laqueur, *A History of Zionism* (London, 1972) chronicle an important reaction of a minority of the Jewish community. Ismar Schorsch, *Jewish Reactions to German Anti-Semitism, 1870–1914* (Philadelphia and New York, 1972) covers the mainstream responses of assimilated Jews. By probing the thought of several German-Jewish intellectuals, Frederick Grunfeld, *Prophets without Honour* (London, 1979) depicts the poignant breakdown of German-Jewish symbiosis in the twentieth century.

The relationship of antisemitism to fascism outside Germany is examined in Walter Laqueur and George Mosse (eds.), *International Fascism* (New York, 1966), F. L. Carsten, *Fascist Movements in Austria: From Schönerer to Hitler* (London, 1977), Meir Michaelis, *Mussolini and the Jews* (London, 1978), and Bela Vago, *The Shadow of the Swastika: The Rise of Fascism and Anti-Semitism in the Danube Basin* (London, 1975).

Material on Nazi antisemitism and the Holocaust is overwhelming in scope. For a grasp of the essentials, the following titles indicate points of departure, at best: François Furet (ed.), *Unanswered Questions: Nazi Germany and the Genocide of the Jews* (New York, 1989), a collection of short articles by the acknowledged experts, deals with all aspects of Nazi persecution. Michael R. Marrus, *The Holocaust in History* (London, 1987) and Yehuda Bauer, *The Holocaust in Historical Perspective* (Seattle, 1978) explain the issues and summarize the continuing debates on their meaning. Gerald Fleming, *Hitler and the Final Solution* (Berkeley, 1984) gathers the evidence on Hitler's personal responsibility for the mass murder of Jews. Analyses of the "popularity" of antisemitism in the Third Reich are Sarah Gordon, *Hitler, Germans, and the "Jewish Question"* (Princeton, 1984), Claudia Koonz, *Mothers in the Fatherland* (New York, 1987), and Ian Kershaw, *The Hitler Myth: Image and Reality in the Third Reich* (New York, 1989). E. Leiser, *Nazi Film* (New York, 1975) touches upon the use of movies as an instrument of antisemitic propaganda. The attitudes of the Western Allies toward the Final Solution is best treated by David S. Wyman, *The Abandonment of the Jews: America and the Holocaust* (New York, 1984). The most meticulous reconstruction of genocide remains Raul Hilberg, *The Destruction of the European Jews* (revised and definitive edition, New York, 1985). The *Yad Vashem Studies on the European Jewish Catastrophe and Resistance* are an important research tool.

Compilations of primary sources afford a direct view of the human motives for inhumanity. Representative collections of translated texts are Raul Hilberg (ed.), *Documents of Destruction* (Chicago, 1971) and Yad Vashem, *Documents on the Holocaust* (Jerusalem, 1981). An ambitious project, John Mendelsohn (ed.), *The Holocaust: Selected Documents* (New York, 1988) contains facsimile reproductions of texts from the National Archives in 18 topically organized volumes. Martin Gilbert (ed.), *Atlas of the Holocaust* (London, 1982) is a valuable source of maps, charts, and other basic data.

Many books address the continuation or recrudescence of antisemitism after the Holocaust. The continuity of officially inspired antisemitism is the subject of Benjamin Pinkus, *The Soviet Government and the Jews 1948–1967* (Jerusalem, 1984). Bernard Lewis, *Semites and Anti-Semites* (London, 1986) attempts to distinguish between anti-Israeli and antisemitic politics in the Arab world. Robert Weisbrot, *The Jews of Argentina from the Inquisition to Peron* (Philadelphia, 1979) and Gregory Martire and Ruth Clark, *Anti-Semitism in the United States: A Study of Prejudice in the 1980s* (New York, 1982) attest to the on-going presence of the problem in the Americas.

Your Excellency, may your mighty influence in Prussia and Germany urge:

1. that the immigration of alien Jews be at least limited, if not completely prevented;
2. that the Jews be excluded from all positions of authority; that their employment in the judiciary—namely as autonomous judges—receive appropriate limitation;
3. that the Christian character of the primary school—even when attended by Jewish pupils—be strictly protected; that only Christian teachers be allowed in these schools and that in all other schools Jewish teachers be placed only in special and exceptional cases;
4. that a special census of the Jewish population be reinstituted.

11. Hamburg Resolutions of the German Social Reform Party (1899)

1. It is the task of the antisemitic party ever to deepen and spread knowledge of the true essence of the Jewish race. We stand only at the beginning of this activity.
2. The strivings of Zionism are a fruit of the antisemitic movement. It acknowledges the so-often-denied national cohesiveness of all Jews. The constitutional strivings of the Zionists merit support only if they give the guarantee that all Jews will be drawn to Zion. Unfortunately that appears to be infeasible. It is intolerable that the Alliance israélite [universelle][1] should become a sovereign power and that it should maintain an ambassador at the German imperial court.
3. Thanks to the development of our modern means of communication, the Jewish question ought to be permitted to become a world question in the course of the twentieth century. As such, it should be solved in common with other nations and result finally in full separation, and—if self-defense demands—in final annihilation [Vernichtung] of the Jewish race. The "true" peace conference will be the one in which the peoples of the globe occupy themselves with the position of the Hebrews. Until then, however, it will be the affair of every individual nation to defend itself against the Jewish plague as best it can.
4. One of the first steps for legislative intervention against the Jewish race must be the legal definition of who shall be considered a Jew. It is racial descent and this alone that determines membership in Jewry. The party congress [of the German Social Reform party] welcomes the

Source: From *Schulthess' Europäischer Geschichtskalendar* (Munich, 1899), p. 142.

[1]See note 9, Document 6.

draft of a Jewish registration law, published in the summer of 1898, as preparation for the solution of this basic task.

5. Point 19 of the party program calls for a statistical census of Jews. It is necessary that this census embrace all facets of Jewish life in Germany so that comparisons to the total population can be made.

6. The congress recommends to the Reichstag faction [of the party] that it make suitable motions in the Reichstag every year in order to compel the individual representatives and other parties to take a stand on the Jewish question.

12. In Defense Against Jewish Ritual Murder (1901)

Our children must be protected from these murderers. It is unacceptable that Jews receive the freedom to enjoy murder. Murderers must be rendered harmless.

Since the most appropriate and radical measures will not be condoned, given our humane upbringing, it is necessary, because of the proven crimes of the Jews and because of their ubiquitous and active solidarity . . . , to strive for *the expulsion of all Jews from the country for all time to come.* Then, at least, we will be secure against these murdering bands in our Germany.

Until the correct understanding of this necessity for mass expulsion has penetrated all strata of the population, thus making legal measures possible, the following ought to be striven for—that is, carried out:

1. *Police supervision* of the most exacting kind for the Jews living among us;

2. Toleration of Jews only in quite small and controllable numbers (no heaping up of Jews in the large cities!);

3. A general prohibition of kosher slaughtering for Jews;

4. Isolation in school and society; dismissal from state offices;

5. Upon the occurrence of a murder where all clues point to the Jews, as in Konitz and Xanten[1], half the wealth of all Jews becomes state property, in the light of the criminal solidarity of Jews;

6. High head tax.

Source: From *Mitteilungen aus dem Verein zur Abwehr des Antisemitismus,* August 21, 1901. Declaration of the antisemitic Reichstag representative, Fritz Bindewald.

[1]Ritual-murder accusations in Xanten in the Rhineland (1891) and Konitz in West Prussia (1900) led to rioting and the arrest and trial of Jewish suspects. In Konitz, members of the antisemitic parties helped instigate violence on the part of the Polish population of the town, which resulted in calling out Prussian troops to restore order.

13. Proclamation of the Alliance Against the Arrogance of Jewry (1912)

The German spirit is outcast,
Victoriously it shall return at last.
Stinging whiplashes will teach you
To know German Strength anew.

The Alliance against the Arrogance of Jewry has been founded because the instances of such arrogance are increasing in number and because the effects on the German nation—its religious, economic, and political life—are immeasurably damaging and horrifying.

The Reichstag elections of 1912 have taken place under the sign of Jewry—that is, under the sign of open and clandestine republicanism and internationalism. "National is irrational" . . . was and is the slogan that misled millions of Germans, blinded by the fraudulent Jewish catchwords of international culture and international progress. That the German nation is politically immature had to be demonstrated by democratic elections. Millions of Germans, confused and naive, followed those blinding phrases without suspecting that they served only to hide the chains with which Jewry wants to saddle our nation.

Jewry is international in the sense of Schopenhauer's phrase: "The fatherland of the Jews is other Jews." It is a net thrown over all the nations. Its mesh becomes all the narrower and stronger the more the national strength and determination of individual peoples diminish. . . . We Germans don't reproach the Jews for being international in this sense. But [internationalism] seeks to weaken individual Germans as Germans and to destabilize the whole national organism economically and politically. This signifies arrogance on the part of a guest people. Against this and all its visible forms, it is the sacred duty of every German to fight with all his strength.

Jewry works systematically and in mighty associations in every area of German life in order to push out or dominate the Germans and to make Jewish influence decisive. This holds not only for the realm of politics and the economy but also for literature, art, theater, science, the whole educational system, the practice of law, and not the least in the workers' and women's movements.

Richard Wagner has told us: to be German means to do a thing for its own sake! The spirit of Jewry is the opposite: to be Jewish is to make a business out of everything. To want to make the Germans like this is an arrogance of the Jewish guest people, an injury and a danger of the most

---

Source: From Gottfried zur Beek [Ludwig Müller], *Die Geheimnisse der Weisen von Zion* (Charlottenburg, 1919), pp. 45–47.

serious kind for our German nation. . . . Jews would like to penetrate into the ranks of the officers and reserve officers of our army—into our German army, the shield of the kingdom, the security of the fatherland, and all the best of its German character! . . .

Whither we turn we meet the same machinations of Jewry, conscious of the goal and with unlimited money means, always aiming at dominance in any form. Its progress and effects are horrifying. National, intellectual, religious, moral, and physical decomposition of the Germans, the growing economic dependence of Germans upon Jews—these are the consequences and the purposes of such actions. To be sure, the ignorant remain untouched by all this; to the fainthearted, the horror of battle outweighs the abhorrence of subjection. Therefore, we want to make knowers out of the ignorant, to strengthen and encourage the timid. The German nation ought clearly to see the danger threatening its noblest possessions. It ought also learn that it only takes the will to vanquish such dangers.

This is the initial work that the Alliance Against the Arrogance of Jewry wants to undertake.

The alliance forswears public agitation. It is directed not against the person and hopes, on the contrary, to avoid such embittering outbreaks. The alliance is thoroughly convinced that German affairs can be served only by German practicality. The immediate objective is dissemination of knowledge about Jewry, about its working methods, its organizations, and its purposes. In this activity the defense against the arrogance of Jewry is contained. The alliance does not want to and will not do injustice to the Jews, nor will it injure justifiable feelings. Our slogan is: protection of the German way of life, inwardly and outwardly, against Jewish *infiltration* and against the Jewish *work of decomposition*. Our struggle is not directed against the Jewish religion but against those characteristics of Jews that operate at the cost of the German nation.

It is high time that conscious Germans unite to inform and prove to their countrymen just how high the time is!

14. Daniel Frymann
If I Were the Kaiser (1912)

Jews under an Aliens Law

The recovery of our nation's health in all areas of life—cultural, moral, political, and economic—and the maintenance of that recovered health is *possible only if Jewish influence is either wholly eliminated or diminished to a bearable level of harmlessness.*

Source: From Daniel Frymann [Heinrich Class], *Wenn ich der Kaiser wär. Politische Wahrheiten und Notwendigkeiten,* 3d ed. (Leipzig, 1913), pp. 74–78.